W9-AAP-914

OPPENHEIMER

The Years of Risk

James W. Kunetka

Prentice-Hall, Inc., Englewood Cliffs, New Jersey 07632

Library of Congress Cataloging in Publication Data

Kunetka, James W. (date).
Oppenheimer, the years of risk.

Bibliography: p.
Includes index.
1. Oppenheimer, J. Robert, 1904–1967.
2. Physicists—United States—Biography. I. Title.
QC16.062K86 1982 530'.092'4 [B] 82-15031
ISBN 0-13-638007-7

This book is available at a special discount when ordered in large quantities.
Contact Prentice-Hall, Inc., General Publishing Division,
Special Sales, Englewood Cliffs, N.J. 07632.

10 9 8 7 6 5 4 3 2 1

ISBN 0-13-638007-7

Printed in the United States of America

Front cover photo by Alfred Eisenstaedt
Life Magazine © Time Inc.

Editorial/production supervision
by Shirley Stein and Rita Young
Interior design by Joan Jacobus
Jacket design by Hal Siegel
Photo insert design by Maria Carella
Manufacturing buyer: Edmund W. Leone

Prentice-Hall International, Inc., *London*
Prentice-Hall of Australia Pty. Limited, *Sydney*
Prentice-Hall Canada Inc., *Toronto*
Prentice-Hall of India Private Limited, *New Delhi*
Prentice-Hall of Japan, Inc., *Tokyo*
Prentice-Hall of Southeast Asia Pte. Ltd., *Singapore*
Whitehall Books Limited, *Wellington, New Zealand*
Editora Prentice-Hall do Brasil Ltda., *Rio de Janeiro*

To J.V.K.

Duffield, Jill Ellman, Art Freed, Gordon Gidley, Dave Heimbach, Louis and Eleanor Hempelmann, Jack Kahn, Jean Kott, Bob and Barbara Krohn, Dorothy McKibbin, John Manley, Carson Mark, Ralph K. Miller, Robert Masterson, Jeannene Mattingly, Frank and Jackie Oppenheimer, Peter and Virginia Oppenheimer, Gilbert Ortiz, Willie Ortiz, Les Redman, Edward Reece, Bill Regan, Bill Richmond, Bill Jack Rogers, Emilio Segrè, Vivian Silverstein, Martha L. Smith, Faith Stephens, Del Sundberg, Donald J. Weidner, and Jay L. Westbrook.

I am grateful to the Southwest Educational Development Laboratory for their support of this project.

I owe a special debt to Bob Krohn for his encouragement and invaluable assistance throughout the years.

Acknowledgment is made to the following for granting permission to reprint material:

Quotations from Robert Oppenheimer, "Atomic Weapons and American Policy," reprinted by permission of *Foreign Affairs*, July 1953. Copyright 1953 by the Council on Foreign Relations, Inc.

Excerpts from the Reith Lectures are used by permission of the British Broadcasting Corporation.

Excerpts reprinted by permission of the publisher from *Robert Oppenheimer: Letters and Recollections*, edited by Alice Kimball Smith and Charles Weiner, Cambridge, Mass.: Harvard University Press, Copyright © 1980 by Alice Kimball Smith and Charles Weiner.

Biographical Chronology

1904, April 22 J. Robert Oppenheimer born in New York City

1912, August 12 Birth of his brother, Frank Friedman Oppenheimer

1921, February Graduated from the Ethical Culture School

1925, June Graduated from the Harvard College, summa cum laude

1925, September–1926, August Studied at the University of Cambridge and Cavendish Laboratory

1926, September–1927, March Studied at the University of Göttingen; received Ph.D.

1927, September–1928, July National Research Council Fellow at Harvard University and the California Institute of Technology

1928, September–1929, June National Research Council Fellow at University of Leiden, University of Utrecht, and the Eidgenossiche Technische Hochschule

1929–1947 Assistant professor, associate professor, and professor of physics at the University of California at Berkeley and the California Institute of Technology

1940, November 1 Married Katherine Puening Harrison

1941, May 12 Birth of son, Peter Oppenheimer

1942, May Named coordinator of fast-fission research under the Office of Scientific Research and Development, S-1 Committee

1942, November Named director of the Los Alamos Laboratory, Los Alamos, New Mexico

1942–1945 Directed Los Alamos Laboratory

1944, December 7 Birth of daughter, Katherine "Toni" Oppenheimer

1945, May–October Member, Scientific Panel, Interim Committee on Postwar Atomic Policy, War Department

1945, July 16 Detonation of first atomic bomb near Alamogordo, New Mexico

1945, October 16 Resigned as director of Los Alamos Laboratory

1945, November Returned to teaching at the California Institute of Technology

1946, January–April Consultant to State Department's Committee on International Control of Atomic Energy

1946–1947 Consultant to the United States Mission to the United Nations Atomic Energy Commission

1946, August Began teaching at the University of California at Berkeley

1947–1952 Member and chairman of the General Advisory Committee of the U.S. Atomic Energy Commission

1947, October Appointed director of the Institute for Advanced Study, Princeton, New Jersey

1948 First major postwar review of security background by members of the Atomic Energy Commission. Security clearance continued.

1952, July Began two 1-year appointments as consultant to the Atomic Energy Commission

1953, December 23 Security clearance suspended by the Atomic Energy Commission

1954, April 12–May 6 Hearing before the Personnel Security Board of the Atomic Energy Commission

1954, June 29 Formal vote (4–1) by the Atomic Energy Commission not to restore security clearance.

1963, December 2 Received Enrico Fermi Award from U.S. government

1966, June Retired as director of Institute for Advanced Study

1967, February 18 Died, Princeton, New Jersey

PART
ONE

1. A Matter of Risk

In a banner headline, *The New York Times* first broke the news to the world on April 14, 1954:

DR. OPPENHEIMER SUSPENDED BY A.E.C. IN SECURITY REVIEW
SCIENTIST DEFENDS RECORD
HEARINGS STARTED
ACCESS TO SECRET DATA DENIED NUCLEAR EXPERT
RED TIES ALLEGED

The lead story revealed that America's preeminent nuclear physicist had been suspended by the Atomic Energy Commission from any further government involvement. Oppenheimer, the wartime director of Los Alamos, the laboratory that developed America's first atomic bombs, and the man named by *Time* magazine as the "father of the atomic bomb," was now suddenly denied access to atomic secrets. A startled public learned that morning that Oppenheimer had been called before a closed hearing of the Commission's Personnel Security Board, where a panel of three men would judge his loyalty and consequently his future involvement in the government's program of nuclear energy development.

This action centered on several major charges, among them his association in the 1930s and early 1940s with Communists, including his brother, Frank Oppenheimer, his sister-in-law, and his wife, Katherine. He was also charged with hiring Communists and former Communists to work on the atomic bomb during the war. Mysteriously, he had also purportedly given contradictory information to the Federal Bureau of Investigation about his own attendance at Communist functions. As well, Oppenheimer failed to report an incident in which he was approached by an alleged Communist who wanted him to pass classified scientific information about the American atomic bomb to the Soviet government. The AEC's charge that Oppenheimer had opposed the development of the hydrogen bomb, even after President Truman had ordered its development in 1950, was especially serious.

It was perhaps this last allegation that puzzled readers most. By the time the war ended and the story of the Manhattan Project* and Los Alamos had been made public, Oppenheimer was a scientist of immense

*The Manhattan Project was the code name for the secret World War II program to develop an atomic bomb.

stature. Since 1945 he had been interviewed in newspapers and magazines and on the radio dozens of times. He had been a member of numerous scientific, military, and diplomatic committees concerned with nuclear weapons. Perhaps no other individual was as closely linked with these weapons as was Robert Oppenheimer.

Official Washington gave few clues or explanations. President Dwight D. Eisenhower did little more than issue a statement through his press office confirming that Oppenheimer's hearing was a result of an executive order on April 17, 1953, which required a review of security clearances for every case where the files contained "substantial derogatory information"; both Eisenhower and the Atomic Energy Commission assured reporters that such information was indeed in the files of Dr. Oppenheimer. The President also revealed that four months earlier he had ordered a "blank wall" between Oppenheimer and all secret government information. This action included dispatching government agents to Oppenheimer's house in Princeton, New Jersey, to remove all classified records, reports, and correspondence from his files. When Eisenhower mentioned that he had consulted former Admiral Lewis L. Strauss, the present chairman of the Atomic Energy Commission, about the Oppenheimer matter, reporters made a crucial connection: Strauss and Oppenheimer had become bitter adversaries over the evolution and control of atomic energy.

Reached at a health resort in Arizona, Senator Joseph McCarthy refused full comment, but did indicate that he had evidence to prove that Oppenheimer was a member of the Communist party. Congressman Sterling Cole and Senator Bourke Hickenlooper, members of the House-Senate Atomic Energy Committee, issued a joint statement that Congress would take appropriate action on Oppenheimer only after the commission finished its hearing. From Missouri, former President Truman offered hestitant support for the beleaguered scientist: "I inherited Dr. Oppenheimer. He was considered a great scientist—one of the greatest—in connection with the atomic bomb. Don't convict anybody by implication or gossip."[1]

To the public, the situation was most perplexing; Robert Oppenheimer was, after all, the quintessential scientist they had read so much about over the years. He was a brilliant and enigmatic man who looked and acted every bit the part: tall, thin, graying, aloof, highly articulate, and always a bit obscure. A child prodigy, he had studied in Europe under Ernest Rutherford and Niels Bohr—two of the greatest names in physics. His wartime record had earned him, justifiably enough, considerable praise for his management of the secret Los Alamos laboratory, whose successes had exploded so dramatically on Hiroshima and Nagasaki. He also displayed remarkable talents as a leader and advisor, roles he conducted brilliantly as chairman of the AEC's General Advisory Committee and as a member of a dozen other high-level advisory bodies within the Departments of Defense and State.

Despite Oppenheimer's commendable record, some people felt that he had a dark side that was potentially threatening. His political past was shaded with Communists, an affiliation that greatly concerned the United States government at a time when the Soviets were seen as an especially pressing threat. This matter was only further complicated when, after working so hard to create an atomic bomb, he suddenly appeared to attempt to stall their further development, and just at the time when the United States' nuclear monopoly had been broken by the Soviets. This angered powerful men in Washington.

Quite clearly, Oppenheimer's "subversive" activities seemed to be a strong contradiction to the scientist's public image—that of a dedicated public servant who had given twelve years of his life to government service. To those who knew him, Oppenheimer seemed to be a man increasingly ambivalent about his role and the roles of his fellow scientists in society. After successfully leading the project at Los Alamos to develop the first atomic bombs, he told Harry Truman in 1948 that he felt as if he had "blood on his hands." In a similarly pensive mood, he told a reporter that the scientists who had developed the atomic weapons had, as a result, "known sin." Beleaguered by newsmen to comment on the possibilities of thermonuclear weapons, he told a *Time* magazine reporter: "If you ask: 'Can we make them [weapons] more terrible?' the answer is yes. If you ask: 'Can we make a lot of them?' the answer is yes. If you ask: 'Can we make them terribly more terrible?' the answer is probably." It was indeed a complicated set of circumstances. The designing and developing of a scientifically remarkable atomic weapon was a project that had interested and excited Oppenheimer as a scientist, but the violent and devastating implications of the weapon presented another matter altogether. It was, perhaps, a situation that greatly complicated the scientist's life.

Oppenheimer's ambivalence could hardly have flattered the scientists he had wooed to Los Alamos during the war, or those he had encouraged to stay on afterward to work on newer, more powerful weapons. Certainly, his behavior could not have pleased the nation's military leaders or men like Lewis Strauss, who believed that the United States urgently needed to protect its strategic interests. What was clear is that Oppenheimer was being attacked by the government he had served for a dozen years.

News of Oppenheimer's hearing surfaced suddenly at a time when the world was greatly concerned with the global balance of power.

Just a few days earlier the press had reported renewed Pentagon interest in Chiang Kai-shek's Nationalist Chinese Army in Formosa. An editorial in *Pravda*, the Communist Party newspaper, suggested that the United States was planning an attack on the Chinese mainland. So far, the deterrent to major military action by either the United States or the Soviet Union was the possession by each of powerful hydrogen weapons. The development of American H-bombs had been held up, according to Senator Joseph McCarthy, for nearly eighteen months by "powerful friends of the Soviet Union" within the United States Government.

President Eisenhower had been forced to turn over most of an early April press conference to Lewis Strauss in order to field questions from reporters on the new H-bombs. Strauss had assured reporters that the recent weapons tests in the Pacific had exceeded expectations. While the tests had been successful, the public did not know that the weapons had been only experimental models which required laboratory conditions to work properly. Few knew that the first hydrogen bomb required a huge multistory building the size of an aircraft hangar to enclose the delicate components of the bomb to protect it from the humid climate. The eighty-eight-ton bomb also required an elaborate refrigeration system to chill liquid deuterium to subfreezing temperatures.

Future bombs, Strauss told eager reporters, would be smaller and deliverable from high-flying aircraft which could, in his words, "take out" a city like New York. Already the Air Force had made secret studies of potential Soviet targets in the United States. Other military studies mentioned the possibility of decentralizing key industries to make certain cities less attractive targets for the Russians. Civilian defense plans called for massive training and "dress rehersals" for the orderly evacuation of cities under threat of attack. Strategic military calculations were discreetly circulated through Congress by Air Force leaders, warning that current radar screens were operational but hardly what one Air Force general called "bomber tight." The United States would have, in an era of aircraft-dropped bombs, perhaps only as little as two hours' warning.

Also unknown to the public was the sequence of scientific and technological events between the end of the war and 1952, when the United States exploded its first thermonuclear device. Oppenheimer's role in these events was hidden in the highly classified Atomic Energy Commission records and in the similarly unavailable minutes and reports of committees and advisory bodies concerned with weapons and national defense. By the time Oppenheimer's security hearing began, the H-bomb was already fact, although its history had been, until only recently, mostly a series of untested theories and uncertain technologies.

A few were aware that the decision to make the hydrogen bomb had not been an easy one. Oppenheimer, among others, had resisted an all-out program like the Manhattan Project for the hydrogen bomb until scientific knowledge was sufficient to commit the vast resources necessary for such an effort. Indeed, the scientific future of the weapon was little more than theory until 1951. By the time the H-bomb became a reality, Oppenheimer and several of his colleagues were strongly opposed to making the weapon. To some this opposition seemed unnecessary and perhaps even disloyal. On April 8, only four days before the hearing, *The New York Times* ran the first public story that recreated the events preceding President Truman's decision to make the H-bomb.

The *Times* article revealed the smoldering history of nuclear weapons that so insidiously engulfed Robert Oppenheimer's life. Four years after Truman's decision, and two years after the United States had created its first thermonuclear weapon, the argument reemerged; Oppenheimer was once again linked to the fact that America had lost valuable time in developing hydrogen weapons. Despite allegations that Oppenheimer's associations and political past were suspicious, the real charge and basis for the hearing was that he had opposed the H-bomb. That his suspicious past had already been cleared once during the war, and again in 1948 by the Atomic Energy Commission itself, did not seem to make any difference.

With anti-Communist hysteria never higher, the government of the United States brought its best known scientist to trial to determine his loyalty—a move that was hardly about to calm the public's fears or guarantee a fair hearing for Robert Oppenheimer.

2. Emergence

Julius Robert Oppenheimer was born on April 12, 1904, in New York City.

He was born to wealthy and cultivated parents. Oppenheimer's father, also named Julius, was an emigré from Germany at eighteen and had become a successful clothing merchant by the time of Robert's birth. His mother, Ella Friedman, came from an established family that had settled in the Baltimore and Philadelphia areas for several generations. Despite a deformed right arm, she studied painting in Paris and became an accomplished artist. They had a second son, Louis, who died shortly after birth. In 1912 the Oppenheimers had a third son named Frank. The family lived in a spacious thirteen-room apartment on New York's elegant Riverside Drive, attended by maids and a chauffeur. The apartment was richly furnished with art objects and paintings, including a small collection of Van Goghs.

It was a family in which artistic and intellectual interests were appreciated and fostered. At a young age Robert became an avid reader; an interest in one book would prompt his father to purchase every other volume by the same author. After his uncle gave him a small collection of rocks and minerals, Robert became a dedicated mineralogist, later joining the prestigious Mineralogical Society of New York, where at age sixteen he delivered a paper to its members, who were astonished by the young man's knowledge.

Both Julius and Ella were nonpracticing Jews, but they were aware of being Jewish, of being different, and both were committed to social justice. They sent Robert and later Frank to the Ethical Culture School, then located on Central Park West. The school, founded by Felix Adler, stressed a philosophy built upon a concept of the goodness of man which was not actually linked to theology. Robert became the school's star pupil. He learned every subject quickly and was especially interested in mathematics and chemistry. In class he was frequently the first to raise his hand, but as soon as the discussion dragged or the exercise became mundane he would respond by becoming quiet and sullen. He was often sickly, staying home in the care of his mother. At school he was not regarded as being particularly rugged; he was known for his dislike of sports and his penchant for riding the school's elevator instead of taking the stairs. His air of superiority, remembers writer and childhood friend Paul Horgan, was nevertheless accompanied by a great charm. Oppenheimer was aware that his parents were proud of his intellect and even, as he later put it, of the fact that he was "highbrow."[1] But his parents also found reason to worry about their brilliant son. Ella wanted Robert to be more like other young boys and one summer succeeded in sending him to camp. His lack of interest in games and his sullenness quickly made him the target of harassment from his peers; summer camp ended abruptly when he was stripped naked and locked overnight in an icehouse by his fellow campers.

In the summer of 1921, Julius took his family to Germany. Robert took charge of Frank, and the two brothers spent their days walking around Cologne and the Ruhr Valley. Toward the end of the summer vacation, Robert contracted colitis after taking a long solitary hike through the Harz Mountains. When the family came home in the fall, he was too ill to enter Harvard University. After recovering, he was rescued from boredom by his father, who arranged for him and a former teacher of the Ethical Culture School, Herbert Smith, to take a long tour through the American Southwest. It was Robert's first trip to New Mexico and Colorado; the vast landscapes, with their muted browns and reds and yellows, impressed him enormously. The trip was a great success; Smith quickly grew to admire his young companion's surprising amount of energy and stamina. Robert demonstrated a toughness he had never displayed before, and in so doing, impressed even himself. The two men spent weeks wandering through the mountains, and Oppenheimer developed a talent for handling horses.

The small village of Cowles, New Mexico, some twenty miles from Santa Fe, high in the Sangre de Cristo Mountains, became particularly important to Oppenheimer. There, Robert and Smith stayed at the Los Piños Dude Ranch, which was run by a woman named Katherine Chaves Page. Like many guest ranches in New Mexico, Los Piños was a rustic lodge primarily for wealthy easterners who came to experience the "Old West." Page, who came from an old and aristocratic New Mexican family, was quick to accept young Robert, which rapidly made him a devoted admirer. Over the next few years he returned again and again to Los Piños, and later, with the help of Page, bought a small ranch located only a few miles from Cowles. The location was spectacular and couldn't have pleased Oppenheimer more; the ranch, situated on 160 acres of land, ran up the side of a mountain to a cliff that was over 10,000 feet above sea level. There was a small cabin just comfortable enough for small groups—two bedrooms upstairs and a kitchen and living room area downstairs. At first, only Frank and Robert spent the summers there, but eventually Robert invited his friends and students for a week or a month of roughing it. To everyone's amusement, he named it Perro Caliente, which means "hot dog" in Spanish.

Many years later he would tell friends that his two true loves were science and New Mexico.

Oppenheimer entered Harvard in 1922 and graduated in just three years. Once again he demonstrated a considerable talent for learning, and learning very quickly. He began studying chemistry, but after a year shifted to physics. He explained that it was the study of order that fascinated him. He was truly a dedicated student, spending many long hours studying alone in his room, subsisting only on chocolate-covered raisins. His contemporaries agreed that Oppenheimer had an exceptional mind. As in high school, he dominated the classes that interested him and withdrew from those that bored him. He was given to showing off intellectually, an immaturity that even Oppenheimer himself disliked. The parts of his personality often struggled against each other; in class he sometimes expressed his love for learning with arrogance or precociousness before his friends. On one particularly hot day, he told an acquaintance, the only thing he could do all day was to lie on his bed and read Sir James Hopwood Jeans' *Dynamic Theory of Gases*, a particularly difficult book. Jeffries Wyman, a fellow science major, at first found Oppenheimer "a little precious, and perhaps a little arrogant, but very interesting, very full of ideas."[2]

Oppenheimer's physical appearance, even at a young age, was as interesting and unique as his personality. He was six feet tall, but his thin build and slightly stooped frame made him seem fragile. He had an exceptional face with an almost startling quality to it; his pale skin was tightly stretched across highly pronounced bones, and his blue-gray eyes were absolutely intense and piercing. Oppenheimer had a certain elegance about him but, surprisingly, allowed his teeth and fingers to become stained yellow with nicotine from years of heavy smoking.

A physics teacher, Percy Bridgman, was the first person to introduce Oppenheimer to the study of physics. Oppenheimer soon became fascinated by the mysteries of matter and motion that are hidden from the eye. It was a good experience for both men; Bridgman, who treated Oppenheimer as an equal, had the gifted student every teacher dreamed of, and Oppenheimer had the teacher and mentor under whom gifted students can grow. His broad reading in science and his quick grasp of the subject matter gave Oppenheimer the opportunity to take advanced classes without first taking the usual prerequisite courses. Later, Oppenheimer liked to tell about the time the Harvard physics department was considering his request to take an advanced course. They expressed surprise at the scope of his reading; one member of the faculty, George Washington Pierce, insisted that Oppenheimer "was a liar if he's said he had read all those books, but he should get a Ph.D. for knowing their titles."[3] Intellectually, Robert had grown tremendously; emotionally, he was still maturing. He graduated summa cum laude. His yearbook quote was brief: "In college three years as an undergraduate."[4]

Oppenheimer decided not to stay at Harvard for graduate work, and even rejected a scholarship. His reasons for leaving were twofold. For personal reasons he wanted to strike out on his own, away from American universities and his family. More importantly, for a student of physics in the 1920s, there was only one place to study at the graduate level—Europe. In 1925 the great universities and laboratories were centered in England, Holland, and Germany. It was an exciting time for science, especially for physics, which was undergoing a revolution. The great work of men like Niels Bohr, Ernest Rutherford, and Max Born was being expanded every day. Oppenheimer arrived at a time when theoretical physics was to make another major step, leaping, as the astronomer Harlow Shapley put it, from the Cenozoic to Psychozoic Age.[5]

One of the great developments of science in the twentieth century was quantum mechanics—the study of the energy and movement of subatomic particles. The evolving theory of quantum mechanics had become the primary concern of theoretical physicists. Since the turn of the century, within just a few decades, scientists had redefined the physical universe and had begun to reveal the intricacies of motion and substance.

In the fall of 1925 Robert Oppenheimer arrived at the Cavendish Laboratory in Cambridge, England. Percy Bridgman had written a personal letter of introduction to Ernest Rutherford on Oppenheimer's behalf. While praising his "brilliant record" at Harvard as well as his quick mind, Bridgman qualified his recommendation by adding that "it is a bit of a gamble as to whether Oppenheimer will ever make any real contribution of an important character, but if he does make good at all, I believe that he will be a very unusual success. . . ."[6] It was a propitious time to be in Europe; during the next five years scientists would further clarify quantum theory in revelations like the Schrödinger and Dirac equations, field theory, and quantum electrodynamics. For Oppenheimer, quantum theory would become an intellectual puzzle to unravel and reassemble.

At Cavendish, Oppenheimer first met Ernest Rutherford, the great Danish physicist Niels Bohr, and Paul Dirac. While theory would become a consuming challenge for Oppenheimer, laboratory work would not. His stay at Cambridge seemed to precipitate an emotional crisis. For a few months he visited a psychiatrist in London, only to give up when the meetings failed to help him. The reasons for the crisis were never clear, even to his friends of the time. Nevertheless, the period was a difficult one for Oppenheimer; he later said that at one point he had even considered "bumping [himself] off." Once, while visiting his friend Francis Fergusson in Paris, Oppenheimer revealed a few factors that may have contributed to his unhappiness: his clumsy efforts in the laboratory and his several unsuccessful relationships with women. On another occasion, Oppenheimer admitted to friends that he had left a "poisoned apple" on the desk of a teacher at Cambridge.[7] No one was poisoned, however, and the event, if it happened, seem to pass without notice. For relief from his problems, Oppenheimer joined old friends from Harvard on a spring holiday in Corsica. They walked the island from one side to the other, stayed in small inns, and talked late into the night.* To John Edsall, one of his companions, Oppenheimer explained that the kind of man he admired most would be one who becomes extraordinarily good at doing lots of things, but still maintains a tear-stained countenance.[8]

Robert changed schools in the autumn of 1926. He arrived at the University of Göttingen in Germany complete with new clothes and a small reputation. Unlike most of his new fellow students, Oppenheimer had experience: He had studied under men like James Franck and Max Born, was elected as an associate of the Cambridge Philosophical Society, and had two of his publications appearing in the journal of the society: "On the Quantum Theory of the Problem of the Two Bodies" and "On the Quantum Theory of Vibration-Rotation Bands."

At Göttingen, Oppenheimer wrote a now-famous paper with Max Born on the approximations involved in the theory of molecules. In less than three years he wrote a number of papers on wave functions, the scattering of electrons, and certain stellar conditions known as "opacities." He made a contribution by way of constructing an original theory of wave motion. His years in Europe were among the most academically productive years he would know. Later, as a teacher, he would produce few original papers, preferring instead to coauthor the papers of his students.

Oppenheimer developed a reputation as an eccentric, but he made many new friends nevertheless. He mastered Dutch and Italian; as a pastime, he read Dante in the original Italian, a habit ridiculed by Paul Dirac. His colleagues Fritz Houtermans and George Uhlenbeck shared his interests in literature. He befriended fellow Americans Ed Condon and his wife, and seemed especially fond of a graduate student named Charlotte Riefenstahl. Karl T. Compton and his wife, Margaret, also became part of Oppenheimer's American colony of friends. When at last he felt ready to take the examination for his doctorate, he discovered that the German Minister of Education would not permit him to do so because he lacked some of the qualifications. Max Born intervened, basing his case on Oppenheimer's exceptional work and his "economic hardship." The minister relented and Oppenheimer passed with honors. He returned briefly to America, professionally enhanced by his European experiences. He had a strong desire to have America replace Europe as the center for the study of theoretical physics.

---

*To writer Nuel Pharr Davis, Oppenheimer apparently confessed to an ill-fated love affair in Corsica. It was an intense relationship; so intense, in fact, that years later Oppenheimer would never do more than allude to it. Frank Oppenheimer, however, does not believe that such an affair ever really took place.

Preface

Few contemporary scientists have achieved the fame and importance of J. Robert Oppenheimer. His stature as a legendary figure of this century is based on little more than a dozen years of public life—years that profoundly influenced the history of contemporary times: His name is linked inexorably with the development of nuclear weapons.

More by luck than by choice, he arrived at the study of physics just as it underwent its greatest evolution. He became a member of the small group of well-educated men and women who made the splitting of the atom one of the great achievements—and threats—of the modern world.

After teaching physics for nearly a decade, he assumed a major role in directing the wartime development of a new and secret application of science, the atomic bomb. Following the war he joined the cadre of policymakers who shaped the arms and defense strategies of the United States. From 1945 to 1954, J. Robert Oppenheimer was one of the most important and influential consultants to the United States Government on matters of atomic energy. He was chairman for six years of the powerful General Advisory Committee of the Atomic Energy Commission; he was a member or the chairman of numerous advisory bodies within the Departments of Defense and State; and he made major contributions to the crafting of the plan for the international control of atomic energy put forth by the United States at the United Nations. He came to be highly respected for the breadth of his vision and his deep understanding of science and society.

But for all of these events, J. Robert Oppenheimer might have escaped his exceptional fame except for a crucial event that occurred in 1954: a security hearing called by the federal government to assess his loyalty. After a dozen years of public service, Oppenheimer was brought to account for both his personal and public lives.

At the heart of the hearing was an examination of Oppenheimer's participation in the development of nuclear weapons. Although he had entered the secret wartime Manhattan Project late, he rose quickly to become its most famous and visible participant. For another eight years he had influenced the individuals and bureaucracy that then built weapons vastly more powerful than those that created the atomic age at Hiroshima and Nagasaki. His influence—which was the real subject of the inquiry—was highly regarded by some and condemned by others; in 1954, however, it was considered inimical to the interests of the United States. The nature and facts of his role in these events are clear only now, with the passage of some thirty years, and with the surfacing of previously secret records from the times.

Perhaps tragically, J. Robert Oppenheimer and nuclear weapons are inseparable, as the 1954 hearing demonstrated with painful clarity. This book, therefore, examines the development of such weapons, from the first crude, hand-built atomic bombs at Los Alamos to the destructive weapons that now dominate international arms talks and peace movements. The book traces, to the extent that the record and individual recollections allow, Oppenheimer's direct involvement with, or influence over, such developments. In this context, his actions and personal views serve only to enlarge his legacy, not diminish it.

Oppenheimer's extraordinary life, his intelligence and enigmatic personality, make him an obvious candidate for biographers. Indeed, he has been the subject of a great deal of popular literature and drama. Those who have written about him have regarded him mostly in terms of his striking and often contradictory personality: brilliant and noble, yet sometimes manipulative and condescending. He is perceived as generous to a fault, yet driven by self-aggrandizement. The private Oppenheimer remains hidden. About his public years he said little; he left no autobiography or diary. His personal feelings and motivations are frequently unknown or veiled behind his facile command of the language. But whatever dynamics were at play, he nevertheless was a participant in momentous historical events.

At the expense of reducing the man and his fascinating life to a dozen years, this history is concerned primarily with the period of time J. Robert Oppenheimer spent in government service: 1942–1954. It is for this period that history will most remember him. This twelve-year period witnessed the man's emerging as director of a unique scientific adventure, a public figure, and a statesman. This book does not examine in detail his earlier life, nor the productive years after 1954 when he returned to teaching and lecturing. It is neither a study of his psyche, nor a definitive statement about his life: no work so close to the events and the individuals could be.

For this interpretation of the man's life and times, the author alone is responsible.

Many individuals provided me with their time, their assistance, and their memories in the preparation of this book. Although the chronology of events is based on documents and records, the interpretation of J. Robert Oppenheimer has been enlarged enormously by memories of the man by his friends and contemporaries who spoke and spent time with me.

I am grateful to Harold Agnew, David Axelrod, Robert Bacher, Hans Bethe, Norris Bradbury, Walter Bramlett, Alice Bullock, Lois Bursack, Oscar Collier, Bill Cunliffe, Anita Dalback, Marge Dube, Priscilla Green

Contents

Oppenheimer's desire to lead the American school of new physics would take more than just interest. He returned to Harvard as a National Research Council Fellow, but realized that further study in Europe would be necessary under the two leading theorists of the day, Paul Ehrenfest at University of Leiden in Holland and Wolfgang Pauli at Zurich's Technical High School. In 1928 Oppenheimer applied for and received a fellowship from the International Education Board, which would begin in the fall at the University of Leiden.

Ehrenfest was quickly impressed with his American student. There was little doubt that Oppenheimer's mind was exceptional, although Ehrenfest believed the young man's mathematics were careless. The results, believed Ehrenfest, were precise enough, but the calculations were rough and messy. He was well respected and liked; his fellow students nicknamed him Opje, and later, in America, the nickname was anglicized to Oppie, or just Oppy. In January, Oppenheimer went on to Zurich to join Wolfgang Pauli. The German scientist exacted great precision from Oppenheimer's thinking, and was fascinated on one hand by its depth and swiftness, and on the other hand by Oppenheimer's lack of concern for exactitude. Nevertheless, the two men worked well together. Isidor Rabi, a fellow American studying in Europe at the same time, thought Oppenheimer's mind was the generation's best in physics: "I was never in the same league," he said.[9]

Homesick, Oppenheimer returned to the United States in the spring of 1929, this time with his reputation well established. He returned, he said, because he had learned a great deal and because he "wanted to pursue [the new physics] myself, to explain it, to foster its cultivation." He had good reason to be pleased with himself: "I had many invitations to university positions, one or two in Europe, and perhaps some ten in the United States."[10] He chose concurrent appointments as an assistant professor at the California Institute of Technology and at the University of California at Berkeley. Teaching at Cal Tech one semester and at Berkeley the following was a pattern he would maintain for the next ten years. He would not return to Europe for nearly twenty years.

Oppenheimer arrived in California in September 1929. For a great part of his life he had been a student, isolated from the larger society around him. His wealth—an inherited income of ten thousand dollars a year—permitted him a life-style far better than most of his colleagues. The powerful social and economic changes that had first swept through Europe and then the United States were of little interest to the scientist. He had noticed the growing tension in German life, but mainly because it had been the topic of a student discussion. "I was," he later admitted, "interested in man and his experience; I was deeply interested in my science; but I had no understanding of the relations of man to his society."

At first he thought only of teaching. He had already discovered two years before that he had a problem working with his students. It was painful for him to be forced to slow down for his students so they could understand him. Certainly it must have been awkward for his students, as well. He also had a curious habit of speaking more softly to make a point, rather than speaking up. Naturally enough, Oppenheimer's first course at Berkeley was in quantum mechanics. It took nearly three months for Oppenheimer to start recognizing the faces of his students and to understand that they were thoroughly perplexed. He sought out Raymond Birge, who had taken the early responsibility of being Robert's mentor. "They're not learning," he told his colleague. Birge suggested patience. "It was," Birge later wrote, "my first intimation not only of the speed with which Oppenheimer's mind worked, but also of his complete failure at the time to realize how slowly, comparatively speaking, the minds of most others worked."[11]

In time, Oppenheimer developed an easier style and took a personal interest in his students. He was never far from his cigarettes—a practice many thought helped him think and talk. As well, he gradually learned to swallow his frustration with teaching. There were times in the beginning when he responded so sharply to silence or to a wrong answer that his tongue-lashing stunned everyone in the room. A few students seemed genuinely terrorized. It took time for Oppenheimer to mature as a teacher. Some friends remember noticing a difference after a year or two. By the mid-1930s, Oppenheimer had secured a good reputation both as a teacher and as a person. He was at ease now, comfortable in the classroom. His style conveyed a sense of excitement and challenge that captivated his students. He became famous for the richness of his courses, and for the elegance of his presentation. He even found himself encouraging students *not* to take his courses a second and third time.

> Starting with a single graduate student in my first year at Berkeley, we gradually begin to build up what was to become the largest school in the country of graduate and postdoctoral study in theoretical physics, so that as time went on, we came to have between a dozen and 20 people learning and adding to quantum theory, nuclear physics relativity, and other modern physics. As the number of students increased, so in general did their quality; the men who worked with me during those years hold chairs in many of the great centers of physics in this country; they have made important contributions to science.[12]

Robert Serber, an early student of Oppenheimer's, remembers that the process of mellowing took five years. "His course [on quantum mechanics] was an inspirational, as well as educational, achievement. He transmitted to his students a feeling of the beauty of the logical structure of physics and an excitement in the development of science. Almost everyone listened to the course more than once."[13]

Hans Bethe, an emigré from Austria and a long-time colleague and friend of Oppenheimer's, remembered his friend's teaching as an emphasis on fundamental problems in physics. His small groups of students and the intense dialogue and range of issues covered seemed to have evolved from Oppenheimer's experiences in Göttingen. "Perhaps he wanted to perpetuate that feeling of continuous discovery which must have pervaded Göttingen. All through his life he was able to convey to all around him a sense of excitement in the quest of science."[14] His excitement extended to life as well. When he organized a picnic or orchestrated dinner, it became a special occasion for those who participated.

He worked best in small groups. In his quantum mechanics class, he might have fifteen students—mostly graduate students, with a few postdoctoral fellows. Meeting with them in his office, Oppenheimer would solicit progress reports from the students on their respective research projects, utilizing the exchange to make inquiries and to introduce material of a broader nature. Serber remembers a class in which the topics discussed spanned electrodynamics, cosmic waves, astrophysics, and nuclear physics.[15] Oppenheimer remembered:

> I found myself in Berkeley and almost entirely at Caltech as the only one who understood what this [theoretical physics] was all about, and the gift which my high school teacher of English had noted for explaining technical things came into action. I didn't start to make a school; I didn't start to look for students. I started really as a propagator of the theory which I loved, about which I continued to learn more, and which was not well understood and which was very rich. The pattern was not that of someone who takes on a course and teaches students preparing for a variety of careers but of explaining first to faculty, staff and colleagues and then, to anyone who would listen, what this was about, what had been learned, what the unsolved problems were.[16]

As his reputation grew, Oppenheimer's circle of friends increased. He became closely involved with some of his students and assuming a parental role he even prepared meals for them, took them out to dinner, and helped arrange for part-time jobs. He joined the University Faculty Club, and became acquainted with faculty members outside of physics and science, mostly classicists and artists. He took on administrative duties in the graduate school and argued for higher pay. Almost single-handedly he built up the theoretical wing of the Physics Department at Berkeley. His successes brought notoriety, which even caused some members of the faculty club to whisper "There goes Oppenheimer" when he passed by.

The young professor's apartment consisted of two sparsely furnished rooms decorated with objects from Oppenheimer's many visits to New Mexico. His rooms were located in a large wooden house built into the wall of a steep canyon on Tamalpais Road outside of Berkeley. The furniture was simple and a few lovely Navaho rugs covered the floors. For visitors, the most arresting feature was a large porch on one side of the house which overlooked the canyon. One could approach the apartment only by descending a series of twisting steps from a parking lot above the house.

In a letter to his brother, he wrote that for diversion from his work he rode horses "once a week" or drove his Chrysler at high speeds. He particularly liked to turn the corners at seventy miles an hour, he added, scaring his hapless passengers "out of all sanity." After several accidents, Julius Oppenheimer finally agreed to buy his son a new car.[17]

Oppenheimer recalled later that it wasn't until 1936 that his interests changed; before that "I was not interested in and did not read about politics and economics." Outside of university duties, he read widely, but mostly novels, the classics, plays, and poetry. With fellow teacher Arthur Rider he studied and read Sanskrit. He was, in his own words, "wholly divorced" from the contemporary political and social scene in America; in his tiny apartment, he had no radio and no telephone. Friends and students had to reach him at his office or by leaving notes for him on his apartment door. Curiously, for someone with such diverse reading interests, Oppenheimer read neither newspapers nor popular news magazines. Reportedly, he didn't learn of the stock market crash of 1929 until some months after it happened. Leo Nedelsky thought Oppenheimer was ignorant of events, rather than naive. "What does politics have to do with truth, goodness, and beauty?" he remembers Oppenheimer saying.

Halfway through the thirties, Oppenheimer changed rather suddenly and became interested in the world around him. His awakening, as some called it, had a quality of immature susceptibility to it; in a sense, this was true. Oppenheimer did rely greatly on others to introduce him to people with philosophies that led them to be active in social and political causes. Nearly twenty years later, Oppenheimer noted: "I had [then] no framework of political conviction or experience to give me perspective in these matters." At least some of his awakening social sense came from the realization that his students couldn't find jobs, or at best, were forced to accept jobs that he unhappily admitted were totally "inadequate." He also learned that more and more members of his family in Germany had become victims of the Nazis. Soon he was using his money to help bring family members to America.

One person who had an important personal influence on Oppenheimer was Jean Tatlock, who was the daughter of an English professor at

Berkeley. She was attractive, intelligent, outgoing, and capable of passionate, if brief, commitments to political causes. She had many friends who were politically active, especially in the embryonic teacher unions and in the American Communist party. She was briefly a member of the party and introduced Robert to colleagues and friends who expanded Oppenheimer's political life. Like his brother Frank, Oppenheimer had become convinced that social conscience demanded activity and believed that it was possible for individuals to effect change. Frank Oppenheimer, forty-five years later, remembers that in the 1930s many people, including his brother, believed that society could be changed for the better. It was novel then for campuses in America to be centers of a wide range of political thought. Jean, like no other woman Oppenheimer had known, seemed to embody this spirit. They soon became intimate and at least twice considered themselves engaged. Frank and his new wife, Jackie, saw Robert and Jean as a couple with a special relationship. Jean seemed especially sensitive to Robert in a rare way. Despite their intimacy, the relationship always appeared to swing between promise and collapse. Robert showered Jean with attention and gifts, almost flaunting his wealth, and Jean reacted by being unkind or by taunting him. The two remained involved until 1939, when Oppenheimer began to see less of Tatlock; the relationship ended with his own marriage in late 1940.

Jean Tatlock also had a remarkable and broadening influence on Oppenheimer's political involvement. Through Jean he became extremely interested in the Spanish Loyalist cause, and became active in the support of the fight against Franco. Support for the Loyalists was popular among campus intellectuals in America. Oppenheimer contributed money to several arms of the relief movement, and even participated in local fund-raising activities, like bazaars. The end of the civil war in Spain and the defeat of the Loyalists caused Oppenheimer, in his words, "great sorrow."

It was through his support for the Loyalists that Oppenheimer met Thomas Addis, who solicited money from the scientist with the understanding that this money would go directly to support "freedom fighters" in Spain. Through Addis, Oppenheimer met the prominent Isaac Folkoff, a man he later told government agents was a "communist." He also met Rudy Lambert, a friend of Jean Tatlock's who was active in the California unions. He would create difficult problems for Oppenheimer in little more than a decade.

As part of his concern for teacher pay, Oppenheimer joined the California Teachers' Union, Local 349, and was active enough to be elected recording secretary. While his involvement with the union continued until 1941, as did his connection with the Loyalist supporters, he gradually began to restrict his political activities. By his own thinking, he had more or less severed most political connections, including those with the California Consumer's Union, by 1941. There seems to have been no formal resignation or dramatic severance. Instead, he could only remember one crucial date: He attended his last Spanish war-relief party on the eve of Pearl Harbor, December 6, 1941.

Throughout his period of political associations, however, Oppenheimer appeared to remain more interested in the philosophy of the cause than in its execution. He gave money freely, taking an outspoken stand in the teachers' union in favor of increasing salaries.* He read voraciously, and to the surprise of some, consumed most of the writings of Marx, Engels, and Lenin in a few weeks. He subscribed in 1938 to the *People's Daily World*, the newspaper of the Communist party in California. His new friends, whatever their value or origin, remained secondary to his first interest: the studying and teaching of physics.

This was less the case for Robert's brother Frank, his junior by eight years. The two had been close since their childhood, Robert usually assuming a fatherly role. In their youth they had done many things together. Frank was very bright and musically talented. He was, in fact, such an accomplished flutist that Robert once remarked that Frank should become professional. Instead, Frank took up physics, perhaps because of his brother, and studied abroad in England and later in Italy. Robert remembered: "We were very close, very fond of one another. He was not a very disciplined young man; I guess I was not either. He loved painting. He loved music. He was an expert horseman. . . . He read quite widely, but I am afraid very much as I did, belles lettres, poetry." Like Robert, Frank had an inheritance that permitted him to study where he liked. When Frank married, in 1936, the brothers' relationship changed. Although they retained their feelings for each other, as Robert saw it, the relationship became "less intimate and occasionally somewhat more strained." Jackie Oppenheimer's background was considerably less affluent and quite different from Frank's; by the time the two met she had made many friends among campus radicals. Like Jean with Robert, Jackie introduced Frank to politics. Together, Jackie and Frank joined the Communist party. The young couple often talked politics with Robert, and once persuaded him to attend a party meeting in their house. Frank, like Robert, would pay a heavy price for his political convictions in the years to come.

Robert's friendship with Haakron Chevalier, a teacher of French literature at Berkeley, would prove to be crucial in a few years. Chevalier had achieved some fame through his translations of the works of André Malraux, including *Man's Fate*, and of a book on Anatole France. The two men became good friends, drawn together by their common love of literature, music, food, and wines. Chevalier was not a scientist—he

*As an example, the salary for one teaching position had been reduced from $750 a month to $600 in 1932 and not raised again.

probably had no real idea of what Oppenheimer did in physics. Instead, he played to the broad range of interests Oppenheimer held. Chevalier was struck by the impression Robert gave of simultaneously possessing youth and agelessness. His expression, Chevalier noted, "could be Christ-like and Mephistophelean. . . ." For Chevalier, the scientist even emanated a spiritual quality.[18] Chevalier seemed as fascinated by the characteristics of the man as he was pleased by the notion of having such a famous man for a friend. Like Jean Tatlock, he introduced Oppenheimer to other men and women interested in liberal causes. For example, he persuaded Robert to join the teachers' union. Even in retrospect, Chevalier believes that Oppenheimer was firmly committed to the causes they both embraced in the 1930s.

The events in Europe, however, made it increasingly difficult for Oppenheimer to defend the actions of the Soviet Union. The Nazi-Soviet Pact of 1939 left many American sympathizers stunned, with no explanation for the abrupt shift of Russian policy toward German aggression. Chevalier remembers an evening when Oppenheimer crafted an elaborate explanation for the Soviet pact; but others, like Hans Bethe, remember a clear cooling of Oppenheimer's support. Friends like Victor Weiskopf and George Paczek reinforced Oppenheimer's hardening views by relating firsthand news of their stay in Russia and of the police-state conditions there.

Undoubtedly the most significant event of the period was Oppenheimer's relationship with Katherine Puening Dallet Harrison. Katherine, called Kitty, was married to Richard Harrison, an English physician studying radiology in Pasadena. The couple were friends with the Richard Tolmans and Charles Lauritsens, both colleagues of Oppenheimer's. Kitty and Robert met in the summer of 1939 at a party given by mutual friends.

Kitty had an interesting history. She had been married twice before; after her first marriage was annulled, she was married again in 1934 to a young man who had been active as a union organizer in Pittsburgh. Joe Dallet, a Communist, quickly persuaded his young wife to join the Communist party. The marriage was soon strained by Dallet's political activities; they separated two years later, and Dallet went to Spain to join the Loyalist forces. With hopes of reuniting, Kitty met her estranged husband in France in 1936; several weeks later he was killed fighting in Spain. She returned to New York, where she spent almost a year working. She lived in the company of her former husband's friends, some of whom were active in the party. One of these was a man named Steve Nelson, who later moved to California and took an active part in Communist activities. In 1938 Kitty married Richard Harrison and moved to Pasadena, near Berkeley, where she met Robert Oppenheimer.

The two quickly fell in love. Like Jean Tatlock before her, she seemed to draw a special response from Oppenheimer. Although less outgoing than Jean, she was bright and strong-willed. Both she and her husband were invited by Oppenheimer to spend a few weeks at his ranch in New Mexico. She arranged to come by herself, however, and joined Robert, Frank, and Frank's family. There they decided to get married as soon as possible. In September 1940 Kitty moved to Virginia City, Nevada, in order to establish the necessary residence to obtain a divorce. On November 1 she legally divorced Harrison, marrying Robert the same day. They returned to the startled community of Berkeley to make a home for themselves and for an expected child. The new baby, named Peter, arrived on May 15, 1941.

Some old friends of Oppenheimer's were somewhat skeptical of the independent Kitty. Some considered her less than a suitable partner for so distinguished a faculty member, but most accepted the news with their good wishes. Throughout her life, Kitty Oppenheimer provoked strong reactions in the people she met. Some found her personality charming and became good friends with her; others accepted her because she was Robert's wife. However, others disliked her and believed she was unpleasant and domineering. Perhaps they disliked the slavish manner in which Robert attended to her or appeared to make concessions to her.

Oppenheimer purchased a beautiful house for his new family at number 1 Eagle Hill Drive in San Francisco. Located on a high knoll, the house was dramatically set, with a garden that fell on three sides into a deep canyon. The Spanish-style home was Oppenheimer's first permanent residence since the family apartment in New York.

The 1930s, which had reshaped Robert Oppenheimer's life, were soon to be overshadowed by a new decade and by a series of remarkable developments. They were a combination of scientific, military, and political events which would open a different world to him.

3. Coordinator of Rapid Rupture

"The U Business is fantastic!" wrote Robert Oppenheimer to a friend in January 1939.[1]

The "business" he referred to was nuclear fission, the process by which an atom is struck by a neutron and caused to split into two fragments. The discovery was made a month earlier by two German scientists working at the Kaiser Wilhelm Institute for Chemistry in Berlin. Days before Christmas, Otto Hahn and Fritz Strassmann accidentally discovered fission while closely examining a sample of uranium which they had bombarded with neutrons; as a result, they discovered a radioactive isotope of barium. The only explanation was that the neutron absorbed by the uranium had caused the atom to split in half. Later, it was learned that the form of uranium split by Hahn and Strassman was the isotope of Uranium 235, a discovery which had momentous implications for both science and the military.

News of fission spread quickly to America and was announced to scientists attending the fifth Washington Conference on Theoretical Physics in January 1939. Scientists quickly realized that fission could lead to a chain, or a self-sustaining reaction. The reaction could become self-sustaining because during a chain reaction, additional neutrons are freed from the nucleus of uranium, releasing enormous amounts of energy. Each newly freed neutron in turn causes another nucleus to split, releasing more neutrons and energy, thereby continuing the reaction. Although it was not known at the time, under certain conditions fission produces another element, called plutonium, which is capable of fission. Scientists thought that Uranium 235—and later plutonium—might be a good atomic explosive. Very simply, they saw that a chain reaction, if controlled, would produce heat and power; if left uncontrolled, the same process would result in a powerful explosion. Oppenheimer, hearing the news from colleagues in California, began to calculate along with his students some of the characteristics that would occur during the fission process.

The possibility of creating a powerful explosion from fissioning uranium had great importance in light of the events occurring in Europe at the time. On September 1, 1939, German armed forces invaded Poland. Two days later, Great Britain and France declared war on Germany, and in little more than a week the Germans had crossed the Vistula River into Poland. In a fireside chat, President Roosevelt announced that the United

States would remain neutral; he could not, however, "ask that every American remain neutral in thought as well."

Several scientists, led by Leo Szilard, sought to obtain government financial support for a large-scale study of fission. If the explosive potential was known to the Americans, it only followed that it would certainly be known to the Germans as well. Franklin Roosevelt, encouraged by a letter from Albert Einstein that described fission, created the National Committee on Uranium in October 1939. Nine months later Roosevelt created the National Defense Research Committee (NDRC) and appointed Vannevar Bush of the Carnegie Institute as its chairman.

Bush had his hands full, with a large amount of work and limited funding. There was still no solid proof that a chain reaction could be created and sustained. There wasn't even a sufficient supply of uranium ore available with which tests could be conducted. In December, Glenn T. Seaborg, Joseph W. Kennedy, and Arthur C. Wahl discovered a new element, which they named plutonium. This new element quickly became another strong possibility for the guts of a bomb, but it could be obtained only through the fissioning of uranium, and both scientists and industry faced the complex task of obtaining a sufficient quantity of Uranium 235, the isotope of uranium necessary to create an explosive chain reaction. There were several possible methods of "separating" the artificially produced Uranium 235, or U 235, from the far more plentiful U 238.* In May of 1941, after almost a year's work, the Committee on Uranium could only report that a bomb made from uranium or plutonium was perhaps three to five years away.[2]

Just a month later, in June, Roosevelt created yet another government agency to coordinate scientific research, including all work in fission. The new organization was called the Office of Scientific Research and Development (OSRD) and was placed under the Office for Emergency Management, directly under Roosevelt. Vannevar Bush was made director, and he asked Karl T. Compton, the former president of the Massachusetts Institute of Technology, to assist him.

Research on fission, however, was still largely the work of individuals and small teams in universities across the nation. Oppenheimer's colleague Ernest Lawrence was confidently at work at Berkeley on an electromagnetic process which could, if successful, supply ample amounts of U 235. Oppenheimer, like his contemporaries at Princeton, the University of Chicago, M.I.T., and a half dozen other universities, studied various aspects of fission, but on a limited basis. From England word came that British scientists were convinced that a weapon could be developed in

---

*It is important to note that U 235 does not occur naturally in isolation. Only one out of every hundred uranium atoms is U 235; the other ninety-nine are the less-desirable U 238, which cannot be used in a bomb. U 235 can be obtained only through a process of separating one atom from the other.

two years or less providing, of course, that a supply of uranium was available. The initial predictions stated that a mass of five kilograms of U 235 would be enough for a chain reaction. Plutonium seemed to offer even stronger hopes for a weapon. Glenn Seaborg, working at Berkeley, was able to report that Plutonium 239, or Pu 239, was 1.7 times more likely than U 235 to undergo fission with what scientists were calling "slow neutrons."[3]

It became clear to Vannevar Bush that only a national, coordinated effort could fully explore the possibilities of fission. With additional monies from Roosevelt in October 1941, Bush accelerated his program to galvanize American science behind the war effort.

Robert Oppenheimer's participation in the swiftly growing fission program was formalized with an invitation from Arthur Compton, of OSRD, to attend a special meeting of the National Academy of Sciences in Schenectady, New York, on October 21, 1941. Along with Ernest Lawrence, Oppenheimer attended a two-day meeting to review the status of fission research. Compton hoped to use the committee's assessment as the basis for a major report to President Roosevelt. Invited at the urging of Lawrence, who thought his friend had important ideas to contribute, Oppenheimer also saw his role as one that assured that "open questions were seen as open and some sketch of a program understood."

Oppenheimer brought with him an understanding of the fission program which was gathered from his own work at Berkeley and from colleagues at other institutions. As a theorist he was certainly aware of the explosive possibility of fission. Rumor had it that he had first learned of the government's large program of fission research when a colleague started to review the work with him, assuming that Oppenheimer was already involved and knowledgeable. In Schenectady, Oppenheimer reported that the amount of fissionable material he thought was needed for a weapon would be perhaps as much as one hundred kilograms and no less than two kilograms. Others reviewed the status of several methods for separating U 235. There were several unknowns: the critical mass of uranium needed, the necessary speed for assembling the uranium and all other components of a bomb, and methods for preventing a process called predetonation, in which the chain reaction begins too early and fizzles. Oppenheimer was known to everyone in the room, to varying degrees. For some, however, his presentation was the first evidence of his amazing ability to synthesize diverse information. He left the meeting as a new participant in the leadership of the government's atomic bomb program.

His involvement, as he now saw it, was twofold. He became an unofficial member of the Lawrence team, working on electromagnetic separation. He met regularly with the program's steering committee and even with its special coordinating team. Using his talent for assimilating information from many sources and diverse disciplines, he contributed an idea after several months which, as he later recalled, "doubled or tripled the capacity, or halved or thirded the price of the [electromagnetic] plant [Lawrence] was building." His second job was to continue his own theoretical work on how to make a weapon. The effort increased his understanding of nuclear masses. Throughout these months, Oppenheimer continued teaching his heavy load of classes, even taking over the classes of colleagues who had left to work on other war-related projects.

The closing months of 1941 brought nothing but bad news from around the world. In late June, Germany had invaded the Soviet Union along a two-thousand-mile front extending from the Arctic to the Ukraine. Within days President Roosevelt had promised aid to the Russians. A month later, in July, the Japanese had occupied French Indochina, causing Roosevelt to freeze all Japanese assets in the United States. The War and Navy Departments sent word on November 27 that a Japanese strike in the Philippines or in Southeast Asia was likely. On December 6 Roosevelt made a personal appeal directly to Japanese Emperor Hirohito, asking him to use his influence to temper the military in an effort to preserve peace. Unknown to Roosevelt, a Japanese carrier task force already had left, on November 26, with plans to attack Pearl Harbor on December 7.

With news of the attack, Bush accelerated his efforts to further coordinate the fission program. Meeting in New York on December 16, just a week after the United States entered the war, Bush reviewed the scattered work for Vice-President Wallace. There was little doubt that a weapon of "superlatively destructive power" could be made, although the scope and size of such destruction was not yet known. Clearly it was time to explore, in an organized fashion, the methods for producing large quantities of U 235. Moreover, Bush argued, the Army should take control as soon as full-scale work on uranium and plutonium production had begun. With some misgivings, Roosevelt agreed.

The difficulties experienced by the projects were discussed at a meeting in Chicago on January 3, 1942. At Bush's suggestion, Arthur Compton called together the research groups from Columbia University, Princeton, and Berkeley, and also Oppenheimer. Compton, as a key member of OSRD's S-1 Committee (for uranium studies), had taken responsibility for coordinating the theoretical and experimental projects concerned with plutonium and making a weapon. Both theoreticians and experimenters faced the same urgent task of proving the value of using uranium in a bomb, as well as guiding the research that was being done on a uranium weapon. Compton, aware of the urgent time element, believed he had less than six months to provide such proof.[4] The outcome of the Chicago discussions was not promising; there was little hope for fast results and there was even disagreement over the findings of some research. Oppenheimer, taking note of this, suggested that some projects be consolidated in a single laboratory. Compton, however, could do little but approve the work already underway, and Oppenheimer continued theoretical studies of fast-neutron reactions at Berkeley. Two weeks later, the news was better. Compton had finally been able to devise a schedule for the next few years: The possibility of a chain reaction must be demonstrated by July 1, 1942; the actual test of a chain reaction concluded by January 1943; and a bomb built by January 1945.[5]

It became clear that the bomb program could be accelerated if all the work was centralized; the widely scattered projects were causing overlapping work and poor coordination. Oppenheimer's arguments were gaining ground.

That same month Compton created a special laboratory at the University of Chicago and made Richard Doan director of what was called the Metallurgical Laboratory, or Met Lab. Fermi, Allison, and Wigner assumed primary roles, and Gregory Breit was made coordinator of fast-fission research—shorthand for work on the bomb itself. Fast fission took on another nickname: the Rapid Rupture Group. As coordinator, Breit oversaw work at six universities, including the work of Oppenheimer at Berkeley.

By March, Oppenheimer was able to report that new calculations suggested that as much as 6 percent of the possible energy that could be released in a bomb might be converted into an explosive force, or yield. This meant that a weapon might now have as much destructive potential as perhaps two thousand tons of TNT, compared to the six hundred tons of TNT projected earlier.

Both Bush and Compton noticed Oppenheimer's solid work as well as his ability to work with his colleagues. His maturation in the eyes of these men came at a time when Breit was experiencing considerable personal difficulty with his project leaders. This was particularly true with several individuals at the Met Lab. As well, Breit had disagreed with Compton over security matters. Breit resigned on May 18, 1942.[6] Oppenheimer was the obvious candidate for his replacement. Compton lost no time in appointing Oppenheimer coordinator of Rapid Rupture; a month later, he received a formal letter appointing him a research associate for the Metallurgical Research Project at the salary of $620 a month.

Just two months earlier, General George Marshall, commander of the Joint Chiefs of Staff, appointed Brigadier General Wilhelm D. Styer the principal liaison between the Army and OSRD's S-1 Uranium Committee. Marshall agreed to the transfer of all uranium and plutonium production, as well as all fission research, to the Army.* General Styer appointed

*OSRD believed that there were four approaches to producing U 235: gaseous diffusion, electromagnetic separation, high-speed centrifuges, and liquid thermal diffusion.

Colonel James C. Marshall (not related to General Marshall), of the Army's Syracuse Engineering District, to head the new fission program. James Marshall was a West Point graduate with field experience in construction. He took command in late June and named the new army program the DSM Project. Shortly thereafter, he moved the project's offices to New York City and renamed it the Manhattan Engineering District or, simply, the Manhattan Project.

Colonel Marshall soon found himself the victim of secrecy, monumental bureaucracy, and low rank. He was unable to obtain a priority rating higher than A-3 for procurement, when nothing less than A-1—the highest priority rating—was needed. He was a colonel in Washington's sea of generals and, of course, only a handful of individuals had ever heard or knew of the importance of the fission program. The only experienced staff member, Colonel Kenneth D. Nichols, was familiar with both scientific research and engineering. But Nichols was only one man.

Bush grew desperate for action. He persuaded General Marshall to replace Colonel Marshall with someone more aggressive and experienced. On September 17, Colonel Leslie R. Groves presented himself to Bush with the announcement that he had been appointed to direct the Army's Manhattan Project. The sight of the corpulent Groves might have concerned Bush, had the colonel not brought excellent credentials with him: He had graduated fourth in his class from West Point and had had an impressive record in the Army's Corps of Engineers in Hawaii, Nicaragua, and half a dozen states. He had recently overseen construction of the new Pentagon building, completing the giant structure in half the time estimated. Perhaps, it had been his personal style, not a lack of talent, that had kept him back in army ranks. His by-the-book personality and acerbic tongue had left him a lieutenant for almost fifteen years. Nevertheless, the man had a quick mind and phenomenal organizational ability; it was his nature, he said often enough, to act first and ask questions later.

Groves sprang into action. A military policy committee was created to oversee the atomic bomb project. Groves insisted that the committee have only three members: Bush, representing the scientific community, would act as chairman; General Styer would represent the Army; and Admiral William R. Purnell, the Navy. Groves would report directly to the committee. From Berkeley, Oppenheimer wondered out loud what manner of army bureaucrat would now command scientists.

As it turned out, Oppenheimer had little time to wonder about the machinations in Washington. As the newly appointed coordinator of fast-fission research, he had to step in quickly after Breit's departure and familiarize himself with work at six universities. He realized that his own theoretical background needed to be balanced by someone knowledgeable in the field of experimental physics. Oppenheimer's talents did not necessarily extend to the laboratory, as he well remembered from his days at Cambridge. Compton agreed, after some discussion, to hire John Manley, who was engaged in work with the Cockcroft-Walton accelerator at the Met Lab. Manley first expressed reservations to Compton about working with the cerebral Oppenheimer. Several years earlier, Manley had heard him deliver a lecture, and while he had been impressed with the scientist's thinking, he had been put off by his aloof personality. When Compton brought the two men together, Oppenheimer seemed to have matured and, eager for help, appeared far more down-to-earth. Manley changed his mind and eventually found himself working well with Oppenheimer.

The two men met again in Chicago on June 6. They agreed that while Oppenheimer would continue his theoretical work at Berkeley, Manley would take over the direction of several diversely located projects that included the work of John Williams at the University of Minnesota, Joseph L. McKibbin at the University of Wisconsin, and Norman P. Heydenburg at the Carnegie Institute. Both men felt a responsibility to visit each project site. The work was fascinating, but involved tedious travel during the next few months.

During a break in his travels, Oppenheimer seized the chance to ask a small group of physicists to join him and a colleague, Robert Serber, at Berkeley that June. It seemed clear to him that there was a sufficient body of information that could now be studied and assessed. Oppenheimer acquired several rooms on the top floor of LeConte Hall for the meetings. For security purposes, he had each window covered with heavy steel mesh and had the only door to the suite fitted with a special lock and key.

The purpose of the meeting was to make some sense of the theoretical and experimental data coming in from the fast-fission projects. Edward Teller, Hans Bethe, Emil Konopinski, and several others attended. They sifted through report after report, filling the blackboards with long calculations and diagrams, finally agreeing that few theoretical gaps remained. Their understanding was sufficiently thorough, indeed, to cause Oppenheimer to note many years later that anyone who entered the room and looked at the blackboard would have had all the information necessary to make a bomb. One key piece of information they lacked was the precise amount of uranium or plutonium necessary to make the core of a weapon. The best guess was little more than what Oppenheimer had suggested a few months earlier: a sphere of plutonium the size of an orange. Such generalities meant a variance of a hundred grams either way. That spread was acceptable at the time, since current production plans called for delivery of uranium and plutonium some time in late 1944.

The far-ranging discussions also revealed the startling possibility that a larger, more powerful thermonuclear, or fusion, bomb could be made with the heat from a fission bomb. Using deuterium, an isotope of hydrogen, a fission bomb could ignite a fire similar to the one generated by the sun. The prospect of such a weapon seemed so important that Oppenheimer made a special journey to Compton's summer retreat in Michigan to give him the news. Compton accepted the news calmly by asking if the weapon could be made in time for use in the war, as did Bush when told of it. Neither man was interested in a weapon that depended upon another not yet developed; the need for an atomic bomb that could be used as soon as possible far outweighed planning for distant "superbombs." By September, Oppenheimer had further information suggesting that the required temperatures could not be reached. He wrote Teller a letter reporting these calculations determined by Hans Bethe.[7]

The meeting in Berkeley reaffirmed the importance of regularly bringing together the results of ongoing research. It also added strength to the growing conviction that the multifaceted fission program needed to be brought together in one location. "We began to notice," Oppenheimer said, "how very much needed doing and how much the little laboratories were suffering from their isolation." By late summer Oppenheimer had become convinced, as had most of his colleagues, that "we needed a central laboratory devoted wholly to [work on the bomb] where people could talk freely with each other, where theoretical ideas and experimental findings could affect each other, where the waste and frustration and error of the many compartmentalized experimental studies could be eliminated, where we could come to grips with chemical, metallurgical, engineering, and ordnance problems that had so far received no consideration."[8]

Oppenheimer approached Robert Bacher and I.I. Rabi with the idea of a central laboratory. Both agreed that the work currently underway could be better managed under a single roof. Oppenheimer queried both of them about how to manage such a laboratory; both were far more experienced than he was at such matters. That fall, in a meeting in New York City, Bacher and Rabi met again with Oppenheimer and the newly promoted General Groves. The general suggested that the proposed laboratory be made a military establishment, where each scientist would receive a commission. Both Bacher and Rabi immediately objected, informing Oppenheimer and Groves that they were both "crazy" if they thought such an idea would ever work. And so, for the moment, the idea was dropped.

Oppenheimer realized that it was essential to first produce the critical materials U 235 and Pu 239. "The first job [is] to make the stuff. But in the hope that [it] would come out all right, we had to have a place where we could learn what to do with it. This was not trivial."[9] At first the talk of a central laboratory centered on using the Met Lab in Chicago; later, in early autumn, the talk focused on Oak Ridge, Tennessee, where the Army was building the large gaseous-diffusion plant for separating U 235 from common uranium. Oppenheimer first thought of a "more or less conventional laboratory," until the time came for ordnance experiments. At that time, another testing ground would be selected away from major population centers. Gradually, he thought about selecting a site that would provide both the space and the necessary conditions for all phases of work: theoretical and experimental physics, chemistry, and ordnance. Such a laboratory, Oppenheimer explained to his colleagues, had to have two characteristics: first, it needed a free and informal atmosphere which would allow people from different projects and divisions to discuss progress and problems; and second, it needed to be secure, isolated, and guarded, if necessary. In early October, Oppenheimer joined Groves, General Marshall, and Colonel Nichols for an all-night conversation in a small, locked compartment on the Twentieth Century Limited train between California and the East Coast. They discussed plans for a laboratory.

The idea appealed to Groves. Such a laboratory would facilitate coordination and management; fewer resources would have to be spent on one large laboratory, compared to a number of smaller ones. As well, the centralization of all work was important because it made security easier. Groves was always conscious of the importance of security and secrecy. Talk of the thermonuclear bomb at the Berkeley conference had spread quickly among scientists at the Met Lab. Groves had little regard for the concept of open discussions among scientists. The idea of a central laboratory also offered the possibility of conscripting key scientists into the military and placing the entire complex on a military reservation.

Oppenheimer, who gradually came to share the general's feelings about security, stressed the value of isolation, especially when it was possible to incorporate the geographical and logistical needs for a test site from the very beginning. As well, Oppenheimer realized that the centralization of work would necessarily avoid duplication and allow everyone to share each other's ideas. It was this last characteristic, more than any other, that would lead to the final successes in 1945.

Groves rejected the notion of building the new laboratory near the Oak Ridge processing plant, fearing that too much activity concentrated in one location would increase the danger of sabotage. Two locations in California had been suggested by Oppenheimer, but were rejected because of their limited space and their close proximity to cities. Groves was wary of placing the laboratory too near any cities because he felt that the scientists would be in contact with too many people, thereby causing possible security leaks. A location in Reno, Nevada, was rejected because of heavy winter snows. The choices narrowed to two locations: Jemez Springs and Los Alamos, both in the north central portion of New Mexico, a hundred miles from each other.

In early November 1942, Oppenheimer joined Groves, Lieutenant Colonel John Dudley, and an enlisted man in New Mexico for a visit to the two possible sites. Jemez Springs—a long, thin valley dramatically hemmed in on three sides by cliffs—was the site favored by Dudley. The valley was part of the Jemez Mountain chain. Although it was a beautiful setting, there were few existing buildings, and Groves estimated that as much as 70 percent of the needed housing would have to be constructed. An army engineering study ordered earlier by Groves suggested that the area was occasionally subject to flooding. Oppenheimer didn't like the choice. From Jemez Springs the quartet drove to the northeast, twisting their way on State Highway 4 through aspen trees turned brilliant autumn yellow. Rising in altitude to nearly eight thousand feet, the car entered the eastern slope of the Jemez Mountains onto a plateau named Pajarito by early Spanish explorers. With the exception of a few ranchers, the plateau was inhabited only by a private school for boys.

For Oppenheimer, it was a return to a part of the country he loved dearly. His own small ranch near Cowles in the Pecos Mountains was little more than a sixty-mile drive from Los Alamos, to the northeast. It was certainly a spectacular location. Pajarito plateau, of which Los Alamos is part, was created in the ash flows of a large volcano millions of years before. Resembling a large, outstretched hand, each finger forms a mesa divided from another mesa by deep canyons some two hundred to four hundred feet deep. Los Alamos mesa rises gently to the west, where it abuts the Sierra de los Valles. To the east is the Rio Grande, and still farther east lies the beautiful Sangre de Cristo mountain range.

Oppenheimer was enraptured by the scenery and both he and Groves thought the location was ideal. The school buildings could form the core of the laboratory. The site was isolated, but still close to roads and rail lines. There was room to grow. And only nine thousand of the estimated fifty-four thousand acres needed for the laboratory had to be purchased. Groves flew to Washington to request approval. The general acted with what Oppenheimer called "unbelievable dispatch" to acquire the Los Alamos Ranch School and the surrounding acreage for a total of $415,000—surely one of the smallest Manhattan Project expenditures of the war.

With the decision to locate the new laboratory in Los Alamos, Oppenheimer entered a period in which he gradually took on the role of laboratory director, but without any formal appointment from Groves. The general, in fact, originally favored Ernest Lawrence, but it soon became clear that Lawrence was necessary to the eventual success of the electromagnetic separation project in California. Compton favored Carl Anderson, a Nobel prizewinner for his work in physics. Both Lawrence and Anderson were men with management experience. Anderson, however, was unimpressed with the prospect of directing a laboratory with such a speculative future and rejected the tentative offer. Oppenheimer had had no practical experience in directing scientific laboratories and, despite his reputation in theoretical physics, he did not have the stature of someone like Lawrence. Nevertheless, Oppenheimer had displayed an unusual ability to learn quickly—a talent he revealed in his rather hurried assumption of the fast-fission projects. Perhaps his most attractive quality was his ability to work with his colleagues and to gain their respect. Groves gradually decided that Oppenheimer was the right man for the job. There was one problem, however, with the appointment: Oppenheimer's political past. Since 1941, Oppenheimer had been under investigation by the FBI and, during the war, by army security men as well. An impressive dossier had been assembled which included information on his activities, his contributions to causes like the Spanish Loyalists, and even on his wife, brother, and sister-in-law. One report—undocumented—even suggested that Oppenheimer might have been in the center of a ring of homosexual teachers and students.* Groves was thoroughly familiar with the contents of the file and was conscious of the need to avoid involving individuals with suspicious pasts in the Manhattan Project. But as Groves saw it, Oppenheimer's past was no more than a little political dabbling, something not unusual for the times. Oppenheimer had become, in Groves's words, "absolutely essential to the project."

In February 1943, Oppenheimer's role as director of the Los Alamos Laboratory was formalized with a letter from Conant and Groves. It announced his directorship and it also empowered the scientist with a statement of purpose to be used in recruiting other scientists and technicians. The February 25th letter became a loose charter for the laboratory; it referred mysteriously to the "development and final manufacture of an instrument of war." Oppenheimer and his colleagues would conduct "certain experimental studies in science, engineering, and ordnance."[10] Fortunately, the letter gave the new director the responsibility of interpreting the vague language himself.

In less than a year and a half, Oppenheimer had moved from minor involvement in theoretical speculations to director of a secret laboratory responsible for a great weapon of war. With German armies nearing Moscow, and with the conquest of Europe complete, the task for Oppenheimer and for Los Alamos was urgent.

---

*While this accusation was not true, it is possible that it stemmed from the fact that Oppenheimer had particularly close relationships with his students.

4. The Secret Record

On the surface, Robert Oppenheimer's stature was never higher, nor his position more secure. His directorship of Los Alamos was not only de facto evidence of his talents, but also of the faith placed in him by the government of the United States. Simmering beneath this faith, however, was a continuing suspicion of Oppenheimer's loyalty by several members of the Army's intelligence team and by the Federal Bureau of Investigation. These suspicions grew from largely circumstantial intelligence information gathered about his past political activities and associations.

Before 1939 the government had no formal concern with the loyalty of its employees; the system worked, simply enough, on good faith until challenged. The Civil Service Commission was more concerned with prior criminal behavior and incompetence than with loyalty. In the 1920s and 1930s there was a good deal of concern over Communist activity in the United States, but there was hardly a formal program designed to "clear" or "approve" government employees. The Hatch Act passed in 1931 only prohibited federal employment to anyone planning a violent overthrow of the government. Once the war began, a growing sensitivity to the character and political beliefs of government employees emerged. Since few expressed allegiance to foreign governments, at least publicly, the issue of loyalty was mostly concerned with past affiliations and friendships rather than ideological beliefs and acts of violence.

This was the case with Oppenheimer. The birth of his social and political consciousness in the 1930s meant a new circle of friends, many of whom fell under the scrutiny of intelligence investigators during the war. The broad-based investigations of so-called "radicals" and Communists in California eventually turned up Oppenheimer's name in the late 1930s. Also discovered were the names Frank Oppenheimer, Steven Nelson, Isaac Folkoff, and a number of Oppenheimer's former students and colleagues. His "history" of involvement became a source of avid interest as his work in fission grew.

After his promotion to coordinator of fast-fission research, Oppenheimer became a major concern of investigators. Curiously, he worked with Lawrence, Breit, and Compton for nearly six months without any formal security clearance. One was finally issued in February 1943 from the security office within OSRD. Groves knew of Oppenheimer's past, but nevertheless permited him unrestricted access to the fission program.

The general closed the book on Oppenheimer, or so he thought, for the duration of the war. Groves had, as Oppenheimer later liked to say, "a fondness for good men."[1] However, other intelligence officials in the Army's G-2 section* were not as prepared to let go of Oppenheimer.

Colonel John Landsdale, Jr., formerly a Cleveland lawyer, was assigned to the Army's Counter Intelligence Group in Washington, D.C., and given the job of screening army personnel. Soon he was assigned to General Groves to work on security matters within the Manhattan Project. Like others in the military establishment, Landsdale became increasingly convinced that Russia would be America's ultimate enemy. One of his first assignments was to investigate Communist infiltration in Berkeley's Radiation Laboratory. Oppenheimer's political activities were quickly uncovered, and Landsdale began to send reports back to Groves.

Another member of G-2 was Colonel Boris T. Pash, a former California schoolteacher. The son of Russian immigrants, as a young man Pash worked briefly in Russia. As a result, he developed profound memories of the horrors of communism. He joined the U.S. Army in 1940 and soon became the chief of Counter Intelligence for the Ninth Army Corps, which was responsible for atomic bomb research on the West Coast, among other things. Pash also quickly learned about Oppenheimer, but unlike Landsdale, he became convinced that Oppenheimer retained his loyalty to communism.

Fellow scientists in the Manhattan Project, unaware of these attentions, considered Oppenheimer's new involvement in fast fission to be evidence that his political background was no longer important. His relationship with men like Haakron Chevalier continued until fission work became a full-time effort. Most of his political ties had been severed by early 1942. Oppenheimer's own memory of this period is that his political interests ended abruptly after Pearl Harbor.

With the creation of Los Alamos, General Groves appointed Major Peer de Silva as the laboratory's new security officer. De Silva shared Pash's suspicions of Oppenheimer. Like Pash, de Silva continued to watch Oppenheimer's moves, seeing in his history and actions a man who was either very naive or very clever. De Silva chose to believe that Oppenheimer was very clever and capable of considerable subterfuge.

Friends, however, saw Oppenheimer more simply. His brilliance seemed matched by a naiveté in political matters. Even his involvement with Jean Tatlock and others, and his financial contributions over the years, seemed only superficial. It is true that he read voraciously about communism, socialism, and even fascism, but never with the depth of interest he had in literature or science. He knew facts, some pointed out,

---

*G-2 was the intelligence division with a special detachment from the Manhattan Project. As the Army consolidated control over fission projects, OSRD no longer issued clearances.

but not implications. Most friends accepted Oppenheimer's explanation when he said his political involvement had been "brief but intense."

What fueled the security apparatus, however, was a series of events that would haunt Oppenheimer for a dozen years.

One key event occurred in January or February 1943, at a time when Oppenheimer was already titular director of Los Alamos. Although the precise date is unknown—neither Haakron Chevalier nor Oppenheimer can remember exactly—the event concerned a conversation they had engaged in at a small dinner party at Oppenheimer's Eagle Hill Drive home. It had been a small group: only Oppenheimer, Chevalier, and their wives. At one point Oppenheimer went into the kitchen alone and was followed by Chevalier, who reported a conversation he had recently had with a scientist named George C. Eltenton. A British citizen working with the Shell Oil Company in Berkeley, Eltenton was friends with Chevalier and only casually known to Oppenheimer. Some days before the dinner party with the Oppenheimers, Chevalier had been approached by Eltenton, who indicated that he had a means of sending scientific or technical information to the Soviet government. Whether or not Eltenton suggested to Chevalier that Oppenheimer be told this information is not known with certainty, although Chevalier later maintained that such was the case and that Eltenton had seemed embarrassed about making the approach. Oppenheimer flatly replied that he wanted no involvement with the scheme. Chevalier claimed that he had raised the issue only so that Oppenheimer would be aware of it. Years later, both men would agree that Oppenheimer unequivocally refused to be involved. What harmed Oppenheimer later was the fact that he did not immediately report the conversation to the authorities, and when he finally did, he refused on several occasions to reveal that Chevalier was the intermediary between Eltenton and himself. Moreover, when Oppenheimer finally told the story, he gave different versions of the event to several security officers.

There were other events that kept reports flowing into G-2 in Washington. In June 1943, Oppenheimer made a recruitment trip to Berkeley, shadowed, in true cloak-and-dagger style, by several agents assigned to follow the scientist. One month before, Landsdale ordered agents to cover Oppenheimer's activities, monitor his telephone calls, and screen his mail. At least one security man traveled with Oppenheimer under the ruse of serving as a bodyguard. Once, while at Berkeley, he received word that Jean Tatlock urgently wanted to see him. He went to see her, largely because of their former relationship. He knew he was taking a risk, but he didn't know that agents were stationed outside Jean's house while he spent the night with her. Jean was unhappy, more despondent than ever. She took him to the airport the next day* and Oppenheimer never saw her again; seven months later she took her own life.

Boris Pash sent an urgent letter to Landsdale warning that Oppenheimer might be persuaded or perhaps blackmailed into turning over secret information to the Soviets. Pash clearly believed that Jean Tatlock, with her Communist affiliations, might well be able to solicit secret information from Oppenheimer. Oppenheimer, he argued, should be "removed completely from the Project and dismissed from employment by the United States government."[2] Similar interpretations were construed from Oppenheimer's innocent contacts with former students and colleagues who were secretly under investigation. Steve Nelson, an old friend of Kitty Oppenheimer's, was active in California's Communist party. He and his wife spent an entire week at the Oppenheimer's home in 1941. Pash briefly thought that a former student of Oppenheimer's named Giovanni Rossi Lomanitz, known from reports only as "Joe,"† was a key member of a West Coast Communist cell. Lomanitz was a bright student who had impressed Oppenheimer enough to be offered a job as his assistant, with the task of taking notes in Oppenheimer's course on electrodynamics. Apparently, he was also known for his outspoken political views. Because Oppenheimer was in Los Alamos, Lomanitz was asked by Ernest Lawrence to become a group leader at the Radiation Laboratory. Within a week of receiving the order, however, Lomanitz discovered that his selective service deferment was being cancelled and he would be drafted soon. He placed an urgent telephone call to Oppenheimer in New Mexico for assistance. In turn, Oppenheimer sent a telegram to Landsdale suggesting that Lomanitz was capable and should be retained at the Radiation Lab in order to prevent anyone from the Los Alamos staff from being sent back to Berkeley as a replacement. He cabled: "Believe understand reasons but feel that very serious mistake is being made." To Lomanitz he wired word that he had argued for a deferment, signing the telegram affectionately as "Opje."[3] Oppenheimer interceded several more times on Lomanitz's behalf.

Landsdale assessed the Oppenheimer matter in a memorandum to General Groves on June 6, 1943. He encouraged Groves to tell Oppenheimer that the Army was aware that the "Communist Party, U.S.A." was

---

*Oppenheimer had been asked by Groves not to fly, because Groves couldn't risk losing Oppenheimer in an airplane crash. He broke his promise in order to make up time in returning to Los Alamos. Groves subsequently "ordered" Oppenheimer not to use airplanes for travel.

†Pash later changed his mind and declared a man named Joseph Weinberg to be the mysterious "Joe."

attempting to learn about the activities of the Manhattan Project. According to Landsdale, it was therefore necessary to remove from the effort all members of the Communist party or those who were "followers of the Communist party line." Landsdale wanted Groves to tell Oppenheimer that the Army had refrained from immediately telling the scientist of their investigations because of Oppenheimer's political past. Landsdale apparently feared that Oppenheimer might share news of Army investigations with some of his colleagues; this news might thereby cause some Communists to go underground. To Groves, Landsdale reiterated Oppenheimer's associations with organizations the Army considered Communist fronts: the American Civil Liberties Union, the Committee to Aid China, the Consumers Union, the Berkeley Conference for Civic Betterment, and the American Committee for Democratic and Intellectual Freedom. Landsdale also listed some ten individuals with whom Oppenheimer had had relationships and people whom the Army considered party members or "connected with its activities." The list included Haakron Chevalier and Jean Tatlock. To Groves, Landsdale suggested: "[Oppenheimer] should be asked . . . who he knows that are members of the Communist party, for the purpose of seeing what, if any, associations he will attempt to conceal."[4]

In the many discussions Landsdale and Oppenheimer had about security, the scientist always assured the security officer of his strong commitment to security and his belief in employing only those scientists who had proven their loyalty. In one such meeting Landsdale urged Oppenheimer to drop his appeals on behalf of Lomanitz. Landsdale and others were concerned about a number of the scientist's former students and fellow teachers, and especially about a new union called the Federation of Architects, Engineers, Chemists, and Technicians (FAECT), located in the Berkeley area. Mention of these concerns caused Oppenheimer to remember his conversation with Chevalier almost half a year before. Eltenton was a member of FAECT and still lived and worked in Berkeley. After some deliberation, the scientist chose an opportunity while in California to visit the Berkeley offices of the Manhattan Project security officer. On August 23, 1943, he met with Lieutenant Lyall Johnson in the new classroom building on the Berkeley campus.

The meeting was brief, but perhaps one of the most fateful moments in Oppenheimer's life. He reported that there was a man in the area who was active in FAECT who perhaps should be investigated by G-2. His name, Oppenheimer said, was George C. Eltenton. Johnson did not press for details. After the scientist departed he immediately called Boris Pash and reported the conversation. Eltenton was already known in Pash's office, but Pash himself was intrigued by Oppenheimer's voluntary offering of the information. He instructed Johnson to set up a second meeting with Oppenheimer for the next day and ordered Johnson's office to be bugged with a hidden microphone and recorder.

Oppenheimer returned the next day and was greeted by Pash as well as by Johnson. Pash began cordially with the comment, "This is a pleasure."[5] Oppenheimer began to reiterate part of the previous day's conversation, focusing on Rossi Lomanitz. Pash cut him off and said he was more interested in other information the scientist seemed to have. Oppenheimer explained that it was his understanding that there was a man in the Soviet consulate who could transmit information back to Russia and added: "Well, I might say that the approaches were always through other people, who were troubled by them, and sometimes came and discussed them with me; and that the approaches were quite indirect. . . ." With no mention of Chevalier, he named Eltenton and said that it might be appropriate to watch him. Pash asked for other names but Oppenheimer resisted, indicating that to do so might jeopardize innocent people whose "attitude was one hundred percent cooperative."

Pash promised anonymity. For peculiar and complicated reasons Oppenheimer then claimed that he knew of several approaches made by nameless intermediaries to men at Los Alamos: "Well, I'll tell you one thing—I have known of two or three cases, and I think two of them are with me at Los Alamos—they are men who are closely associated with me." These men, he added, were contacted not by Eltenton, but by another party. This party was a member of the Berkeley faculty, but not a member of the Manhattan Project. He also added that these approaches were not necessarily treasonable in that they might have been made in an atmosphere of support for Russia, one of America's allies in the war against Germany. Whatever the nature of the contacts, however, Oppenheimer left the distinct impression that as many as three other scientists had been approached by the mysterious "intermediary." This information, however, was entirely false. Pash put his question to Oppenheimer: "Well now, could we know through whom that contact was made?"

Oppenheimer demurred; he thought such a statement would be a mistake. "I think I have told you where the initiative came from and the other things were almost purely accidental and that it would involve people who ought not to be involved in this."

The interview ended with a wish from Pash to Oppenheimer for "the best of luck." The conversation appeared—at least to Oppenheimer—to be a comfortable one; he had, after all, reported a potential threat to security without jeopardizing his friend. In fact, the conversation had momentous implications. Oppenheimer would soon reveal that what he had told Pash was a "cock and bull story." He would be forced to reconstruct and explain the events again and again. It was also momentous for the mysterious intermediary, Haakron Chevalier. The question remained: Why had Oppenheimer chosen to protect Chevalier by constructing a tale more injurious to both himself and Chevalier? Pash immediately sent a long message to Groves, reporting the substance of the conversation, which suggested that Oppenheimer was covering up his own involvement.

Barely a week later, in early September, Oppenheimer joined Groves and Landsdale on a long train ride from Cheyenne, Wyoming, to Chicago. Security was their major topic of conversation. Oppenheimer disavowed further support of Lomanitz and deflected questions on the intermediary used by Eltenton. He argued that he wanted to protect an innocent man, but agreed that he would tell Groves if so commanded. Groves elected not to press for the name. Landsdale was unhappy with Groves's decision but deferred, for the moment at least, to his superior officer.

Landsdale raised the question again, however, in a few days, this time during a meeting in Washington, D.C. As Pash had done weeks before, he began warmly: "Well, now I want to say this—and without intent of flattery or complimenting or anything else, that you're probably the most intelligent man I ever met. . . ."[6] The officer revealed that their intelligence process had suggested that several people had transmitted information to the Soviet government. He said, after some preliminary discussion: "All right, now I'll tell you this: They know, we know they know about Tennessee, about Los Alamos, and Chicago." Oppenheimer explained that his brother Frank, unlike some Communist members, had totally severed his membership at the beginning of his war duties. He was not so sure about Frank's wife, however, though he thought it unlikely that she still kept in contact with the party. The conversation turned to Eltenton and to the "channel" referred to by Oppenheimer.

Landsdale: Now you can, therefore, see from our point of view the importance of knowing what their channel is.

Oppenheimer: Yes.

Landsdale: And I was wondering, is this man a friend of yours by any chance?

Oppenheimer: He's an acquaintance of mine, I've known over the years.

Landsdale persevered. How could the government be sure that the mysterious channel wasn't approaching others? The approach, as Oppenheimer put it, wasn't any more than a "cocktail party channel"—that is, the sort of off-handed and casual chatter that goes on at parties. Landsdale indicated that the government knew of many channels for the Soviets, but not the one Oppenheimer had raised as a possibility: "Now, that's a simple reason why I want that name, and I want to ask you point-blank if you'll give it to me. If you won't, well OK, no hard feelings."

Oppenheimer held firm. "No. I've thought about it a good deal because Pash and Groves both asked for the name, and I feel that I should not give it. I don't mean that I don't hope that if he's still operating that you will find it [the channel]. I devoutly do. But I would just bet dollars to doughnuts that he isn't still operating."

Once again, under direct questioning, Oppenheimer had protected Chevalier. The same protection was not given to his other colleagues. Pressed by Landsdale to reveal the names of other individuals who were party members, Oppenheimer indicated that he knew of two persons: "I learned on last visit to Berkeley that both Lomanitz and [Irving] Weinberg were members." Oppenheimer then added that he "suspected that before, but was not sure. I never had any way of knowing." These words would be embarrassing for him a decade later.

Oppenheimer continued to volunteer names, including that of Jane Serber, wife of his old student and friend, Robert Serber. Asked by Landsdale if he would react to a list of names, Oppenheimer agreed. But first Landsdale asked Oppenheimer if he had ever been a member of the Communist party. Oppenheimer replied firmly that he hadn't.

Landsdale: You've probably belonged to every front organization on the Coast?

Oppenheimer: Just about.

Landsdale: Would you in fact have considered yourself at one time a fellow traveler?

Oppenheimer: I think so. My association with these things was very brief and very intense.

Asked if he had ever been approached by someone to pass "a little information to the party," Oppenheimer replied: "If it was, it was so gentle I did not know it." Other names were offered to Landsdale: Rudy Lambert; Hannah Peters, wife of Bernard Peters, who was working at Berkeley on a fission project; and Steve Nelson. Landsdale also mentioned Haakron Chevalier.

Landsdale: What about Haakron Chevalier?

Oppenheimer: Is he a member of the party?

Landsdale: I don't know.

Oppenheimer: He is a member of the faculty and I know him well. I wouldn't be surprised if he were a member, he is quite a Red.

Landsdale sought to reassure Oppenheimer: "I may say that I've made up my mind that you yourself are OK, otherwise I wouldn't be talking to you like this, see?" Oppenheimer replied drolly: "I'd better be—that's all I've got to say." Landsdale then asked the scientist if he would be willing to give information on persons within the Project who still might be members of the party. "Not in writing," Oppenheimer said, "I think that would make a very bad impression." Landsdale also intimated that the government knew more about Oppenheimer than they let on.

Landsdale: Now I say this, that we have been fairly sure for a long time that you knew something you weren't telling us.

Oppenheimer: How did you know about it because I wouldn't have known. . . . How did you know that?

Landsdale: Well, you don't mind if I don't tell you.

After nearly two hours of conversation in the hot office, the interviewed ended. For Oppenheimer, his reticence was a matter of "past loyalties."

Oppenheimer had no idea that the two-hour conversation had been recorded and that his comments would be matched, word-for-word, with previous statements. Moreover, his frankness, which seemed to indicate a growing personal concern for his reputation, would ultimately lead to the assessment that he was less than truthful.

The matter of the mystery contact was concluded, for the time being at least, on December 12, 1943. On a visit to Los Alamos, General Groves ordered Oppenheimer to reveal the name of the intermediary between himself, the three scientists Oppenheimer had referred to, and Eltenton. It was a strange set of circumstances. Groves toured the laboratory, sat through several lengthy briefings, and then asked Oppenheimer to accompany him on the twisting road back to Sante Fe. This time, however, Groves made it clear that only Oppenheimer was to make the trip. Robert's personal secretary watched them leave the administration building in early darkness.

Oppenheimer complied with the general's request and revealed the name of Haakron Chevalier. Of this there is no doubt. Yet there is no certainty that Oppenheimer also revealed to Groves that the story of the three other scientist-contacts was untrue. Oppenheimer maintained that he had confessed the full story to Groves on that night. There is some reason, however, to believe that he did not. The following day Colonel Kenneth Nichols sent three telegrams from Washington labeled "Secret" to security offices at Berkeley, Oak Ridge, and Los Alamos. The first telegram went to Lieutenant Lyle Johnson at Berkeley. It read: "Landsdale advises that according to Oppenheimer professor contact of Eltenton is Haakron Chevalier. . . . Oppenheimer states in his opinion Chevalier engaged in no further activity other than *three original contacts*." (Emphasis added.)[7] Presumably the telegram reflected Groves's conversation with Oppenheimer. Substantively, the other two telegrams said the same thing: Chevalier was the intermediary and Oppenheimer believed no other contacts had been made except the original three. The telegrams sent by Nichols suggested that Oppenheimer revealed Chevalier's name and continued with his original story. Oppenheimer would later maintain that he had repudiated the entire story.

Both Groves and Landsdale later admitted that they believed Oppenheimer was covering up for somebody else. Groves personally believed that the reason for Oppenheimer's hesitancy was Frank Oppenheimer: "It was always my impression that he wanted to protect his brother, and that his brother might be involved in having been in this chain, and that his brother didn't behave quite as he should have. . . . He always felt a natural loyalty to him, and had a protective attitude toward him." The reluctance to reveal *any* names, in fact, was seen by Groves as the "typical American schoolboy attitude about telling on your friends."[8] In any case, the result of Oppenheimer's actions was painful and expensive. By lying, he was guilty of a felony in a technical sense; by enlarging the events beyond the facts, he unduly implicated Chevalier.*

The final discovery that Chevalier was the contact between Eltenton and Oppenheimer did not curtail the government's interest in Oppenheimer. Far from it; in fact, if anything, the scientist's confession only confirmed the suspicions of Boris Pash and Peer de Silva. A month after Groves's interview with Oppenheimer, Peer de Silva sent a telegram to Landsdale stating that Oppenheimer was not to be trusted: "His loyalty to the Nation is divided." Pash was even more passionate: "J.R. Oppenheimer is playing a key part in the attempts of the Soviet Union to secure, by espionage, highly secret information which is vital to the security of the United States."[9]

Pash was later transferred to a secret mission in Europe known as ALSOS, whose purpose was to gather intelligence information on German fission work and, where possible, to follow advancing Allied troops into Germany to interrogate German scientists. In January 1945, Peer de Silva was transferred to another post but not before he left a full report on Oppenheimer for his successor.

Groves would later recall that security matters consumed only 5 percent of his time during the war. Oppenheimer, for the first time in his life, began to think of protecting himself and began to keep a file of important conversations and communications. One of the first entries consisted of correspondence relating to his appeals on behalf of Rossi Lomanitz. Even this would be interpreted by some members of the government as the canny work of a man with divided loyalties.

---

*The government took no action against Chevalier at the time.

5. The Director

The official opening of Los Alamos on April 15, 1943, was, in one word, chaotic. Throughout the winter, while the Ranch School was still in session, the Albuquerque Engineering Corps had moved in to begin the construction of a technical complex consisting of an administrative building and several laboratories and shops. The Army had decided to keep the largest of the school buildings, called Fuller Lodge, to serve as a dining hall as well as a small hotel which could be used to accommodate visiting scientists and military officials. Just south of the lodge were a small pool of water called Ashley Pond and a small stone building which had once served as an icehouse for the school. Across a dirt road from the icehouse, the engineers built the main technical building, known as T Building, which would serve as headquarters for Oppenheimer, his administrative staff, and the Theoretical Physics Division. Plans called for other laboratories for chemistry, experimental physics, cryogenics, and the Van de Graaff and Cockcroft-Walton accelerators which had been "borrowed" from several universities. On April 15 only a few of these buildings were actually ready for use. Some had walls and roofs, but were unheated and contained no furniture. Housing for newly arriving staff was virtually nonexistent. Many staff members and their families were shipped off to dude ranches in the area. The comfortable motels in Sante Fe had been declared off limits by Groves, who feared fraternization with local residents. The laboratory buildings were generally constructed in what the Army called "modified mobilization style." Each had a drab exterior of clapboard siding and a simply pitched roof of asphalt or wood shingles. Few of the Tech Area buildings were air-conditioned or dustproof. The new buildings for army personnel were even less attractive.

Oppenheimer's primary responsibility was the organization of the entire operation at Los Alamos. Despite repeated requests from Manley to expedite the process, Oppenheimer stalled for weeks before coming up with a basic organizational plan for the laboratory. Finally, after an acerbic exchange with Manley one night, Oppenheimer appeared the next morning with a sheet of paper and said, "Here's your plan!" Originally, Oppenheimer and Manley envisioned a laboratory of about one hundred scientists and their families. Groves had tried to discourage families at Los Alamos, thinking that wives and children would distract men from their work. Oppenheimer, however, was forced to disagree. He argued that it would be difficult, if not impossible, to recruit staff if they were forced to part with their families. Even more of a threat to recruitment, however, was

Groves's renewed insistence that the laboratory be made a military installation. He quoted James B. Conant as supporting the idea. Conant, who had experience during World War I in military laboratories, saw no problem in the suggestion. Groves even considered making Oppenheimer a lieutenant colonel and all division directors, majors. Oppenheimer did not immediately object and even took steps toward becoming an officer at army offices in San Francisco. But the implications for recruitment soon overshadowed all other concerns. Rabi and Bacher continued to object in the strongest terms. Bacher's letter of acceptance for a job at Los Alamos contained in the last paragraph a statement of his resignation, to become effective if the laboratory was ever turned into a military installation. The argument by Rabi, Bacher, and all others was straightforward: A military organization would be rigid and inevitably inimical to an exchange of ideas. How, for example, could an enlisted man offer a new idea to an officer? Would an officer be able to admit to a mistake? In some cases, enlisted men could be expected to have better experience than officers.

With some adroitness, Oppenheimer persuaded Groves and Conant to keep the laboratory a civilian enterprise, at least for the time being. Oppenheimer quickly dropped any support of Los Alamos as an Army installation. Clearly, the opposition from men like Bacher and Rabi was too strong. Groves agreed, but with the understanding that the laboratory's staff could still possibly be inducted into the Army at a later date, perhaps as early as January 1944. Fortunately, no military conscription occurred, and Los Alamos remained a civilian institution within a military reservation.

Oppenheimer organized the laboratory around the major tasks involved in building a weapon. Along with his former student Robert Serber and Richard Tolman of the National Defense Research Committee, he reviewed the status of uranium and plutonium research in order to reveal those areas where work was needed. With this information he was able to draw up an initial work program as well as a series of orientation lectures for new staff. Oppenheimer created four divisions: Experimental Physics, Theoretical Physics, Chemistry and Metallurgy, and Ordnance. The leaders of each of these divisions reported to the director. Each division, consisting of various units or groups among whom work was divided, had considerable independence. Oppenheimer guarded against too much independence through the novel use of a governing board.

The job, as Oppenheimer saw it, was one of "being sure that people understood and that the decisions were properly made, and there were many not easy decisions. We did this through a system of groups, divisions, and coordinating councils and a steering committee which finally made the determination of laboratory."[1]

As the director, Oppenheimer chose a small corner office in T

Building, with an adjacent office for his personal secretary, Priscilla Green. Green had been secretary to Ernest Lawrence and had worked with Oppenheimer for the first time during the summer conference at Berkeley in 1942. She handled all of his correspondence, attending all meetings as recorder, and for a while even operated the laboratory's telephone switchboard. She also took dictation from Oppenheimer during some of the drives over the harrowing road to Sante Fe. Oppenheimer had her record his conversations with Groves until the general caught on and instructed Oppenheimer to "get her off the line." Green became indispensable. To colleagues, Oppenheimer joked: "I don't know what we're going to do about Priscilla's lust for power."

Urged by Groves, Oppenheimer hired Edward Condon of the Westinghouse Laboratories, a member of the S-1 Uranium Committee, as associate director to handle administrative matters at Los Alamos and to act as liaison with the military commander of the post. Condon clashed with both military and scientific personnel almost immediately and stayed only six weeks. Groves, forced to assume responsibility for the unfortunate appointment, chose to believe that Condon left because he feared the project would fail and damage his reputation.[2] After such a bad experience, it took Oppenheimer months to find a replacement. As an interim measure he selected David Hawkins from the University of California to take on the job. This troubled security officials, who had discovered Hawkins's earlier left-wing political activities.*

As soon as he could, Oppenheimer appointed division leaders. He relinquished his temporary directorship of the Theoretical Division and formally placed Hans Bethe in charge. Born in Germany, Bethe was now an American citizen and had been with the Radiation Laboratory at M.I.T. Robert Bacher, who had been working on radar, came to Los Alamos as leader of the Experimental Physics Division. United States Navy Captain William S. Parsons took over the Ordnance Division. He had experience in radar and proximity fuses, and also an invaluable knowledge of explosives as a result of his previous work at the U.S. Naval Proving Ground. Joseph Kennedy, who had been a student under Glenn Seaborg, assumed the directorship of the Chemistry and Metallurgy Division.

One of Oppenheimer's most innovative ideas was to create a committee called the Governing Board, which was established to counsel, plan, and conduct the technical effort and to act as a directorate for cooperative decision making. Members of the board included the laboratory director, all division leaders, and administrative and technical liaison officers. The board served to expose all senior men to the progress and

---

*Years later David Hawkins told Congressional investigating committees that he had been a member of the Communist Party before World War II.

problems of each division. The first few meetings hardly touched on research and development, however. Instead, they had to deal with housing snags, construction failures, poor morale, and personnel complaints.

On June 17, Oppenheimer told the Governing Board that he was creating a second committee, to be called the Laboratory Coordinating Council. The council was not a decision-making body like the board, but could have policy matters referred to it. The council's concern was with administrative and social matters. Most of the twenty members had at least the status of group leader. Bacher was asked to prepare the agendas, and either he or Oppenheimer would preside over the meetings.

In the spring, a third group was added to the laboratory organization. Suggested by Bethe, the colloquium was created as a forum for the exchange of ideas among scientists. It was also intended to develop a sense of common effort and cause, with younger men acting as equals to their seniors in the contribution of ideas or criticisms. The first meeting was called for May 30; it promised overviews on the most promising methods of manufacturing uranium and plutonium, as well as the ordnance characteristics of certain explosives.[3] Anyone attending these sessions would have a substantially complete understanding of the laboratory's work and progress.

Groves immediately expressed shock at the prospect of such open discussion; regular attendance would give any participant a view in detail of atomic weapons. Such information was antithetical to Groves's preference for compartmentalization and, he thought, an invitation to security failures. Against a barrage of letters and telephone calls from Groves, Oppenheimer stood firm. He argued that it was critical for the scientists in each division and group to be aware of the successes and failures in other groups. There needed to be an atmosphere in which everyone would have a chance to make contributions.

To placate Groves, Oppenheimer agreed to limit colloquium membership and place all participants on a strict honor system. Membership was limited to staff members and individuals with scientific degrees or equivalent experience. These individuals, as he said, were regarded as "contributors to or beneficiaries from an exchange of information."[4]

Groves continued to grumble from his office in Washington. In late June he raised the question of the colloquium with his military policy committee. They were of two minds: They could not dispute the benefits of open dialogue among scientists, but such an environment could also open the door for security leaks. Bush was asked by the committee to discuss the matter with Roosevelt, who in response wrote a letter to Oppenheimer with encouragement and with a plea for caution. Los Alamos, he said, was a "secret among secrets." Groves, for his part, did not trust scientists to keep secrets. He remembered a twelve-hour train ride from Chicago to Lamy, New Mexico, in which he lectured the great Niels Bohr on what *not* to say. Within five minutes after his arrival, Bohr had said everything he had promised he would not say.[5] The general finally relented, but remained disgruntled. Ten years later he would claim that the lack of compartmentalization at Los Alamos was the reason why "criticial information" could have been passed to the Soviets by spies.

Oppenheimer had more than Los Alamos security to be concerned with. In addition to the lack of basic scientific information, there was a disturbing lack of communication between Los Alamos and other Manhattan District laboratories because of the heavy security restrictions. This was particularly true of information on the production of uranium and plutonium. In June, Groves relented slightly and agreed with Oppenheimer that some interchange between sites might be helpful. The precise information that could be exchanged, of course, would have to be heavily controlled. After a few months Oppenheimer was even permitted to visit Oak Ridge, where the Manhattan Project was producing U 235 that Los Alamos hoped to use in a weapon. Oppenheimer's staff fought the same battle as well. Bacher finally convinced Groves that it wasn't necessary to have all reports from each laboratory go to the general's offices in Washington, D.C., where they would be rewritten, and then sent on to selected sites.

There were other handicaps as well. Los Alamos concealed its existence and the identities of its staff when making inquiries of agencies outside the Manhattan Project. Blind addresses were used, long-distance telephone calls were made through a telephone number in Denver, and government identity cards were specially made with false names and series numbers. The laboratory had to rely heavily on the procurement offices of the University of California. The small offices in California were soon overburdened with complicated requests for unusual equipment and for suspiciously large amounts of certain chemicals and explosives.

In the midst of assembling the new laboratory, Oppenheimer found time to note one small extravagance: his salary. In an exchange of letters between the University of California—the prime contractor between the government and Los Alamos—and General Groves, the director pressed for fairness, especially when salaries at Los Alamos were loosely following a salary scale prepared by OSRD. "In peacetime," he wrote to Robert Sproul, president of the University of California, "I was a professor of physics and not a director of anything. Thus my present salary exceeds by a little over two hundred dollars a month that which I would get if we applied our unusual formula to my peacetime salaries."[6] His salary, set by the War Department when he assumed leadership of Los Alamos, was a mere ten thousand dollars a year. After several months of consultation, his salary remained at ten thousand dollars, and Groves wrote a letter thanking Oppenheimer for his offer and complimenting his generosity in offering to reduce his salary.

Robert Oppenheimer's most tiring task the first year was recruiting staff. To Tolman he wrote in late November 1942, "The job we have to do will not be possible without personnel substantially greater than that which we now have available, and I should only be misleading you and all others concerned with the S-1 Project if I were to promise to get the work done without this help."[7] Between conferences with Groves and Tolman, overseeing construction at Los Alamos, and beginning work with the small staff already there, he set out on long recruitment trips. It was not an easy task. Because the laboratory was new, with no history, many scientists were reluctant to come. The Met Lab at Chicago and the Radiation Lab at Berkeley could at least capitalize on their university affiliations. Many scientists of note were already working on important war efforts such as radar. The cadre of scientists working with Oppenheimer during the Rapid Rupture days were for the most part already at Los Alamos. Although he had few budget constraints, his preeminent problem was recruiting personnel. To get them, he concentrated on attracting the biggest names he could, knowing that it would be easier to convince others to come if they realized that there were major figures already there or committed to join them.

"I traveled all over the country talking with people who had been working on one or another aspect of the atomic energy enterprise, and people in radar work, for example, and underwater sound, telling them about the job, the place that we were going to, and enlisting their enthusiasm." But sometimes his offers were met with skepticism. Despite his own reputation as a scientist, he lacked the public fame that others enjoyed. Los Alamos was unknown, located in a place that no one had ever heard of, and although Oppenheimer played it down, it was a project closely linked with the military. Some men were rightfully concerned with their reputations: What if Los Alamos failed?

Robert Bacher arrived with advice from his boss, Lee DuBridge, to "check out" Los Alamos. Many of his colleagues working on radar didn't believe that the laboratory would work on anything that would prove important to the war. In fact, Bacher sensed that many scientists were skeptical of the entire fission program.

"The real problem," according to Oppenheimer, "had to do with persuading people to come. There was a great fear that this was a boondoggle which would in fact have nothing to do with the war we were fighting." Fortunately, few people turned him down. Once Bacher arrived, for example, he was able to assist Oppenheimer in the recruiting. Hans Bethe offered help, as did Bethe's wife, Rose, who offered to set up an employment agency. In order to give people some idea of what to expect in Los Alamos, Oppenheimer prepared a long letter for Hans Bethe, which in turn could be used in recruiting staff. Housing, for example, would be largely two- and four-family units with living rooms fourteen by eighteen feet. Hot air would heat the units in addition to a fireplace, and some furniture would be available. Unfortunately, although Oppenheimer didn't know it at the time, the type of housing he described would be limited, and families arriving later in the war would be forced to live in a variety of housing that ranged from modified quonset huts to small apartments.[8]

After the war Oppenheimer noted that "the last months of 1942 and 1943 had hardly hours enough to get Los Alamos established. The real problem had to do with getting to Los Alamos the men who would make a success of the undertaking."

Who did Oppenheimer finally convince to come?* It can be said that on this one point alone Robert Oppenheimer could justify his directorship of Los Alamos. During the war years, an impressive number of eminent scientists and Nobel prizewinners came as residents or as consultants, luminaries like Sir James Chadwick, Sir Geoffrey Taylor, Enrico Fermi, Niels Bohr, I.I. Rabi, John von Neumann, and Ernest Lawrence. These men helped create the mystique that years later would envelop Los Alamos during the war years. For some, the laboratory would become the cardinal experience of their lives; for others, like Groves, it was a gathering place for prima donnas. In reality, it was an unusual institution, filled with a hodgepodge of mostly young theoreticians and experimenters whose average age was under thirty.

Even in late 1942, before his official appointment as director, Oppenheimer had some idea of the men he wanted to head the major arms of the new laboratory. He sent Groves a memorandum on November 9 suggesting specific men for key leadership positions: Edwin McMillan, Marshall Holloway, Joseph Kennedy, Emilio Segrè, John Williams, Robert Serber, Eldred Nelson, Stanley Frankel, Edward Teller, and Hans Bethe.[9] All came, although a few served only as visiting consultants.

Oppenheimer had the continuing help of John Manley, who soon joined the Experimental Physics Division. Enrico Fermi and Robert Bacher were early choices—Bacher was one of the first arrivals at Los Alamos. Robert Wilson came from Princeton University, where he had been directing a project, and brought his entire staff with him. Bacher invited former colleagues from Cornell University. Oppenheimer even persuaded Niels Bohr to come in 1944, along with his son. Bohr, who became known as Uncle Nick, was a living legend for most of the scientists at the laboratory, for it had been Bohr who at age twenty-eight corrected Ernest Rutherford's atomic theory. He was also the man to whom the Germans

*After the war, when asked this question by a Congressional Committee, Oppenheimer responded simply, "Everyone." He meant, of course, almost everyone with a reputation in physics.

Meitner and Frisch had rushed with news of the discovery of fission. For help with explosives, Oppenheimer sought the aid of Groves, who assigned Captain Parsons from the Navy. Two others would soon arrive with explosives experience: Norris Bradbury and George Kistiakowsky.

The British also sent a team to Los Alamos. The move climaxed two years of negotiations between Churchill and Roosevelt. During 1941, when much of the fission work in America seemed unproductive, the British had remained optimistic, choosing the code name Tube Alloys for their work. Oppenheimer had been impressed with their work, although its scope had been limited by the heavy drain on resources in Britain. Kenneth Bainbridge, another new arrival at Los Alamos, had spent a year working with British scientists and was able to report directly on their work.

One of the more revealing aspects of Anglo-American cooperation was the hesitation on the part of American political and scientific leaders to be fully frank about their work. Churchill reluctantly had been forced to admit that the war effort was a top priority in England and that only America had the resources to undertake both uranium production and weapons development. In the fall of 1943 a combined policy committee was established in Washington. With Groves's permission, in November, Oppenheimer sent a report to Rudolph E. Peierls, director of the Tube Alloys project; his report reflected a hesitancy on Oppenheimer's part to tell the full scope of American work. He did not, for example, disclose America's theoretical work on the hydrogen bomb. Oppenheimer explained to a colleague the entire situation with delicacy: "We had the problem of relations with the British."[10] By December, several teams of British scientists had arrived in the United States for assignment to several Manhattan District laboratories. A group, including Otto Frisch and Ernest W. Titterton, went to Los Alamos. As more men arrived, Oppenheimer's early caution served no purpose: As members of the colloquium, they soon learned the full nature of the work.

Sir Geoffrey Taylor spent lengthy visits at Los Alamos, as did Sir James Chadwick, the discoverer of the neutron. Oppenheimer originally envisioned a separate administrative structure for the British mission at Los Alamos, perhaps under pressure from Groves. The need for scientists in all areas soon necessitated assignments in every division. The team soon numbered twenty men and reported directly to American group and division leaders. Peierls assumed a titular leader position.

The staff at Los Alamos was surprisingly international. Fermi, Bruno Rossi, and Emilio Segrè were from Italy; from Hungary, Teller and von Neumann; Niels Bohr and his son were from Denmark; and Stanislav Ulam from Poland. Victor Weisskopf and I.I. Rabi were from Austria, and Hans Bethe and Rolf Landshoff were German refugees.

George Kistiakowsky had come to the United States from Russia as a small child.

Klaus Fuchs, who would later warrant a special historical mention, came to Los Alamos as a member of the British mission. Born a German, he became a naturalized British citizen after his escape from the Nazis. After the war it was learned that even before his arrival in Los Alamos, Fuchs had transmitted American and British plans for uranium separation to the Russians. He had gathered this information through his fission work in Great Britain. Once at Los Alamos, Fuchs quietly sent detailed information on the laboratory's implosion bomb to the Soviets. His actions were ironic, given the extreme nature of the security measures imposed on all members of the staff.

Fuchs hardly seemed the type to do such a thing. At Los Alamos he was hard-working, quiet, and for the most part kept to himself. Occasionally he baby-sat for the children of married friends. One Los Alamos wife dubbed him Poverino—the unfortunate one.

Unknown to Fuchs and to the complex array of security officials and agents, another man also passed secrets to the Russians during the war years. David Greenglass, an American G.I. stationed at Los Alamos, agreed—for money—to send explosive secrets by way of his in-laws, Julius and Ethel Rosenberg. Fuchs, however, acted out of loyalty to his philosophical beliefs and never accepted money. Both Fuchs and Greenglass escaped detection until 1950.

Even though there were many foreigners, most of the scientists at Los Alamos were Americans. Men like Darol K. Froman, Alvin Graves, Luis Alvarez, Norman F. Ramsey, Eric Jette, and Joseph Kennedy left good posts at universities to come. Kenneth Bainbridge returned from England and joined the staff. Norris Bradbury, who would assume leadership at Los Alamos after the war, came from the Naval Proving Ground, where he had worked under Parsons. Seth Neddermeyer came from the National Bureau of Standards, and Donald Hornig left the Underwater Explosives Research Laboratory in Virginia.

Younger men left graduate and even undergraduate studies to come to Los Alamos. Harold Agnew, who had worked with Fermi in Chicago, arrived when he was barely twenty-one years old. Robert Krohn came from the University of Wisconsin with a new bachelor of science degree. Raemer Schreiber left a Manhattan Project at Purdue University; and Berlyn Brixner, an engineering job in Albuquerque. Al Van Vessen and Bill Norwood came as G.I.'s. Even Oppenheimer's brother, Frank, came to Los Alamos from the Oak Ridge uranium separation project.

Many men arrived with their families. For the first few months, families had to stay near Los Alamos or were crowded into small apartments where they shared kitchens and bathrooms. With a few exceptions, Groves ordered that for security reasons no laboratory staff should stay in

Santa Fe; however, because of the disarray of the mesa, now known as the Hill, he allowed a small office to be opened at 109 East Palace Street, near the city's ancient square. The Santa Fe office was managed by a congenial and patient woman named Dorothy McKibbin. She greeted the daily arrivals with warmth and attempted to allay their confusion.

Oppenheimer and his wife, Kitty, arrived in mid-March, and his secretary and young Peter arrived a few days later. At first, Priscilla Green was located in a room next to the Oppenheimers' room at the La Fonda Hotel in Santa Fe. There was a connecting door between the rooms, which Oppenheimer used when conducting business with Green. A short while later, Kitty Oppenheimer casually informed Green that the adjoining door would be locked.

From Santa Fe, everyone made the tortuous thirty-five-mile trip to Los Alamos by car or bus. Most of the very few official cars and trucks were old and apt to break down on the road to Los Alamos. The road not only had dangerous switchbacks, but was layered with sharp rocks. The roads on the mesa and to the surrounding canyons were even rougher and had never been paved. The Los Alamos Ranch School had prided itself on maintaining as natural and rustic a setting as possible. The same conditions prevailed for most of the war, even after the arrival of the Army. Getting to the housing areas and remote sites from the technical area was equally difficult, as these roads were also unpaved or little more than dirt trails. Roads laid in the winter when the ground was frozen turned to mud in the spring. When it rained, the plateau staggered in mire, slowing all movement to a crawl; hardly a home or office failed to have a telltale trail of mud on the floors and carpets.

For new arrivals, the first reaction was usually one of culture shock. All had been told, of course, that the laboratory was located in New Mexico, at high altitude and in a "charming" setting. Some also learned that the new laboratory would be located in the Jemez Mountains. This name was particularly useful for security reasons: To non-Spanish speakers, the word *jemez* sounds like *haymos*, and no map of New Mexico revealed such mountains. While the drive to Los Alamos was dramatic and often beautiful, the initial view of the small town certainly looked military and rather squalid. The anxiety increased when many were shunted off to rustic guest ranches, with furniture either en route or stuck somewhere in storage. Most modern necessities were not readily available or even apparent: sewerage systems, schools, stores, laundry facilities, post office, garbage disposal, medical services, and policemen. Until the end of April telephone conversations, over an old forest service line, were possible only between Los Alamos and the Sante Fe office. Brief requests or instructions could be shouted, while more complex conversations were impossible, requiring a seventy-mile round trip.

The laboratory opened in April when the weather seemed to

hover between cool and cold. Few buildings were heated. The proposed commissary had not yet been built, and box lunches had to be ferried from Santa Fe each day.

Oppenheimer faced what seemed to be one problem after another. The original assessment of Los Alamos as a laboratory for "about one hundred scientists" became a joke. No sooner had men and machines arrived than the water supply ran short. Winter weather had frozen and shattered pipelines. The reservoir on the mesa grew algae. One huge water tank and later another were finally built. As soon as scientists began work, they ordered additional construction. The first contractor had been able to complete 54 percent of its contract in two months; the remaining 46 percent took another year. Each request for expanded or new facilities delayed progress while construction teams were shifted from project to project. Oppenheimer's only solution was to hire more contractors.

Oppenheimer's recruiting efforts required a double, almost contradictory, effort: to warn each prospective staff member about the need for thorough security, but somehow, in the process, to downplay its pervasiveness. Life at Los Alamos would mean restrictions on personal mobility as well as on communications with family, friends, and colleagues. Most men and their wives received a memorandum from Oppenheimer that was labeled "Restricted." In it, the reader found that Los Alamos was located at 7,300 feet and on a strip of mesa nearly two miles long. The weather was pleasant—an average of 67.7 degrees—and ordinary clothing should be supplemented with "rough, country clothes." Oppenheimer then urged each person to strictly regard the need for tight security. In reality, this "regard" meant no mention of Los Alamos as a location, certainly no mention of one's work (or a husband's work), no travel beyond Sante Fe, and, eventually, censorship of the mails.

To further obscure the association of certain men with secret war work, Oppenheimer assigned code names. Enrico Fermi became Henry Farmer and Niels Bohr, Nicholas Baker. Everyone took on the job description of "engineer" for tax forms and driver licenses. All mail to Los Alamos was addressed to P.O. Box 1663, Sante Fe, New Mexico.

On July 20, 1943, Oppenheimer received a letter from Groves marked "Secret." He was informed that he should not fly in airplanes of any description, nor should he drive more than a few miles without a "competent, able bodied, armed guard." These rules would become even stricter later in the war, when Oppenheimer's house in Los Alamos would be assigned full-time guards. Even Kitty had to have a pass to enter her own home.

Oppenheimer reminded everyone to be discreet. As director, he was particularly careful not to give Groves any reason to believe that he was careless with information. Bacher saw Oppenheimer once fasten a classified memorandum to his hip pocket with a safety pin in order to prevent its accidental loss.

To hide the actual work of the Hill, as Los Alamos came to be called, the laboratory created a story that was to be circulated in Santa Fe. In April 1943, Oppenheimer informed Groves that the story agreed upon was that Los Alamos was developing a new type of rocket. In part, this story would help to explain the program of testing explosives, which would soon start. Still another story involved the development of an "electromagnetic gun."

The workday began every morning at 7:30 A.M. with a shrill siren sounding from the Technical Area. The official work week was six days, but often men disappeared into their laboratories on the seventh as well. As the laboratory grew, it was necessary to build certain sites—such as those for manufacturing explosives—far away from the Tech Area. Los Alamos made good use of the many canyons that subdivided Pajarito Plateau, taking on the military's penchant for simple designation: X, Z, Omega, and S sites. When he was in Los Alamos, Oppenheimer was always in his office before anyone else.

Oppenheimer determined that there were four major research areas facing the staff: critical mass, the conditions that affected nuclear reactions and detonation, the chemistry and metallurgy of uranium and plutonium and the possibility of producing a thermonuclear or hydrogen bomb. A special "review committee" appointed by Groves agreed that these were the major tasks. The summary also provided Oppenheimer with the basis for a series of lectures to be presented beginning on April 15 to new staff. General Groves was present and greeted each member of the new staff with a handshake. As a laboratory, Los Alamos was barely functional. It was, as one scientist recalled, one hell of a mess. Buildings were incomplete, there were few roads, and the weather had not yet softened into spring. Meeting in a drafty lecture hall, the staff sat in wood and canvas chairs facing a small stage where Robert Serber stood. He had been handpicked by Oppenheimer to deliver most of the initial lectures.

Serber was self-concious, but the material he presented carried itself. The work at Los Alamos would center on deriving explosive energy from U 235 or Pu 239.* Oppenheimer's team at Berkeley had by then theorized that the energy release from one kilogram (about 2.2. pounds) of

---

*Such an explosion would come from the fissioning of the nuclei of uranium or plutonium under certain controlled conditions. Fission occurs when the nucleus of a fissionable isotope absorbs an additional neutron, becomes unstable, and divides, usually in half. Together, the fragments have somewhat less mass than the original nucleus plus the additional neutron. Most of this difference in mass is converted into kinetic, or explosive, energy.

U 235 equaled the energy release from the detonation of seventeen thousand tons of TNT.

A chain reaction occurs only when a critical mass of the fissionable material is present. Conventional explosives like TNT burn equally well in large or small amounts, but this was not true of nuclear material. Los Alamos scientists would have to determine the minimum amount, or critical mass, for both U 235 and Pu 239. No explosion would occur if too little material was used.

A source of neutrons, other than those that occur naturally in the environment or from cosmic waves, needed to be placed at the center of the bomb to trigger a chain reaction by releasing, at the proper instant, a large supply of neutrons. A shield, or tamper, was needed to prevent unwanted expansion of the uranium or plutonium and to "reflect" neutrons back into the heart of the bomb. For a chain reaction to be explosive, one fission has to follow another as rapidly as possible, therefore "fast" neutrons are elemental to the process. Moreover, the actual uranium or plutonium has to be "subcritical" in the initial stages in order to prevent a premature chain reaction. At the right time, the subcritical material is forced together—or assembled, as Los Alamos called it—into a critical and then supercritical mass.

Serber outlined the two most promising methods of assembling a critical mass in a bomb. The first was a "gun" method, in which one subcritical mass of fissionable material is fired rapidly into another, causing a supercritical, or explosive, reaction. The gun would have an explosive charge and a subcritical mass on one end, and a second subcritical mass firmly locked into position on the other end.

The other method was called implosion, in which a slightly subcritical sphere of fissionable material is surrounded by high explosives. Spreading the force of the detonated explosives inward compresses the subcritical mass into a supercritical lump that, in turn, explodes. Because the sphere has to be uniformly compressed, the process is difficult to achieve. This latter process captured the imagination of Seth Neddermeyer, Oppenheimer's former student and a former employee of the National Bureau of Standards, who soon became a major advocate of the implosion bomb.

Edward Teller also reported on the possibility that a far more powerful weapon could be built. The thermonuclear bomb, or superbomb, as he called it, would require a small fission weapon to create the enormously high temperatures needed to ignite a substance like deuterium or lithium. Deuterium, which is an isotope of hydrogen (the lightest element), is twice as heavy as the hydrogen nucleus. Teller pointed out that the obvious advantage of using deuterium in a superbomb is that it has the lowest ignition temperature—about 400,000,000° F—and once ignited, it is at least five times as explosive as U 235.

Like several of his colleagues at Los Alamos, Teller had come to America in the 1930s to escape the growing anti-Semitism in Hungary and Germany. He had been invited by Oppenheimer to come from the University of Chicago to join the Theoretical Division at Los Alamos. From the very beginning Teller's brilliant mind was captivated by the possibility of creating a superweapon. He rapidly persuaded Oppenheimer to assign him a small staff to study only thermonuclear problems. Oppenheimer agreed despite the great amount of work involved. There would be a cost for the new weapon, and even Teller dryly referred to it in a new term: megabucks. Some ill will would come from colleagues because of his narrow interest, but Teller's persistence earned him a major role in the superbomb's development after the war.

Teller's energy and quickness of mind was similar to Oppenheimer's. At their first meeting in 1937, Teller was struck by what he considered the "overpowering" quality of Oppenheimer's mind.[11] When they first worked together at Los Alamos, they considered each other as friends. Their eventual separation during the next three years was the result of differing philosophies and perhaps because of secret competition. On the surface, the differences seemed to be more a matter of Oppenheimer's concern for expedient development of a fission weapon versus Teller's imaginative devotion to a superweapon.

For the moment at least, the laboratory was concerned with developing its most promising possibility: the gun bomb, which they believed could use either uranium or plutonium. The implosive alternative was a less certain possibility.

No doubt the excitement of those first days created a sense of magic for everyone. Oppenheimer mixed old and young people, those who were experienced and those with little more than a college degree. The colloquium revealed for the first time the awesome possibilities of atomic energy. Most came to be aware of, if perhaps only during the war, the glitter of the weapons they were creating and their power to unleash the most elemental forces in nature. And it was a power, as Freeman Dyson later noted, that scientists would bring into being with their minds.

6. The Task at Hand

As director, Robert Oppenheimer's primary responsibility at Los Alamos was to guide development of an atomic bomb. For the first few months of 1943, his general approach was to divide the resources of the fledgling laboratory between the two available alternatives—the gun and implosion weapons—with the bulk of the manpower and money supporting the gun project. The simplicity of the gun approach made it the most straightforward technological undertaking and the one that promised the earliest success. Implosion was intriguing, but far more complex. No one had ever tried to uniformly compress a ball of metal using high explosives. In fact, during most of 1943 the Governing Board reflected the divided opinions of scientists regarding the feasibility of the implosion.

At first it was thought that the gun weapon could use either uranium or plutonium. As long as that proved true, the gun would clearly be top priority, implosion remaining as the second-best choice. By late fall, however, Oppenheimer had mounting evidence that plutonium would not work in a gun. The problem lay in the inability of the current production and refinement methods to remove all or most of the impurities from plutonium. An imaginative piece of work by Emilio Segrè at Berkeley in 1942 had already suggested that plutonium might be likely to fission spontaneously because of the neutrons that are released prematurely from impurities in the substance.* The only way to overcome this condition was to bring two subcritical pieces of plutonium together so quickly that the possibility of spontaneous fission could be overcome. Staggering as it was, conventional guns could only throw one piece of material into another at three thousand feet per second; in a gun using plutonium, the speed would have to be considerably faster.

Implosion research was hampered in part by a lack of plutonium and uranium samples, which were necessary for experiments. Stan Ulam witnessed the day the first sample of Pu 239 arrived. He was leaving his office in the administration building when he saw Oppenheimer running excitedly down the corridor holding a small vial. In it, not yet processed into a metal, was a murky substance lying unimpressively at the bottom of a clear liquid. For months Robert Bacher's group had had the laboratory's

*In 1942, Segrè had suggested the possibility of spontaneous fission in plutonium without access to an actual sample of Pu 239; the possibility was inferred from work on other fissionable elements.

total wealth of U 235 in the form of a very thin, very small square of metal foil. Even a year later, when the laboratory's supply included several pieces of U 235 foil, the supply of Pu 239 amounted to only a few small specks.

But even with such a small sample, Segrè was able to confirm that the plutonium then being produced by Manhattan District reactors would definitely undergo spontaneous fission.* For Oppenheimer, the reality was simple: There was not enough time to build another major plutonium purification plant in Los Alamos. Reluctantly, he was forced to cancel all work on the plutonium gun, a decision that meant plutonium could be used only in an implosion weapon. For those men working on the Pu 239 gun, the decision came as an unfortunate but sadly necessary rejection of their year's work. Across the laboratory, in fact, the news seemed to severely darken the promise of quickly developing and delivering a weapon for use in the war.

Oppenheimer couldn't afford to be disheartened, at least not publicly. He pointed out the few promising signs that indicated that implosion could somehow be made to work. On the Fourth of July, 1943, scientists began conducting experiments designed to use explosives to compress metal objects. Early results suggested that in these explosions considerable compression could occur. Early IBM computers arrived and though they were crude, they eliminated much of the tiresome calculations for theoretical work that previously had to be done by hand. At times the computer data offered promising mathematical models for the implosion-bomb designers. In another development, Jim Tuck, a member of the British team at Los Alamos, offered a creative solution to the problem of fabricating explosives for implosion. In order to uniformly compress the plutonium sphere, Tuck suggested using explosives shaped to look like five-sided pyramids with their tops cut off. When assembled around a nuclear core to make a second layer and ignited, the shock waves would converge at some hypothetical point in the center. Because the effect was one of focusing shock waves, the explosive charges were nicknamed "lenses."

There was pressure to use plutonium in a bomb because current production rates for both uranium and plutonium suggested that the latter would be available in greater supply in early or mid-1945. Projections by Groves indicated that only enough U 235 would be available in 1945 for one weapon; as many as two or three weapons could be made using plutonium.

Oppenheimer placed his old colleague Seth Neddermeyer in charge of the implosion program. When the plutonium gun was abandoned, Neddermeyer's team suddenly grew vastly in size and stature. Although he

*The impurity that would cause spontaneous fission was the plutonium isotope, 240.

was an excellent and creative scientist, Neddermeyer was not a manager. Work stagnated and faltered; complaints about Neddermeyer started to make their way to Oppenheimer. By May 1944 the situation had become critical: Several groups in the laboratory found themselves hampered at every turn by administrative snarls and seemed on the verge of mutiny. From Washington came continuing pressure to proceed with the implosion program even if the explosive potential was low; Conant told Oppenheimer that even a bomb with a force of several hundred tons of TNT would be acceptable.[1]

Oppenheimer's first decision was to reorganize the implosion program. He succeeded in convincing George Kistiakowsky, one of the few explosives experts in the nation, to move to Los Alamos in the early summer and take charge of the implosion effort under William Parsons. Privately, Oppenheimer assured his colleagues that Neddermeyer would be moved to a less sensitive position. On June 15, 1944, Oppenheimer announced his reorganization to the staff; a month later he met with Groves, Conant, Colonel Nichols, and Fermi in an emergency meeting in Chicago to defend his actions. There was little discussion or need for defense: However, everyone agreed that Los Alamos needed to concentrate its efforts on developing the implosion weapon without jeopardizing the completion of the uranium gun.

Oppenheimer returned to Los Alamos and effected sweeping changes in the total organization of the laboratory. He dissolved the Governing Board and replaced it with a series of committees. Kistiakowsky was given his own division, called X Division, which was specifically responsible for the implosion bomb. Oppenheimer fought back against the sagging spirits: The problem with Los Alamos, he announced to his senior staff in August, was laxity rather than discontent. He created a special top-level committee consisting of staff from several different divisions, which he called the Cowpuncher Committee. Its purpose, he said, was to "ride herd" on implosion. In a rare move, Oppenheimer stood up against Groves's strong opposition to have Enrico Fermi transferred to Los Alamos from Chicago's Metallurgical Laboratory to become an associate director. Rumor had it that Groves was afraid Fermi would oppose using the bomb once it was developed.[2]

That summer, scientists still believed the Germans might produce an atomic bomb, although the war on both fronts had shifted in favor of the Allies. Allied troops, for example, had driven far into France from Normandy; in Italy, they had liberated Florence. Japan now seemed a more likely target for an atom bomb if one could be completed in time.

The reorganization of the implosion project was enough to create at least a sense of progress. Oppenheimer reported to Groves in August 1944 that three weapons were now under serious development at Los Alamos. The MARK I was a low-yield, low-power uranium gun bomb; the

MARK II was a more sophisticated gun weapon with greater explosive power; and the MARK III, which would use plutonium, was an implosion bomb requiring relatively little fissionable material but having a comparatively greater explosive yield. After talking with Oppenheimer, Groves assured General George Marshall that a MARK II would definitely be available by August 1945, and that if implosion experiments were successful, a MARK III would be available sometime between March and June of 1945.[3]

One result of the August reorganization was an independent work team under Edward Teller, called the Super and General Theory Group. Teller was generally regarded as gifted and imaginative, but also temperamental and single-minded. He had an argumentative nature which was really only a part of his thinking process, but from time to time it offended others. Teller's insistence on working only on the thermonuclear weapon alienated many who felt his talents were needed on the atomic bomb. This included Hans Bethe, who until August 1944 was Teller's boss. Oppenheimer, realizing that Teller was not purposefully trying to be abrasive, gave in and assigned Teller his own group. Teller had been granted his request but he had to pay a price for it; his relationship with Oppenheimer began to deteriorate. Later he recalled, "When I got to Los Alamos my friendship with Oppenheimer was already practically at dead end."[4]

Teller had pressed Oppenheimer to support the study of the thermonuclear bomb since early 1943. His fascination with the superbomb dated from a lunchtime discussion with Fermi in 1942. After almost a year of work at Los Alamos, Teller was able to report some encouraging news. Emil J. Konopinski, working with Teller, had suggested that the ignition temperature for the detonation of liquid deuterium could be lowered by adding an artificially created element, tritium. With a lower ignition point, the probability of deuterium igniting increased by a significant degree.

Teller had made an impassioned appeal to Oppenheimer and the Governing Board in September 1943 for more support. He cited recent intelligence reports from Europe as evidence that the Germans had an interest in deuterium and were very possibly working on Nazi superbombs. Oppenheimer was hesitant to embark on any substantial program, however, because of the decided need to emphasize the fission program. Teller was given a small staff to study only the super and was mollified for the moment by the promise of eventual independence.

After the laboratory's reorganization, Teller was freed from all responsibility so that he could study the thermonuclear bomb exclusively. Whatever the attitude toward him in Los Alamos, he was not without external support. The prospect of a superbomb could not fail to interest Groves and Tolman, who saw the weapon as a momentous development in explosive power. Groves believed that "the super cannot be completely forgotten if we take seriously our responsibility for the permanent defense of the U.S.A."[5] On October 6, Teller wrote to Tolman: "If work on the super gadget should be pursued in peacetime, it is my opinion that a staff of approximately 100 scientists and technicians would be sufficient to carry out work on the super gadget."[6] Another defender of the superbomb was Luis Alvarez, who wrote a supporting letter to Tolman at the same time. "I feel strongly that the next war will be fought with supers (if one can call it fighting), and then battleships and submarines will be as useful as rowboats."[7]

Teller reported some gruesome projections in the spring of 1945. A superbomb might be capable of generating forces as great as ten million tons (ten megatons) of TNT—a projection that proved to be remarkably accurate. To put this into perspective, Teller reminded his colleagues that such an explosion would not be the greatest ever witnessed on earth. A search of historical records revealed that the Krakatoa volcanic eruption in 1883 generated an explosion heard three thousand miles away. The large meteorite craters in Arizona and Siberia were evidence of explosions larger than that of a ten-megaton superbomb. On a relative scale, Teller thought that if an ordinary fission bomb could produce a blast equivalent to ten kilotons of TNT in an area of ten square miles, a superbomb could produce a similar effect over 1,000 square miles. One superbomb, for example, could easily destroy New York City. Even more awesome was the thought that if a super burned a ten-meter cube of liquid deuterium at the height of three hundred miles, the blast would equal one thousand "ordinary" superbombs detonated at the height of ten miles. The potential damage could waste one million square miles.

While work on the fission bomb was hardly complete, Oppenheimer wrote to Tolman on September 20, 1944, urging further development of the super. "I should like . . . to put in writing at an early date the recommendation that the subject of initiating violent thermonuclear reactions be pursued with vigor and diligence, and promptly." While Los Alamos could not at present start the work until the fission bombs were complete, the laboratory could very well accelerate work after the war. For scientific and political reasons, "the extent to which energy can be released by thermonuclear reactions is clearly of profound importance."[8]

Considering these comments, it seems ironic that a decade later Oppenheimer would be defending himself against charges by the United States government that he had resisted the development of a thermonuclear weapon.

There was indeed a remarkable quality to the leadership exercised by Robert Oppenheimer at Los Alamos, which both admirer and detractor would later admit. His effectiveness came as a surprise to those who remembered Oppenheimer's first years as a teacher, when he could hardly comprehend why his abstruse lectures failed to teach his students. For a man who had had little management experience before the war, Oppenheimer did very well; he quickly developed a style and manner that capitalized on his talent to follow developments in dozens of scientific and technical areas and on his ability to charm and persuade. He personally recruited most of his senior staff (Parsons was one exception), and was able to remember most of the other staff by name. The affectionate nickname "Oppie" was carried to Los Alamos; he still delighted in his dialogues with young men, perpetuating an image from California that he acted like a mother hen with chicks.

One result of Oppenheimer's leadership was his re-creation of a university atmosphere at Los Alamos. Of course, this was a world he knew intimately; he had never worked anywhere but in a university. For young men it was a continuation of college study, but obviously it required a great deal more involvement. Bob Krohn, one of the young men brought to Los Alamos straight from the campus, saw the special relationship between student and teacher continue, with respect growing out of what one knew or contributed, rather than from any particular work assignment.

To his credit, Oppenheimer always seemed to generate optimism, particularly when promising leads vanished or important developments seemed at an impasse. He displayed an amazing talent at mediating differences among his bright and eccentric staff. He seemed sensitive to the moment when his presence or words would be useful in surmounting a theoretical or personal obstacle. He was able to generate a great deal of spirit by just talking, and John Manley remembered him as "a great guy to take advantage of a stage. He continually used words for their auditory effect."

Yet from time to time, a side of him emerged that was not so kind, encouraged perhaps by tension. It was a quality that close friends remembered from earlier days. Oppenheimer could vacillate quickly between encouraging his staff's successes and chaffing them with a snobbery or sense of intellectual superiority. Piqued by slowness or timidity, he could be caustic. Harold Agnew remembers an occasion when Oppenheimer lashed out at one staff member so suddenly that others in the room were stunned and embarrassed. Norris Bradbury never saw this happen with scientists, but was aware of the verbal sharpness Oppenheimer directed toward the military. Colonel Kenneth Nichols, who would later become the general manager of the Atomic Energy Commission, was particularly "the butt of strong language from Oppie." Manley's impression was that Oppenheimer "had an impatience with stupidity, which was understandable, and an impatience with fumbling: fumbling in expression, thinking. In no case was it deliberate to cause pain."

These incidents were rare, but they were remembered, and most knew the director had his human side as well. His facilitating manner, which was used so successfully in mediating differences, caused a few staff to take notes while talking with Oppenheimer, not only to avoid being deflected in their requests or protests, but to be able to offer proof later of an Oppie decision in their favor. His own hesitation to deal quickly with Neddermeyer seemed an odd contrast to his constant urgings for decisive action among his staff. Few can remember Oppenheimer ever giving a direct compliment.

The work took its toll. Oppenheimer's weight fell in two years from a slender 130 pounds to a gaunt 110.* His smoking increased so that he was never without a cigarette or pipe in his hand. Prone to illness, he once even caught the chicken pox. Some noticed his disturbing habit of letting his mind wander in long meetings. By the summer of 1944, Oppenheimer seemed particularly tired. Bacher suspected that he was on the verge of resigning and tried to bolster his ego by insisting that only Oppie could finish the job. Bacher and others believed that at this critical stage only Oppenheimer could manage the laboratory.

His wife, Kitty, and Peter, his young son, were almost the only private world left to him. On December 7, 1944, a second child arrived; the Oppenheimers named their new daughter Katherine, after her mother, and nicknamed her Toni. Close friends, like Louis and Eleanor Hempelmann (who had been asked by Robert and Kitty to care for their children should something happen to both of them) would occasionally visit for a weekend. They offered companionship and shared an interest in the Oppenheimers' horses. Horseback riding, in fact, was one of the few pleasures Robert and Kitty made an effort to continue at Los Alamos. They kept a stable of horses, bought and sold them to friends or citizens of Santa Fe, and turned over the care of the horses to the Hempelmanns and a few select others only with the greatest admonitions not to let anything happen. Priscilla Green was responsible for reminding purchasers of Oppenheimer horses to pay their bills.

During the war, Oppenheimer served the role of buffer between his fellow scientists and Groves and the military. Oppenheimer courted Groves, flattered him, and acted as the punctilious director. Both men responded to each other with a distant warmth. The two were very different, and little in their past or manner would suggest that either could work productively with the other. Groves was Protestant, had a technical education, and was thoroughly immersed in military operations. Oppenheimer was Jewish, intellectual, and delighted in divergent thinking and discussion. Standing by one another, they were an odd pair to look at.

*Oppenheimer apparently possessed an extraordinarily slender physique. John and Kay Manley remember that Robert was the only adult they knew who was able to sit in the antique child's highchair they kept in their house.

Both were generally the same height, but Oppenheimer was slender with loose-fitting clothes. Groves was corpulent, with carefully tailored uniforms. Despite their differences, they both recognized the strengths in the other. Groves had a director capable of leading brilliant men, and Oppenheimer had a chance to exercise the full range of his talents. Despite their close working relationship, they always addressed one another formally as Dr. Oppenheimer and General Groves.

Given the nature of the work being conducted at Los Alamos, the general was an obvious target for jokes and for frustration, although some people did recognize Groves's better side. Bradbury, for example, realized his enormous management skills and believed that Groves deeply wanted to be liked by those around him. Bradbury even remembers that the general occasionally tried to be funny, but without much success. Bacher noticed that Groves was always more deferential to Oppenheimer than to other scientists like Compton and Lawrence.

Oppenheimer later reflected that his best times at Los Alamos were those spent touring the laboratory's scattered offices and sites. Within months the laboratory had spilled off the mesa, expanding into nearby canyons. Oppenheimer could be seen walking from his home to work every day before most others arrived, sometimes spiritedly engaged in a conversation with a companion. Visiting S Site or Pajarito Canyon, he drove a military jeep or his own large black Buick. His informal visits would allow him to sit in the back of the room smoking his ever-present pipe or cigarette, nodding approvingly at promising reports. Although his presence intimidated some, most welcomed his ability to see quickly the dimensions of a problem.

At Los Alamos, Oppenheimer created a myth about himself, just like he did during his earlier teaching days. One often-told incident has him walking into a room where physicists had spent a long, tiring day on one problem: their blackboards were covered with complex calculations. Oppenheimer studied the blackboard for a moment, walked to the board and corrected a figure, and walked out without saying a word. Another time, Oppenheimer was sitting in on a meeting of metallurgists and after listening calmly for a while, smoking his pipe, he summed up the various arguments so thoroughly that the solution to the problem became obvious. During one meeting with young scientists, Harold Agnew ventured to ask why plumbers at Los Alamos were making nearly three times as much as staff members with college degrees. Oppenheimer said wryly that plumbers did not know the importance of the laboratory's work and the scientists did. That, the director said, was worth the difference in pay.

Part of his magic was an ability to give ordinary events an extraordinary quality. He could articulate a problem or a condition with such style that listeners would be enraptured. Whether it was a description of some new aspect of the bomb or simply mixing his famous martinis,

Oppenheimer could, if he chose, make the event memorable.

His charm did not, of course, eliminate the difficulties of living on the Hill: housing remained in perpetually short supply, salaries were never brought into line, supplies never caught up with demand, and so on. Oppenheimer even received reports that young women were propositioning men at the laboratory's PX. As the weeks grew longer, Oppenheimer found himself giving more and more of his famous "pep talks."

The social life at Los Alamos offered some relief from the hardships. There were parties almost every weekend, occasional plays, musical groups, and even a low-wattage radio station. Robert and Kitty hosted a number of parties in the beginning and then began to withdraw. When she chose to be, Kitty was a talented hostess and cook. On rare occasions Robert and Kitty were able to escape from the Hill and make the drive down to the valley for a dinner at a small tearoom run by a woman named Edith Warner. Her house, which included a small dining room, was near the west bank of the Rio Grande, where the road from Los Alamos crossed over. Warner had lived there since 1928, originally making a meager living by operating a small stop called Otowi Crossing for the Denver and Rio Grande Railroad. Oppenheimer had met her when he was younger, and the two of them developed a lasting friendship. During the war she agreed to serve dinner to eight or ten people from Los Alamos several nights a week. The Oppenheimers always had a standing reservation, but as the war wore on, it became a pastime they were able to exercise less frequently. By late 1944 events were moving so rapidly that time with Peter and Toni was limited to fleeting moments.

There was, undeniably, a peculiar fascination with "the gadget," as the bomb was called. Whether it was the uranium gun bomb, nicknamed Little Boy, or the plutonium implosion weapon, called Fat Man, they were both intricate puzzles. The small sphere of plutonium that would form the very heart of the Fat Man was warm to the touch, a quality reported by some as being "trembling, almost alive." Each part of the implosion device was exactingly crafted to fit together like parts of a complex machine. The uranium gun was far simpler; it utilized a dull-black gun barrel to house the explosive charges and two pieces of uranium at either end, called the male and female plugs for their shapes.

Oppenheimer was as captivated as anyone with the intriguing qualities of the new weapons. There was a strange, almost dark beauty to the highly machined and silvered spheres of plutonium and plugs of uranium. In Building TA-22-1 at S Site, where Fat Man was assembled, a special ceiling track and hoist had been installed to move the enormous, yard-thick implosion gadget from one assembly point to another. While escorting Groves or some other privileged visitor, Oppenheimer would describe the bomb in terms of its components: charcoal-dark explosive lenses, uranium tamper, dull-silver plutonium core, and so forth. For their value, both in terms of money and human effort, they could even be described lovingly.

Because of the unusual openness at Los Alamos, most men had a chance to see the weapons at one stage of development or another. A few men, like those in Otto Frisch's Critical Assembly Group, worked with nuclear materials on a daily basis. In a canyon distant from Los Alamos, Frisch's men had the task of determining how much plutonium or uranium was needed to achieve a critical mass. They did this by creating imaginative but dangerous experiments to bring subcritical pieces of U 235 or Pu 239 together for a fraction of a second in order to make them critical. In that brief moment, a dozen scientific instruments measured the level of radiation and gave a further clue to the specific amount needed.*

The frantic pace at Los Alamos stopped briefly on April 12, 1945, when news of Franklin Roosevelt's death came over the radio. Oppenheimer was walking down a street when he was given the news by a young scientist. Three days later, at a nonsectarian Sunday service, he spoke about the President's passing:

> In the Hindu scripture, in the *Bhagavad-Gita*, it says, "Man is a creature whose substance is faith. What his faith is, he is." The faith of Roosevelt is one that is shared by millions of men and women in every country of the world. For this reason it is possible to maintain the hope, for this reason it is right that we should dedicate ourselves to the hope, that his good works will not have ended with his death.[9]

Roosevelt died less than a month before the end of the war in Europe. Berlin fell on May 2, and the war ended officially in Europe on May 8, 1945.

With the arrival of May there was a refreshing sense of expectation. Oppenheimer believed that his laboratory would be able to deliver a bomb on schedule. Frisch's group was close to achieving the first critical assembly of U 235, which would confirm several years of theoretical speculation. Bacher's tests of the explosive lenses proved that symmetrical shock waves occurred with the shaped charges. Another Los Alamos team seemed to have perfected reliable detonators. On June 24, Frisch reported to Oppenheimer the precise amount of plutonium needed for Fat Man.

Parson's men completed the exterior shells or casings for both Fat

---

*The only death at Los Alamos during the war was that of Harry Daghlian, a young scientist working for Frisch, who accidentally let two hemispheres of plutonium fall together amid a pile of uranium bricks, which made the assembly briefly supercritical and deadly. Daghlian died twenty-eight days later from the effects of radiation.

Man and Little Boy. Fat Man would be sealed in an egg-shaped outer shell utilizing nearly 1,500 bolts. With fins added to the shell for stability as it dropped, the entire weapon would be 12 feet long and 62 inches in diameter; it weighed nearly 10,000 pounds. Little Boy was in actuality a modified gun barrel, sealed at both ends and enclosed in a large cylindrical tube. With fins, it was 10 feet long and 28 inches in diameter; it weighed 9,000 pounds.

With work nearing completion on so many fronts, Oppenheimer could take time to assess Los Alamos and make tentative recommendations for the postwar period. He had more than 4,000 civilian and 2,000 military personnel working in 200 buildings, 37 of which were in the Tech Area alone. The scientists and their families lived in 620 rooms in more than 300 apartment buildings, as well as in 200 trailers and 52 dormitories.

In May he reported to General Groves on the progress of the laboratory, the work yet to be done, and some plans for Los Alamos after the war. At present, he wrote, all work was being devoted to completing the first models of Fat Man and Little Boy. Unless large supplies of U 235 were to become suddenly available, Los Alamos would continue to produce mostly plutonium-based weapons. There was, quite obviously, a considerable amount of work that could be done to improve Fat Man, considering the fact that the model under completion was little more than prototypic—clumsy, difficult to assemble, and overweight. Already Los Alamos knew how to make the Fat Man three times more powerful and how to improve the explosive lenses. Oppenheimer also reported that Los Alamos was still far from knowing how to make a hydrogen bomb. Despite Teller's elaborate theorizations, the laboratory had no firm idea how to make a superbomb. Indeed, it wasn't certain that thermonuclear reactions could even be made to take place on earth, or if such a reaction could be sustained to cause an explosion. With intense study, however, it was believed that the superbomb could be available in less than a decade.[10]

For the moment, Oppenheimer was concerned with delivering a weapon. Much depended upon the success of his laboratory during the next few months.

7. The New Age

As Oppenheimer and his laboratory neared success, Washington turned its attention to the diplomatic implications of the atomic bomb; quite clearly it had both military and diplomatic meaning. Both Roosevelt and Churchill were aware of its dual nature when they had signed the Quebec Agreement in August 1943; in a secret protocol they had agreed to a "full sharing" of information on bomb developments with Canada, but not with a third party. Stimson quietly told his colleagues that the bomb could possibly force concessions from the Soviets.[1]

Oppenheimer himself was in a quandary over matters of philosophy. As a scientist, he could favor sharing information with Allied nations, much as he had before the war, but as director of Los Alamos he also could understand the hesitation Roosevelt, Bush, and others expressed about giving information to anyone other than the closest friends of the United States. At the Yalta Conference in January 1945, Roosevelt suggested to Churchill that the two countries brief Stalin on the general nature of the Manhattan Project. Churchill professed to be shocked and refused adamantly. He was afraid that if the Russians had this information, they would not feel a need to cooperate in the war against Japan. Moreover, the Prime Minister feared that sharing information with one ally would necessarily mean having to make a similar revelation to the French.[2] Despite Oppenheimer's distance from involvement in global planning, he was under pressure from within the Manhattan Project to support an exchange of information. Niels Bohr and Leo Szilard, among others, were quite outspoken about the need for sharing atomic secrets with all nations; it was an integral part, they argued, of any postwar hopes for an international agreement.

Truman, no less than Roosevelt, was urged by advisors to keep the new weapon a secret. While Roosevelt fostered a spirit of cooperation toward the Russians, he yielded nevertheless to pressures from Churchill and his own advisors to withhold information on the American enterprise. Truman saw that secrecy and the sole possession of a bomb could mean considerable advantage to the United States at war's end. Stimson, who thoroughly briefed Truman on the Manhattan Project when Truman became President, reflected that the United States ". . . must find some way of persuading Russia to play ball."[3] Fat Man and Little Boy could be important to such an argument. Oppenheimer, occupied with events at

Los Alamos, chose to assume a neutral stance, for the moment, in the growing debate over postwar policy.

In March 1945 America learned that the U.S. Third Army had crossed the Rhine into Germany at Remagen. Within a month it was the Elbe. From the Pacific came news that over four thousand American soldiers had died on the tiny island of Iwo Jima. Stimson and his planners estimated that as many as two hundred thousand American casualties might be sustained by an Allied assault on the Japanese islands.

Oppenheimer received encouraging news that the German atomic bomb had been no more than a phantom. Scientific investigators in Europe, including Boris Pash, had interviewed captured German scientists and had learned that bureaucratic fumbling and internecine fighting among scientists had prevented a unified and successful effort. Perhaps more important, Adolf Hitler had failed to develop an interest in the possibilities of such an intricate device, remaining far more interested in the spectacular V-1 and V-2 rockets.

There was still a nagging uncertainty at Los Alamos about whether Fat Man would work. Oppenheimer sensed this in his colleagues' repeated requests for an experimental test of the device and in the discomforting pleas for more time to perfect one component or another or to conduct just one more experiment. Oppenheimer carefully approached Groves for permission to conduct a full-scale firing of a Fat Man.[4] Groves weighed the advantages and disadvantages. Enough plutonium would be available that summer for at least two, possibly three Fat Men of current design. Successful tests would confirm the work in Los Alamos and prevent any surprises of a dud in Japan. The general wired back his approval.

Oppenheimer appointed Kenneth Bainbridge to be responsible for the implosion test. Bainbridge quickly assembled his own group and began looking for an appropriate site. Oppenheimer joined the team for a round of visits in May 1944. Several island possibilities off California and Texas were rejected in favor of a large block of land in southern New Mexico, not far from the White Sands National Monument. There was nothing to purchase: All of the necessary land was under government control as part of the Alamogordo Bombing Range, where B-17 and B-29 crews practiced before assignment overseas.

Oppenheimer named the test area Trinity, recalling several lines from John Donne's *Holy Sonnets*:

> Batter my heart, three person'd God, for, you
> As yet but knock, breathe, shine, and seek to mend.
> That I may rise and stand, o'erthrow me and bend
> Your force to break, blow, burn and make me new.

Within months a small city appeared in the desert. Since Fat Man would be exploded from the ground instead of from an airplane, a one-hundred-foot metal tower was built and the spot nicknamed Ground Zero. Three major observation posts were constructed ten thousand yards away at the north, west, and south compass points. The command shelter for Oppenheimer, Bainbridge, and others was located at the south shelter. Ten miles away, down one of the few paved roads at Trinity, was base camp, with laboratories, storerooms, a mess hall, several dormitories, and a meeting room. All supplies were trucked down from Los Alamos in a series of daily runs that each took half a day. An elaborate security and pass system was created; strict instructions were handed out to everyone going to Trinity from Los Alamos and returning. There were to be no stops for gasoline or telephone calls, no adventures en route. The one approved stop was Roy's Cafe in Belen, where everyone believed Groves had placed a G-2 agent as chef.

The explosion was expected to generate temperatures in the range of 1,000,000°F. In less than one hundredth of a second, the central fireball would expand to about 800 feet in diameter and cool down to 15,000°F. In two minutes the fireball would dissipate into the atmosphere, forming a cloud and reaching a peak altitude of 15 kilometers, cooling down further to 8,000°F. Scientists on the ground and those in observation planes were instructed not to look into the explosion until after the first fireball had formed.

In April, Frank Oppenheimer arrived at Oak Ridge to act as assistant to his brother. Frank was assigned the tiring job of jumping from one problem to another as a resource person. Like Isidor Rabi, Frank had been asked by General Groves to come to Los Alamos to offer support to the nervous director. Despite Frank's past record as a Communist party member and California activist, Groves permitted him to come to Los Alamos during one of its most crucial phases. For most of June and early July, Frank stayed at Trinity, making rounds in the oppressive heat and earning a small reputation as an excellent troubleshooter.

An early test date, set in March, of July 4 was abandoned when schedules clearly indicated that a delivery of a final weapon by that date would be impossible. Oppenheimer assured Groves that a test would be conducted as soon after July 15 as possible. Groves was mindful that Truman hoped to have favorable results to report in mid-July at the meetings with Churchill and Stalin in Potsdam. On the morning of July 2, Oppenheimer anxiously telephoned Groves in Washington and requested a delay of three days: Fat Man, he said, would be ready by July 18. After some discussion, Groves insisted that the original test date of July 16 had to be maintained. But Oppenheimer's request seemed so anxious that Groves consulted his superiors; when they supported Groves, the general called back and reaffirmed a July 15 or 16 test date. Oppenheimer and Los Alamos were pushed to the limit.*

The work schedules at Los Alamos and Trinity became frantic. The daytime weather was hot, often soaring over 100°F. Any delay at Los Alamos meant overtime at Trinity in order to make up the loss and stay on schedule.

Groves organized a trip to the West Coast to visit Manhattan Projects there in order to provide a cover for a detour to Trinity to observe the Fat Man test. President Truman, already at Potsdam, prepared for his first visit with Stalin. From the East Coast, Tolman, Bush, Conant, and Arthur Compton made clandestine preparations to come. Only a few days were left.

Trinity was located in the middle of a sun-bleached valley named the Jornada del Muerto, or Dead Man's Route, by early Spanish explorers. During the summer day the sun beat down mercilessly; at night, the dry air carried a chill. The vast desert contained little more than low shrubs and other parched flora native to the heat and dryness.

Oppenheimer arrived at Trinity on Sunday, July 15. He appeared tired and fretful. Wandering around the site, he visited Ground Zero, base camp, and several of the observation shelters, causing ripples of anxiety wherever he went. At Ground Zero, he nervously watched as scientists slowly assembled Fat Man for the last time. Silently, a young photographer took movies of Oppy as he watched the black sphere from the edge of the small group of sweating men. A few months earlier, Bainbridge had been asked by Tolman and General Farrell—apparently under orders from Groves—to keep Oppenheimer away from the final assembly of Fat Man and the tower at Ground Zero once the bomb was in place. They expressed a fear that under pressure or in a fit of anxiety, Oppenheimer might make an unwarranted action or decision. Bainbridge balked. The bomb belonged more to Oppenheimer than to anyone else, and under no circumstances would he forbid his director's presence during any phase of the test.[5]

Oppenheimer was indeed nervous; he spent some time talking with Bush. Turning somber for a moment, he translated a few lines from a Sanskrit poem for his elder colleague:

> In battle, in the forest, at the precipice in the mountains,
> On the dark great sea, in the midst of javelins and arrows,

---

*This bit of black humor circulated through the laboratory in July:

From this crude lab that spawned a dud
Their necks to Truman's axe uncurled
Lo, the embattled savants stood
And fired the flop heard 'round the world.

> In sleep, in confusion, in the depths of shame,
> The good deeds a man has done before defend him.[6]

Groves and Conant arrived later in the day, while several busloads of scientists and visitors went to the top of a small mountain twenty miles away called Compañía Hill. A few unmarked cars were dispatched to Albuquerque to pick up the notables. Among them were Charles Thomas, the Manhattan District's coordinator of chemical research; Ernest Lawrence; Sir James Chadwick; and William L. Laurence of *The New York Times*, the only newspaper reporter permitted to cover the Trinity story. The test was set for 5:30 A.M. Monday.

In the dark of early morning, just thirty minutes before the final countdown, Bainbridge completed the final steps that would arm the Fat Man. Donald Hornig, a young scientist who had spent the night babysitting the bomb in the tower during a rain and lightning storm, was relieved and sent back to the south shelter. At the tower, Bainbridge threw the final switch that connected all the electronic leads. The sleeping Fat Man was now tied by an electrical umbilical cord to a control panel at south shelter. A bank of searchlights was turned on, illuminating the tower and its cabin for miles. Oppenheimer, unable to sleep, had spent most of the night pacing base camp. At dawn he moved with Groves to the control bunker. Bainbridge, Farrell, Kistiakowsky, and Bush huddled nearby in a dirt-and-concrete building. Outside, men took shelter in small trenches or lay flat on the ground with their feet pointing at Zero. A few made light conversation.

As the final seconds approached, somewhere amid the maze of electronic devices and wiring, the final crucial connection was made.

From the darkness came a brilliant burst of fierce light many times brighter than the noonday sun. Instantly the desert and distant mountains were bathed in white brilliance. Even those with their eyes closed were able to sense the explosion of light and feel the warmth of it on their bodies. Those who recovered first turned to see, through dark squares of colored glass, a huge ball of fire, like the sun at close range, rising from the desert in a swirling inferno of reds and oranges and yellows. Shortly thereafter there was a loud crack as the sound of the explosion reached the viewers and turned into a mighty roar.

Oppenheimer, who with Groves and the others stumbled outside of the shelter, stood mutely watching the play of lights. He remembered a line from the Hindu *Bhagavad-Gita*: "I am become death, the shatterer of worlds." Bainbridge, who was standing nearby, turned to Oppenheimer and said that they were now all sons of bitches. Kistiakowsky rushed up to Oppenheimer and reminded him of the bet they had made: Kistiakowsky had bet his salary for a month against ten dollars from Oppenheimer that the bomb would work. All around them, the men of Los Alamos broke into cheers and rounds of congratulations.

Groves had hoped to use the hours after the test as a time to assess the explosion with Oppenheimer, Bainbridge, and a few others, but he had little chance for such a serious discussion. The months of hard work and the shattering success left everyone giddy. Oppenheimer surprised everyone with a complete reversal of mood; he seemed as jaunty and energetic as ever. After numerous handshakes he left in a private car for Los Alamos, smiling and with much of the tension gone from his face.

From Albuquerque, Groves cabled his secretary in Washington with news of Fat Man. In turn, she cabled Secretary of War Stimson in Potsdam:

> Operated on this morning. Diagnosis is not yet complete but results seem satisfactory and already exceed expectations. . . . Dr. Groves pleased. . . .[7]

A week later Oppenheimer met with Groves and Tolman in Chicago to review a dozen reports on the Trinity test. They learned that at ten miles the brilliance of the explosion had been that of one thousand suns, and that enough gamma radiation had been emitted to be lethal to every living thing within a radius of two thirds of a mile. The dark side of Enrico Fermi's earlier prediction—that there was one chance in thirty of Fat Man destroying New Mexico and one chance in one thousand of destroying the world—was not fulfilled. Fat Man had produced an explosive yield of seventeen thousand tons of TNT.

President Truman waited eight days before mentioning to Stalin the success at Trinity. America shared General Groves's lengthy report with the British as soon as it arrived, and Churchill broke the news to his people on July 16. In response to Truman's casual mention of the bomb, Stalin merely said, "Good," and expressed the hope that it would be used against Japan. Neither the Americans nor the British knew that for two years Klaus Fuchs and David Greenglass had been passing secret information on the bomb to Soviet agents.

Trinity had proved Oppenheimer's anxiety to be unwarranted; now there was only one other task—Japan.

As Fat Man blazed in the desert, other Los Alamos scientists were already making final preparations on Tinian, a small island in the Pacific, for the bombing of Japan. For Groves, the question of where to drop the bomb was purely a military concern, but he chose to involve Los Alamos scientists in the selection process. A Target Committee was created, with General Lauris Norstad presiding and with Generals Groves and Farrell representing the Manhattan Project. Oppenheimer, a full member, was given permission to invite scientific colleagues as needed. He was unable to attend the first meeting in Washington on May 2, but sent John von Neumann, Robert Wilson, William Penney, and Joyce Stearns from Los Alamos. The Committee agreed that the bombings needed to be visual and conducted in the daylight. Weather trends suggested that six or seven days in the first half of August would provide the best climatological advantage. Hiroshima emerged as the first choice of target because as of May it had not yet been bombed by the 21st Bomber Command, whose responsibility included Japan. The cities of Yawata, Yokohama, Tokyo, and Nagasaki, among others, were also suggested.

A second meeting was held a week later, on May 10, in Oppenheimer's cramped Los Alamos office. The Army Air Force had suggested five "optional" targets which could be reserved for Los Alamos. The first was Kyoto, the country's ancient cultural and intellectual center. Hiroshima was an important army depot and a port of embarkation. Yokohama had not yet been bombed and contained aircraft and electrical equipment factories; it was also one of the most heavily defended cities in Japan. The Kokura Arsenal was a fourth choice, with heavy concentrations of light product manufacturing within the city. Niigata was another important port city on the northwest coast of Honshu. Oppenheimer and several members objected to Kyoto because of its historical value and the thought that a bombing there might solidify Japanese resistance to the prospect of surrender. Secretary of War Stimson also favored sparing Kyoto as a target.

Earlier in May, Stimson had created a new advisory body called the Interim Committee. Its purpose was to advise the secretary on "postwar research, development, and control, and on legislation necessary for these purposes." Stimson would act as chairman, with George L. Harrison, the president of the New York Life Insurance Company, as alternate chairman. Other members included Vannevar Bush; James F. Byrnes, director of War Mobilization; William L. Clayton, assistant secretary of state; Karl T. Compton; James Conant; and Ralph A. Bard, an undersecretary in the Navy Department. Stimson called a meeting of the Interim Committee for May 31 and invited Oppenheimer, Lawrence, and Fermi to attend.

The meeting was important not only for its discussion of whether or not to drop the bomb, but also because of the far-reaching discussions on postwar policy. Stimson saw the meeting as a reinforcement of the idea that "we were looking at this [the use of the bomb] like statesmen and not like merely soldiers anxious to win a war at any cost."[8] The day's agenda would cover the issues of temporary control of the bomb, postwar research, controls, and future nonmilitary uses. Oppenheimer arrived with Lawrence, Bush, Conant, Karl Compton, Arthur Compton, and Enrico Fermi. Oppenheimer led the discussions on weapon development; the availability of the next generation of weapons—smaller, more powerful, with explosive forces between ten and one hundred megatons—was simply a matter of time.[9] In terms of postwar plans it was clear that the Manhattan Project should be maintained; Los Alamos was needed to continue researching larger weapons and to continue amassing a stockpile. When the subject of sharing information with Russia was raised, Oppenheimer reiterated Niels Bohr's belief that Russia must be told about the new bomb, but perhaps without detail. Several people agreed with this opinion until Secretary of State James Byrnes, who joined the meeting late, strenuously objected. Most realized that America's exclusive use of the weapon would give America leverage with the Soviets. This might have an important effect on postwar negotiations.

It was over lunch that the question of actually using the weapon was raised for the first time. One alternative offered, and one which had some support at Los Alamos and at the Met Lab, was that the bomb be used in a nonmilitary demonstration. A Fat Man, for example, could be assembled on an island near Japan and attention drawn to the weapon prior to detonation. Oppenheimer disagreed, arguing that a display could not rival the impact of a city destroyed by a single bomb; moreover, surprise was important. A test explosion would not necessarily convince the Japanese leadership that a single weapon had been used. After all, the Japanese could hardly be invited to inspect the weapon. Finally, it was agreed that the bomb would be used and that it would be used *without* warning.

On June 15, Oppenheimer forwarded several reports representing the views of the scientific panel to George L. Harrison, alternate chairman of the Interim Committee. Led by Oppenheimer, the panel acted as advisor to the Interim Committee. One report projected immediate postwar need for weapons research at twenty million dollars; another report urged greater spending for a broader program of nuclear research and development, expected to cost nearly a billion dollars a year. Oppenheimer also cited the panel's recommendation for use of the bomb on Japanese cities. He made it clear that he was not alone in the recommendation; scientists like Ernest Lawrence, Arthur Compton, and Enrico Fermi also believed that a military use of the weapon was the only practical alternative. The same report stressed that Russia and America's other allies be told first before use of the bomb.

> We said that we didn't think that being scientists especially qualified us as to how to answer this question of how the bombs should be used or not; opinion was divided among us as it would be among other people if they knew about it. We thought the two overriding considerations were the saving of lives in the war and the effect of our actions on the stability, on our strength and the

> stability of the postwar world. We did say that we did not think exploding one of these things [a bomb] as a firecracker over a desert was likely to be very impressive.[10]

Apparently, the Interim Committee agreed; planning continued for the drop on Japan.

On July 24 the target list was narrowed to four cities: Hiroshima, Kokura, Niigata, and Nagasaki. Oppenheimer reported to Groves that a Little Boy would be ready for use soon after August 1 and that a Fat Man would be ready by August 5. He assured Groves that the bombs would be more powerful than the one detonated at Trinity, which produced an explosive force of 17,500 tons of TNT.

At 9:14 A.M. on August 6, the bombardier of the *Enola Gay* released the Little Boy uranium weapon over Hiroshima. A few minutes later there was a brilliant flash, which lit the inside of the strike plane; seconds later the *Enola Gay* was jolted twice by shock waves. The large ball of fire, at first seeming to churn within itself, quickly mutated into swirling purple clouds and boiling flames that surged upward. The mushrooming cloud reached thirty thousand feet in less than three minutes.

Three days later, on August 9, another strike plane, *Bock's Car*, left Tinian's long airstrip. At 11:50 A.M. the second Fat Man fell toward Nagasaki. There was the same bolt of brilliant light, followed a few seconds later by shock waves. Unknown to the United States, two Americans who were prisoners of war in a camp erected near the city only weeks before died in the blaze.

Los Alamos experienced a combination of relief and jubilation. On the day of Hiroshima, Oppenheimer called the laboratory staff together in the auditorium in Delta building. On the podium he clasped his hands together over his head in victory and read from a message flashed by Parson fifteen minutes after the drop:

> Clearcut results exceeding TR test in visible effects, and in all respects successful. Normal conditions continued in aircraft after delivery was accomplished.

Hiroshima was indeed a devastating strike: 60 percent of the city had been flattened; 37,000 persons were missing and 78,000 were dead. Nagasaki suffered less destruction, but more than 100,000 persons had been killed or injured. The city had burned in a raging storm for more than a day. The time for a more somber assessment of Hiroshima and Nagasaki was not yet here. Even Oppenheimer seemed caught up in the apparent success. If his personal feelings were different from his public demeanor, he did not reveal them.

Shortly thereafter, Los Alamos prepared several Fat Men for shipment to Tinian. The recent arrival of quantities of plutonium, however, provided the necessary substance only for a third core. On August 10, Groves wrote General Marshall that the third weapon would be ready to be dropped on a target after August 24. Marshall returned the letter the same day, with a handwritten note penciled on the bottom:

> It is not to be released *over* Japan without express authority from the President.
>
> G.C. Marshall[11]

As it turned out, however, the bomb would not be needed: On August 14 the Japanese surrendered. When word of the surrender reached Los Alamos, all work was abruptly halted for the day. The Tech Area siren sounded, and anyone near a horn blew it. Kistiakowsky set off a round of old explosives in a canyon below the mesa. Scientists hastened from the laboratories into the streets. Word spread quickly in the small community.

Days earlier, shortly after the Hiroshima bombing, Oppenheimer had received a telephone call from Groves in Washington:

Groves: I'm proud of you and all of your people.

Oppenheimer: It went all right?

Groves: Apparently it went with a tremendous bang. . . . Yes, it has been a long road and I think one of the wisest things I ever did was when I selected the director of Los Alamos.

Oppenheimer: Well, I have my doubts, General Groves.[12]

Oppenheimer perhaps sensed a certain fear that others too would soon come to feel: While Hiroshima and Nagasaki were proof that the Los Alamos project had been entirely successful, it also meant that the world would never again be the same. Most importantly, the nature of war was forever altered. A nation now possessed the means of destroying another nation without resort to armies and navies. A single airplane could deliver the deathblow. And international politics had irrevocably changed. For the moment at least, America possessed the supreme power.

At Los Alamos, Oppenheimer called it "winding down." Now that the war had ended, the sense of urgency was gone; there was no need for six- and seven-day work weeks. Suddenly, the men who had created and worked on the bomb had to consider what to do next: Oppenheimer could, of course, return to teaching at Berkeley or even perhaps continue his work in Washington, a position that had been increasing steadily. Senior men like Fermi, Bacher, and others could also return to academic posts at major universities; Parsons had his military career; and others would return to colleges to complete degrees or earn new ones. But many had to face the prospect of returning to civilian life.

As early as the fall of 1944, Oppenheimer was aware of the problems of returning to normal life. He did not think he could maintain employment of the fragile coalition of men much beyond the end of the war; Los Alamos did not necessarily contain the elements for everyday life. On December 7, 1944, he directed the Administrative Board to consider a plan to help the laboratory staff find jobs in the postwar world. He knew that it would not be easy: Most of the staff's work had been top secret, and the elaborate security system would no doubt hamper fair competition for subsequent jobs.

There was, of course, still work to be done at Los Alamos. In a letter to Groves on May 7, 1945—the same day Germany surrendered—Oppenheimer tried to establish what he called "cognizance" of the laboratory's future. He told Groves that Los Alamos would continue its efforts to produce additional Fat Men, as well as to perfect both the plutonium and uranium weapons. Nevertheless, it would be necessary, he argued, to establish contracts with outside firms in order to systematically transfer most of the production tasks to commercial businesses.

Oppenheimer increasingly began to see that a centralized government agency—perhaps some evolved form of the Manhattan Project—would be necessary for the work to continue in the nuclear sciences. In May, at least, it seemed clear to Oppenheimer that continuing the laboratory in its present form would be a mistake. Within months, however, he would alter his view. Oppenheimer also took pains to persuade Groves that some members of the present staff should be persuaded to continue work at Los Alamos. "I think that there will have to be a very great change in the way in which the Laboratory is set up and very probably an actual shift in its physical location." At the time, Oppenheimer believed that most of the staff at Los Alamos considered themselves to be occupied with a job that would last only as long as the war, with no plans beyond that. "I also know," he wrote to Groves, "that the whole organization, temper, and structure of Site Y Laboratories [Los Alamos] is singularly unsuited for peacetime perpetuation." His letter ended with an announcement of his intention to leave Los Alamos:

> In particular, the Director himself would very much like to know when he will be able to escape from these duties for which he is so ill qualified and which he had accepted only in an effort to serve the country during the war.[13]

It was perhaps a self-effacing statement, but in May the pressures at Los Alamos were nearing their peak.

With the end of the war Oppenheimer began to take steps to deal with the sudden relaxation of pressure and with the declining inventory of work. He ordered a halt to all new research efforts until postwar plans for Los Alamos could be cemented. He also ordered that a Los Alamos "encyclopedia" be written as a technical history of the work and a "how-to-do" manual on weapons. Hans Bethe received the thankless task of editing this project. Work on refining Fat Man continued, but at a slower pace.

Kistiakowsky sent a lengthy memo to his staff titled "What to Do Now." He was careful to add that the "what" might well be changed "on instructions from Washington." In August employment opportunities suddenly opened up, leaving Oppenheimer and everyone else surprised and pleased. Job offers poured in; Los Alamos personnel suddenly realized that their last year or two had brought them invaluable experience, unobtainable at any university in the world.

The end of the war also brought a magnification of the hardships of living at Los Alamos. Oppenheimer had managed to persuade most of the residents that the value of the work at Los Alamos far outweighed the disadvantages and hardships. Secrecy, the perpetual shortages of water and many food items, and the poor housing had brought major grievances from the staff throughout the war; now, without the urgency of war, they were barely tolerable. Disenchantment grew daily, and Oppenheimer was hard pressed to keep the laboratory functioning.

Groves had already decided to keep Los Alamos as it was. Bombs would still need refinement and a stockpile would still need to be amassed. Oppenheimer's persistence about resigning presented a problem to Groves, but it also provided him with the opportunity to select a new director, perhaps one, Groves thought, who would be more amenable to a military view. It was clear that selecting Oppenheimer had been a brilliant decision, and with the success of Japan, a proven one. The general's exceptional act of waiving all evidence of Oppenheimer's suspicious political past had paid off. Oppenheimer's departure would free him to lobby in Washington, a setting where his quick mind and articulate tongue would serve him well. Because Los Alamos was still under Manhattan District control, Groves would have the final say over a new director to replace Oppenheimer.

Finding a replacement, however, was more difficult than Groves had expected, and, with the staff dwindling every day, he needed to act quickly. Many of the laboratory's best men were leaving to return to academic posts. Groves solicited recommendations from Oppenheimer, whose disappearing staff left him few choices. High on his list was Norris Bradbury, who had come to Los Alamos as a lieutenant commander in the naval reserves. Bradbury had had an outstanding career at Pomona College, the University of California, the Massachusetts Institute of Technology, and Stanford University. He had come to Los Alamos as a physicist as well as one of the laboratory's few weapons experts. He had played major roles at Trinity and in Project Alberta, and had flown in the observer airplane over Nagasaki. Groves was impressed with his military background, as well as with his credentials in science. Oppenheimer recommended him as a scientist, a natural leader, and someone who could stand up to what were looming as strong pressures from Washington from many corridors of government. Bradbury, however, was startled when Oppenheimer offered him the job.

Oppenheimer was adamant in insisting that Los Alamos must continue under the leadership of *one* director. When Groves suggested to Oppenheimer that perhaps selecting both an interim director and a coordinator might be the best solution, Oppenheimer reacted strongly, placing an urgent telephone call to Groves in Washington. Groves was not available and, shunning diplomacy, Oppenheimer left a terse message with a startled aide. There was only one job, he said firmly, and that was as interim director *and* coordinator, an opinion that was supported by the staff as well. Oppenheimer went on to say that when he and Bradbury came to Washington to meet with Groves, it would be with the assumption that there was but one job, and that if Bradbury were selected, he would be selected "for the one job." With that, Oppenheimer hung up. The aide noted on the call sheet that he had never before heard Oppenheimer "feel so strongly" about any matter.[14] With considerable need to keep as much of the laboratory intact as possible, Groves offered a compromise: Bradbury would serve as interim director for six months. To assure cooperation from remaining staff, Groves announced that he expected Oppenheimer and division leaders to choose a permanent director from their ranks.

Groves visited Los Alamos on a peacemaking mission on September 18. Speaking to Oppenheimer, Bradbury, and division authorities, he reviewed the legislation pending before Congress to place atomic energy within a civilian agency and expressed his own perceptions about the future of Los Alamos. There was no doubt, he said, that the laboratory would remain a vital center for weapons research and for some production of bomb parts. Whatever long-term changes might occur, Los Alamos had a future of three or four years, at least. Groves then announced his acceptance of Oppenheimer's resignation, to become effective October 16, and the interim appointment of Bradbury as director.

On the day of Oppenheimer's resignation, Norris Bradbury made a major policy presentation to the staff of the laboratory. Oppenheimer sat quietly in the room listening to Bradbury, unaware that he would soon become the center of a vicious storm over the development of the superbomb. Already he was a national figure, hailed by the press as a hero. His laboratory, which had worked so hard to hide itself and cloak its work, was now suddenly on the map. His presentations before Congress on the behalf of legislation supporting civilian control had further spotlighted his position as spokesman for nuclear energy. At the moment, however, listening to Bradbury's careful and sometimes light presentation had a salutary effect on the retiring director, as well as on the laboratory's assembled staff.

Festivities were planned for Oppenheimer's departure. Groves arrived with several important officials to present to Los Alamos a certificate of appreciation from the Secretary of War. October 16 found Los Alamos with bright, cool weather. Fuller Lodge was decorated with flags and colorful bunting. From a low platform in front of the lodge, Groves presented the certificate to Oppenheimer and made a brief speech acknowledging the important work that had been completed by the men and women at Los Alamos. The ceremony honored the man as much as his work. Quietly, the directorship shifted to Norris Bradbury. Priscilla Green noticed that Oppenheimer was nervous as he accepted the award and made a brief speech.

Later that evening, at a large party in his honor, Oppenheimer was surrounded by old friends and colleagues. He was given a handcarved chest of wood that staff members had purchased from the La Fonda Hotel in Santa Fe. The party was joyous, at least superficially. Many of those attending felt that the evening was tinged with sadness, an atmosphere fostered subtly by the serious speech Oppenheimer had given earlier that afternoon. The success at Los Alamos, he said, had been both promising and ominous. Accepting the citation from Groves, he spoke in a low, careful voice. He thanked Groves on behalf of the laboratory's men and women, expressing the hope that everyone could look at the scroll in the future with pride. "If atomic bombs are to be added to the arsenals of a warring world, or to the arsenals of nations preparing for war, then the time will come when mankind will curse the names of Los Alamos and Hiroshima." But then, after a pause in which the audience could hear the bunting flapping in the wind, he added a note of hope:

> The peoples of this world must unite, or they will perish. This war, that has ravaged so much of the earth, has written these words. The atomic bomb has spelled them out for all men to understand. Other men have spoken them, in other times, of other wars, or other weapons. They have not prevailed. There are some, misled by a false sense of human history, who hold that they will not prevail today. It is not for us to believe that. By our works we are committed, committed to a world united before this common peril, in law, in humanity.[15]

With the war, Oppenheimer became engaged in a whole new drama. While he was now a hero, soon to develop considerable prestige and influence, he would never again have the control over events that he wielded at Los Alamos. That, too, intensified his somber words.

PART
TWO

8. The Spokesman

Robert Oppenheimer left Los Alamos for a world reeling from the changes created by World War II. The United Nations charter, negotiated in San Francisco earlier in 1945, had taken effect within days of Oppenheimer's parting speech to the Los Alamos staff. The first meeting in London of the Council of Foreign Ministers had failed to produce any agreement on treaties with countries such as Bulgaria, Hungary, and Italy, and ultimately dissolved in disagreement over whether or not China and France would participate. Two months later, in December 1945, the council met again in Moscow and debated, among other topics, the international control of atomic energy.

The notion of control was very much on the minds of Americans. In mid-1946, for example, public opinion polls revealed that half of the population believed that the United States would fight in another war within 10 years. Three-quarters of the public believed that American cities would become victims of atomic attacks with weapons far more powerful than the ones used against Japan. Not surprisingly, the public revealed little confidence in international control and inspection of atomic weapons, and the vast majority of Americans believed that the United States should retain the "secret" of the bomb as long as possible.[1]

The future of atomic energy was, obviously, a highly critical issue. Oppenheimer was no longer the director of Los Alamos, but he was still very much involved with the atomic energy program, and, like most everyone else, was opinionated. Certainly, he must have felt a strong responsibility considering that he was so intricately involved with the project from the start. He argued for a sane policy of civilian control of nuclear energy and for an international body to make the benefits of the new energy available to all nations. He believed strongly in not keeping the bomb a secret and spoke out to warn the public: "You cannot keep the nature of the world a secret; you cannot keep atoms secret." Oppenheimer wanted to reaffirm the value of science to society and the importance of continued involvement by scientists in the concerns of society.

His feelings were not without foundation. As 1945 was drawing to an end, the elaborate Manhattan Project apparatus was still under General Leslie Groves and the United States Army. In Washington, Vannevar Bush and others were pressing for a comprehensive policy of control of both weapons and atomic research. In a departing statement, Secretary of War Henry Stimson expressed the importance of international cooperation; sharing the atomic "partnership," as he called it, was not only inevitable but mandatory. Maintaining exclusive Anglo-American control over the weapon was, he felt, an invitation to a "secret armaments race of a rather desperate character."[2] President Truman was already under pressure to bring the question of control before the United Nations. Within his own borders, however, the President was caught in a fray of political, military, and scientific demands over the future of weapons development and control. Oppenheimer felt strongly that he and his fellow scientists should be involved in the decision making.

Oppenheimer framed some of these ideas on postwar policy in a perceptive speech he delivered on November 2 to some five hundred members of the newly created Association of Los Alamos Scientists. Speaking to a packed audience in the laboratory's largest auditorium, Oppenheimer stressed that Los Alamos meant something "major" to scientists and to science itself. Nuclear discoveries had been made at an incredibly fast rate, and their application to weapons development had been just as quick. Indeed, the discovery and eventual mastery of the atomic bomb had a uniquely profound effect on the world—especially on those responsible for it—not only because it was a scientific breakthrough of the highest sort, but also because of its drastic and far-reaching military implications. At Los Alamos, scientists had taken their new knowledge and with it had conceived, designed, and constructed the weapons with their own hands—but they had created more than just a scientific wonder. The sheer success of the weapons in Japan brought the world new knowledge "with such shattering reality and suddenness that there was no opportunity for the edges to be worn off." Why had men done this?

> But when you come right down to it the reason that we did this job is because it was an organic necessity. If you are a scientist you cannot stop such a thing. If you are a scientist you believe that it is good to find out how the world works; that it is good to turn over to mankind at large the greatest possible power to control the world and to deal with it according to its lights and its values.[3]

Secrecy, Oppenheimer offered, ran contrary to what science was all about. Scientists must always be prepared to share their knowledge and to risk the consequences. As scientists, they were better prepared to accept change, even radical change. In a sense, this acceptance of change, and particularly of a change of spirit, was at the heart of any notion of international agreement. People simply had to remember their common bond with human beings everywhere else. "I think it is true to say that atomic weapons are a peril which affect everyone in the world, and in that sense a completely common problem."

Oppenheimer, now playing the dual role of scientist-statesman, proposed four points he felt were an essential part of any international arrangement. First, any proposals ought to be regarded as an interim solution. Second, participating nations needed a "joint atomic energy commission," operating under broad directives from the individual states, but with a collective power to pursue research and development. Third, there should be concrete machinery for forcing an exchange between scientists and students—a mechanism, as Oppenheimer said, to strengthen the "fraternity of scientists." And fourth, no more bombs should be made. These, in simple terms, naive or not, were the basics of Oppenheimer's philosophy. There was no doubt, he said, that following the bombing of Japan, a good measure of momentum had been lost when the United States failed to issue a clear statement of policy. This was an argument he would turn to again in the new few years.

Closing his speech, Oppenheimer reminded his audience that not all scientists were in agreement over these matters. In a comment that would take on great significance for him personally, he said: "Such disagreement is healthy. But we must not lose the sense of fraternity because of it; we must not lose our fundamental confidence in our fellow scientists."

A few days later, with Kitty, Peter, and Toni in tow, Oppenheimer left the plateau and returned to the house on Eagle Hill outside Pasadena.

What would he do next? The most obvious alternative was to return to teaching, and he initiated a few tentative inquiries in late August. For the first time in four years, Robert and Kitty took a vacation. The last four years had taken their toll on Oppenheimer: his weight had fallen to 110 pounds and his hair had begun to turn gray. He was 41 years old. He and Kitty left Peter and Toni with friends in Los Alamos and drove to their mountain cabin at Cowles for a few days of well-deserved isolation. He took with him a great pile of personal correspondence that had accumulated at Los Alamos. There were many letters of congratulations from family, friends, and old colleagues. He took pleasure in responding to these personal letters. He also wrote a long letter to Charles Lauritsen at the California Institute of Technology, seeking some clarification of his status there. Would he be welcome back? And if so, at what salary? As well, he wanted to know what the conditions of support would be for graduate students and research? He received a tentative offer from Cal Tech on August 31, but they delayed a decision for nearly six weeks. Interestingly, Robert Millikan, president of Cal Tech for twenty-four years, had needed persuasion: In a letter to Richard Tolman, Millikan questioned whether or not they should offer Oppenheimer the job because he was concerned that Oppenheimer was a bad teacher and that perhaps Cal Tech already had "enough Jews" on its faculty. Anyway, Millikan argued, two younger men could be had for the price of Oppenheimer.[4]

When their firm offer did arrive, Oppenheimer felt a need to seek reassurance from others. In a letter to Robert Sproul, president of the University of California, he requested a "frank expression of your views [regarding his return to Cal Tech]." In the meantime, he turned down another lucrative offer from Harvard University. To James Conant, he professed that Harvard's offer "was one of the hardest things to say no to."[5] Oppenheimer formally accepted Cal Tech's offer on October 16, and in November moved back to California. In August 1946 he resumed his professorship at the University of California at Berkeley. Oppenheimer's hesitation seemed, in part, to be a reflection of his suspicion that his welcome was in question. In discussions with Ernest Lawrence, the two had exchanged somber words, especially relating to the relationship between Los Alamos and the University of California. Oppenheimer certainly had long been aware of Millikan's feelings. In part, too, he was concerned with Cal Tech's opinion toward his emerging role as advisor to what he was calling "policymakers" in Washington. In his letter to Lauritsen he directly asked if Cal Tech would welcome and support his "advisory participation in future atomic national policy?"[6] Already he was spending more time in Washington than in either Los Alamos or Pasadena.

Finally, in April 1947, Oppenheimer received word from Princeton University's Institute for Advanced Study that they were interested in the possibility of his assuming directorship of the institute. Oppenheimer weighed the advantages: a major post, one with proximity to Washington and New York, as well as ample room for his involvement in national affairs. He accepted in the early spring; Raymond Birge announced Oppenheimer's resignation from Cal Tech a month later. It was, he said, "the greatest blow ever suffered by the Department."[7]

Oppenheimer's name had been pushed enthusiastically for directorship by Admiral Lewis L. Strauss, a member of the board of trustees. Strauss, who first met Oppenheimer in Washington, had been very impressed with the scientist's mind and his thinking. During a special meeting to consider applicants, Strauss dominated the conversations with complimentary comments about Oppenheimer. With the board's approval, Strauss personally offered the position to Oppenheimer while he was visiting California.[8]

The family moved in October. They took possession of the director's residence, Olden Manor, on the edge of the beautifully landscaped grounds of the institute. For the moment, it seemed as if Oppenheimer had returned to the quiet life of the academician.

Oppenheimer and his family spent New Year's Day of 1946 in California with his brother, Frank, and his family. It was the first time in several years that the two families had been able to spend time together.

Robert and his family stayed in a large building next to Frank's house, which Robert called the "barn." It was an innocent family holiday, typical for millions of Americans, but it was later construed as evidence of Oppenheimer's alleged Communist activities. In fact, he was eventually charged with spending the afternoon at Frank's house with two other members of the American Communist party.

A few months later, in San Francisco, Robert and Kitty spent an evening with Haakron Chevalier and his wife at Stimson Beach. It was the first time Oppenheimer had seen his old friend since before he had become the director of Los Alamos. Chevalier had never received the necessary clearance during the war to work with the Office of War Information. He until recently had served as a translator at the Nuremburg war trials and was just back from Germany. The two couples had dinner and shared experiences.

Several weeks following this meeting, Chevalier was visited by two men from the Federal Bureau of Investigation. After much prodding and several specific questions about George Eltenton, Chevalier related the so-called kitchen incident to the FBI.

At a party at the Oppenheimers' Eagle Hill house a few weeks later, Chevalier related his incident with the FBI to Oppenheimer and revealed that he had confessed to the Eltenton approach. Oppenheimer appeared tense and anxious, but reassured Chevalier that he had done the right thing and revealed that he also had told the story to army security men. Oppenheimer was so tense, in fact, that he barked at Kitty when she interrupted him to say that other guests were arriving.[9]

Oppenheimer received his questioning by the FBI on September 3. During the interrogation he admitted that in his earlier interviews with Boris Pash and John Landsdale he had not been entirely truthful: Chevalier, he confessed, had approached only Oppenheimer, not three men, as he had previously claimed. He did not answer questions about his attendance at parties after the war where Communists were alleged to have gathered. When asked about Joseph Weinberg, Oppenheimer acted surprised that Weinberg was suspected of having had Communist affiliations. This was later charged as being a deliberate falsification on Oppenheimer's part.

It was becoming increasing clear to Oppenheimer that he was being watched. His phones were tapped and his movements were under surveillance. Later he told a friend that the government spent more money tapping his phone than they ever paid him at Los Alamos.[10]

Oppenheimer's departure from Los Alamos occurred at a time in which the United States was grappling with the implications of the new weapon and trying to create a posture for international agreement. Neither question had an easy solution for scientists or statesmen.

Public reaction was inevitably a mixture of awe and concern. The atomic bomb had played a part in ending the war; for this, the public was thankful and even made heroes of Oppenheimer and the others involved. There were others in the government and the news media who forewarned of the dangers of nuclear annihilation. An even greater division of opinion existed within the scientific community.

For almost a year, scientists at the University of Chicago's Metallurgical Laboratory had discussed the postwar implications of the new weapons. In July, Leo Szilard—who five years earlier had used his influence to persuade Einstein to write to Roosevelt—circulated a petition among Met Lab employees urging that the United States *not* use the weapon for future military bombing. The petition, eventually gathering sixty-nine signatures, was sent to Arthur Compton in Washington, who in turn shared it with Groves. The general viewed the petition as useless, if not damaging, but nevertheless sent it along to Secretary Stimson. Groves also sent the results of a poll taken among Met Lab employees in which over 60 percent favored military use of the atomic bomb.

After Hiroshima and Nagasaki, of course, these discussions were moot. On August 12, President Truman approved the release of a lengthy report, prepared by Henry D. Smyth, on the development of the atomic bomb. It was ponderously titled *General Account of the Development of Methods of Using Atomic Energy for Military Purposes*. In his preface Smyth argued that the full technical and scientific secrets would of necessity remain secret, but the political and social implications of the technology were open for all men to discuss.

Discussions about future use of the bomb eventually turned into arguments for its control. The Interim Committee within OSRD, appointed by Secretary of War Stimson, had already prepared a draft of tentative legislation for a "commission on atomic energy." This early legislation proposed a twelve-man commission nominated by the president with representation by scientists, civilians, and the military. Such a commission would have substantial power to control production of nuclear materials, the transfer of these materials to other agencies or governments, and the responsibility to conduct experiments to explore the new energy force. Whatever its range of powers or the shape of its organization, one vital element would be the commission's relationship with the United Nations. Some scientists argued that the control of atomic weapons should be placed in the hands of an international body. A letter from Oppenheimer to Secretary Stimson on August 1, 1945, proposed just this. Stimson, however, like George Harrison and others, felt that any sort of fair discussion of international control was months away, at least until after the Potsdam Conference. Of more immediate concern was a national agency that could assume the responsibilities of the Manhattan Project. Shown a copy of Oppenheimer's letter, Secretary of State designate James

Byrnes* reacted by instructing Harrison to tell Oppenheimer personally that "for the time being his proposal about an international agreement was not practical and that he and the rest of the gang should pursue their work full force." This included, as far as Byrnes was concerned, work on the superbomb.[11]

Another version of an atomic energy commission bill prepared by the War Department lawyers was even more sweeping than that of the Interim Committee. For example, virtually no work on atomic matters would be allowed to occur outside of the commission without permission, and all employees would be exempt from Civil Service regulations. Both Bush and Conant felt the proposed plan was too comprehensive and too restrictive. Vannevar Bush was now the director of the Office of Scientific Development and Research and, during the war, had been the chairman of the Military Policy Committee, which had overseen all of the Manhattan Project effort. No one possessed as broad a view as Bush on atomic energy matters. To him, the most dangerous element of the War Department plan was the possibility that such a commission could ultimately find itself with contradicting responsibilities: control and regulation on the one hand, and conducting research and development on the other. A redraft of the bill eliminated some of his objections, but the cautious Bush still found the proposed bill too broad in its powers.

Reporting to the nation on his trip and negotiations at Potsdam, Truman again stated that the recipe for the atomic bomb would remain secret, but that a commission would be created within the federal government to control atomic energy. Truman made clear that resolving domestic issues was the first priority, and only after that would international control be approached. There was, of course, more at stake than just the secret of the bomb. In 1945, at Manhattan laboratories across the nation, directors like Norris Bradbury were having a hard time keeping their staff; few wanted any part of the hastily assembled wartime laboratories which now were floundering in uncertainty. From Washington, Groves expressed his opinion that the government had to act soon to establish a permanent body for nuclear work. Nonetheless, pressure continued from every side to establish an international agreement; there was too much to lose, it was argued, unless all nations subscribed to the same principles.

On the afternoon of September 25, Oppenheimer and Harrison met with Acting Secretary of State Dean Acheson in the State Department building. They touched on the delicate question of whether or not to negotiate with the Russians over control of atomic bombs. Acheson, utilizing his own resources, had prepared a statement for Truman's use which urged making an overture to the Soviet government, however slim the chances were of success. In part, it echoed Stimson's thinking and

---

*Byrnes would follow Henry Stimson as secretary of state in September 1943.

preliminary plans; Harrison, in fact, thought the statement was practically a paraphrase of Stimson's draft. Acheson also expressed grave concern over the future of atomic-bomb development; he almost ended the meeting. It was clear, he said, that weapons could be improved or developed that could destroy the world by igniting the atmosphere. Oppenheimer hastened to calm Acheson; it was not likely that such weapons could be developed.

Acheson appeared mollified, if only superficially, and permitted the discussions to continue. One concern was the manner in which the United States government would approach the Russians. Could, for example, the U.S. give the Soviets all scientific data relating to nuclear fission minus the technical plans on bomb assembly, implosion, and the like? Oppenheimer thought this was a possibility, but added that sooner or later the Russians would have this information as a result of their own research.[12] He added that with Russia just recovering from a devastating war, it was unlikely that the Soviets could make a weapon in the near future.

But Oppenheimer knew, as did many of his colleagues, that the scientific discoveries at Los Alamos and Oak Ridge were the result of imaginative but straightforward scientific inquiry. The ingenious manufacture of weapons—the notion of implosion, for example—would occur to any body of scientists in any country with a certain level of scientific and technological sophistication.* Reports by Samuel Goudsmit from occupied Germany revealed that scientists there understood the general principles of fission. American scientists realized that it was probably only a matter of time before the Soviets would have this same information.

The estimates of when Russia would have an atomic bomb varied from three to twenty years. Unfortunately, as Oppenheimer perceived it, much of the discussion and planning for the control of atomic bombs was based on the assumption that the United States would have a long-term monopoly on what the press insisted on calling the "secret" of the atomic bomb. Oppenheimer pointed out again and again that the failure to establish a national commission for nuclear energy only supported the false impression that weapons technology could be withheld from other countries for years. The heavy security that pervaded the Met Lab and Los Alamos was under attack by scientists themselves, an attitude that indirectly added to the opinion that the United States should use its new knowledge to barter a favorable relationship with Russia.

Oppenheimer brought his ideas together in a report he prepared for the Interim Committee. One motivating force for the scientists who

---

*The careful reports made to the Soviets by Klaus Fuchs were not yet known.

developed atomic weapons during the war, he wrote, was the hope that the new weapons would help avoid war. He agreed with Dwight Eisenhower, who had recently said that the new weapons might "blackmail mankind into peace." With regard to secrecy, Oppenheimer believed that scientists were not convinced "that keeping secret the scientific elements or technical details of our present knowledge ... will assure us of technical leadership, or make it impossible for other powers to carry through a terrifying development of atomic weapons." There was no real protection against such weapons except through international control. The United States must act quickly to create such control; the present time was, in Oppenheimer's words, "uniquely favorable" to such an effort. Oppenheimer believed that other nations might initially exaggerate their difficulties in obtaining atomic weapons. He then struck at the heart of the arguments for international control:

> If time is allowed to elapse before suitable steps are taken with a view to establishing world-wide control, some of the other powers may have developed methods and installations that will give them a vested interest in maintaining their national autonomy in this field. For this reason alone we are not confident that any future time, however favorable to the political developments in the world, would be more suitable than the present.[13]

America's leadership was certainly divided on the idea of international cooperation. As Russia would obviously want a bomb of their own, Stimson favored enjoining them to become "full partners" in the peaceful development of atomic energy. Stimson felt that the Soviets could quite possibly be persuaded to forego weapons development and instead participate in the exploration of atomic energy as a peaceful tool. In order to do this, it would be necessary for the United States and Great Britain to act quickly. It would be possible, he believed, to impound the American arsenal of weapons if Britain and Russia would agree not to use the bomb for warring purposes. Others did not agree. Secretary of State Byrnes was adamantly opposed to the idea of cooperation with the Russians; the political gyrations at Potsdam had convinced him that Russia was not to be trusted. James Forrestal, secretary of the Navy, thought that the government should not give away secrets, which he believed belonged to the American people, without first getting some sense of how the public felt. Secretary of Commerce Henry Wallace favored a policy of sharing information with America's allies. Truman favored some sort of attempt to wrest an agreement from the Soviets. Aside from that, it was clear to the President that a policy for control of atomic energy was urgently needed—first at home, and then internationally.

The disagreement in Washington over the future of atomic weapons and control was paralleled among scientists. The end of the war and the sudden public announcement of the existence of the bomb did not provide the scientists with time to sort out their feelings on both their wartime contributions and their perceptions of what ought to follow. In September 1945, Oppenheimer told Acheson and Harrison that many of his colleagues strongly opposed doing any further work on atomic bombs or on the superbomb envisioned by Teller. He shared with them his earlier letter to Stimson, which described his colleagues' hope for cessation of further weapons work. Oppenheimer believed that the restlessness among the Los Alamos staff was due less to a lack of national legislation than to a fear that they would be asked to continue perfecting a weapon that was against their principles. This was particularly true of the superbomb. It was never clear how many scientists Oppenheimer spoke for, but he urged that a commission for atomic energy, along with a statement of national purpose, would certainly help others to make up their minds.

The argument offered by Oppenheimer perhaps appeared contradictory to some: scientists had willingly made the atom bomb during the war but now wanted no part of it. Groves, for example, found the stance hypocritical. For most, however, the bomb had been a necessity of war, especially in light of the possibility that the Germans would have developed a weapon first. What mattered now was the promise of atomic discovery. Oppenheimer accepted both points and argued further for atomic energy to be placed into the hands of all nations. But unlike many scientists, Oppenheimer seemed more aware of the dual qualities of atomic energy; while it offered considerable future promise, it also existed at the moment as a powerful weapon. Moreover, it was as much a political weapon as a military one. Of immediate concern to Oppenheimer was the realization that those responsible for policy in America were rapidly taking control of the weapon. Scientists were no longer in control, and that fact troubled Oppenheimer more than most. In a world recovering from global war, it was an alienation that he thought a sane man could not accept.

In a letter to General Groves, Los Alamos scientist John Manley expressed his concern that policy decisions on atomic matters were being made without the involvement of scientists. Manley reflected the feelings of many Los Alamos scientists when he implied that separating policymakers from the men who had done most of the work was itself the worst kind of policy. Manley's letter echoed the Met Lab petition that had been submitted to Bush and Groves. On September 1 seventeen scientists, including Fermi and Sam Allison from the Met Lab, met in Chicago to press the government for more freedom in research. Atomic scientists did not want to be restricted to studies of weapons, but wanted the freedom to explore the full range of possibilities of the atom. For most scientists, nuclear physics was on the threshold of even greater discoveries with immense promise for mankind. In a now-famous comment, Allison warned that unless security provisions were eased, scientists would be reduced to studying butterfly wings. Groves immediately sent his aide, Colonel Nichols, to Chicago to forestall further "butterfly" comments.

Scientists were not persuaded that early talk in Congress over legislation to establish an atomic energy commission suggested any more than a new "unsecret" Manhattan Project—hardly the free, unhampered atomosphere for research sought by scientists. As a result, the scientists at the Met Lab organized themselves into the Atomic Scientists of Chicago; those at Los Alamos organized a similar group.

To all of this, Oppenheimer seemed to be of two minds. Clearly he felt that the scientists should be involved in making policy decisions or that they should at least have a voice. On several important occasions he expressed his feelings, and the representations of others, on behalf of international control and sharing information between scientists. A statement endorsing the exchange of information with the Soviets was sent to leaders in Washington with a cover letter written by Oppenheimer. Despite his involvement, he seemed to take a backseat in the scientists' movement to organize. While he certainly did not reject the idea of organization, he turned down offers to become involved in their creation or to act as their chairman or spokesman.

He did not choose to explain his position. Instead, he took a complicated path in which he supported scientists, but also kept active behind the scenes, maintaining his access to government leaders. It was an example of his extraordinary ability to work with several different, and often opposing, groups. Through the arguments he saw a common goal: to control and to explore the new energy. As an emerging statesman, he saw the necessity for formulating policy amidst conflicting forces; as a scientist, he agreed with the need for freedom and for the pursuit of pure science. For the moment, however, his talents were more urgently needed in Washington.

On the morning of September 25, Oppenheimer met with Harrison and Robert Patterson, the new secretary of war.* They discussed the elements of former Secretary Stimson's plan and helped redraft recommendations to be made to Truman. Patterson expressed his own wish that action be taken immediately to introduce legislation in Congress.

At the same time Acheson asked Herbert S. Marks, a young lawyer, to draft a presidential message to Congress which would contain elements of a plan for both national and international control of atomic energy. In the message, Marks generally drew on the concept of a commission appointed by the President which would control all domestic activity in

*Stimson had retired on September 21, 1945, at the age of seventy-eight.

atomic matters. Kenneth Royall and William L. Marbury, of the War Department staff, had proposed the same type of commission. Marks's draft contained few details over which disagreement could occur. Proposing the concept of international control, Marks spoke of atomic energy as a "revolutionary" new force, which meant that nations could no longer "rely on the slow progress of time to develop a program of mutual control among nations."[14] There had to be an international agreement or the bomb had to be rejected; to fail to act would mean a weapons race of monstrous proportions.

On October 4, Truman formally submitted a message to Congress and placed himself on record as a supporter of a combined program of national control and international cooperation. The concerns over philosophy now shifted to practical concerns over passage in Congress.

Truman's recommendations became known as the May-Johnson Bill, after Congressman Andrew Jackson May of Kentucky and Senator Edwin Johnson of Colorado, who respectively introduced the measure in the House and Senate. Almost immediately, discussions of the bill in the Senate became entangled in a contest of power between Senators Edwin Johnson and Arthur H. Vandenberg of Michigan. Under the leadership of May, the hearings in the House began promptly on October 9. General Groves testified first, followed by Patterson, Bush, and Conant.[15]

The Congressman, the White House, and the War Department were shocked at the sudden outcry. The Chicago *Sun* ran a story claiming that the government was trying to push legislation through without soliciting advice from scientists. Groups of scientists at Oak Ridge and the Met Lab issued statements warning against hasty legislative action, and many of them expressed disappointment with elder statesmen of atomic energy such as Oppenheimer and Bush for not supporting a more pro-scientist position. Alarmed, Patterson called Harrison. Harrison, who had already talked with Conant, suggested an immediate meeting of the Scientific Panel in Washington. Patterson asked Harrison to telephone Oppenheimer to discuss strategies for presenting alternative views from the scientific community before Congress.

Their long-distance conversation captured the essence of the opposing views within the community. Oppenheimer agreed with Harrison that a meeting of the panel would be helpful, as would—as Harrison had suggested—a follow-up visit to Oak Ridge to meet with the dissenting scientists. Oppenheimer revealed that he had known as early as the week before that there would be an outburst, and that he had already reported this to General Groves. As well, Oppenheimer reported that he had spoken with Leo Szilard—the leader, as he saw it, of the protesting scientists. Szilard's view, as Oppenheimer perceived it, was that it was his duty to press Congress to keep the possibilities open for international agreement.

After hearing Truman's message to Congress, Szilard altered the direction of his arguments to oppose the extraordinary power proposed for the new commission. To Harrison, Oppenheimer confided that he thought Szilard's views were "trivial."[16]

Harrison felt that a telegram from the Scientific Panel would be helpful, considering that all of its members were respected leaders. Oppenheimer agreed to call each person to ask permission to add their names to a telegram supporting quick passage of the bill. Oppenheimer did not know Fermi's views, but agreed that a telegram would be sent with the names of all concurring members. As it turned out, only Compton refused to sign, though not necessarily out of disagreement, but rather because he was unsure of the need for such haste. At the end of the day Oppenheimer sent a telegram to Harrison on behalf of most of the members of the panel. Signed by Oppenheimer, Fermi, and Lawrence, the telegram urged "the prompt passage of the legislation now before Congress." With wisdom, they suggested,

> ... Operations can be carried on within the framework of the proposed legislation safely, effectively, and in the best interests of this Nation. We believe that the broad powers granted the Commission by the legislation are justified by the importance and the perils of the subject. We think it is necessary for the American people to understand in full the implications of the new technical situation.... We assure you that in our opinion the legislation as presented represents the fruits of well-informed and experienced consideration.[17]

The panel met again in Washington on October 17. All the members had read the bill during the intervening period. The implications of the legislation now seemed clearer and, frankly, to some, less encouraging. There were reservations over the control of scientific and technical information. Oppenheimer and Fermi met later in the afternoon with Harrison, Groves, General Royall, Lieutenant Arneson, and Secretary Patterson to discuss ways to lessen the growing dissatisfaction in scientific quarters; perhaps some changes in the proposed legislation would help? Oppenheimer offered to talk with Szilard, Herbert Anderson, and Harold Urey, who had served on the S-1 Committee, before they testified in Congress in the next few days. It was clear to Patterson that delays in passing the bill would almost certainly mean tighter restrictions later on for scientists. Congress clearly favored heavy government controls on atomic research as well as on the preservation of secrets. Fermi's objections to the specter of destructive government control of private research was answered by a proposed amendment. It was Oppenheimer's job to persuade Szilard and the others; if a united front could not be achieved, Oppenheimer needed to be prepared to testify personally on behalf of the legislation.[18]

Szilard was the first to testify when the May-Johnson hearings reopened on October 18. The committee members seemed to play with Szilard, questioning him unnecessarily on the scientist's long-standing dispute with the U.S. Patent Office. Oppenheimer testified late in the afternoon. In his first appearance before Congress, he portrayed himself well as an articulate and self-confident man, a posture that would add to his public personality. He spoke strongly in defense of the bill, an act that would bring criticism from some of his colleagues. Asked by committee chairman May about his qualifications, Oppenheimer replied sheepishly, "I have practically no qualifications, Mr. Chairman." To polite laughter, he added, "In 1941 I became interested in the possibility of making atomic weapons, and since the inception of the laboratory at Los Alamos, I have been its director. So I know a little bit about the making of bombs."[19]

There were two reasons for swift passage of the bill, he argued. First, there were many things scientists wanted to do with atomic energy, both in the military and scientific realms, which could not be done as long as the new energy source was "tied up under absolute secrecy at Los Alamos." The second reason, one which Oppenheimer offered on behalf of all scientists, was that "the greatest possible future safety of this nation against atomic weapons will rest in international control of atomic weapons." Those with the responsibility to negotiate this agreement would prefer to do so with a satisfactory national organization for atomic energy. While Oppenheimer himself did not help to draft the bill, it did have the supervision of both Conant and Bush. "I think," he said, "if they liked the philosophy of this bill and urged this bill, it is a very strong argument. I know that many scientists do not agree with me on this, but I am nevertheless convinced myself." While the bill lacked some specificity which Oppenheimer thought necessary, that could come later; the very subject of atomic energy was, after all, quite new.

Representative Chet Hollifield of California, a member of the committee, pressed Oppenheimer on civilian versus military control.

Hollifield: Don't you feel that if research and development were to be completely in the control of the military, it might be done along military lines rather than along civilian lines?

Oppenheimer: It might, it would certainly be so—

Hollifield: Naturally, would it not?

Oppenheimer: No. I was going to say that if the administrators were chosen as representatives of the services to carry out work of consequence to the services, then it might be so.

Hollifield agreed that the military should have control of military applications; he was still hesitant, however, to have "all control over development and research and channel it into the hands of the military."

Oppenheimer: That may be. You see, this legislation is legislation to get control of the project out of the War Department, not to put it into the War Department.

Hollifield: I am not so sure of that.

Oppenheimer: That is what my friends of the War Department, for whom I have labored, tell me.

May: The War Department discovered the weapon. Why can they not keep the secret?

The hearings ended that day with this pledge of faith in the military. He left the hearings pleased with his performance; his appearance, he believed, had made a strong impression on the members of the committee.

Unfortunately, his testimony failed to generate the sense of support desired by the bill's drafters. If anything, the rough handling of Szilard only served to strengthen opposition by scientists who already believed the government was attempting to shove the new commission down their throats. Oppenheimer had not succeeded in lessening discontent.

In the Senate, members overcame Vandenberg's parliamentary maneuvers to foil creation of a special committee to study atomic energy legislation. Suggested by Senator Brien McMahon, a freshman senator from Connecticut, the committee was finally approved by the Senate on October 23. Two days later McMahon was named chairman; ten other senators were appointed. James R. Newman, formerly with the Office of War Mobilization, was asked to serve as a staff member to educate the committee members on atomic energy. At the same time, in the White House, Truman was receiving reports of strong objections to the May-Johnson Bill from within his administration. One report noted that the proposed legislation overemphasized military developments, while another report stressed that there would be a lack of "executive control" over the commission once it was established. With this information, Truman withdrew his support from the bill, although he offered no alternative measure. The May-Johnson Bill was not going to survive.

At the same time, the various independent associations of scientists from laboratories at Chicago, Los Alamos, and Oak Ridge began to see the need for some form of organizational consolidation for coalescing political influence as well as maximizing their limited finances. Interestingly, much of the movement to consolidate, as well as to speak out before Washington's policymakers, came from young men with little experience in lobbying. John Simpson and William Higinbothan, from the University of Chicago and from Los Alamos, respectively, were examples of this new breed of scientist-politician. From a preliminary meeting of representatives from Chicago, Columbia, Oak Ridge, and Los Alamos stemmed the Independent Citizens Committee of the Arts, Sciences, and

Professions. Their charter inevitably was to warn the world of the dangers of nuclear weapons and to encourage an international understanding and cooperation in which the new energy could be exploited to benefit mankind. On November 16 the growing organization formally split into two permanent organizations: the Federation of Atomic Scientists (FAS), composed of scientists, and the National Committee on Atomic Information, which represented nonscientific organizations such as the League of Women Voters, the National Education Association, and the National Farmers' Union.

As the weeks went by without passage of legislation, new battles began to emerge to complicate the possibilities for settlement. Groves and McMahon differed strongly over the matter of access to classified information, which Groves refused to release. Truman was persuaded to accept a change in the membership composition of the proposed commission: Where previously there would have been nine commission members, with representation by the military, now there would be an entirely civilian body. Oppenheimer, Bush, and others were drawn into the battle in the hope of winning support for the administration's views. The possibilities for legislative action now seemed more remote than ever.

Oppenheimer was caught in the middle. He had been persuaded to support—with enthusiasm, some critics charged—the May-Johnson Bill, along with its commission structure, its restrictions on research, and its heavy penalties for the release of classified data. Along with the wartime scientific leadership with which he had become identified—Bush, Compton, Lawrence—Oppenheimer was in a vulnerable position as support for the May-Johnson Bill dropped with each day. He was clearly aware of the mounting opposition to government overcontrol. He was in close contact with every major figure in FAS, for example, but his vaunted position in Washington left him less maneuvering room than he would have liked.

A break in the stalemate occurred in mid-December when Senator McMahon introduced his new legislative proposal as Senate Bill 1717. From scientists, the reaction was favorable: There was a strong emphasis on international control; research could occur within the commission or in private hands; there appeared to be a minimum of restrictions on information, and patents control was acceptable. There were to be five full-time commissioners appointed by the President. Hearings were scheduled to start on January 22, 1946.

The political atmosphere for the debate was tense. The War Department had failed to muster the strength in Congress to pass May-Johnson; there was a growing distrust of big-name scientists such as Oppenheimer and Bush, who were believed by some to have sold out to the military. Truman had moved away from his concentrated concern for national legislation and was now preoccupied with achieving an international agreement. The newly formed FAS group had demonstrated unusual sophistication in pressuring Congress, especially for such a young organization. General Groves, still titular leader of the Manhattan enterprise, was increasingly seen as the symbol of military domination of atomic energy. The battle was now becoming one of civilian versus military control. In Congress there were those who felt that the control of atomic energy should be in civilian hands, but with military representation on the commission. And while Truman appeared to support the new bill, there had been no affirmative word from the administration until February 1, when Truman released to the press a letter to McMahon which complimented the senator on the impartiality of his hearings and stressed the urgency for civilian control. McMahon had the support of the President, but hardly the support of his committee. The conservative background of most of its members prevented an out-and-out acceptance of a commission that totally excluded the military and perhaps seemed to stray from focusing on defense needs. The arrest of twenty-two persons in Ottawa by the Canadian government for disclosing secret atomic energy information hardly helped the debate in Congress. Senator Vandenberg finally suggested a compromise: to have the newly renamed Military Advisory Committee members be appointed by the secretaries of the military services.

In early April, with the bill to establish a new atomic energy commission apparently well on its way to passage, Oppenheimer made another appearance before the Special Senate Committee on Atomic Energy. David Lilienthal, the chairman of the Tennessee Valley Authority (TVA), who was invited as well, noted that Oppenheimer had adapted his philosophy to the new legislation and had spoken out with clarity.[20] On June 1 the bill was passed unanimously in the Senate.

Sent to the House, the bill was delayed in a bitter effort by some legislators to tack on amendment after amendment. Information released by the House Un-American Activities Committee suggested certain members of the Manhattan laboratories were advocates of "world government." Supporters of the bill had barely recovered from defending it against these assaults when the patent provisions came under attack, with some Congressmen charging that they subverted America's free-enterprise system. Finally, on July 20 the bill was approved by a vote of 265–79. On August 1, 1946, Harry Truman signed the Atomic Energy Act.

Oppenheimer now faced the question of what role he would be permitted to play in the nation's infant atomic program.

9. A Matter for the World

Oppenheimer and his colleagues were satisfied that legislation had been passed to control domestic atomic energy, but they were concerned that so little progress had been made in the effort to obtain international control.

Oppenheimer forcefully declared his vision for international control at the May 1945 meeting of the Interim Committee. As a consultant to the committee, he was in a good position to keep abreast of progress through his conversations with Bush and Compton. There was pressure on the administration to make atomic energy a world endeavor, not only from men like Oppenheimer, but from other governments around the world as well.

Truman's political maneuvering in the last months of 1945 had done little to reassure America's allies that the United States was firmly behind the efforts to establish international agreement. The solidification of even a national policy of atomic energy had been prevented because of delays within the administration.

The new Prime Minister of Great Britain, Clement Attlee, was due for a high-level conference in Washington with Truman and the Canadian Prime Minister Mackenzie King on November 11, 1945. King believed Canada should participate in the talks; after all, he argued, Canada was a wartime partner in the development of the atomic bomb and one of three nations to possess the secret of the weapon. Oppenheimer was adamant that the United States quickly needed to clarify its position on international agreement. The Quebec Agreement of 1943 had outlived its usefulness and needed to be replaced by a newer statement of agreement between the wartime allies. In fact,there was a great deal of confusion and controversy over which role the United States should play in its relationship with Great Britain. Certainly it was difficult to explain to Congress—or to anyone else, for that matter—the complex relationship created by Roosevelt and Churchill earlier in the war. But more importantly, the Soviet Union had to be brought into the negotiations for international control. Oppenheimer believed that one first step was to use the United Nations as a forum for the creation of an international agency that would disseminate information on energy. Scientists would be encouraged to share the results of their work. Secondly, assuming that an international body in charge of inspecting national nuclear projects was created, information could be made available on atomic energy. And last, if all went well, fissionable material would be made available to nations for use in reactors for the production of power. On November 20, 1945, Truman announced that the United States would request the creation of a special international agency for atomic energy at the first meeting of the United Nations early in 1946 in London.

On December 1, Secretary of State James F. Byrnes organized a working group within the State Department to begin policy planning for the international agreement the United States would offer at the U.N. The group included Carroll Wilson, who had been Vannevar Bush's assistant at OSRD; Herbert Marks; and Joseph E. Johnson, chief of the State Department's Division of International Security Affairs. For scientific assistance Byrnes invited Oppenheimer and Henry Smyth to join. Undersecretary of State Dean Acheson was given responsibility for the overall development of the plan.

Acheson formalized the outside technological and scientific support with a panel coined the Board of Consultants. Acheson invited five men to join: David E. Lilienthal, director of the Tennessee Valley Authority, as the panel's chairman; Charles Thomas, vice-president of Monsanto Chemical Company; Harry Winne, a vice-president of General Electric and someone with considerable familiarity with the Oak Ridge gaseous-diffusion plants; Chester Barnard, president of New Jersey Bell Telephone Company; and Robert Oppenheimer.[1] The board was charged with creating a system for control which would alert authorities to activities by any nation that suggested the development of atomic weapons. There were many questions to be answered. First, of course: How could such a system work? What were the effects of secrecy? How soon would other nations in the world community have a bomb or bomb potential?

Lilienthal met Oppenheimer for the first time on January 22 at the Shoreham Hotel in Washington, the day before the board's first meeting. They met in Oppenheimer's hotel room and, over drinks, discussed the assignment facing them. Lilienthal was immediately impressed with Oppenheimer's thinking. He had heard about Oppenheimer before, but was startled by his nervous habit of pacing the floor and speaking loquaciously in short, intense bursts. He even noticed Oppenheimer's quirk of making funny little noises with his mouth.[2]

The board met as a group the next day in the somber offices of the secretary of state. After a preliminary meeting the group adjourned to meet in New York City, on the top floor of the American Trucking Building, where Oppenheimer had spent several days briefing his colleagues on atomic energy. For everyone but Thomas it was the first time they were able to understand the true nature of fission, the difficulties in manufacturing materials like plutonium and uranium, and the complexities involved in making a weapon. Lilienthal was utterly fascinated and impressed with Oppenheimer's ability to organize and synthesize such complex information. No "fairy tale or book," he wrote in his private diary, could compare to the first seven-hour session he spent under Oppenheimer's spell.

One point Oppenheimer stressed particularly was that the technology necessary for making a weapon was relatively simple; the manufacture of Pu 239 and U 235 was technically complex. A major consideration, therefore, of any system of control must be the production of fissionable materials. Oppenheimer's colleagues agreed. They realized that a prototypic system would be one that lay somewhere between maintaining total secrecy and making all information available. Both extremes, they knew, would almost certainly lead to a mass race to develop weapons.

On February 2, Oppenheimer put some of these thoughts into a memo to Lilienthal.

> It has become clear to us that not only politically but scientifically and technically as well, the field of atomic energy has witnessed very rapid change and very rapid progress. I believe that this will be the case in the future, too, and that no organization and no proposal can be effective which does not have a flexibility adequate to these changes. . . . Against this background of the difficulties of control as an isolated and negative function, I have thought it essential at least to consider combining the functions of development and of control in a single agency.[3]

Oppenheimer expressed his views publicly in an article which appeared in the June 1946 issue of the *Bulletin of the Atomic Scientists*, entitled "International Control of Atomic Energy." The arguments for international control were clear: the awesome destructive power of the atomic bomb, the weaknesses of contemporary defenses against such a weapon, and the impossibility of a permanent monopoly by the United States. Two methods of control, regulation and retaliation, were inadequate. Regulation was insufficient because it would be extremely difficult to control every action a nation might take. In the article, Oppenheimer explained, "It's very hard to tell whether a man is mining uranium because he is interested in cancer or interested in war."[4] To retaliate against a nation that was preparing to use an atomic bomb or even just developing one would be difficult in light of the international context of aggressive and defensive behavior. Atomic weapons were hardly a means of policing nations. The best choice, he urged, was to create an international agency to control and develop atomic energy. This sort of agency could quickly begin the business of exploiting the benefits of atomic energy, mine and control uranium sources, provide inspection services where necessary, and permit other nations to conduct safe research such as in the area of the medical sciences.

What kind of security could such a system provide? Certainly it would not eliminate war. But it would be "a guarantee that at a given time there are no atomic bombs, that no nation is either mining uranium, producing fissionable material, manufacturing bombs, or set up to do any of these things."[5] The price, however, would be the immediate surrendering of American security—the possession of weapons—against the long-term gain of assurances that no one else had such weapons.

> It is quite clear that this is a long road. I have the feeling that we have come something of a road already, but it is also quite clear that to reach the end will call for a spirit rather different from that that has animated most international discussion, in which the separate national interests have been the overwhelming consideration.[6]

Oppenheimer voiced these ideas at the next meeting of the board and took the lead in suggesting the framework for an agency that would provide control as well as an ordered exploration of nuclear technology. He saw developmental work as being roughly categorized as both "harmless" and "dangerous."[7] Experiments using a small laboratory reactor might be classified as harmless, whereas a large gaseous-diffusion plant to produce U 235 would be dangerous. And an international agency would concern itself with controlling the industrial plant rather than the campus reactor. Another safeguard would be established if mining and shipping of radioactive raw materials (uranium, for example) were under the control of the agency. Oppenheimer succeeded in engaging the interest of everyone present. This type of system, he proposed, could be modeled after a world corporation, which nations would join as stockholders. Meeting on February 1, the board agreed that such a system would form the basis of the recommendations they would make to Acheson. They also agreed, however, that a plan with specific details was not really their responsibility; as such, their recommendations would include alternatives as well as an assessment of each alternative.

When the board met again a week and a half later, each man had prepared a report discussing in detail one assigned aspect of international control. The members began to refer to their collection of documents as "the notebook." Lilienthal wrote the opening section, which introduced the general problem. Oppenheimer prepared "A Primer on Atomic Energy," which recaptured his lectures of two weeks before. Other sections reviewed raw materials and the production of fissionable materials, the elements of a system for control, and the requirements for security. Both Oppenheimer and Thomas argued for an agency that would perform active functions, such as development, as well as one that would monitor and safeguard nuclear materials. Oppenheimer argued forcefully that the proposed organization should control the world's monopoly of raw materials. Equally important, the agency should continue work in nuclear explosives in order to understand what possibilities existed. Without this, the agency's knowledge base would quickly become out-of-date, and the staff would be unable to understand any developments that might possibly be made by an aggressive nation. Another major activity would be the exploration of atomic energy for electrical and motive power and for industry.

Lilienthal felt that an active policy was essential; merely outlawing the bomb would be too simplistic and almost certainly would encourage nations to develop atomic weapons of their own. The board obviously wanted to recommend a policy that would not allow the new weapons to be controlled by the military. Oppenheimer's ideas were accepted by the board, who then decided to recommend to Acheson the concept of an international body whose work would be divided between strict control functions and positive work in the area of developing nonweapons uses for atomic energy. Carroll Wilson was asked by Lilienthal to combine the papers by Oppenheimer, Winne, Barnard, and Thomas into a unified report. The board then left for a tour of Los Alamos and Oak Ridge. For three of them—Lilienthal, Barnard, and Winne—this was the first visit to the top-secret installations of World War II. Only when they rambled through the vast halls at Oak Ridge and entered the Mesa laboratories of Los Alamos did the full extent of the nation's vast atomic energy enterprise fully strike them. Oppenheimer's question—would the nation produce war weapons or use the energy for peaceful purposes—now had a deeper meaning.

Sober but exhilarated, the board returned to Washington to review the revised draft prepared by Wilson. They were under pressure to deliver: A meeting with Acheson and Byrnes was scheduled for March 7, only a week away. The final report now ran to four thick volumes. Although Oppenheimer's ideas were incorporated throughout the volumes, each author left his own mark. It was a curious blend of personalities and perceptions.

The first volume proposed an international agency for the control and development of atomic energy. The second volume consisted of Oppenheimer's lectures on the principles of atomic energy, relabeled *The Scientific Basis of Atomic Energy Development*. The third volume was a series of recommendations prepared by Secretary of War Stimson's Interim Committee on work that might be conducted in the field. The last volume was a report by Carl McGowan entitled *Current Proposals for the International Control of Atomic Energy*.[8] Oppenheimer joined Lilienthal in urging Acheson to release the report to the public as soon as possible.

On March 7 the Board of Consultants and Acheson's committee met together at Dumbarton Oaks, in Washington's Georgetown section. Lilienthal's plan called for each member of the board to read a portion of the first volume out loud. He began with a review of the board's work and explained that they were fully aware that their recommendations were by nature limited and could not provide all answers. Barnard felt that inspection and police work alone were not sufficient to prevent nations from conducting clandestine weapons work. Oppenheimer spoke about the control of two basic elements—uranium and thorium, the only two substances that could produce fissionable materials. The control of both elements clearly meant the control of all nuclear work. Winne touched at the heart of the report: competitiveness between nations could be eliminated or controlled, at least, only by taking atomic energy out of national hands and placing it into the hands of an international authority. Thomas explained the distinction between dangerous and harmless work. A final round of presentations offered details on various aspects of a world organization: control of materials, conduct of research, licensing, operation of laboratories and production plants.

Acheson's committee granted qualified approval, but not without discussion. Groves believed that monitoring raw materials would prove to be almost impossible, since he saw several ways to circumvent the plan. Bush was concerned that Russia's large standing army would be made more powerful if America put aside its new weapons. With any plan, he argued, they would have to be able to pull out of their agreement if and when evidence revealed that the plan was failing. The board was willing to admit that there were indeed risks involved. Russian participation at the highest levels of an international agency would mean access to weapons information. Any plan would need to be implemented in steps; checks at each step would prevent compromising American security. Oppenheimer found a way of incorporating arguments by Bush and Conant into a revised plan. A revised plan was promised in ten days.[9]

Over the weekend Oppenheimer assisted Marks and Wilson in preparing the draft. An entirely new section was prepared which treated the process of transition from American monopoly to world authority. It was clear that any plan, once implemented, would shorten the time that the United States would have a monopoly on nuclear weapons. What would happen if a nation tried to develop its own weapon while the plan was being implemented? Fortunately, security relied upon both scientific knowledge and technological or industrial capacity. As the German experience during the war had shown, theoretical knowledge was relatively easy to come by. Building plants to produce U 235 or Pu 239 was a more complicated and expensive process. Releasing scientific information in order to evaluate the American plan was not substantially dangerous. Of greater concern were the industrial and technological mechanisms created by the Manhattan Project: Oak Ridge, Hanford, Los Alamos, and the existing stockpile of weapons. The board's plan for implementation needed critical scheduling to prevent even a momentary loss to American security should the entire plan collapse.

Oppenheimer opposed adding a schedule for the transition, a move he thought premature, especially because it would restrict the freedom he believed would be necessary during the negotiation process. Bush, like Groves, believed strongly that the American delegates to the United Nations needed a timetable to guide them. Acheson tried to forestall an impasse and suggested that a timetable could be added later, after Truman and other had seen the plan and approved it. For the moment the present members might be better to reconsider the plan paragraph by paragraph. In the end the plan was submitted without major changes.

Oppenheimer had reason to be pleased. The report contained much of what he personally felt were the crucial elements for success. His vision of an international agency to conduct both monitoring and research and development activities had won its way through the contesting views of the State Department. Now the report had to win approval from the United Nations.

President Truman took the advice of Secretary Byrnes and invited Bernard Baruch to take the post of representing the United States and its plan. Some, like Lilienthal, opposed the idea, but Baruch was a man with deep roots in government service. A close friend of Franklin Roosevelt, he had served as adviser to the President and in early 1944 had worked closely with Byrnes to draft plans for postwar government policy. In his midseventies, Baruch accepted the position with trepidation, specifying that his work would be limited to several hours in the morning and again in the afternoon. Certainly he would need scientific advisers as well as an assistant.

Baruch was especially interested in Oppenheimer for the position of senior scientific adviser. Baruch found Oppenheimer's mind to be one of the "most brilliant" he had ever encountered. The scientist had made a particularly strong impression when giving a talk to the representatives of the United Nations Atomic Energy Commission: "For sheer intellectual virtuosity, it was a performance that could hardly be surpassed."[10] The two men had a private session on April 4 that led Baruch to believe he had a strong mutual understanding with the scientist.[11] Oppenheimer, however, was not eager to assume a protracted role as consultant; privately, he was not pleased with Baruch's appointment. "That was the day I gave up hope, but that was not the day for me to say so publicly."[12] While not rejecting the offer outright, the scientist did carefully indicate he was concerned that the President should make the right policy decisions. Moreover, Oppenheimer didn't find Baruch's staff entirely competent. In a meeting with them, he heard a barrage of odd ideas, such as making the UN the repository for atomic weapons for "retaliation purposes." This wasn't what Oppenheimer wanted to hear from the men who would be closest to Baruch. He formally rejected the offer on May 6.[13] Baruch finally secured Richard Tolman as scientific adviser and let the word out that he had found Oppenheimer "uncooperative."

On May 17, 1941, Baruch and Acheson convened a high-level conference at the Blair-Lee House in Washington. Along with Tolman, Bush, and a few others, every member of the Board of Consultants attended. After some preliminary conversations on a survey of global uranium deposits, Baruch asked if any member of the State Department Committee on the board wished to change any portion of the report. Oppenheimer, still remembering his rejection of Baruch's offer, appeared to voice more objections than anyone else. The section on implementation, for example, seemed too dictatorial on the part of the United States, and what would be the effect of a veto on the commission's administrative and technical work? Others offered their thoughts. Herbert Swope, a member of Baruch's staff, asked why the plan failed to name penalties for violations. What would keep nations in line? The question had considerable import, of course, but what penalty could realistically be brought against a superpower? Oppenheimer felt that the penalty would be war. The meeting ended at nightfall and resumed the next day. By the third day Lilienthal, Oppenheimer, and the other members of the board prepared a summary statement reducing the report to the twelve most important elements.

By the end of May, Baruch, who was called "the old man" by the Board, had accepted a large part of the Acheson-Lilienthal report. Baruch assured Oppenheimer on May 19 that he had no intention of "deviating" from the board's proposed plan. In fact, he felt that many of the proposals put forward by his staff were "nonsense." Oppenheimer, despite the reassurances, was not optimistic about the outcome of the negotiations.[14] There were still differences between Baruch and his staff and the State Department's committee and board. Contrary to his promise to Oppenheimer, Baruch prepared a revised plan which stipulated penalties for treaty violations and urged international control by the new commission of all uranium ores. Throughout, there were subtle differences of language, enough so that the board found it necessary to offer counterdrafts. The discussions reached a stalemate after a few weeks; at one point Baruch complained to Byrnes that if the State Department insisted on leaving the plan unchanged, they could present it themselves to the United Nations. There was only a week left before the United Nations met to consider the plan, and Byrnes was forced to call a special meeting in Washington.

Baruch stressed his complaints: The existing plan was too weak on penalties and lacked adequate measures for detection of violations.

Truman, to whom the battle was brought, went through both plans paragraph by paragraph. In the end he endorsed Baruch's version with the postscript: "Above general principles approved June 7, 1946. Harry S. Truman."[15] Baruch had won this battle with the understanding that he was now bound by the principles just agreed upon unless changed by the President himself.

At the first meeting of the UN's Atomic Energy Commission, on June 14, the nations represented included Australia, Brazil, Canada, China, Egypt, France, Mexico, the Netherlands, Poland, the Soviet Union, the United Kingdom, and the United States. Trygve Lie, the secretary general of the UN, invited Bernard Baruch to take the podium for his presentation. Oppenheimer, who sat with the American delegation, heard Baruch open somberly with the words, "We are here to make a choice between the quick and the dead." The speech went well. It had been reviewed the day before by the State Department and some errors corrected. At one point it had been necessary to contact Oppenheimer in California for information just as he was leaving to attend the opening proceedings.[16] His presence, of course, was particularly ironic; he was, after all, the wartime director of Los Alamos, the very institution that had created Fat Man and Little Boy and had made this present debate a necessity in the first place. In his mind remained the question of whether or not the United States would be able to break Soviet implacability in order to negotiate a viable agreement.

He waited, like everyone else, for the Soviet response. Within the United Nations the response to the so-called American Plan was very good. Nationally, the reaction was mixed. A few critics believed the proposed plan would do little more than give away American secrets—the same sort of charge tossed around by members of Congress and some of the press. One newspaper chain described the plan as "imbecilic."[17] The Russian reaction came on June 19. In a speech amazingly free of polemics, Andrei Gromyko proposed a counterplan which in essence prohibited the production and therefore the use of nuclear weapons. In fact, existing stockpiles would be destroyed within three months of signing the agreement. Only America had weapons, of course, a point not lost on Gromyko's listeners. Moreover, two committees in the Atomic Energy Commission would disseminate scientific information and monitor developments in nations to prevent the production of weapons. The permanent members of the Security Council* would retain their veto over atomic matters.

Oppenheimer joined the American delegation in planning a response. For the moment, at least, there was no detailed criticism of the Russian proposal. More important was assessing whether the Russians

*Members: China, France, USSR, United Kingdom, and the United States.

would be willing to negotiate some compromise between both plans. From Gromyko's speech it seemed evident that Soviets would accept penalties or sanctions as part of a treaty. Would they stand firm, however, on maintaining the right to cast a veto in the Security Council? Oppenheimer thought they would continue to insist on veto rights. Five days later the commission members took up discussion on the two plans before them. Almost immediately, the discussions polarized between East and West. By July 2, Baruch was sufficiently disgusted to send Truman a status report on the Russian stance: "If we accept the Russian position, the atomic race would really then be on, because there would be nothing but the so-called good faith of nations' pious wishes and no enforcement or knowledge of what anyone else was doing."[18]

In the view of the United States, voting to outlaw weapons and to destroy the American stockpile was insufficient action; a complete system for the control and development of atomic energy was needed. The U.S. could hardly destroy its few weapons and release all information relating to them merely on the promise by other nations not to make or use weapons. The American appeal for a larger system seemed doomed by repeated calls for a treaty to outlaw weapons. Within the various committees and subcommittees discussing the proposals there appeared to be a reluctance to study key aspects of international agreement systematically: control, inspection, exchange of information, and the relationship between the commission and the Security Council. And veto power was crucial to maintenance of the United Nations charter. Patient but anxious to explore all possibilities for agreement, the American delegation suffered through week after week of repetitious discussion and eventual stagnation. Oppenheimer continued to act informally as consultant with Richard Tolman—a role greater than he had envisioned when he rejected Baruch's offer months before—in the preparation of a report for the commission on which controls might be exercised over key activities like uranium mining and production of nuclear materials. By December, however, the Soviets still refused to consider any meaningful action beyond their own plans.

Oppenheimer became less and less hopeful that anything useful would come from the debates at the United Nations. He became, Lilienthal observed, in "deep despair" over the negotiations. The two men met in Washington on July 23. Oppenheimer, just back from the deliberations at the UN, confessed his belief that the American delegation did not understand the intricacies of the plan and that Baruch had dwelled—at great price—on the question of punishment for violators and insistence on no veto power. When Lilienthal urged the scientist not to admit despair, Oppenheimer replied that a "reservoir of hope" did not exist. As they parted, Oppenheimer told Lilienthal: "I am ready to go anywhere and do anything, but I am bankrupt of further ideas. And I find that physics and the teaching of physics, which is my life, now seems irrelevant."[19] Had Oppenheimer, new to diplomacy on such a grand scale, experienced some personal enervation or burnout? Or perhaps, having been exposed to so much public attention, had he suddenly discovered that he could no longer return to mere teaching? His mood gave no clue.

On December 30 the United Nations Atomic Energy Commission met in plenary session to consider the "First Report of the Atomic Energy Commission to the Security Council." Baruch stayed firm on the matter of no veto; other items in the report reflected changes meted out during the arduous six and a half months. The final vote to report out the document was 10–0, with two abstentions: Poland and the Soviet Union. Several days later Baruch submitted his resignation. Some critics charged that his firm stand on the veto may have been less useful than Baruch himself had insisted it was. Russia's insistence on maintaining the integrity of the UN Charter, and thereby the veto itself, was not without some strength and validity. Objections by the United States suggested to many nations, especially the smaller ones, that the United States was not dedicated to achieving world disarmament merely because of parliamentary squabblings. Oppenheimer's pessimism now seemed justified: American promotion of its own plan seemed mishandled and there appeared to be little chance of agreement at this stage.

The American Plan had barely been introduced to the United Nations when the United States detonated its first atomic weapons since the wartime drop on Nagasaki nearly a year before. The test, part of a scientific and public-affairs extravanganza called Operation Crossroads, occurred in early July. Unlike those at Trinity and over Japan, this series of explosions, using Fat Man weapons, was conducted publicly in the Pacific and observed by thousands of press and public officials.

Oppenheimer had been asked to serve on the President's Evaluation Committee for Operation Crossroads in February 1946; originally he had declined the invitation, but was urged to stay on the committee. Uneasy with this duty, the scientist wrote a lengthy letter to Truman, asking once again to be relieved of his position on the committee. He made this request ". . . lest the nature of my misgivings make my position on your committee not a help to you but an embarrassment."

Oppenheimer was opposed to the tests, objecting to Crossroads on four grounds. The tests were conducted ostensibly to determine the effectiveness of atomic weapons in naval warfare. Considering the limited amount of weapons in America's stockpile and the cost projection (one hundred million dollars) of the tests, there certainly were cheaper ways to obtain the same data by using model tests. The same scientific data expected from the tests could be obtained by laboratory experiments or by a test specifically designed to collect such information without the complications of naval arrangements. In fact, the tests would use implosion weapons employing no new characteristics or innovations since Fat Man. Also, using atomic weapons against ships was not very effective; they were essentially weapons to be used against cities or centers of industry. And last, the weapons intended for use in the Pacific had one chance in fifteen of fizzling. Newer weapons with enhanced characteristics were available, but were not going to be used. What would happen to American prestige if a dud actually occurred?

Of course, there was perhaps another more important factor: The Crossroads tests were entirely military in nature. Were these tests perhaps not somewhat ill-timed, considering the American efforts at the United Nations? Oppenheimer believed they were neither timely nor useful. He closed his letter with an appeal:

> It could well be most undesirable for me to turn in after the tests are completed, a report to this effect [failure or low utility]. You may believe, as I do, that under the circumstances I can better serve you if I am not a member of your committee than if I am, and may therefore wish to excuse me. It is my earnest desire to be helpful to you every way possible.[20]

A few days later he resigned, but not without the feeling from some people that perhaps, like Lady Macbeth, he was washing his hands too often for past sins.

With passage of the Atomic Energy Act imminent, Truman turned his attention to possible candidates for the five AEC commissioners. Aides on Senator McMahon's committee submitted a list of candidates which included David Lilienthal; other lists circulating in Washington included Oppenheimer, Bush, and Conant. By the end of July, Truman had selected Sumner T. Pike, a former member of the Securities and Exchange Commission, and Lewis Strauss, an attorney and former Navy admiral with wartime ordnance experience. Both men accepted Truman's invitation. By late September, Truman had decided on Lilienthal as chairman and on Robert Bacher, one of Oppenheimer's key scientists at Los Alamos during the war. Bacher hesitated at first—research was his chief interest at the time—but after talking with Oppenheimer he changed his mind and agreed to serve on the commission. A few weeks later the President selected William W. Waymack, editor of the Des Moines *Register and Tribune.* On October 28, Truman held a press conference to announce his nominees for the AEC's first commissioners.

The nominations were well received; all five men were individuals with strong reputations and successful careers. Of the five, the most controversial was Lilienthal, whose directorship of the Tennessee Valley Authority had made him the target of conservative attacks in the House and Senate. Truman expected trouble from men like Senator

Kenneth McKeller of Tennessee. Despite the lack of staff and budget, temporary offices were quickly located in the Old State-War-Navy Building. On November 7 the Treasury made available one million dollars in Army funds; the new commission was now in business. Lilienthal held his first meeting on November 1 in Oak Ridge, Tennessee, where he and his colleagues went on a tour of Manhattan facilities. Two weeks later they convened in California for meetings and a dinner hosted by Oppenheimer in his Eagle Hill house.

One of Lilienthal's first acts was to recommend to the President the names of nine men to serve on the commission's influential General Advisory Committee, whose task it was "to advise the Commission on scientific and technical matters relating to materials, production, and research and development." His first choice was Robert Oppenheimer. Also recommended by the commission were James Conant, Enrico Fermi, Glenn Seaborg, Cyril S. Smith, Hood Worthington, Lee A. DuBridge, Isidor I. Rabi, and Hartley Rowe. Most of these men had been associated with the wartime effort: Fermi, Smith, Rowe, and Rabi had served under Bush at OSRD; Worthington and Seaborg had been engaged in other Manhattan projects; and DuBridge was now the president of the California Institute of Technology and an old friend of Oppenheimer's.

Without delay, Truman appointed Oppenheimer, Conant, and DuBridge to six-year terms; Rowe, Fermi, and Seaborg to four-year terms; and Worthington, Rabi, and Smith to two-year terms. The Secretaries of War and the Navy made their nominations to the Military Liaison Committee. The director of military applications was, under the new law, to be an individual in the armed services. Groves saw to it that Colonel Kenneth T. Nichols, his talented assistant during the past four years, was the War Department's only nominee. Nichols won approval, but only after several months of delay. The key position of general manager went to Carroll Wilson, whose committee work the last year or so had made him quite familiar with the purpose of the AEC.

Groves and the commission members spent most of December arguing over what Army installations would be transferred to the AEC. While Groves was indeed prepared to transfer thirty-seven Manhattan District facilities, he proposed to withhold weapon storage facilities, the Army's special intelligence operation on atomic energy, and Sandia Base in Albuquerque, New Mexico, because it was argued to be a key installation in the military's plan for stockpiling weapons. The deliberations lasted almost until the end of the year. Both Sandia Base and the intelligence operation were put under the AEC's control. Weapons custody remained an issue of debate. On December 31, 1946, President Truman signed the executive order that brought the Atomic Energy Commission into legal existence.

On the first day of the new year Lilienthal and his four colleagues on the commission were in full charge of a rambling organization not yet freed from its military dependency, and fraught with managerial and philosophical problems. Groves, despite all of his efforts and guidance during the last four years, was now formally separated from the Manhattan organization he had created. Oppenheimer, who held a key position on the AEC's Advisory Committee, could look forward to a role guiding the nation on atomic matters. He had done so as wartime director of Los Alamos; the view from Washington, however, as he once said to a friend, was quite different.

10. The Public Man

The newly created Atomic Energy Commission began operating even before its five commissioners had been formally confirmed by the United States Senate. With hearings scheduled for the end of January 1947, Lilienthal and his colleagues were already responsible for atomic energy—weapons, laboratories, a mammoth industrial empire, and thousands of employees working through the commission's contractors.

The first meeting of the General Advisory Committee had been called for January 3, 1947, in the new War Department Building in Washington, D.C. Robert Oppenheimer, Robert Bacher, and Lee DuBridge were unable to attend because they were detained in the West by a large winter storm. In his absence, Oppenheimer was nominated chairman of the committee for one year. Hartley Rowe agreed to act as temporary chairman until Oppenheimer arrived. Meeting with the commissioners for the first time, the committee found the setting and conversation congenial. Oppenheimer arrived with barely enough time to learn that the GAC would meet again in a month, with him acting as chairman. He protested his new election, just as he would protest all of his other nominations that would occur during the next five years. He always offered to let someone else chair; he was always refused. As one committee member said, there was just never anyone else to consider. At the end of the meeting he left with James Conant, who was then president of Harvard University, for the first meeting of the Atomic Energy Committee of the Joint Research and Development Board.

The Joint R & D Board was Vannevar Bush's creation, an interim body designed to promote some degree of coordination between the scientific and technical activities of the military, hopefully preventing duplicate work in weapons development. As a member, Oppenheimer joined Bush; Crawford H. Greenewalt, a Du Pont executive; Lloyd V. Berkner, the board's chief administrative officer; and military representatives from each of the branches. The board was intended to work closely with the AEC's Military Liaison Committee, which felt that its chief task at that time was to instruct the military on atomic weapons.

The Joint R & D Board, much like the GAC, reflected a healthy representation of Manhattan Project alumni. Both Oppenheimer and Conant served on the GAC; Bush had directed the overall effort during the war under General Groves; and other board members included Fermi, Bacher, an AEC commissioner, Rabi, Rowe, Cyril Smith, and Seaborg, who were all wartime participants. In early 1947, a year and a half after the end of the war, the nation's atomic energy program was still under the influence of men who had helped create it. Oppenheimer especially had overlapping appointments, placing him in an unusual position in the government.

In February, just as the Senate's confirmation hearings for the five new AEC commissioners were under way, Carroll Wilson, the AEC's general manager, ordered the formulation of a personnel security system. Thomas O. Jones, who had been in charge of security at Los Alamos during the war, was hired to draft some basic guidelines. On February 14, Wilson approved a system that granted three security clearance levels: a P clearance for individuals at AEC installations (such as Oak Ridge) who had no access to restricted information or technical operations; S clearance for frequent visitors to AEC installations who did not have access to restricted data; and the much more important Q clearance for all commission employees or consultants who did have access to the most secret information or laboratories. In addition, a new personnel security questionnaire was created and given to all existing personnel and all new employees, regardless of their wartime role. Wilson projected that individual security checks, which were to be performed by the FBI, might take as long as four weeks. In reality, the process ran more often to six weeks or more. While most employees completed the PSQs, as they were called, and were granted clearance at one level or another, the investigations inevitably revealed that some people had questionable pasts and would have to undergo more elaborate scrutiny. The most difficult cases were brought to the commissioners for approval or disapproval.

General Groves had already forewarned Lilienthal that wartime pressure had necessitated granting clearances, issued by the Army during the war, to certain individuals with questionable pasts. Wilson certainly knew that the AEC was under considerable pressure to hire only the most virginal of individuals; Lilienthal's confirmation hearing, for example, raised charges that he had a Communist past—charges that were untrue, but which nonetheless made the commission anxious to avoid any trouble in this area. It was clear to Lilienthal and Wilson that the commission needed to act carefully in screening both old and new employees, whether they were located at commission headquarters or offices and laboratories in the field.

It was an unpleasant surprise when Lilienthal received a telephone call from J. Edgar Hoover on March 8, 1947. Robert Oppenheimer, the FBI director reported, had a past that might well disqualify him from any post with the AEC. Lilienthal was startled; why had the FBI waited until now to reveal the scientist's background? Later in the day Thomas Jones received a heavy file and a letter from Hoover, which read: "I thought it best to call to your attention [to] the attached copies of summaries of information contained in our files relative to Julius Robert Oppenheimer . . . and his brother, Frank Friedman Oppenheimer . . . obtained from confidential sources."[1] The contents of the file were ominous indeed, containing detailed accounts of Oppenheimer's involvement with left-wing political groups in the 1930s as well as the information that his brother, Frank, Frank's wife, and his own wife, Kitty, were members of the American Communist party. Perhaps even more threatening were the carefully analyzed transcripts of interviews between Oppenheimer and various members of the Army's security organization and the FBI. Lilienthal was particularly shocked by the Chevalier incident. This information was especially disturbing in light of the recent Senate confirmation hearings and charges that the AEC had previously hired individuals despite records of their "suspicious pasts."

On Monday morning Lilienthal quickly called his fellow commissioners together in an executive session. The file, along with Hoover's letter, was given to each member to read. Bush and Conant, because of their wartime association with Oppenheimer, also were asked to join the commissioners later in the afternoon. Both men agreed that when Groves hired Oppenheimer, he had been fully aware of most of Oppenheimer's background. They stressed that the scientist had performed a critical service for the United States during the war and that after the war there was no information which in any way cast suspicion on the scientist's actions or loyalty. Lilienthal was unable to reach Groves by telephone because he and his wife were on their way to Florida for a vacation. Lilienthal then called Secretary of War Patterson.

Obviously, Truman also had to be informed. Oppenheimer was a presidential nominee, and certainly a public disclosure of the scientist's dubious past would cause considerable embarrassment to the White House. Lilienthal reached Clark Clifford, Truman's assistant, on Monday afternoon and gave him the facts. On Wednesday, Clifford called Lilienthal back—the President had the information, but wanted a few days to think matters over. Meanwhile, on the basis of support from Bush and Conant, Oppenheimer's loyalty could not be perceived as being in question.

Both Bush and Conant formalized their support for the scientist in letters written to Lilienthal on March 11. Bush referred to Oppenheimer as ". . . one of the great physicists of this country, or of the world for that matter," and stressed his invaluable contribution to the nation's war program. He was, wrote Bush, ". . . a man of excellent judgement and a real leader in the entire effort." Conant was more direct:

> I can say without hesitation that there can be absolutely no question of Dr. Oppenheimer's loyalty. . . . I have no knowledge of Dr. Oppenheimer previous to the summer of 1941, but I say unhesitantly that whatever the record might show as to his political

> sympathies at that time or his associations, I would not deviate from present opinion, namely, that a more loyal and sound American citizen cannot be found in the whole United States.[2]

Groves was finally reached in Florida and ordered back to Washington. He prepared a memorandum for Patterson, entitled "Loyalty Clearance of Dr. J. R. Oppenheimer." He bluntly stated that when he had taken control of the atomic bomb program in September 1942, there were indeed a number of people who had not received proper security clearances—and one of these men had been Oppenheimer. Despite the information on the scientist and the reluctance on the part of the Army's G-2 section to clear him, Groves decided it would be "in the best interests of the United States to use his services." Groves, after personally reviewing the case, felt that Oppenheimer was fundamentally a "loyal American citizen." He added, "Since then, I have learned many things amplifying that record but nothing which, if known to me at that time, would have changed my decision."[3]

Lilienthal met with Hoover to review the matter on March 25. He provided the results of their internal review, as well as the letters from Bush, Conant, and Groves, to the stolid director. The only real source of concern was the Chevalier incident; there was no other evidence that Oppenheimer had maintained or in any way continued his political connections from before the war. Moreover, he did indeed have an outstanding record at Los Alamos. Hoover did not disagree, but he did have reservations about Oppenheimer's failure to immediately report the Chevalier incident at the time it occurred. Frank Oppenheimer, however, was considered "undesirable."[4] The AEC finally decided to grant clearance to Robert Oppenheimer, but was forced to formally register its action on the record at its August 6 meeting. Now it was a matter of record that Oppenheimer had been formally cleared.

For the moment, Lilienthal had done all he could to save the situation so that they could continue to use Oppenheimer's services in the AEC: The President had been alerted; the AEC itself had conducted an intensive but brief review and had decided that Oppenheimer's loyalty was not in question, although matters in his past were indeed troublesome. Lilienthal, in fact, had suggested to his colleagues, as well as to Clifford, that a special review panel could examine the case, even members of the Supreme Court. For the time being, the matter was closed. Oppenheimer continued his role as a member of the GAC and as a consultant to various government efforts, but the matter of his past did not stay quiet for long.

Oppenheimer called the second meeting of the General Advisory Committee to order on February 2, 1947. It was the first official meeting of the committee since the organizational gathering nearly a month before. It was a dramatic moment as well; Bacher, just back from Los Alamos, was scheduled to give a report on the precise number of atomic weapons the United States had presently stockpiled, as well as the current production rates for all bombs. In effect, Oppenheimer and his colleagues—every member was present—were determining, within certain limits, United States full nuclear capacity; its ability, in other words, to destroy an enemy. This information was the nation's second greatest secret, the actual design and assembly of weapons being the first. Lilienthal was presenting this highly classified information only to the commissioners, the GAC, and selected members of the military. No one was allowed to take written notes. The setting of the meeting only added to the drama: The auditorium of the new War Department Building on 23rd Street in Washington had three-story-tall ceilings and dark-panelled walls that seemed to dwarf the men, who sat at a large conference table. As a precaution, Lilienthal permitted the numbers to be given only with an accuracy of "plus or minus 20 percent."[5] No doubt everyone except Oppenheimer was shocked when they learned that the United States arsenal actually had very few weapons at its disposal, not one of which was fully assembled and ready for use. The "great arsenal" described by the politicians and press had obviously been nothing more than talk.

After Bacher's sobering presentation, Oppenheimer reviewed the general status of weapons development as well as other lines of non-weapons research, such as reactor development. There were few new developments in either fission or thermonuclear weapons, he reported, and few results in reactor research. Both weapons and reactors were important, Oppenheimer argued. Government research could not focus only on weapons. Fermi agreed, but voiced what others felt: Weapons had top priority. Also high on the list of priorities was the continued production of uranium and plutonium, without which further weapons work would be stalled. Even the thermonuclear weapon needed more study. It had been decided that Los Alamos should be maintained for continued research and development, but Oppenheimer himself was unsure whether or not the world did, in fact, need newer and more powerful bombs. There was little reservation among the others, who felt that weapons were a necessity in the ever-darkening international scene. Reluctantly, Oppenheimer had to agree that Los Alamos needed both encouragement and support from the AEC. The laboratory also needed a clearer statement of policy from the commission. This support was particularly important if the United States wanted a thermonuclear device. For the present, reactors, while important, would have to take a backseat to weapons.

For Oppenheimer and the other members of the GAC, the news from laboratories in the field was discouraging. Los Alamos had a new leader—Norris Bradbury, a man endorsed by Oppenheimer. Despite Bradbury's determination to revitalize Los Alamos, the laboratory suffered from low morale, lack of guidance from Washington, and the steady exodus of senior and mid-level men whose experience and administration during the war had made the project so successful. John Manley, working at Los Alamos, had been invited by Oppenheimer to become secretary to the committee. Manley accepted and left for Oak Ridge only to discover many of the same conditions as at Los Alamos, except at Oak Ridge they were exacerbated by the larger number of employees. The situation at Los Alamos seemed even gloomier when news reached the committee of the deaths of two scientists in two separate accidents in less than a year. There could be no doubt that the nation's laboratories had to be rebuilt if they were to serve their purpose as the central point of the energy program.

At the next meeting of the GAC, on March 28 and 29, Carroll Wilson reported on the steps that had been taken during the previous weeks to improve the conditions of the laboratories and plants. The agenda covered a wide range of topics.

Oppenheimer summarized the discussions the next day. Weapons were the clear priority for the commission's work. Los Alamos would need special assistance in order to stabilize and grow. Thermonuclear studies would continue and new uses for uranium 235 must be found, especially in light of the present demands on plutonium and the overworked production facilities at Hanford. The new reactor at Argonne, employing a new technological approach called redox, was the next priority, followed by new reactor construction at the Hanford, Washington, site. These recommendations were in turn made by Oppenheimer to the AEC commissioners. There was little doubt that the GAC's recommendations would carry great weight before a body of men still learning to master the complex technological and industrial details.

Exhausted, Oppenheimer left the meeting to return to California by way of Los Alamos. Together with Conant, Rowe, Rabi, Manley, and General James McCormack, the AEC's director of military applications, he arrived at the laboratory on April 3. It was Oppenheimer's first visit in almost a year and a half, but there was no time for nostalgia. This was an important visit; he was determined to make a firsthand assessment of the status of weapons development and production. One good piece of news greeted the men upon their arrival on April 3: The Senate Committee on Atomic Energy had approved the President's nominations for AEC commissioners. A formal vote by the Senate as a whole was set for six days later.

The visit to Los Alamos was crucial for both laboratory staff and for Oppenheimer's committee. With advance notice from Oppenheimer,

Norris Bradbury had prepared an agenda which dealt with the key questions: "What rules should be set up for the relation between the *efficient* use of active materials, and *amount* of active material, the *size* of the bang, and the *availability* of active material?"[6] Bradbury and his staff needed to know just how much uranium or plutonium they could expect to have available to them, since the explosive power in weapons was generally related to the amount of fissionable material in any given weapon design. Bradbury was all too aware of the production difficulties both at Oak Ridge and Hanford, but the demands from the military to amass a stockpile were almost frantic. Obviously there was pressure on Los Alamos to develop efficient weapons—that is, weapons designed to produce powerful explosions using relatively small amounts of fissionable materials.

Oppenheimer's group was guided by a thorough report prepared by Bradbury and distributed before the meeting at Los Alamos, which summarized the wartime program, with its Fat Man and Little Boy models, and then described nine new models which appeared to show great promise. These new devices would improve the implosion bomb, as well as make the uranium 235 gun weapons more efficient. Bradbury had also taken the unusual step of inviting most of his senior staff to the meetings with the GAC. Oppenheimer agreed with Bradbury's motives; it was not so long ago that he himself had found it necessary to insist to General Groves that compartmentalization would not work at Los Alamos and that the colloquiums were an important part of the work process.

The GAC was also briefed on Teller's theoretical work on a thermonuclear weapon. There had been little time during the war to study the complex problems of fusing isotopes such as deuterium and tritium, which were light elements that could be brought together only under very high temperatures. Since the war, Teller and a small staff had been able to devise two approaches to the thermonuclear weapon: one called the Super, and another called the Alarm Clock.

Oppenheimer and colleagues were able to quickly agree that Bradbury was correct in calling for immediate testing of existing weapons and for development of more effective versions. Los Alamos did not need to deplete its energies by undertaking vast new weapons programs. Existing fission weapons could be made more powerful through careful refinement. Certainly the work on thermonuclear weapons could continue, although Oppenheimer feared that inherent problems were complicated enough to prevent a successful weapon from being completed for many years. The immediate task was to strengthen the existing weapons and to free Los Alamos from as many production tasks as possible, such as manufacturing detonators and fabricating bomb parts. Late that night, following the meetings, Oppenheimer and Manley prepared a report for

Lilienthal summarizing the discussions and recommendations from Oppenheimer's team.

The next day they toured Sandia Base, adjacent to Albuquerque's airport, where the nuclear weapons were scheduled to be outfitted with their explosive lenses and stored in concrete and dirt "igloos" south of the landing strips. The visit was not reassuring to Oppenheimer: Most of the buildings were of war vintage and made of wood. Security seemed light, especially compared with the elaborate fence-and-guard system at Los Alamos. Considering that this was the nation's entire stockpile of atomic weapons, there was cause for concern.

Before catching a plane for California, Oppenheimer called Robert Bacher at the commission offices in Washington to say, in guarded language, that the trip had been very successful and that General McCormack was carrying his report back to Washington. The recommendations urged by Oppenheimer and the committee deserved quick "concurrence." At last, he added, they "could see the bottom of the barrel."[7]

In his report, written as a letter to Lilienthal, Oppenheimer reported that "the work at Los Alamos has a priority second to none." Fission weapons were the main target, but the GAC had considered thermonuclear weapons as well.

> We have come to appreciate that rapid progress in the development of thermonuclear explosives is not to be anticipated; nevertheless, we are convinced that, at least for the present, studies bearing on this problem are contributing to the health of the Los Alamos Project, and laying the foundations for further progress in the future.

At this point, Oppenheimer and his committee members viewed the hydrogen bomb as a tentative but interesting possibility. His report, however, could not be characterized either as an effort to stall or kill the further study of the hydrogen weapon—a fact lost several years later when his role in the development of the thermonuclear weapon was under question.[8]

The GAC visit had been useful for Los Alamos. There was a consensus on the need for testing and for developing reliable weapons that could be turned into production models. Oppenheimer's handling of the discussions also had lessened some of the pressures from the military on Bradbury. The military had had a chance to voice their needs and concerns. Army planners envisioned a wide range of weapons, and the Air Force was seeking support for a nuclear-powered airplane. Throughout the expression of these demands, the theme of increasing production of uranium and plutonium hit home again and again. Clearly, the GAC would have to study closely the projections for reactor developments.

If weapons, in fact, were the commission's first priority, the GAC was prepared to argue that reactors should be its second. Reactor research was the key to increased fissionable materials production as well as for a myriad of scientific and technical achievements which might one day include cheap electrical power. Oppenheimer was interested in finding peaceful uses for atomic energy; this had been one of his themes for a long time. Isotopes were the relatively inexpensive by-products of reactor operation, and could be used by the public in areas such as medicine and industry. Both Oppenheimer and Conant also agreed privately that airborne reactors for use in airplanes were highly unlikely any time soon. They chose to discourage this work where they could, although it was clear that each military service was quickly trying to claim a share of the atomic pie; there would almost certainly be battles over this.

Oppenheimer called his committee together again over Memorial Day weekend. After covering the preliminary agenda, Oppenheimer raised the question of how the AEC might support fundamental research by scientists in universities or small laboratories. Since the end of the war, many requests had flooded into the government from hospitals and universities for small amounts of radioactive substances. The substances were not related to weapons and, therefore, with the passage of the Atomic Energy Act, could legally be made available. One critic of this concept, however, was Commissioner Lewis Strauss, who feared that isotopes might in some way contribute to weapons research or be used as radioactive poisons in warfare. Oppenheimer strongly discounted this argument; in no way did he favor releasing fissionable materials. Isotopes, on the other hand, were not useful in weapons and were contributing to research. He even favored making these substances available to scientists in foreign countries. His reasoning was sound: Work with isotopes would help to expand fundamental research in nuclear physics. Making these substances available also demonstrated that the United States had a genuine interest in using nuclear energy for purposes other than weapons.

The use of isotopes was only one part of what Oppenheimer envisioned as a broad-based program of support for fundamental research. He argued his case personally in May with the commissioners in an effort to get support, which AEC staff had recently projected might cost the commission some nineteen million dollars a year. In what Lilienthal registered in his diary as a brilliant defense of the effort, Oppenheimer proposed a program that included taking control of Navy accelerators and generously making available isotopes to legitimate researchers. Lilienthal remained in awe of Oppenheimer's abilities, calling the one-hour presentation "as brilliant, lively, and articulate a statement as I believe I have ever heard. He is pure genius. Even the great brains joined in the amazement and delight we all felt at this wonderful piece [Oppenheimer's presentation]."[9]

While most people appreciated Oppenheimer's argument, there were other more pressing demands for the commission's resources. Weapons were a preoccupation of the military. Tests of advanced weapons were scheduled for the Pacific soon, and there was some opposition to sharing radioactive materials with anybody, much less with foreign scientists. For the moment, Oppenheimer's eloquent plea was lost in preparations for Project Sandstone, a series of tests scheduled for 1948. Support for nonessential research would simply have to wait.

Oppenheimer's reaction was to believe that part of the delay in acting on a program of support for nonweapon-related research stemmed as much from a lack of understanding of nuclear principles as from poor communication between the GAC and the commission. Robert Bacher, who shared Oppenheimer's concern for support of research, was a scientist himself; he volunteered to lay the groundwork for a thorough discussion of the request at a special meeting of the commissioners and the members of the General Advisory Committee on July 28. At that meeting, Oppenheimer again brought up the subject. It was important, he added, for the AEC to educate the public. He used as an example the unrealistic expectations, promoted daily by newspapers and magazines, that nuclear power was just around the corner. He was certain that such expectations would lead to disappointment; power from reactors was, in fact, far in the future.

His projections on the utilization of atomic energy to generate power struck a nerve, as this was something the Congress and the public expected from the commission. It was certainly a dimension that helped to soften the AEC's image as a group concerned only with weapons of destruction. Oppenheimer agreed to draft a report on the subject which the commission could consider later in its two-day meeting.

Oppenheimer's draft, prepared with the help of John Manley, was not encouraging. The shortage of uranium meant that supplies for power reactors were a distant bet at best. Alternative means, such as the so-called breeder reactor,* were at least ten years away in terms of development of acceptable reactor technologies. Lilienthal was disappointed by the report, finding it very negative. The authors of the report, Oppenheimer and Manley, seemed particularly negative. Some of the criticism was political, Lilienthal thought; the statements helped mitigate criticism from foreign scientists who believed America was keeping atomic power to itself. "It is curious," he wrote, "how political reasons motivate scientists and savants, though they would be surprised if you pointed it out to them and probably deny it. Wishful thinking—which so largely characterized political thought—is no monopoly of politicians or mortal men."[10]

*The breeder reactor produces more fissionable fuel (e.g., plutonium) than it consumes.

Strauss throught that a report critical of the AEC would mean considerable difficulties in requesting appropriations from Congress. Oppenheimer remained adamant against these objections; the commission, he said again, had a responsibility to educate the public. Still, the commissioners would not be pushed, agreeing only to consider the report during the following two months.

Less than a month later the commissioners, the members of the GAC, and the directors of the six national AEC laboratories—Argonne, Ames, Brookhaven, Los Alamos, Schenectady, and Clinton—met on August 17 at a private ranch north of Berkeley. Oppenheimer, unlike his colleagues on the GAC, was given a private room, as were the five commissioners. Without a formal agenda, the participants were free to raise any question they wished. Oppenheimer again called for the support of basic research. Strauss, again in discord with his colleagues, objected to a motion that called for the distribution of radioactive isotopes. Strauss was very emotional about the issue and even threatened to resign. He revealed that he was trying to gather support from the State Department to kill any effort by the AEC to make isotopes available to foreign scientists. Lilienthal even had to make a special effort to have a private chat with Strauss, encouraging him not to resign.[11] Beyond the matter of isotopes, the meeting seemed to be moving toward a consensus that the AEC should support independent research outside its own laboratories. Oppenheimer reaffirmed the GAC's support of such a program, even at the cost of thirty million dollars a year. Despite Strauss's objections, the commission finally voted to make available limited quantities of isotopes to researchers.

The discussion also turned to reactor developments. At Oppenheimer's request, Fermi and Cyril Smith had prepared a revised version of the GAC's report on reactor development while they were at Los Alamos. Instead of directly stating that uranium reactors would never be cost-effective, the revised report stated that present designs could not efficiently utilize uranium as a fuel. Support came from an unexpected corner: General Nichols believed that the report would help to soften European criticism. The GAC finally adopted a five-page statement on November 23. In it, two reactors then under development—the high-flux and the breeder models—were described as being capable of producing power within a few years. More sophisticated reactors, including those that could efficiently use uranium, were years away.

There was division within the GAC on which alternative should be adopted in exploring reactors. Conant favored quick action, even at the expense of detail. Oppenheimer and Fermi thought that considerable scientific research had to underlie any extensive program. Both Oppenheimer and Rabi suggested that a reactor committee should be created within the AEC to oversee the rapid but orderly exploration of development. Ernest Lawrence was nominated as its chairman, a position he quickly accepted. The commissioners bought the notion of a committee, but created one within their own organization and named James Fisk, the AEC's director of research, as its chairman. Fisk moved quickly and his arguments eventually forced a reversal of Oppenheimer's committee decision to locate a new AEC research reactor at Clinton instead of at Chicago. Despite Oppenheimer's manipulations, the GAC suffered a rebuff.

Another key question facing the General Advisory Committee was weapons custody. Clearly the AEC designed and field-tested weapons, and laboratories like Los Alamos manufactured some components of weapons. The wording of the Atomic Energy Act was vague on the matter of custody, but the military was making a strong argument for what its people called "surveillance," or the inspection and maintenance of weapons. Already, at Kirtland Field in Albuquerque, the Air Force maintained storage igloos and provided security. Lilienthal wanted the commission to have the custody of weapons, as did scientific leaders like Norris Bradbury. The AEC's Military Liaison Committee, backed by the Joint Chiefs of Staff, was pressing hard for military possession.

If the commissioners wanted support from the GAC, they were disappointed. Oppenheimer began the tenth meeting of the committee on June 4 by stating that he and his colleagues could not take a formal stand on the matter of custody. What they could do, he offered, was evaluate the merits of civilian control versus military control. The committee appeared to favor retaining custody of the weapons within the commission—in other words, civilian custody. Oppenheimer offered a compromise of sorts: It did seem possible that part of the present stockpile could be turned over to the military. This suggestion hardly answered the question of whether weapons would be military or civilian property. This issue was particularly urgent; at the same time, the Soviets were blocking all rail traffic between West Germany and Berlin, and within a week, they had succeeded in sealing off Berlin entirely.

The matter finally found its way to Truman, who met with the commission and the military's representatives on July 21. The President, however, had already made up his mind; two days later, he issued a formal statement: The weapons would remain with the AEC.

The GAC had other matters to deal with, including an evaluation of the Sandstone tests a month before. The apparent success of the models now meant that the United States had a prototype, the Mark IV, which could now go into production. No longer would the components of each bomb need to be laboriously crafted by hand. Tests on even more innovative weapons suggested that a newer, lighter-weight bomb could be produced to meet the specifications of the new Air Force bombers. These new weapons would mean a change of defense policy.

Indeed, the rules of the game had changed, a fact that Oppenheimer learned quickly. Along with the Pentagon, the AEC was able to identify a number of qualities of the new weapons that would now shape the nation's war plans:

> 1. Naval vessels and large bodies of troops were not primary targets for atomic bombs.
> 2. There would be little defense by large urban or industrial centers against the new weapons.
> 3. The weapon could eliminate a substantial number of people and leave few structures intact.
> 4. The element of surprise would be greater with every increase in the size and potency of weapons. Atomic weapons had the "supreme value" in this regard.
> 5. Acts of war or imminent acts of war should result in defensive actions.
> 6. The standing orders for the Commander in Chief needed redefinition in order to launch adequate defense and retaliation actions against a nuclear attack.
> 7. Atomic weapons were by far the most effective device for the creation of fear and panic. The most effective use of these weapons would, therefore, involve social patterns which heretofore had not been considered.[12]

Oppenheimer's activities extended beyond his involvement with the AEC and the General Advisory Committee. Although less involved since Bernard Baruch's resignation in January 1947, the scientist continued to do some work with the U.S. delegation at the United Nations. Warren R. Austin, the representative to the Security Council, was appointed to replace Baruch as the American representative to the UN Atomic Energy Commission. As deputy, Secretary of State George Marshall appointed Frederick H. Osborn, the wartime director of the Army's education and information program. Most of the previous year had been spent in tedious, often dilatory deliberations over the American and Russian proposals. The United States had won a small victory in February when the Security Council voted to take up discussions on the American plan; only Poland and the Soviet Union had abstained. Nevertheless, the discussions remained at a stalemate, with both the Americans and Russians intransigent in their positions. The stalemate seemed more to serve the Soviet propaganda interests well, as they continued to call for total disarmament.

Oppenheimer had realized months before that the Soviets were only delaying and that they had no intention of conceding to the critical points of the American plan—inspection and no veto. The scientist made an urgent call to Osborn to arrange for a meeting to discuss the matter. Meeting at Osborn's country home for the weekend, Oppenheimer explained that he thought the Baruch plan would not work unless each nation committed itself to inspection. In his view, the Soviets would never open their country to others, especially for the purposes of arms inspection. Taking an extreme position, Oppenheimer felt that the United States should break off negotiations with the Soviets. To continue, he suggested, would only serve to weaken the Baruch Plan and gain propaganda value through their continuing call for disarmament. Oppenheimer felt very strongly about this.

Osborn was surprised by Oppenheimer's adamancy. "The general background was that [Oppenheimer] was now certain, after watching the Russians for 3 or 4 months, that the Russians had no intention of accepting any plan for the control of atomic energy . . . which would mean lifting the Iron Curtain . . . for to do so would mean the end of the regime." If this was the case, Oppenheimer explained to Osborn, *any* plan of international control would be exceedingly dangerous to the United States.[13]

Oppenheimer believed that the United States' efforts to turn atomic energy to good purposes had been thwarted, likening the situation to the tale about Confucius and the woman whose son had been eaten by a tiger. Offered comfort by Confucius, the woman added that her husband also had been eaten in the same forest a year before, and a year before that, the same thing had happened to her father. Confucius, realizing the dangers of the forest, asked why she did not move away. The woman replied, "The forest is bad, but the government is excellent!" The bright promise of the benefits of nuclear energy foreseen at the discovery of fission had been subverted by the world's preoccupation with weapons.

Oppenheimer felt that one reason for the failure was the single-mindedness of the United States in pursuing an international agreement only in the United Nations. Outlining his ideas in an article in the *Bulletin of the Atomic Scientists*, Oppenheimer suggested that the United States had formulated its policy just as the profound differences between the two nations had revealed themselves: differences of values, different perceptions of national security, and the belief by the Soviet Union that conflict was inevitable. A nation could hardly destroy its stockpile of atomic weapons when, as Oppenheimer pointed out, the "normal practices" of the Soviets "involve secrecy and police control." Regarding the plethora of "alternative" proposals for international agreement, Oppenheimer had harsh words:

> It is my view that none of these proposals have any element of hopefulness in the short term. In fact, it appears most doubtful if there are now any courses open to the United States which can give our people the sort of security they have known in the past.[14]

Only a "reorientation" of Soviet policy and a corresponding change in American policy, could create the sort of international agreement that the United States had struggled so hard to promote in the United Nations.

Osborn was not in a position to cut off negotiations. His superior, Warren Austin, would need approval from the State Department and the President. Moreover, Osborn had learned that a number of smaller nations had resented Baruch's heavy-handed approach toward promoting the American Plan. There was little choice but to continue American efforts to negotiate an international agreement. Perhaps there would eventually be a break in the impasse.

Osborn felt that the United States should continue working toward an agreement, leaving the details to be worked out during the implementation stage. Care should be taken to protect the balance of power between East and West. General Groves, attending a meeting with Osborn, Oppenheimer, Conant, and others, firmly objected to this sort of thinking; agreement on strategic balance and the like was, he felt, impossible between the two major powers. Oppenheimer favored a public statement to the effect that the United States would be willing, at any time, to discuss the prevention of nuclear war, but that the argument over proposals in the United Nations was wrong "in principle."[15] On September 11, 1947, the UN Atomic Energy Commission voted to send its report on the American Plan to the Security Council. The Soviet Union, however, voted against it; Poland abstained.

On September 17, 1947, Oppenheimer made a presentation at the National War College in Washington, D.C., in which he tried to explain the American Plan.

> The cornerstone of our proposal is an institution which requires candidness and great openness in regard to technical realities and policy. It involves a maximum effort to abolish national rivalries in the field of atomic energy, and in all dangerous areas of atomic energy it involves a total and genuine international action.

In the event that his audience felt that he was ignorant of Soviet character, Oppenheimer carefully explained that the "sacrifices" that would be required from the Soviet Union were in "very gross conflict" to their present government policy. And it was highly unlikely that the Soviets would make such sacrifices.

> The whole notion of international control presupposes a certain confidence, a confidence which may not be inconsistent with carrying a gun when you sit down to play poker, but at least is consistent with sitting down to play poker. In the year and a half since the efforts on these problems started, we have found ourselves forced by the Soviet moves and by the changing political situation throughout the world over and over again to take steps which were in essence a repudiation of that confidence; and the

> Soviet has taken ever more grave steps in repudiating that confidence.[16]

It was depressingly clear that the Soviets were not about to make any concessions. Oppenheimer reiterated this in another speech to the New York Bar Association in February 1948; the United States proposals "manifestly" were simply not going to be accepted.

Three quarters of a year later, in May 1948, the UN Commission on Atomic Energy voted on its third report, which flatly stated that negotiations were at a stalemate and that hope for an international agreement through the United Nations was dead. Explaining this failure to a meeting of New York City lawyers several years later, Oppenheimer said, "The failure to persuade the Soviet government to alter its procedures was anticipated by many. Yet we should not forget that this is an objective not only of the past but of the future as well."[17]

While the negotiations at the United Nations were a failure, Oppenheimer stressed that the desire for international cooperation was a worthy endeavor. In a radio interview with Eleanor Roosevelt on February 12, 1950, Oppenheimer expressed his belief in the value of the effort.

> The decision to seek or not to seek international control of atomic energy, the decision to try to make or not to make the hydrogen bomb, these are complex technical things, but they touch on the very basis of our morality. It is a grave danger for us that these decisions are taken on the basis of facts held secret. This is not because those who contributed to the decisions or make them are lacking in wisdom; it is because wisdom itself cannot flourish and even the truth not be established, without the give and take of debate and criticism. The facts, the relevant facts, are of little use to an enemy, yet they are fundamental to an understanding of the issues of policy. If we are guided by fear alone, we will fail in this time of crisis. The answer to fear can't always lie in the dissipation of its cause; sometimes it lies in courage.[18]

The first report of the Chevalier incident appeared on the front page of *The New York Times* on October 31, 1947. The story emerged from sources within the House Un-American Activities Committee, which was holding hearings on alleged Communist infiltration in the motion picture industry. Eltenton's name had emerged, as had Chevalier's and, inevitably, Oppenheimer's. Committee spokesman Louis Russell made it clear, however, that Robert Oppenheimer had rejected the proposal from Chevalier. The information had come, according to the newspaper account, originally from FBI sources. Oppenheimer, from Princeton, chose not to comment, but issued a terse message that indicated he would not speak on the matter as long as it was under investigation by the government. The incident seemed to typify the increasing concern over Communism and Communist infiltration in America.

However ominous the implications of the HUAC hearings, Oppenheimer continued to receive public honors. In 1947 alone, he had been made vice-president of the American Physical Society—the same organization to which news of the German fission discovery first had been made in America—and honored with the Willkie Memorial Building Award and honorary membership in the Goethean Literary Society. He had received honorary doctorates from the University of New Mexico and Harvard University. He had made talks at Princeton University, the University of Denver, the All University Conference at Davis, the National War College, and the Massachusetts Institute of Technology. In addition to his membership on the General Advisory Committee, he served on the Committee on Atomic Energy for the Research and Development Board and on the Oak Ridge Institute of Nuclear Studies. The new year had every promise of being equally bright.

As 1947 ended, Oppenheimer could look back on the activities of his committee and assess their accomplishments and failures. The guidance provided by the GAC to Los Alamos had resulted in the successful Sandstone tests. More powerful and efficient weapons were now available to the military. There was at least some beginning of a program of support for research. Despite strong opposition from some members of the commission, isotopes in limited form and number were being made available to hospitals and research centers in both the United States and Europe. Progress on reactor development was uneven but hopeful. For the moment, at least, weapons remained within the custody of the AEC. And the committee, despite some unpopular stands, retained its influence with the commissioners.

This assessment reflected the interests and perceptions of the General Advisory Committee as well. There were also, of course, several disappointments. The military continued to call for an expanded weapons program, often ignoring the sheer inability to produce fissionable materials. Congress was calling for an increase in the American stockpile, not in the hundreds, but in the thousands—a move that could only cause further battles over resources. More subtle, and of more concern to Oppenheimer, was that the atomic bomb would soon be the cornerstone of defense policy. For him, as for others, this change obviously had profound implications.

Uncomfortable perhaps with these developments, but still philosophical, Oppenheimer spent New Year's Eve preparing a letter for the

President, reviewing the progress and difficulties of the previous year. While a great deal had indeed been accomplished, there had also been difficulties which were at least in part a result of the commission's "inheritance." He wrote:

> We very soon learned that in none of the technical areas vital to the common defense and security, nor in those looking toward the beneficial applications of atomic energy, was the state of development adequate.[19]

This state of affairs, as he put it, could be explained in part by the delay until 1946 in formulating a "national policy." The wartime installations, useful as they had been during the war, were not adequate to more contemporary needs. Improved weapons were under development, as was the construction of a new testing ground in the Pacific. Reactor developments were promising, but slow to take place. Oppenheimer predicted that many years would elapse "before our work in this field has the robustness and vigor which its importance justifies."

Major steps had been taken to make radioactive isotopes—a delicate subject for some—available in the United States and abroad. "We see in this a prudent but inspiriting example of the extension to others of the benefits resulting from the release of atomic energy, an extension sure to enrich our knowledge and our control over the forces of nature."

The pervasive effects of secrecy were important to address. The "adverse effects" of secrecy, and of "the inevitable misunderstanding and error which accompany it," were more debilitating at that point than they were at the start of the year. Secrecy could not be maintained at the cost of error and stagnation. "Only by such re-evaluation can the development of atomic energy make its maximum contribution to the securing of peace, and to the perpetuation and growth of the values of our civilization."

11. Threat from the East

The great hopes for peace that had characterized 1945 had been replaced in early 1948 by the ever-increasing fear that the world was again on the verge of war. Soviet aggression in Poland, Czechoslovakia, Hungary, and a half dozen other states made many Americans anticipate that another major confrontation was at hand. This specter haunted the Atomic Energy Commission and its advisers. Despite all of Oppenheimer's eloquent pleas for the peaceful exploration of atomic energy, the overriding concern during the commission's first year had been with weapons.

At the end of the war the United States had two workable weapons: the implosion bomb, utilizing plutonium and a complicated mechanism for detonating it, and the less complex but uranium-hungry gun model. The implosion bomb was by far the more efficient of the two weapons: The great force of imploding waves made assembly of the critical mass much more swift and deadly. Oppenheimer, even as early as May 1945, had told Groves that newer models, utilizing varying interior amounts of tamper and critical mass, were available. The great wartime push had, by necessity, produced two bombs which were hardly production models. Each weapon, in fact, was assembled by hand, sometimes with last-minute adjustments made for differences in lathing or manufacturing. These models could hardly be considered standard stockpile issue. The job had become one of streamlining old weapons and perfecting newer ones. As part of its experimental program, Los Alamos moved its testing site from the desert of New Mexico to the lonely atolls of the South Pacific.[1] Unlike Trinity, almost a year before, Operation Crossroads in July 1946 was covered extensively by the military and the press. The tests involved 200 ships, 42,000 men, and 150 aircraft; over 1,000 newsmen witnessed the event. In April 1948 a second round of tests occurred, code named Project Sandstone.

The weapons detonated in Sandstone represented the first major redesign of nuclear weapons since Fat Man. Three versions were tested, each employing technological innovations. To scientists, perhaps the most striking result of Sandstone was that all three weapons worked. The first weapon alone, for example, had produced a TNT effect of thirty-seven kilotons, more than twice the explosive yield of the Trinity Fat Man. The second weapon, called Yoke, achieved a yield of forty-nine kilotons. To Oppenheimer and the AEC, the results clearly indicated that the existing stockpile of weapons was virtually obsolete. Los Alamos would now be capable of making newly designed weapons utilizing less fissionable material and with greater explosive power, far more powerful than the Nagasaki bomb. Sandstone had indeed introduced a superior weapon into the American arsenal.

The new year had barely begun when Oppenheimer's GAC was once again forced to consider progress in reactor development. It was the major topic of discussion at the February 8, 1948, General Advisory Committee meeting. The problems with centralizing reactor research and development at the Argonne Laboratory outside Chicago were still in part unresolved. The new data associated with the large, powerful reactors under development—materials, heat stress, prolonged use, and safety—presented many unknowns.

At the time Oppenheimer met with the GAC, Edward Teller, now at the Institute for Nuclear Studies at Chicago, was chairing a committee on safeguards on the so-called high-flux reactor. This device was important to the experimental reactor program because of its ability to use nuclear fuel more efficiently than the natural uranium reactor. Teller and his committee were concerned that existing safeguards would not permit such a reactor to operate at more than a thousand watts or so, at least not with the nation's second largest city nearby.

Oppenheimer and his committee members also heard reports on the utilization of reactors for powering aircraft and submarines. Oppenheimer—who months before, with Conant, had discouraged aircraft reactors—once again repeated his objections and obtained a recommendation from the AEC which stalled any major work on such a reactor until a comprehensive study could be completed. Two weeks later the commission agreed with Oppenheimer's recommendation and approved Project Lexington, an aircraft reactor study. Reactors remained on the committee's agenda throughout 1948. There were discussions over possible designs, continuing concerns over reactor safety—one of Teller's reports was believed to have exaggerated the dangers of the Argonne reactor, for example—and finally, a preliminary assessment of the Lexington study, which projected that development of an aircraft reactor would take fifteen years and over one billion dollars.

The final Lexington report, which arrived eight months later, reaffirmed the high cost of developing nuclear-powered aircraft—a cost, as the report put it, that "cannot rationally be expended at the present." The best the GAC could do, much to the anger of the Air Force, was to resume further close study of the possibilities.[2]

The problems with conventional reactor designs were challenging enough. Within each basic reactor, such as the fast-flux or breeder, there were many options for design, such as using neutrons at differing levels of energy or of utilizing different moderating materials. More difficult to understand, at least from Oppenheimer's point of view, was the commission's hesitancy and indecision; regularly, the alternatives were presented to the AEC for a decision. More often than not, the commission seemed to hesitate. Oppenheimer, Fermi, and others on the GAC were increasingly appalled by the lack of progress. There appeared to be a lack of spirit, or zeal perhaps, among scientists and administrators alike. The spirit of the late 1930s and early 1940s was gone; in its place there seemed to be a general feeling of being oppressed by the bureaucracy and by a commission that was concerned only with weapons.

There were other problems as well, some of which helped to explain the difficulties faced by the commission in making decisions. The Joint Committee on Atomic Energy continued to press for reports of progress and made a barrage of requests for supplemental funding. There were also the never-ending complaints that security was too lax within the commission. General Groves, who was now head of the Armed Forces Special Weapons Project, found it difficult not to offer advice on weapons and on policy. Even Oppenheimer, who was fond of the General, found Groves's meddling more than he could take. In February he told Lilienthal that the time had come to get rid of Groves. Oppenheimer forced a meeting with Secretary of the Army James Royal and Secretary of War Forrestal to press the point. They agreed and eventually named Kenneth Nichols to assume Oppenheimer's old mentor's position.[3]

Oppenheimer took time in late February to participate in the Vanuxem Lecture Series at Princeton University. Not surprisingly, he chose to make recent developments in atomic physics the subject of his talks. It was a grand gathering; Niels Bohr attended, as well as Albert Einstein, who was fascinated with Oppenheimer's description of the new universe. Lilienthal, who attended and represented the AEC, saw the venerable Einstein chuckle as Oppenheimer described neutrons as "those creatures." Once again, Oppenheimer had captivated his audience with his special sense of the beauty of the physical universe. He was, even amid the somber politics of Washington, still a showman and a visionary.

In March 1948 the commission received word through Walter Zinn, the AEC's chief reactor authority, that the British were pressing forward, admittedly on a limited basis, with the production of atomic weapons. The British reactor development plan emphasized the production of plutonium, the key ingredient in fission weapons. This announcement did little to ease the difficulties that already existed between the United States, Canada, and Great Britain over cooperative efforts in atomic energy. Despite the close wartime ties, the postwar world and the passage of the Atomic Energy Act had clearly changed the American position on the issue of sharing information. Many members of the military, and Strauss as an AEC commissioner, felt that British possession of weapons was not in the best interests of the United States. Britain's proximity to mainland Europe as a battleground could mean that the Soviets could quite possibly take possession of the Isles and whatever weapons Britain had. The situation was further complicated by American dependence on British uranium ore reserves in South Africa and in Canada. Without this ore, the United States could not meet the production levels set for producing U 235 and Pu 239. The Canadians had only a limited interest in weapons; they were, however, interested in reactors. Since 1948 the United States and Great Britain had acted under a modus vivendi, agreeing that some limited exchange of information would occur between nations and that the U.S. would not use an atomic weapon without British consent.*

Oppenheimer was invited to participate in a review of Anglo-American cooperation when he was asked to chair a two-day meeting at Princeton involving representatives from the Departments of State and Defense and the commission. Originally the meetings were intended to be a small working group, but by July 24 it had grown to include George Kennan, R. Gordon Arneson, and George Butler from the State Department; Wilson, Volpe, Lilienthal, and Conant from the commission; and Generals Lauris Norstad and Nichols from the Department of Defense. Locked away in a safe building at Princeton, the discussions presented the belief that helping the British with atomic energy would not aid the Russians and might prevent the British from wasting their scientific and economic resources. This spirit seemed to suggest that a stronger program of cooperation might be encouraged. The day ended with dinner at Oppenheimer's house on campus. Conversations the next day were equally noncontroversial. There was agreement that it was foolish to try to block British efforts. Instead, a closer coordination of programs among all three nations—Canada included—inevitably meant a stronger defense. The meeting was even more remarkable for the support offered by Norstad and Nichols.

During the evening Oppenheimer was able to host a reunion of sorts with his colleagues on the State Department's board of consultants: Lilienthal, Winne, Bernard, Thomas, and Wilson were there. Oppenheimer launched into a subtle exploration of the popular argument that the

---

*This delicate relationship was further jarred by what became known as the "Cyril Smith" incident. Smith, a chemist and Los Alamos alumnus, was scheduled for a trip to England. James Fisk, director of research for the AEC, heard of Smith's visit and permitted him to stop at Harwell, the British reactor site, to discuss plutonium metallurgy—a topic of interest to reactor development as much as to weapons. With Smith en route, Strauss heard of the projected visit and adamantly objected. The AEC contacted Smith just in time and ordered him to cancel his meetings with no explanation. The incident hardly helped Anglo-American relations.

atomic bomb was "just another weapon." The weakness in that argument, he offered, lay in a failure to determine just how and why such a weapon would be used. The atomic bomb, he argued, was far different and far more dangerous than conventional weapons.

Lilienthal thought the meetings were convivial but without much substance. He did nevertheless enjoy the informal atmosphere and conversations in Oppenheimer's home. He was particularly touched and amused by an incident involving Oppenheimer's young son, Peter. Apparently, years before, Kitty Oppenheimer had made an electric game for Peter consisting of lights, buzzers, and switches, called "the gimmick." On the night of the meeting, Peter sat on the floor trying but failing to make it work. Kitty came out of the kitchen to help, but had no success either. She returned to the kitchen, and Robert sat on the floor and began to fool with the wiring; he had his ubiquitous cigarette with him. Young Peter rushed into the kitchen and in a not-so-quiet voice asked: "Mama, is it all right to let Daddy work the gimmick?"[4]

A week later the AEC commissioners discussed the results of the Princeton meeting. Strauss reiterated his objections to the further exchange of information with the British, at least for the period during which the matter of appropriate policy was still under discussion at the State Department. No weapons data could be made available, he argued, until there was an agreement on stockpiles and plutonium production. Lilienthal took the discussions and Strauss's objections to the State Department. The policy that eventually evolved reflected America's dominance of atomic energy: Reactors and weapons laboratories were to be located in the United States and Canada to the extent possible; Great Britain and Canada should consume no more than 10 percent of the supply of uranium ore for the next five years. While Strauss continued his objections, Truman eventually approved the proposals on April 4, 1949. The real test would come through approval in Congress.

The British were not so easily persuaded to accept the American plan for cooperation. Technically, they knew how to make weapons. Their scientists had, after all, been at Los Alamos during the war and had recently participated in the Sandstone tests. Months passed until the British offered counterproposals: They were willing to accept a "completely integrated" program involving Canada, the United States, and themselves, but also wanted two production reactors, a low-level gaseous-diffusion plant, and a system whereby they would be allowed to keep atomic weapons in Great Britain according to a formula to be worked out. Their proposal came at the end of December 1949. The timing, however, was unfortunate.

On November 1, 1949, the commission received word from the FBI that the British government was exploring a case involving atomic espionage. Three months later to the day, the AEC again received information from the FBI that the British had a confession from Klaus Fuchs, a member of the Harwell reactor group. Fuchs had been at Los Alamos during the war and, as a member of the British team, had been privy to the whole range of fission developments. He was in a position to give critical information to the Soviets on basic nuclear reactions, weapons design, and even the laboratory's preliminary thinking on thermonuclear weapons. Fuchs, who had passed information to the Soviets since the early 1940s, had done so in a spirit of assisting socialism and not for personal gain. The damage, however, to Anglo-American relations was severe. No significant working relationship was to emerge between the two countries. America would continue as the dominant leader; Britain would struggle along as best it could.

Spies and Communist infiltration into the government were popular issues both in the press and in Congress in 1949. Senator Bourke Hickenlooper, chairman of the Joint Committee on Atomic Energy, expressed his continuing concern that the commission was not taking enough steps to protect America's vital atomic secrets. The Joint Committee's interest in security was matched, although with less élan, by the House Un-American Activities Commission, led by Congressman J. Parnell Thomas. One target of the committee was a purported Communist cell at the Radiation Laboratory at Berkeley.

Oppenheimer was called before the House Un-American Activities Committee on June 7, 1949. The meeting was supposed to be in executive session, although Oppenheimer's testimony leaked out in a matter of days. The room itself seemed designed to intimidate witnesses; the members of the committee and their staff sat on a raised platform that ran in a semicircle around the witness table. Oppenheimer had been called to provide information on certain individuals who had been employed by the Radiation Laboratory. Some of the individuals under investigation by the committee were Rossi Lomanitz, David Bohm, Bernard Peters, and Joseph Weinberg—all men Oppenheimer knew from teaching or war days. Oppenheimer was accompanied by Joseph Volpe, the AEC's general counsel, who sat next to him at the witness table.

Early questioning, led by Frank S. Tavenner, Jr., of the committee staff, was rather light in substance. Oppenheimer was asked about his knowledge of the alleged Communist cell at the Radiation Laboratory and about men like Lomanitz and Weinberg. Asked how he knew that Bernard Peters was once a member of the Communist party in Germany, Oppenheimer replied that it was a well-known fact, and for that matter that "he [Peters] told me." He was then quizzed about Eltenton and Chevalier. Oppenheimer repeated the story of the kitchen conversation. There was surprisingly little exploration of the event until later in the morning, when Congressman Harold Velde asked Oppenheimer if he had ever reported the incident to security officials. Oppenheimer replied: "I did, first to the security officers at Berkeley; second, to Colonel Landsdale; and third, to General Groves." He did not mention, however, the delay in reporting the incident, nor the discrepancies in his various accounts. Oppenheimer was finally asked about his brother, Frank. To the best of his knowledge, he said, Frank was not currently a member of the Communist party. But asked if he had been, Robert replied, somewhat to the surprise of the committee:

> I ask you not to press these questions about my brother. If they are important to you, you can ask him. I will answer, if asked, but I beg you not to ask me these questions.[5]

The committee backed off; the question was withdrawn. The session ended, in fact, when Congressman Richard Nixon expressed "appreciation" for Oppenheimer's work and for his role in the nation's atomic energy program. With that, all members of the committee came down to shake his hand. For the moment at least, a crisis created by his past had been forestalled.

Several days later, after Bernard Peters testified, he stopped in Princeton to see his former teacher. Oppenheimer assured Peters that he had not said anything injurious. Within days the testimony of both men leaked out, and Oppenheimer was quoted as calling Peters "quite Red." Peters had denied membership in the Communist party during the hearings. Oppenheimer then received letters from Ed Condon, Bethe, Victor Weisskopf, and his brother, Frank, disapproving of his testimony. He chose to recant. In a letter to another newspaper—the Rochester *Democrat-Chronicle*—he cited Peters's denial before the committee and offered his apologies for anything that might have damaged the young scientist's career. Some saw this merely as evidence of Oppenheimer's susceptibility to influence.[6]

On June 14, Frank Oppenheimer and his wife, Jackie, appeared before the House Un-American Activities Committee. News of Frank's party membership in the 1930s had broken to the press in July 1947. At first, contacted by a newspaperman at 1:30 A.M., Frank denied ever having been a member of the Communist party. Later he corrected his story, but not without creating a bad impression.

The environment was far less friendly for Frank than it had been for his brother. Frank indicated he had joined the party in 1937 by sending in a newspaper coupon and had dropped his membership in 1941. He had not, he admitted, revealed his membership to wartime security officers. The real contest came when Frank was asked if he knew certain individuals and knew them to be members of the Communist party. He replied again and again that he would not answer questions about affiliation; these individuals, he insisted, could be asked directly about their pasts. His wife, Jackie, testified separately, but also refused to answer questions about alleged party affiliations. Later in the day, Frank Oppenheimer learned from a newspaper reporter that his resignation had been accepted by the University of Minnesota.

Just a few weeks later, on July 7, Robert and Kitty Oppenheimer spent the day with Haakron and Barbara Chevalier at Stimson Beach, California. They met again in August, this time only with Chevalier, and then spent the night alone in Chevalier's cabin. Chevalier found Oppenheimer warm and friendly, but physically pale and emaciated. It seemed to Chevalier, at least, that Oppenheimer was carrying some great burden with him.[7]

In mid-1948, Lilienthal was forced to turn his attention to the problems of renomination. Under the Atomic Energy Act, the five commissioners served for one full year before switching to a system that staggered the terms of individual commissioners over a period of five years so that only one person resigned and one person was nominated each year. In Congress the most objectionable of the present commissioners was Lilienthal, openly disliked by Hickenlooper and Taft. Truman, for reasons of his own, did not choose to consult with Congress before he announced he would nominate each commissioner again under the staggered plan. Hickenlooper was outraged at not being consulted; he was particularly disturbed at the renomination of Lilienthal. In a compromise, the Senator offered to extend the terms of the existing commissioners by two years. He even took his plan to a meeting with Compton, Bush, Rabi, DuBridge, and Oppenheimer on April 28. The scientists were firmly in favor of the President's renomination plan, rather than a mere extension of terms. Under the circumstances, however, it was clear that such a proposal would only be tied up in bitter debates in Congress; they had to give in to political pressures. Oppenheimer and the others drafted letters of support for the Hickenlooper plan. Oppenheimer called it a "week of idiocy."[8] His letter to Truman reluctantly supported Hickenlooper:

> I have become convinced that what the Commission most needs is a certain measure of stability and of reassurance, that without these it will have neither the authority nor the confidence to establish sound policy, to put it into execution, and to take and respond to the inevitable criticism which those responsible for an undertaking such as this must expect and will always meet. . . . I write to you in this as one who deeply shares your hopes and concern, and who has been close enough to the work in atomic energy to have a firm opinion.[9]

Despite grumblings in the Senate, the body passed the amendment and Truman signed it on July 3. The commission would now serve two more years.

The debate on extending the terms of the commissioners coincided with the June 4, 1948, meeting of the General Advisory Committee. There were several important topics to be covered, including progress on the thermonuclear weapon, custody of weapons, and the organizational difficulties of the commission itself. In his report to Lilienthal, Oppenheimer wrote:

> Of the various models of such weapons [thermonuclear] . . . one and only one appears to be capable of fairly rapid development; this is the so-called Booster. . . . With the scope of effort now available, the other weapons are at best in the remote future; and in the absence of clear, well-defined, and over-riding military requirements therefore, and of an increase in the personnel available for their development, scheduled and active work upon them hardly appears practicable.

The GAC therefore recommended the Booster, which the committee believed might be ready for a test in two or three years.

The matter of custody of atomic weapons was less clear. The GAC did not believe it was in a position to rule on who should have possession of weapons. This matter of "policy" was an important one, wrote Oppenheimer.[10]

On the question of the commission's organization, however, the GAC had much to say. Oppenheimer told Rowe, Conant, and DuBridge to prepare a report for the commissioners reflecting the committee's review. Oppenheimer himself was to present the report for the GAC to the commission the following day. Although it was not personal in nature, it was critical of the commission and its management.

Oppenheimer, with the GAC assembled, addressed the commission, using his most diplomatic style. The commission had failed to tackle the difficult problems of security, reactor development, and the laboratories. Other members of the scientific community were also concerned. The GAC was unanimous in its recommendations. At the heart of the problem was the failure to use the advice of the GAC effectively. Because decentralization was not working, Oppenheimer called instead for five key positions within the AEC: general manager and directors of weapons, reactors, research, and production. The four directors would have line responsibility. He said:

> We are afraid we can be of little use to the Commission under the present organization. We despair of progress in the reactor program and see further difficulty even in the areas of weapons and production unless a reorganization takes place.[11]

Oppenheimer followed his report with a letter to Lilienthal on June 18. Suspecting that the commission would now be on the defensive, Oppenheimer suggested that the unanimity of the report by the GAC was evidence of how strongly nine knowledgeable men felt about the matter; and if the GAC felt so strongly, was it not reasonable to assume that much of the outside scientific community felt the same way? Lilienthal had mixed feelings; there were successful organizations using the AEC administrative model, but still, there was so much to consider regarding the lack of progress in many areas. On June 25, Oppenheimer called Lilienthal long-distance from California to apologize for the "great sorrow" caused by his committee's report; the GAC was aware, he suggested, of the difficult environment in which Lilienthal and the other commissioners were forced to make decisions. It was, Oppenheimer explained, a case of withholding comment for so long that when they finally spoke, "what bubbled out" tended to be not a balanced appraisal, but only the criticisms. Oppenheimer emphasized that the GAC had "great confidence and affection" for the commission, but what they had said was still true.[12]

The commission eventually acted on the criticism. On August 5, Carroll Wilson issued an announcement of the new organization—still far from complete, but with major components now in place. Fisk retained responsibility for research; reactor development, now divorced from research, was to go to an as yet unnamed director; production would go to Walter Williams; and weapons, or military applications, would go to McCormack. Carlton Shugg was made deputy general manager.

In September 1948, Oppenheimer made his first trip back to Europe in twenty years. He and Kitty attended the Solvay Conference for Physics in Brussels. While ostensibly giving a talk on electron theory, he was determined to assess European opinion toward the American atomic effort. What he discovered was no surprise; many of his European colleagues believed the United States was unnecessarily concerned with security and with keeping the secret of atomic energy—whether related to weapons or not—as a purely American secret.

As scientist, preeminent adviser on nuclear physics, and individual, Oppenheimer was invited to join, sponsor, or direct numerous causes representing both scientific and social programs. His credentials for 1948 were impressive: In addition to his membership on the GAC, the Research and Development Board, and the General Board of the Navy Department, he was a member of the council of the National Academy of Sciences, the Social Science Research Council, New York Academy of Sciences, advisory committee to the New York University Institute for Mathematics and Mechanics, and chairman of the board of sponsors of the *Bulletin of the Atomic Scientists.* He served, more humbly perhaps, as a member of Miss Fine's School's board of trustees, the S. Kisada memorial scholarship committee, and the Nassau Club in Princeton. Adding to his honors of the year before was another honorary doctorate from the University of California at Berkeley, and the King's Medal for Service in the Cause of Freedom from the British Government.

The commission—and especially its chairman, David Lilienthal—received a boost on November 3 when Harry Truman was reelected to his first full term as President of the United States. The election, plus Democratic House and Senate victories, now meant that membership and leadership on the Joint Committee on Atomic Energy would shift.* Brien McMahon, for example, would replace Hickenlooper as chairman.

The new leadership in Congress had hardly taken control when, in early 1949, a series of events took place which had profound implications for the commission and for Robert Oppenheimer. The fifth semiannual report by the AEC to Congress was delivered amid anger from conservative legislators on the Joint Committee about the information that had been released in the report. While the document was unclassified by law, some felt that the data and photographs were in violation. Pictures of an accelerator, for instance, were offered as examples of Lilienthal's carelessness. Lilienthal tried patiently to explain that no information in the report was classified; indeed, many of the photographs had been published elsewhere. Oppenheimer and his fellow committee members made a special trip to the Hill to state their satisfaction with the report. Subtly, Oppenheimer tried to make a case for releasing more information, not less. Wryly he suggested that there were, of course, difficulties in making information available to others, but he wondered if even the United States' own military had enough information to devise adequate war plans?[13]

In the midst of the arguments over the semiannual report, Waymack and Bacher resigned from the commission and were replaced by Gordon E. Dean, a professor of law at the University of Southern California, and Henry DeWolf Smyth, author of the 1945 Smyth Report. Their nomination hearings spilled over into a battle over Frank P. Graham, president of the University of North Carolina and head of the Oak Ridge Institute of Nuclear Studies. In his role as director, Graham was required to have a security clearance; eventually he was issued one by the AEC. Fulton Lewis, the radio news commentator, stated publicly that Graham had once been a member of some organizations now alleged to be Communist-infiltrated. This charge was picked up by the Joint Committee, only adding to the continuing attacks that the AEC was careless in its employment

*The Democratic victories were particularly important to Truman in terms of support for his legislation; the previous 80th Congress, for example, had overridden his veto of the Taft-Hartley Act.

practices. Charges of carelessness always touched a sensitive nerve. Oppenheimer was one case that the committee quite clearly hoped would not fall into public light.

On February 7, 1949, employees at the Argonne Laboratory discovered that a bottle containing 289 grams of uranium was missing from a security vault. Suspecting that this was due to carelessness by the laboratory, the institution did not report the loss to AEC officials until a month and a half later. On April 27 the AEC finally decided to notify Senator McMahon. Inevitably, the missing uranium made the news on May 17. Despite a rigorous check, which turned up all but four grams, Senator Hickenlooper called for Lilienthal's resignation and charged the AEC with "incredible mismanagement." The series of "crises" that had befallen the commission were severe enough for some members of the committee to call for a hearing on the matter.

The hearings had a good deal of political value for some; Hickenlooper, for example, was up for reelection in November. McMahon's role as chairman of the Joint Committee and as guardian of the nation's atomic energy program was indirectly under attack. The hearings were set for May 26. Lilienthal responded with a letter "welcoming" the investigation; he felt it would prove that the leadership and management they had provided had been exemplary. McMahon opened the hearings with somber words:

> We meet this morning as a result of charges against the Atomic Energy Commission and numerous congressional demands that the Chairman of the Commission be removed from office. . . . I need not emphasize that we are dealing with matters of grave import. This would seem to be a good time for an impartial and independent committee reevaluation of the nation's atomic energy project.[14]

Lilienthal led the witnesses with a prepared statement on the achievements of the commission. Lewis Strauss gave testimony on June 8 and 9, largely focusing on his objections to the commission's decision to make radioactive isotopes available to foreign countries. The original focus of the hearings—the management of the commission—quickly broadened into a rambling consideration of atomic energy topics. The notion of isotopes and their availability, for example, became one of the major themes of discussion during the committee's investigations.

Oppenheimer spoke on June 13, with most of the Joint Committee and with all of the AEC commissioners in attendance. The first substantive question directed at Oppenheimer concerned isotopes. He was unequivocal: Twice the General Advisory Committee had discussed making isotopes available and twice it had recommended to the commission that such a program be undertaken. The GAC had even criticized the commission for its conservative stance. As well, at no time had the GAC—or the commission, for that matter—recommended making isotopes available that could be used in fission (e.g., in a weapon); isotopes were to be available to researchers working in medicine, biology, physics, chemistry, and metallurgy. To Hickenlooper's prodding he added:

> No one can force me to say that you cannot use these isotopes for atomic energy. You can use a shovel for atomic energy; in fact you do. You can use a bottle of beer for atomic energy; in fact you do.

Out of approximately six thousand shipments of isotopes, not one was used for military or defense purposes in this country. Isotopes were initially made available for research purposes, not for military ones; if they were to be used in a military capacity, Oppenheimer suspected that the United States would be in a position to know this well in advance because of the country's level of scientific understanding. There was a long chain between research and military purpose, he argued, and for a moment there was a humorous exchange in the otherwise lugubrious proceedings:

Senator Milikan: There is a long chain between the chicken salad and the gleam in the eyes of the rooster, but they all have relation with one another.

Oppenheimer: You could not be more right, Senator.

Hickenlooper wasn't prepared to give up the argument yet; he continued to press Oppenheimer on the meaning of the phrase "atomic energy" and the specific provisions within the Atomic Energy Act that prevented the "exchange of atomic energy information" with other nations for industrial purposes. The term "atomic energy" had been construed to mean all forms of energy released as a result of "nuclear fission or transformation." To Hickenlooper, isotopes meant atomic energy and therefore a forbidden entity.

Other members of the Joint Committee quizzed Oppenheimer, who remained unflappable throughout the proceedings. Senator William Knowland asked him if it was not true that the overall national defense of a country rested on more than secret military development. Oppenheimer replied, playing to his audience:

> My own rating of the importance of isotopes in this broad sense [of national defense] is that they are far less important than electronic devices, but far more important than, let us say, vitamins, somewhere in between.

Many people in the room laughed, but one man did not; several days earlier, Lewis Strauss had made a strong, almost emotional argument for his personal belief that isotopes should not under any circumstances be exported. Whether intentional or not, Oppenheimer's statement only further strained his already poor relationship with Strauss. To observers and colleagues of Oppenheimer, it seemed to be a very expensive performance by the scientist. Whatever his reason, Oppenheimer's harshness with Strauss was an indication of his occasional tendency to be hard and insensitive. No one could fail to notice Strauss angrily leaving the hearings.

Oppenheimer continued his testimony with answers to questions on the relationship between the commission and the General Advisory Committee. Oppenheimer reported that the two groups had a good rapport and occasional differences of view. In fact, there had been no recommendations made to the commission to which the commission was diametrically opposed. For himself, however, Oppenheimer could think of many instances of opposition: the commission's failure to act on reactors, a program of support for independent research, and the like.

Oppenheimer did stress the good condition and quality of staff at Los Alamos:

> I think that it is generally regarded by my colleagues that Los Alamos is the best Federal laboratory and the best laboratory working on a military job that there is in the country.

And regarding the laboratory's work:

> I am very much satisfied. Quite a number of very important improvements in atomic weapon design and atomic weapon manufacture have been worked out. The present program of the laboratory is to carry this further and to get into some new and more difficult things. It is a sound program; it is soundly conceived; and it is going forward full steam ahead. It is not a wartime effort. It is not the kind of 100 percent, everybody-in thing that we had in the war; but we could not expect that. And it is a very, very good laboratory.

Oppenheimer left the hearing pleased with his performance. The investigation would wind down without any remarkable conclusions or insights.* It did, however, serve the purpose of widening the differences between men like Strauss and Oppenheimer and, in general, between those who believed atomic energy should serve national interests above all others and those who believed it should serve humanity.

It is no surprise that these two men had such different perceptions of the meaning of atomic energy. What made the conflict both terrible and fascinating at the same time was that scientists like Oppen-

*On October 12 the Joint Committee voted 9–6, along party lines, that the Hickenlooper charges were without foundation.

heimer were so involved in determining, along with politicians, American military policy. Given their backgrounds and training, these scientists and politicians could easily have rather different understandings of the world and therefore of atomic energy. For Oppenheimer, now, more than ever, it was an exceedingly difficult task to balance his philosophy as a scientist interested in benefiting all mankind, with his politics, as a patriotic American interested in aiding his country. These differences were exacerbated even further by a startling event which occurred in early September.

On September 3, 1949, specially outfitted airplanes picked up telltale signs of radioactive debris in the atmosphere. These airborne units had been created the year before at the insistence of Strauss, who believed that long-range detection of nuclear explosions was a crucial part of American intelligence. The system the AEC created combined data from sonic, seismographic, and air-sampling sources. Radioactive evidence had been picked up by an Air Force weather reconnaissance plane that was flying from Japan to Alaska. At first the filter samples could do no more than suggest a radioactive count that was higher than normal. Two days later, however, newer samples clearly revealed that fission isotopes were present. These isotopes were evidence of either an atomic explosion from a weapon or a reactor of some kind. In order to learn the source—bomb or reactor—the Air Force sent every available plane to the Pacific to gather further air samples.

William Webster, deputy secretary of defense for atomic energy, suggested to the AEC that a panel of experts be gathered to study the results; Carroll Wilson, general AEC manager, agreed. Vannevar Bush would be asked to be chairman.* Robert Oppenheimer, former AEC Commissioner Robert Bacher, Admiral Parsons, members of the Air Force's Long Range Detection System, and a group of British scientists under William Penney comprised the panel. The group met on September 19, nearly two weeks after the Air Force had picked up the first suspect air samples. There was little doubt in anyone's mind that the Soviets had successfully detonated an atomic device. The data analyzed had been collected across a broad geographic area. While it was not yet possible to determine where or precisely when the test had occurred, it was clear that a fission weapon had indeed been detonated. Oppenheimer took the lead in drafting the report: "The origin of the fission products was the explosion of an atomic bomb."[15] The test had most likely occurred on August 29, 1949. Oppenheimer and members of the panel agreed that the public

*Ernest Lawrence remembers Vannevar Bush telling a story that he had been appointed to head the Russian A-bomb panel because the Air Force didn't trust Oppenheimer; Luis Alvarez, recalling the story differently, said that President Truman appointed Bush as chairman because Truman didn't trust Oppenheimer.[16]

should be informed immediately about the Soviet test, which was given the code name Vermont.

Lilienthal was summoned back to Washington from his summer retreat on Martha's Vineyard. When he ran into Oppenheimer at the AEC offices on September 19, the scientist looked drawn and was "frantic." Lilienthal was pressed to quickly inform the public; as Oppenheimer and Bacher said, there were already more than three hundred persons who knew the Soviets had exploded an atomic bomb, and there most certainly would be a leak of some kind soon. An afternoon meeting with Truman on September 20 produced only another stall. The President was reluctant to announce such a serious event during this time of distressing international crises and news from Britain that the pound was soon to be devalued; the news had to wait. Lilienthal returned to brief the commissioners, Oppenheimer, and Bacher. Everyone was disappointed, especially Oppenheimer; this was precisely the sort of "secret" that caused the public to misunderstand atomic energy. To Lilienthal, Oppenheimer nervously said: "We mustn't muff this chance to end the miasma of secrecy. . . . holding a secret where there is no secret." He also confessed that he had been "very surprised" at the Russian success.[17]

Truman finally scheduled a release of the news for Friday, at the weekly meeting of his cabinet. Simultaneously, the news would be released to the press. Oppenheimer, in Washington for the September meeting of the GAC, joined Senator McMahon and members of his Joint Committee for the announcement. The President tried to put the Soviet achievement in perspective. American scientists had known since the end of the war that such an achievement was just a matter of time, and the fact that the Russians now had a bomb only emphasized the need for an international control of nuclear energy. The announcement before the Joint Committee produced shock and anxiety nevertheless. The moment was made even more dramatic by a loud thunderclap outside the Capitol in one of the city's late summer storms.

Oppenheimer left the Joint Committee meeting to return to his session with the General Advisory Committee. There was a consensus that the news would most likely have an important effect on the committee's work. Certainly there would be a public outcry for a renewed emphasis on developing—quickly—larger and more powerful weapons. This in turn would accelerate the burden on the production plants, already pressed for uranium and plutonium. Henry Smyth suggested that the public might now take a greater interest in civil defense. Oppenheimer spoke for all committee members when he expressed the hope that the Russian bomb would only serve to improve America's security policies. One result, for example, might be a better working relationship with the British. Oppenheimer scheduled the next GAC meeting for December, but asked that all members be on call in case something important occurred. He knew well that the news just announced to the public would have far-reaching consequences and would soon involve the committee and the commission in major decisions. He did not, however, realize just how extraordinary these decisions would be nor what price they would exact from him personally.

12. Quantum Leap

By and large, news of the Russian atomic bomb was reported without histrionics. National heroes like Omar Bradley effectively calmed some of the public's reaction by stating that the Soviet achievement was in and of itself not surprising and, in fact, was inevitable. Some of the press reported that the bomb came as much as two years before American intelligence had predicted it. The more important reaction, one hidden from public view, came from within the government itself. Lilienthal tried to reassure members of the Joint Committee that weapons superiority was the first priority of the Atomic Energy Commission. He proposed no new starts, but rather a "speeding up" of production of fissionable materials and an acceleration of work on new weapons design.

McMahon was not so sure that merely accelerating work was enough. A report prepared by McMahon's aide, William L. Borden, called for increased production and enough weapons to bomb both military and industrial targets. Most importantly, the report called for a new all-out effort to develop the thermonuclear bomb. Discussions within the commission had focused for some time on strengthening the Los Alamos effort on hydrogen bombs. Oppenheimer's name inevitably came up as an important source of help, perhaps even as director of a concentrated program to develop such a weapon. Lilienthal had doubts, however. Men of Oppenheimer's stature could not be shoved into a thermonuclear program at the laboratory without straining the entire organization's morale. Oppenheimer, like Fermi and Bethe, could better serve as a consultant.

The thermonuclear weapon itself was still theoretical. The several design principles developed earlier at Los Alamos could be tested in two or three years as part of other weapons tests in the Pacific. Such a weapon, even if successful, might produce the force of a million tons of TNT but would require nothing less than a railroad to deliver it. As part of one design, scientists were presently envisioning an elaborate refrigeration system to supercool isotopic material. In order to achieve the temperatures and controlled environment necessary to "fuse" atoms, a building the size of a small gymnasium would probably be required. The technological problems involved were so immense that the commissioners were hardly comfortable about recommending specific steps for Los Alamos. Strauss favored an all-out effort; others, like Pike, weren't sure.[1] Strauss liked to talk about the United States making a "quantum leap" in weapons development; he became a champion of the new device. Fearing that there would be no action within the commission—he had been a minority before—he contemplated ways to bring the superbomb, as the thermonuclear weapon was called, to the attention of the President. In a letter written on October 5, 1949, he urged the commission to seek the advice of the General Advisory Committee. Strauss wanted an "intensive effort" comparable to the Manhattan Project and was not without allies.[2] The military was interested. McMahon and his Joint Committee showed even greater interest now that the Russians had their own atomic bomb. Edward Teller was a strong advocate of the thermonuclear program; it had been his passion at Los Alamos. Ernest Lawrence and Luis Alvarez were two others who favored rapid development of the weapon.

Lawrence and Alvarez decided to take their arguments directly to Washington. On October 7 both men stopped at Los Alamos en route from California to talk with Edward Teller. George Gamov, Stanislaw Ulam, and John Manley, who was representing Norris Bradbury,* were also present. Teller reported that the theoretical work was by no means done, but that it offered several promising leads. Ulam was hard at work on a mathematical theory to describe the interactions of elements during the thermonuclear process; Teller already had a series of experiments on the drawing boards for the proposed Pacific tests in 1951. Later that night, at the Albuquerque Hilton Hotel, Teller urged his colleagues to push the development of a reactor that could produce large quantities of tritium. Lawrence and Alvarez arrived in Washington in the midst of a storm for visits with General McCormack, members of the commission, and Pitzer, the AEC's director of research. Over lunch with McMahon and Congressman Carl Hinshaw, they explained their ideas and successfully generated a considerable amount of enthusiasm. McMahon told Lawrence to call him if they experienced any difficulty with their plans for the tritium reactors. Lawrence was delighted; he wanted the reactor located at Berkeley under his direction.

On Monday, October 10, Lawrence and Alvarez met with members of the commission, but Lilienthal appeared disinterested. In his diary Lilienthal confessed that he found interest in this weapon "distasteful." Apparently he found it so distasteful that during the conversation he turned his chair around and faced the window.[3] The meeting ended without an endorsement. The final stop for Lawrence and Alvarez was a meeting with Isador Rabi in New York. Rabi, a long-time friend of Oppenheimer's, agreed that the Russian success had changed the context of America's nuclear work and was glad that America's "first team" was going back to work.[4]

When Oppenheimer learned of their visits, he was displeased;

---

*Teller, excited by the prospect of talking with Lawrence and Alvarez about his pet project, failed to observe protocol and did not notify Bradbury of the visit.

Lawrence and Alvarez had taken on the role, in his words, of being "promoters" of the new weapon. He especially did not like the fact that they had conducted a meeting with the military and with the chairman of the Joint Committee *before* meeting with the commission. Moreover, the two men seemed to speak for a growing group of scientists in favor of a "crash program" to develop the thermonuclear weapon.

At Los Alamos, scientists were surprised by the news of the Russian success. John Manley, for example, pointed out that the tacit understanding among his colleagues had been that the Russians would not have a weapon in 1952. On October 13, Edward Teller prepared a long memorandum for members of the laboratory's Technical Council. For Teller, peaceful settlement with the Russians would be possible only if the United States possessed "overwhelming superiority." The solution, he felt, to the sudden Russian accomplishment was rapid development of the superbomb. "It seems quite possible that the bottleneck in making a superbomb will be lack of theoretical knowledge and lack of technical know-how." This view, however, was not held by Norris Bradbury, among others. John Manley believed that "an acceleration of the present program may be the best protection of our position for the short-term." The laboratory's program could not jeopardize future success by concentrating on short-range objectives. "For this reason it would be unwise to choose a *single* course of action for the whole laboratory effort [emphasis added]." Manley did not believe Los Alamos should abandon all of its programs simply to concentrate on the thermonuclear bomb. "A vigorous effort in all departments by this country could possibly result in a test by 1951."[5]

At Lilienthal's urging, Oppenheimer called a special meeting of the General Advisory Committee for October 30. There had been a definite attitude change in Washington which now favored an expansive program to reassert American weapons dominance. Lilienthal hoped to obtain some sense of perspective and clarity with his committee of experts. All but Seaborg, who was in Sweden, would be able to attend. Oppenheimer also invited several friends to Princeton for special talks a week earlier, hoping to benefit from their objective opinions. Word of Oppenheimer's meeting spread quickly. A confidential telegram was sent by McCormack to Los Alamos: "You can be sure," he wired, "that the Teller-Lawrence approach will be high on the agenda."[6]

In an October 14 letter to Lilienthal, Oppenheimer confirmed the dates of the meeting and explained that while he understood the urgency of the situation, the end of the month was the only time that all members, except Seaborg, could attend. "I have, however, made arrangements to obtain from him [Seaborg] in writing, and, if necessary, consultation, his views on the subjects of the meeting."[7]

On October 20, Norris Bradbury and John Manley arrived from

Los Alamos; John von Neumann, whose work on computers promised to accelerate the massive mathematical calculations needed for thermonuclear work, was already a member of the faculty at the Institute for Advanced Studies at Princeton and planned to attend. The next day Hans Bethe came from Cornell and Teller from Chicago; Teller hoped to use the meeting to present his views and to urge Bethe to join the effort at Los Alamos.

The meeting on October 20 was sobering. Both Bradbury and Manley gave a straightforward report on the work thus far completed at the laboratory. While there were several new theoretical insights into the superbomb, there was no clear course of action to propose. Bradbury indicated that progress was, at this stage, largely dependent upon completion of a variety of mathematical programs—calculations that would require the assistance of computers. Support among the staff, he reported, ranged from urging an all-out effort to following the present plan of research and development.

Bradbury could sense that he and Oppenheimer were drifting apart philosophically on the issue of the H-bomb. Bradbury found it impossible to stop thinking about the superbomb and, in that sense, impossible to stop work on it. "Oppenheimer thought I was bellicose; I thought him naive."[8]

The following day Oppenheimer drafted a letter to James Conant in which he summarized his own views, a letter which would, incidentally, have great importance five years later. Addressing Conant casually as "Dear Uncle Jim," Oppenheimer indicated that he wanted his colleagues to have "one bit of background" as preparation for the upcoming GAC meeting. "The Super," he wrote, "is not very different from what it was when we first spoke of it more than 7 years ago: a weapon of unknown design, cost, deliverability and military value." Because of the recent change of opinions regarding the weapon, encouraged in part by Lawrence and Teller, the Joint Committee had been urged to believe that "We must have a Super, and we must have it fast." A congressional subcommittee, in fact, was heading to Los Alamos and Berkeley to hold emergency meetings on the super. What concerned Oppenheimer, however, was not the technical problems per se:

> I am not sure that the miserable thing will work, nor that it can be gotten to a target except by ox cart. It seems likely to me even further to worsen the unbalance of our present war plans. What does worry me is that this thing appears to have caught the imagination, both of the congressional and of military people, as the answer to the problem posed by the Russian advance.[9]

Oppenheimer then added strong language, suggesting perhaps that others might even read the letter:

> It would be folly to oppose the exploration of this weapon. *We have always known it had to be done*; and it does have to be done, though it appears to be singularly proof against any form of experimental approach. But that we become committed to it as the way to save the country and the peace appears to me full of dangers.[10] [Emphasis added]

This was hardly the sort of information men like Teller and Strauss wanted to hear from the chairman of the General Advisory Committee. For its purposes, the commission wanted to know if present programs or program components should be altered or stopped in order to meet new defense requirements. Should, for example, the AEC authorize the start of a major program on the super even if it proved to be a detriment, for example, to present reactor development? In a letter to Oppenheimer, Acting Chairman Pike asked the GAC bluntly if a hydrogen bomb could in fact be built, and if so, what role would it play as part of America's defense system, compared to conventional fission weapons? He also asked for the GAC's opinion on an expansion of current reactor programs which would include those that could produce tritium.

Glenn Seaborg, who would not be able to attend the emergency meeting, drafted a letter to Oppenheimer on October 14 stating his impressions "for what they may be worth. . . ." Indicating that the United States might already be behind in the development of a thermonuclear weapon, Seaborg noted:

> Apparently this possibility has begun to bother very seriously a number of people out here [Lawrence, for example], several of whom came to this point of view independently. Although I deplore the prospects of our country putting a tremendous effort into this, I must confess that I have been unable to come to the conclusion that we should not. My present feeling would perhaps be best summarized by saying that I would have to hear some good arguments before I could take on sufficient courage to recommend not going toward such a program.[11]

"I have been unable to come to the conclusion that we should not." Was that support or not? Seaborg was clearer in endorsing Lawrence's reactor project, as it did not interfere with any other efforts then underway at the AEC. He also believed that if there was less secrecy the work might proceed at a faster pace. While Seaborg did not seem to completely reject the idea of a super, he failed to give it outright support.

The GAC meeting began October 28 with discussions on the Soviet Union and the role of atomic energy in foreign policy. Discussions on the thermonuclear weapon began the next day. General Omar Bradley and the chairman of the Joint Chiefs of Staff, joined the meeting, as did

Robert LeBaron, chairman of the Military Liaison Committee. The GAC seemed split on what to do. Conant was against the idea of a crash program and so was Rowe. Oppenheimer did not voice an opinion, but Lilienthal sensed that he too opposed it. Rabi felt that the decision to make the super would be made; his question was who was willing to join in it. Fermi believed that an all-out program would damage the current fission development program.[12] The military obviously favored the weapon, although Bradley believed that the advantage of such a weapon—one a thousand times the size of Hiroshima—was largely psychological.[13]

The meeting broke for lunch, and Oppenheimer joined Alvarez and Serber. Alvarez was shocked to learn that Oppenheimer was not in favor of building the hydrogen bomb; as far as Alvarez knew it was the first time Oppenheimer had ever spoken out on the subject. His reasoning, as Alvarez remembered, "was that if we built a hydrogen bomb, then Russia would build a hydrogen bomb"; in other words, if we didn't, they wouldn't.[14] Alvarez was also surprised to hear that Serber too had changed his mind. It was clear to the Californian that the thermonuclear program was not something that "the top man in the scientific department of the AEC" wanted.

The meeting continued to educate the committee and the commissioners; there were intelligence briefings on Soviet activities, further elaborations on the super, and a gradual emergence of views. On Sunday, Oppenheimer delivered a summary report to the commissioners. It was also decided that each GAC member would refrain from making public statements for one week in order to guarantee the commission freedom to consider all the alternatives. Lilienthal saw the change in views happen overnight. He realized that as of Saturday four members, which was less than half of the committee, were going to vote in favor of an all-out program on the super. By Sunday they were all opposed to it.[15] The GAC discussions had been closed to Lilienthal and everyone but members of the committee. Oppenheimer spoke out, but did not seek to dominate the frank arguments. Years later, no participant in the discussions could remember any pressure from Oppenheimer.

A formal written report was drafted that afternoon by Oppenheimer and Manley; it contained the majority and minority reports. The committee decided that the unique nature of the reports necessitated a top secret classification. The report itself was in three parts. The first dealt with some general considerations on production of materials and on the use of fission weapons for tactical use. The second and more critical part dealt with the so-called superbomb. The third spoke to the differences in approach to the problem as perceived by the GAC members.

Regarding production, the report recommended exploring thoroughly which uranium- or plutonium-producing capacities were not being fully utilized and what methods could be used to accelerate their productivity. Atomic bombs could be used more extensively for tactical purposes, but these weapons needed to be designed to fit the carrier, whether it was an airplane or the tip of a missile. Small fission weapons, for example, would be specifically designed and built to fit the new ground-to-air missiles that were under development by the armed forces. They supported neutron-producing reactors, such as those advocated by Lawrence. This reactor would be used for the generation of U 233,* radiological warfare agents, a mechanism for testing reactor components, the conversion of U 235 to plutonium, a secondary facility for making polonium (used in initiators†), for the production of tritium for boosters—a more powerful weapons design, and for superbombs.

The booster program was an alternative of sorts to the super, or hydrogen bomb. It employed tritium to obtain certain thermonuclear conditions, which in turn would produce a more powerful explosion than simple fission weapons. A standard fission bomb, however, would still be necessary to provide the high temperatures needed for ignition. The so-called classic superbomb was a thermonuclear weapon which would use a fission bomb to ignite tritium, which then would ignite deuterium. Theoretically, this weapon could be made infinitely powerful simply by adding larger amounts of deuterium as a fuel. Part I of the report favored the booster program but deplored the super:

> With regard to the use of tritium in the superbomb, it is our unanimous hope that this will not prove necessary. It is the opinion of the majority that the super program itself should not be undertaken and that the Commission and its contractors understand that construction of neutron producing reactors is not intended as a step in the super program.[16]

Part II of the report, even more strongly worded, opposed the superbomb program. "No member of the Committee was willing to endorse this proposal [to pursue a high priority push on the Super]." The reason for this view was largely technical. Not only would a substantial amount of tritium be necessary in each weapon, but many theoretical and engineering obstacles needed to be overcome. There were questions over whether or not scientists could even begin the elementary ignition process with conventional fission weapons because of the fact that tritium was needed to ignite deuterium. Only actual tests of various weapon devices would prove or disprove the workability of the design. "An imaginative and concerted attack," the report read, "has a better than even chance of producing the weapon within five years."

Beyond these technical problems there was another reason for

*U 233 is another fissionable isotope of uranium.

†The initiator is the source of neutrons in a weapon.

disapproval of the superbomb: Its sheer destructive power was nothing short of awesome. Such a weapon—limited only by the ability of the nation to deliver the weapon—could easily have a destructive and radioactive force "some hundreds of times that of present fission bombs," and a damage-area capacity of "hundreds of square miles." It was no longer a weapon that would be used against only military targets; a substantial portion of the civilian population would be destroyed as well. Superbombs of less destructive power could be made, providing, of course, that the essential triggering mechanism could be made to work. This kind of weapon would not be an economic alternative to fission weapons; after all, the recent Sandstone tests had demonstrated that a more powerful bomb was already available. Oppenheimer wrote:

> If one uses the strict criteria of damage area per dollar and if one accepts the limitations on air carrier capacity likely to obtain in the years immediately ahead, it appears uncertain to us whether the super will be cheaper or more expensive than the fission bomb.

Part III was the most controversial:

> Although the members of the Advisory Committee are not unanimous in their proposals as to what should be done with regard to the super bomb, there are certain elements of unanimity among us. We all hope that by one means or another, the development of these weapons can be avoided. We are all reluctant to see the United States take the initiative in precipitating this development. We are all agreed that it would be wrong at the present time to commit ourselves to an all-out effort toward its development.[17]

Two statements of view were appended to the report: The first statement was signed by Oppenheimer, Conant, Rowe, Smith, Bridges, and Buckley; the second by Fermi and Rabi. The superbomb, they wrote, transcended any potential military advantage and would completely lay waste to its target area. Defense tactics of this sort were actually nothing less than genocide. If the Russians would develop their own superbomb:

> We would reply that our undertaking it [development of the super] will not prove a deterrent to them. Should they use the weapon against us, reprisals by our large stock of atomic bombs would be comparably effective to the use of a Super.[18]

In their statement, Fermi and Rabi agreed and added a philosophical note that "the use of such a weapon cannot be justified on any ethical ground which gives a human being a certain individuality and dignity even if he happens to be a resident of an enemy country."[19] The United States, they argued, must obtain an international agreement with all nations not to develop such a weapon. This strong wording reflected Fermi's personal opinion "that one should try to outlaw the thing before it was born."[20]

Oppenheimer's cover letter to Lilienthal addressed the charge of the emergency meeting: "to consider some aspects of the question of whether the Commission was making all appropriate progress in assuring the common defense and security" of the country. Oppenheimer reviewed each individual consulted and briefly touched on the organization of the report itself. Attached were "certain comments on which the Committee is unanimously agreed." While the unanimity referred to was accurate, it involved only the committee members present; it did not include Glenn Seaborg, who attended none of the meetings. Oppenheimer's only reference to Seaborg was in his cover letter to Lilienthal: "Dr. Seaborg's absence in Europe prevented his attending this meeting." There is no official record in the minutes that Oppenheimer shared Seaborg's October 14 letter with other members of the committee. It will never be known if Seaborg would have agreed or disagreed with the committee if he had attended the October meetings. Lilienthal noted a change in the spirit of the committee over the weekend. Rabi, to Alvarez at least, earlier had seemed to be in favor of the effort, as had Serber. Whatever the case, Oppenheimer did not read the letter into the record. Later, however, he thought he had read it out loud. Cyril Smith, who was present at the meeting, recalled Oppenheimer doing so.[21] In four years, Oppenheimer would be charged with withholding information from his colleagues in order to kill the superbomb program.

Unaware or perhaps unconcerned with the views Seaborg expressed two weeks earlier, Oppenheimer was satisfied with the report. The three-day meeting, fraught with so many possibilities for the delicate position of the nation's future, had produced an intelligent plea for sanity. The United States must exercise the leadership to insure peace, or it would plunge the world into an unparalleled arms race.

Oppenheimer's concern was now for the commission: Would they be able to withstand the mounting pressure from Congress and the military? Would Lilienthal, who looked forward to retirement in a few months, be up to the task of defending the report before its critics? Privately, he may have believed Lilienthal lacked the energy to lead such a battle. To his close friend, Supreme Court Justice Felix Frankfurter, he confessed in December 1949 that Lilienthal was "quite reluctant to subject his major problems to analysis," and was "uninterested in the analysis which others have tried to make for him." Oppenheimer even chose to quote his wife, Kitty, who thought Lilienthal would serve best in a "college or small university."[22] Producing a consensus among eight men in secret in three days was one thing; selling the consensus to a sharply divided and fearful nation was another.

For Lilienthal, it was more than a matter of generating enough personal energy; it was a matter of linking an essentially negative assessment to some greater national policy issue. He met with Acheson on November 1 and indicated his perception that the decision on the super was not one just for the AEC, but really a matter of policy for Acheson and Truman. Moreover, Lilienthal had to combat increasingly strong pressure from Congress. Senator McMahon responded to the GAC report by dismissing it as naive: The Russians, he felt, would inevitably involve the United States in a war. The super was the only defense for the U.S. now that the Soviets had weapons of their own. Teller continued his own campaign. He arrived in Washington for a meeting with McMahon, who told him that the GAC report made him sick. Manley opposed the meeting between the scientist and the senator, feeling it was inappropriate during the delicate deliberations within the AEC. He made a call to Chicago, trying to convince Teller not to come, arguing that it was impolitic. But Teller refused and made the trip anyway.[23] Four days after the GAC meeting, the commissioners met to discuss the report.

Strauss remained convinced that the United States needed the superbomb. He thought it was inconsistent for the nation to develop larger and more destructive fission weapons and yet shy away from the super. Smyth believed the military value of the new weapon was questionable, but seemed to favor exploration of the bomb, as long as he could reverse his support in a year or so if nothing fruitful emerged. Gordon Dean believed that the United States should tell Russia that the nation would not develop the weapon if an international agreement could be achieved; failing this, the President should go ahead with the super program. Pike had not yet made up his mind, but leaned toward a negative vote; he saw little evidence that the military actually wanted such a weapon. Besides, the cost of producing tritium, as compared with plutonium, appeared to be perhaps eighty to one hundred times as great, gram for gram. There was also the realization that larger bombs did not necessarily mean greater damage.[24] It was clear to Lilienthal that he did not have a consensus on what action to recommend; no report could be made at this time. The next day he attended a meeting arranged by Oppenheimer with Acheson to discuss the implications of the super as a quid pro quo for international agreement.

By Friday, Lilienthal still had no agreement from his commissioners. Dean and Strauss both still felt the super needed immediate development. The commissioners met with Oppenheimer and the General Advisory Committee on Monday, November 7, but, unfortunately, the meeting was strained and nonproductive. The meeting ended amicably, but still without any consensus.

Lilienthal finally took a document to the President which consisted of each commissioner's views. The very idea of the superbomb was likely to be a public issue sooner or later—with McMahon's enthusiastic support, probably sooner. A public discussion, Lilienthal argued, was therefore desirable. Lilienthal, Smyth, and Pike recommended against development of the super and urged the President to make his decision as soon as possible. Strauss and Dean favored secret diplomatic approaches to the Soviets to explore the possibility of agreement; failing that, the President should order the immediate development of a hydrogen bomb.

Submission of the report coincided with Lilienthal's decision to resign. He had spent over nineteen years in government services and was tired. The battles ahead, compared to the difficulties of the last three years, promised to be even more trying. Truman understood, but asked Lilienthal to stay until a successor could be found, or at least until the middle of February. Lilienthal confessed in his diary a "selfish" reason for wanting to resign: "Lewis [Strauss] had made it almost impossible to enjoy the Commission as a family, as we did when we started out, something I worked hard to develop."[25] Lilienthal warned Truman that a crucial battle was ahead; a decision on the super would not wait.

McMahon, in fact, began the series of visits to AEC installations he had promised earlier in the month. He arrived in Los Alamos for a meeting with senior staff, led by John Manley. In preparation for the visit, Manley was asked by Carroll Wilson to share with Los Alamos staff the recent GAC report and other selected documents. Manley did so, sharing the information with J. M. Kellog, Carson Mark, Teller, Robert Kimball, Alvin Graves, and Darol Froman. McMahon arrived on schedule, with Borden, his aide. Manley quickly learned that both men had been outraged by the GAC's report. Teller was surprisingly objective when he reviewed progress on the super, calling chances for success "about fifty-fifty." Nevertheless, the scientists expressed strong convictions that the work should be undertaken without delay. Manley reported to Oppenheimer that night by telephone that there was no doubt that McMahon would do all he could to press for the super.

The first public word of the new weapon was inadvertently leaked on November 1. In a television interview, Senator Ed Johnson revealed that scientists were working on bombs a thousand times more powerful than the one that fell on Nagasaki. His source of information, of course, was the Joint Committee.

Oppenheimer and his GAC members continued their discussions in Washington. The previous month had produced a flood of reactions—mostly negative—to the GAC report. If anything, the proponents of the super had been forced into consolidating their support. The network of scientists, military, and politicians rumbled. McMahon's support for the hydrogen bomb, never greater, was generously displayed during his tour of the AEC installations, where he criticized the GAC for their folly. The Senator even prepared a four-thousand-word letter to the President summing up his convictions. Teller continued to press from his position as concerned scientist. General Omar Bradley, responding to the Joint Chiefs of Staff, wrote to Secretary of Defense Johnson that Russian possession of a super without similar American possession was unacceptable. Security outweighed the philosophical objections. In this atmosphere, the GAC again met to reconsider their earlier position.

By the end of the three-day discussions, Oppenheimer was able to report to Lilienthal that the committee stood by its earlier recommendations. As supporting documentation Oppenheimer included four reports representing the views of three individual committee members and John Manley. Rowe thought the super might lead the public into a false sense of security. Other reports argued that the super did not have sufficient advantages over large fission devices to be worth the considerable cost in time and resources and current projects that would be sidetracked. Fermi asked whether there were enough large targets to even make the super useful.

Within the commission Paul Fine, from the division of military applications, undertook a detailed study of the super, discussing its military value and probable cost. Manley, who served as a member of the commission's working group on the super, made his own evaluation. On January 13 the Joint Chiefs of Staff released their own assessment, criticizing the GAC's report. While not pressing immediately for an all-out program, the Chiefs believed that systematic study of the super, even with its technical difficulties, was needed. True, such a program would put a strain on the nation's resources, but this was capable of being absorbed. Morally, the super was like any other weapon, only more powerful.

Strauss wrote a personal letter to Truman in late November. He thought it unwise to "renounce, unilaterally, any weapon which an enemy might reasonably be expected to possess." Attached to the letter was a memorandum arguing the case for the super. Strauss thought the weapon had a fifty-fifty chance of being developed in two years in an all-out effort.[26]

With both sides pressing their arguments, the press broke news of the bitter fighting on January 14. Drew Pearson reported on the Lilienthal-Strauss differences, as well as on the differences between various branches of the government. Newspapers from coast to coast ran the story as headline news. The Associated Press story, reprinted in many newspapers, alerted readers to the prospect of a similar Russian program. Unlike fission weapons, which contain technology transferable to peaceful uses, the AP story stated that the hydrogen bomb "could be charged only to national defense. Such a project would deal in death only."[27] A *New York Times* story managed to surface government concerns over whether or not the United States should even make a last push for international agreement. Whatever the contents—and it varied from day to day—the stories did force the President into action.

There were strong differences aired between scientists in public. Hans Bethe and Robert Bacher both raised questions about constructing a hydrogen bomb in articles in *Scientific American* in early 1950. A dozen scientists at the 1950 meeting of the American Physical Society criticized those who had urged the President to decide in favor of the weapon. Edward Teller argued for the quick development of the bomb in an issue of the *Bulletin of the Atomic Scientists*.

With the Joint Committee and the Defense Department in support of the Super, the State Department was the only influential group that had not yet taken a formal stance. A study group appointed by Acheson and under the direction of Gordon Arneson studied the opinions of both the AEC and Defense establishments. Their assessment was that there was little doubt that the Soviets would continue to develop the super as part of their own arsenal. The State Department also believed that such a program within the United States promised to show the weapon's feasibility within three years without seriously damaging fission developments. Why not, they suggested in their final report, encourage the President to direct a super program which would begin at a pace and scale to be set by the AEC and the Defense establishment?

On January 27 the commissioners met with the members of the Joint Committee. It was an unpleasant meeting: The commission was forced to put on the record that three of its members had voted against an all-out program and two had voted for it. The decision, they decided, was now up to the President. The position of the General Advisory Committee could no longer be supported. The arguments ended in a meeting on the morning of January 31 between Lilienthal, Defense Secretary Johnson, Acheson, and the National Security Council selected by Truman to advise on the H-bomb. The group recommended to the President:

> 1. That the AEC be directed to determine the feasibility of the thermonuclear weapon, at a pace and scale to be determined by the AEC and the Defense Department.
> 2. That the Secretaries of State and Defense be directed to undertake a reassessment of the nation's objectives in peace and war, especially in light of fission and possibly thermonuclear weapons.
> 3. That a public announcement be made of the intention to explore thermonuclear weapons.

A draft press release was prepared after Lilienthal urged that wording be added to make any program on weapons appear as "continuing." His compliance, however, did not mean full agreement. Civilian control of atomic energy was still the intent of the law, he argued; the nation should not make a decision on such a weapon on the basis of military requests without also taking into account its implications to foreign policy. The present defense conditions of the United States must be examined *before* making a decision on the super. At the heart of this argument was Lilienthal's concern that nuclear weapons would become the basis for foreign policy, a fear shared by Oppenheimer and others.[28] Acheson could not disagree, but saw no alternative to the weapons under the present circumstances.

At 12:30, Lilienthal, Johnson, and Acheson met with Truman; within ten minutes the President made his decision to proceed with the hydrogen bomb. There was simply no other course to take, he said, looking at Lilienthal. Oppenheimer was disappointed, but not surprised. Some members of the GAC asked if they shouldn't resign under the circumstances, but Lilienthal thought that would be inappropriate. As they talked, Truman informed the press. Headlines later that day read:

TRUMAN TELLS AEC TO BUILD H-BOMB

"I have directed," he said, "the Atomic Energy Commission to continue its work on all forms of atomic weapons, including the so-called hydrogen or super-bomb." These weapons were to be developed "until a satisfactory plan for international control of atomic energy is achieved."*

Strauss was jubilant; the hydrogen bomb he thought so essential to American defense and security was now going to be a reality. Celebrating his fifty-fourth birthday on the day of Truman's decision, Strauss threw a party at the Shoreham Hotel, where he announced that he planned to retire soon. Lilienthal himself was due to retire on February 15. Oppenheimer attended the celebration even though he and Strauss were hardly the best of friends. Ernest Lindley, the newspaper columnist, approached Oppenheimer and asked him why he appeared less jubilant than the others. It was an important question, although Lindley did not know just how much Truman's decision violated Oppenheimer's beliefs nor the difficulty of his negotiations over the past three months. After a pause Oppenheimer turned to Lindley and responded: "This," he said, "is the plague of Thebes."[30]

At last Strauss had made the first step of the "quantum leap" he so urgently wanted for this nation, but to some it seemed to be a fatal leap in the wrong direction.

---

*In 1975, Edward Teller cited three individuals as "responsible" for overturning the decision of the General Advisory Committee: "Senator Brien McMahon, Lewis Strauss and Klaus Fuchs."[29]

PART THREE

13. Technically Sweet

The American public received another shock within days of President Truman's announcement on the hydrogen bomb. On February 3, 1950, major headlines in the press revealed that British scientist Klaus Fuchs had confessed to giving secrets of the atomic bomb to the Russians. Fuchs had been under investigation for several months by the British government, and he had just confessed to British authorities that he had given his Russian contacts information on British fission work during the early forties, as well as information regarding his own work while at Los Alamos until 1946. Both McMahon and Congressman John Wood, chairman of the House Un-American Activities Committee, promised quick investigations into the Fuchs affair. Truman's press secretary revealed that the President had known of the matter for a few days, but there was absolutely no connection, he said, between the President's decision to make the H-bomb and the news of Klaus Fuchs. General Groves was hastily summoned to testify before the Joint Committee the following day.

A report prepared by General Nichols suggested that the information Fuchs had been privy to had probably accelerated the Russians' production of an atomic bomb by as much as a year or two. While at Los Alamos, Fuchs had had knowledge of most of the major events and discoveries and had certainly been well-informed on the process of implosion. After the war he had participated in talks on thermonuclear weapons. Nichols's report ruefully concluded that the Russian thermonuclear program was probably much closer in progress to the American program than they thought earlier. Secretary of Defense Johnson took the report and his conclusions to the White House; he urged that the thermonuclear program must be accelerated with all haste.

It was possible to see Fuchs's villainy as an indirect indictment of Oppenheimer's management at Los Alamos. Groves, who had strenuously opposed Oppenheimer's colloquiums and the general lack of compartmentalization at the laboratory, no doubt remembered this as he prepared to testify before the Joint Committee. Oppenheimer, however, stood by his management; even if the laboratory had practiced compartmentalization it would not have prevented Fuchs from informing—his own department was a key area of the implosion program. Even if he had transmitted no more than a record of what his unit was doing, he would still have revealed to the Russians the most important work at Los Alamos. The issue was to come up at Oppenheimer's security hearings in four years.[1]

Of more immediate concern was exactly which information on thermonuclear weapons Fuchs might have passed on to the Russians. While many believed that critical information had been sent, this belief could not be supported by the facts. Even in early 1950 the state of thermonuclear development at Los Alamos had been limited by uncertainty and theoretical gaps. At best, Fuchs could have reported only on the wartime thinking and given his speculation on subsequent events.

Three days later, on February 6, the House Un-American Activities Committee released its "Report on Atomic Espionage." There was brief mention of Katherine Puening (Kitty Oppenheimer's maiden name), as a woman who had been a friend of Steve Nelson's and as someone married to a key scientist in the country's atomic bomb project. The report, however, was careful to note that neither the wife nor the scientist-husband had in any way engaged in subversive activity; their loyalty, the report read, was not in question.

Toward the end of February, Oppenheimer and Haakron Chevalier exchanged letters. Chevalier had written to his old friend to express his eagerness to return to teaching; but he was encountering difficulties. Chevalier had read recently that Oppenheimer had testified before the House Un-American Activities Committee to the effect that in the so-called "kitchen incident," Chevalier had approached the scientist not to solicit information, but to report the conversation with Eltenton. Chevalier sought clarification from Oppy. Oppenheimer replied on February 24 that he could not send a transcript of the proceedings because the committee had decided to keep them secret. But he told Chevalier:

> I said that as far as I knew, you knew nothing of the atom bomb until it was announced after Hiroshima; and that most certainly you had never mentioned it or anything that could be connected with it to me. I said that you had never asked me to transmit any kind of information, nor suggested that I could do so, or that I consider doing so. I said that you had told me of a discussion of providing technical information to the USSR which disturbed you considerably, and which you thought I ought to know about. . . . These were, I think, the highlights; and if this account can be of use to you, I hope that you will feel free to use it.[2]

The letter from Chevalier, an old friend, was understandably disturbing to Oppenheimer. The national phobia over Communists and Communist infiltration was increasing. In February, Senator Joseph McCarthy of Wisconsin made his first charge of "205 known Communists" working in the State Department. Oppenheimer's security investigation file, which by now was several feet thick, was no longer just the property of the Atomic Energy Commission and the FBI. Others, including the members and staff of the House Un-American Activities Committee, were beginning to piece together bit by bit a growing portrait of Oppenheimer's past.

Oppenheimer's General Advisory Committee was holding its nineteenth meeting just as Truman announced his approval of the H-bomb program. Oppenheimer's report of the meeting to Lilienthal was not particularly enthusiastic:

> "... The determination of national policy to proceed with the development of the super-bomb occurred during the course of this meeting and many of the consequences of this determination could not be fully explored at this time."

The GAC did authorize a high-energy, high-current accelerator at Berkeley, a device that could answer several design questions as well as produce polonium for initiators. The members also commented on the proposed program of research and development at Los Alamos. The "principal feature" of the program, as Oppenheimer described it, was the development of the super. The committee suggested that the upcoming tests in the Pacific, scheduled for 1951, should contain an experiment to see if deuterium could be burned; in other words, it should be a test of thermonuclear propagation. The possibility of conducting the proposed program, however, depended on obtaining as much as 250 grams of tritium, and the GAC did not think it would be feasible to produce this amount in less than a year or so. Only the Hanford reactor, which was reactivated with enriched uranium, could produce the amount needed, but they did not know how long it would take. Los Alamos had to either conduct its thermonuclear tests in 1951 with 150 grams of tritium, or alter its program.[3] This assessment from Oppenheimer's committee had an effect on the meeting scheduled for February 23 at Los Alamos.

At Los Alamos, Bradbury described the program he had designed for the laboratory: maximum effort on the super, but continued work on fission weapons which were near completion. He hoped for a test of thermonuclear principles in 1951, even though he realized that it depended on achieving the starlike temperatures needed to ignite deuterium, an element that could be produced rather cheaply. Tritium, which burned at temperatures achievable with a fission bomb, would then be used to burn deuterium.* It was difficult to determine just how quickly Los Alamos could solve these problems inherent in the program.

Bradbury pointed out that there were several physicists who had moral reservations about working on the bomb. Teller, who attended the meeting, agreed with Bradbury, adding that he felt some of the older

---

*Both deuterium and tritium are isotopes of hydrogen.

scientists—Oppenheimer, for one—were to blame for the lack of personnel: They had failed to use their position to encourage bright men to work on the super program. For Teller, nothing less than a complete "reorientation" of the laboratory could serve the all-out effort he envisioned. Fission work could continue, he explained, but not at the expense of the super. He remained convinced that the Russians were hard at work on a thermonuclear weapon of their own.[4] This was the heart of the differences between Teller and Oppenheimer. Teller believed that America had to develop a thermonuclear weapon at all costs, and with a program filled with scientists similar to the wartime Manhattan Project. Oppenheimer believed that thermonuclear weapons should be explored, but not to the detriment of perfecting fission weapons already under development. To Oppenheimer, the evidence amassed thus far did not support Teller's arguments that a super could be developed, and developed quickly, if only "the right men" were at work on it. Oppenheimer was not alone in his assessment of the super's feasibility. Working on the super at Los Alamos was Carson Mark who believed "There was nothing to build in 1945; nothing in 1949; nothing in 1950." Mark, in fact, thought Oppenheimer wanted the thermonuclear bomb explored: It was just that "if there wasn't such a thing, then that would be the desired outcome for Oppenheimer."[5]

To what extent did Oppenheimer support development of the super? Clearly he never sought to contradict the President's mandate to proceed. In fact, his attitude that spring, like much of the year before, was one of reasoned caution: did the scientific evidence collected so far permit a complete restructuring of the nation's weapons establishment? He could hardly deny the intrinsic attraction of exploring, scientifically, thermonuclear reactions. But was the attraction of scientific discovery sufficient to warrant spending the vast resources projected for such an effort? Oppenheimer voiced these arguments whenever he could, but no one ever heard him flatly say the weapon shouldn't be built.

Bradbury had the difficult task of making sure the thermonuclear program was successful within the existing framework of the laboratory; not all programs could be, or should be, dropped simply to make way for the H-bomb. In March 1950 he created the "family" committee to oversee work on the thermonuclear program. The committee, chaired by Teller, would be responsible for monitoring the activities of the various divisions and groups that were engaged in one aspect or another of the super program.[6] Bradbury believed that Teller lacked the ability to manage large numbers of people; there was no way he could give Teller full direction of a program as complex as the one at hand—developing a thermonuclear weapon. "I couldn't afford to put Teller in charge," Bradbury recalled years later; "I would have had a full-scale mutiny on my hands."[7]

Now that the program was underway at Los Alamos, the GAC could turn its attention to reactors. There was a need for a reactor that could produce large quantities of neutrons. There were several possibilities, but the Hanford reactor still appeared to be the best for producing tritium. However, reactors also needed to produce plutonium in case the super program failed. The Chalk River reactor, on the Canadian border, could produce enough plutonium for a fission weapon the size of Fat Man in less than a year; material for a gun-type weapon could be produced in a year from this same reactor. The committee finally decided that the natural-uranium, heavy-water-moderated reactor gave the most promising chance.[8] In mid-March the AEC and the Department of Defense asked President Truman to approve two heavy-water reactors for the long-term production of tritium; in the meantime, the Hanford reactor could produce enough of the substance for the 1951 weapons tests in the Pacific.

Oppenheimer remained uncomfortable with the nation's preoccupation with weapons. True, the time seemed to call for such concerns, but in the process, the growth of scientific knowledge seemed to be stifled. The nation's resources were channeled toward instruments of destruction rather than toward instruments of peace. Oppenheimer captured some of these feelings in an article he wrote for *Science* magazine in March. Science could eliminate hunger, he said, yet it seems to have its greatest impact on warfare.

By the middle of 1950, Los Alamos seemed to have lost some of its earlier optimism for a quick development of the H-bomb, now nicknamed "Daddy." Work on the super had not progressed very well. The central problem seemed to be the difficulty of understanding the complexities of a thermonuclear explosion. Bradbury had stressed in February that the problems were theoretical or scientific, and not technological. Teller, however, was forced to admit in August that "the required scientific effort is clearly much larger than that needed for the first fission weapon . . . theoretical analysis is a major bottleneck to faster progress."[9] By the end of 1950, Los Alamos had assigned thirty-five full-time staff members and several full-time consultants to the problem. The laboratory needed a detailed understanding of the thermonuclear process during an explosion. Carson Mark, who headed the laboratory's T—Theoretical—Division, believed that "without this, no conclusive experience was possible short of a successful stab in the dark, since a failure would not necessarily establish unfeasibility, but possibly only that the system chosen was unsuitable, or that the required ignition conditions had not been met."[10]

The calculations they needed taxed the limits of existing computers. The Navy ENIAC (electronic numerical integrator and calculator) consumed a large room and nineteen thousand vacuum tubes; it worked slowly and had no memory storage. John von Neumann was already working on an improved model, but completion was perhaps a year away. Using only desk calculators and pens and paper, a team of scientists under Stan Ulam estimated that fission reaction had a fifty-fifty chance of continuing to burn in early 1950.[11] These difficulties had a harsh effect on the scientists, but this served to drive Teller harder. To William Borden, on the Joint Committee, Teller complained that members of the GAC had not exactly been helpful in recruiting the staff he believed was necessary to complete work on the super.[12] Oppenheimer and Conant, he argued, could do a lot to help or hurt the effort. His anxiety was not assuaged by new calculations provided by Ulam: Theoretically, the present design of the super did not appear to work. Von Neumann concluded that the only solution would be to add more tritium. On June 24, Bethe wrote to Carson Mark: "I believe that the last calculations by Ulam . . . definitely indicate the dying out of the reaction."[13] Indeed, the prospects for the super looked more and more gloomy as the year wore on.

With Lilienthal's resignation as chairman of the AEC, Oppenheimer's name again surfaced as a possible candidate for the job. Conant and Arthur Compton were mentioned as well. Truman had to recommend a new chairman for the commission, as well as a commissioner to replace Lewis Strauss. Oppenheimer felt that Joseph Volpe, the AEC's general counsel, should be given a position on the AEC and wrote a laudatory letter to Truman on February 23 offering Volpe's name and certifying his "tact, wisdom and ever-growing understanding of the AEC's problems."[14] On March 20 Truman nominated Thomas E. Murray, a director of the Chrysler Corporation and a mechanical engineer, to finish Lilienthal's unexpired term. In June, Pike, Dean, Murray and Smyth were re-nominated with Dean appointed chairman. T. Keith Glennan, president of the Case Institute of Technology, was named the fifth member of the commission.

Just as the commission was in the process of reorganizing, there were also new appointments to be made to the General Advisory Committee. Oppenheimer and Conant were secure, as were Smith, DuBridge, and Rabi—they were all members of the original Committee. Fermi's, Seaborg's, and Rowe's terms, however, would soon expire. Oppenheimer believed that William Libby, a chemist at the University of Chicago, would be the best man to replace Seaborg; should Fermi decide against remaining for a second term, Oppenheimer thought Bacher, Bethe, and von Neumann would all be solid substitutes. Except for Libby, Dean favored others. He wrote to Truman and supported Libby; Walter G. Whitman, a

*Incidentally, the 1950 calculations, which took one and a half months and two months of personnel time with an IBM 602, in 1974 took only thirty minutes and fifteen minutes of staff time using more sophisticated computers.

chemical engineer and director of the Lexington Project; and Eger V. Murphee, who had first assisted in the Manhattan project in 1942.

In the midst of this shuffling, the FBI arrested Harry Gold, who was charged with being the link between Klaus Fuchs and the Soviets. His confession led to the arrest of Julius and Ethel Rosenberg, as well as a Soviet consular official, and David Greenglass, who was a former Army G.I. and machinist at Los Alamos during the war. To the public the arrests seemed clear evidence of Communist infiltration; it was certainly fuel for the oratorical fires of men like Senator Joseph McCarthy and the members of the Joint Committee on Atomic Energy.

On May 9, Sylvia Crouch, whose husband had once been a Communist party member, testified before the California Senate Un-American Activities. She claimed that she and her husband had once attended a secret, closed Communist party meeting in Oppenheimer's California house in July 1941. The participants, she stated, were very important people—so important, in fact, that their names had been withheld from lower-level party members. She identified Oppenheimer from photographs the FBI showed to her. She further testified that Joseph Weinberg had also been at the party in Oppenheimer's house. The following day a former Communist presently employed as a truck driver, Alfred Barbosa, testified that he had seen Oppenheimer at a New Year's Eve party in the home of an individual named Kenneth May.

Oppenheimer immediately issued a denial through the Atomic Energy Commission: He had never been a Communist, nor had he ever hosted a party of Communist officials in his home. He did, however, admit to having had friends in "left-wing" politics and had even belonged to some of these organizations. However, all of Oppenheimer's political activity that was now under question had ceased before he became involved with the nation's atomic energy program in 1942.

While the California testimony only added to the suspicions several people had about his past, the charges also produced quick support from friends and colleagues. Norris Bradbury wrote to say that everyone at Los Alamos was "deeply distressed" to read of the charges; he hoped that "good sense and decency" would prevail and offered to help in any way he could. General Groves, already retired from the Army and now an official at Remington Rand, wrote a similar offer of help. "If at any time," he wrote,

> you would feel that it were wise, I would be pleased to have you make a statement of the general tenor of that which follows:
>
> > General Groves has informed me that shortly after he took over the responsibility for the development of the atomic bomb, he reviewed personally the entire file and all known information concerning me and immediately ordered that I be

> cleared for all atomic information in order that I might participate in the development of the atomic bomb. . . . at no time did he [Groves] regret his decision.[15]

Oppenheimer replied to Groves that "these are indeed troublesome days for all of us." The problems faced during the war were not the hardest "that we in this country will have to face." Surprisingly, support came from a Republican member of the House Un-American Activities Committee, Richard Nixon. "Dr. Oppenheimer," he said to a political gathering, is "a completely loyal American to whom the people of the United States owe a great debt of gratitude for his tireless and magnificent job in atomic research." Congressman Nixon, who was then running for the Senate, expressed "complete loyalty" to the scientist.

Despite this public and private support, Oppenheimer realized that it would be necessary to do more than merely deny the allegation that he had attended a "closed Communist meeting" sometime in July 1941. Both he and Kitty ransacked their files for evidence of their whereabouts during that period. To the best of their recollection they had been at their cabin in the Pecos Mountains of New Mexico. In Sante Fe their old friend Dorothy McKibbin interviewed people looking for evidence to substantiate that the Oppenheimers had been vacationing there at the time. Finally, from interviews and from odd sources like telephone bills and receipts, they were able to confirm the fact that they had been in New Mexico during the period mentioned in her testimony. A letter written by Kitty to her mother in Germany on August 7, 1941, surfaced, revealing a series of minor disasters that had plagued the Oppenheimers that summer: Robert had fallen off a horse and had twisted his knee, and Kitty had run the family car, called Bombsight, into a truck—a sequence of events that had forced them to cut their vacation in New Mexico short by one week.

Oppenheimer was interviewed twice by the FBI regarding his activities nine years before, in July 1941. He claimed that he did not even know Weinberg was a Communist until it had been made public. This information, however, was contradictory to what he told John Landsdale on September 12, 1943. This discrepancy was quickly noted by nameless security men, adding to what they believed was mounting evidence of the scientist's disloyalty.

On June 25, Communist troops from North Korea invaded South Korea across the 38th parallel. The United Nations Security Council ordered an immediate cease-fire and withdrawal of North Korean forces. On June 27 the council called upon members of the UN to furnish arms and men to repel the armed attack. The same day Truman ordered troops to South Korea; by June 30 they had been authorized to undertake missions above the 38th parallel. The government announced that by July

7 the draft would be reinstated to quickly build up American armed forces. This rapid series of events accelerated the demands for weapons superiority, including, of course, the hydrogen bomb. Truman's first move was to authorize the release of atomic weapons—without their nuclear cores—to Britain; in the event of an emergency, the cores could be shipped to Great Britain for quick assembly.

In June, Oppenheimer planned a trip to Los Alamos with several members of the General Advisory Committee. They met the week following the Fourth of July. Oppenheimer and his colleagues found Bradbury's presentations interesting, but the work on the super remained inconclusive. Bradbury emphasized that work was proceeding, but that the goal of a test weapon with a reasonable chance of success was still not there. Certain other advances had been made, such as developing an external initiator, and in enlarging the explosive yield of fission weapons by altering the amount of fissionable material.

The GAC planned to meet on September 19 in Washington for a "quite informal" review of progress on the super and on various fission projects. Bradbury attended and presented reports on the super prepared by key staff members Edward Teller and John Wheeler. Despite the limited results from the tedious calculations by Ulam and others, there was still no clear indication that success was imminent. Quite a different picture emerged on fission weapons. As reported to Oppenheimer in July, Los Alamos now knew how to make fission bombs that were lighter, smaller, and considerably more destructive than Fat Man and Little Boy, giving a greater explosive return for smaller amounts of fissionable material. This breakthrough meant the military now had a larger arsenal of weapons at their disposal, including smaller weapons that were easily adaptable to field artillery or aircraft use.

The successful fission program had strong implications for military planners. With a more diverse array of atomic bombs available, the Defense Department might reassess its reliance on the large, cumbersome weapons such as the hydrogen bomb, and instead adopt a broader-based plan in which small field weapons would supplement troops, conventional weapons and equipment. Korea was already revealing the possibility of using atomic tactical weapons.[16] With the super still in the shadows, the quick improvement of fission bombs was the decided alternative, and one that was within the nation's grasp. This decision, however, only further revealed the differences in view toward the value and ability of atomic weapons. Aside from the GAC, Oppenheimer's objections to the hydrogen bomb were viewed as nothing more than resistance to American weapons superiority. Even his rational assessment of the slim chances for success and the value of fission weapons was regarded as subversive by military leaders.

The issue of thermonuclear versus fission weapons dominated the meeting of the GAC on October 30. Gathering at Los Alamos, the committee heard from Bradbury, Mark, Teller, Wheeler, and several other members of the laboratory's staff. The theoretical work so far could be confirmed only by the 1951 tests, now called Greenhouse. Oppenheimer and the committee believed that the program outlined by Los Alamos for the next year or so was suitable, but Oppenheimer again stressed the importance of continuing work on fission weapons. As the super was still in doubt, fission weapons were a useful alternative, one that meant the current stockpile of weapons could be increased without a severe hardship on the production of uranium and plutonium. Bradbury, however, claimed that the stockpile directives received from the military did not reflect this thinking. The military, Oppenheimer pointed out, could hardly be expected to understand the complexities of making a super and that their interest in thermonuclear weapons was based largely on the belief that sheer explosive power would compensate for targeting errors. General McCormack agreed in part by offering a hunch that tactical situations would suggest a stockpile comprised of many relatively small-yield bombs and a few very large ones for large targets.

Both Bradbury and Bethe preferred many small weapons for attacking "river crossings and landings"; large bombs had the disadvantage of overkill by not giving uniform coverage to the target area. Teller argued that the area damage "per kilogram of fissionable material" was larger for big bombs. Bethe disagreed; weapons that were two hundred kilotons or larger did not increase efficiency. Oppenheimer believed that larger weapons were mostly useful against "strong targets." General McCormack added that he did not foresee disappointment from the military if large fission weapons resulted from the laboratory's work.

Calculations at Los Alamos suggested that a thermonuclear reaction was possible; the question now was whether the current design for the super would be able to achieve it. There was a strong possibility that the thermonuclear reaction, once ignited by a fission weapon, would start but then fizzle out. The amount of tritium needed had already been increased several times as theoretical work revealed more about the complex process. Teller saw the difficulties, but believed that further work would bring solutions. "The field of uncertainties is very great indeed," he said. He was especially concerned that there simply were not enough people of the right caliber working on the weapon. There was even discussion of the usefulness of creating a second weapons laboratory to concentrate solely on the problems of the super. For the moment, with little but theory to offer the promise of eventual H-bombs, the sure advantages of a well-developed stockpile of atomic weapons appealed more to men like Oppenheimer.[17]

Oppenheimer felt that if the United States had a diverse stockpile of atomic weapons, the nation would be prepared for different kinds of conflict. He articulated his views in a letter to the General Board of the Navy:

> "Whatever our hopes for the future, we must surely be prepared . . . to meet the enemy in certain crucial, strategic areas in which conflict is likely, and to defeat him in those areas . . . to engage in total war, to carry the war to the enemy and attempt to destroy him."[18]

He stressed that reliable information on the Soviet military potential would be continually needed.

Oppenheimer continued this theme as chairman of a committee under the Research and Development Board whose purpose was to assess long-range military objectives and the use of the atomic bomb. Oppenheimer served with many of his fellow scientists: Bacher, Alvarez, Lauritsen, William Parsons, and Wilbur Kelly. Also serving were members of the military establishment: Generals Nichols, McCormack, and Roscoe Wilson. Oppenheimer's appointment as chairman had been made by Robert LeBaron, an assistant to the secretary of defense, who knew in advance that the appointment would cause opposition from those involved in atomic energy who favored the H-bomb. Oppenheimer had served on a similar panel in 1948.

> We sat down, the three generals, the admiral and I, and called in other people whose help would be useful and wrote our best opinion as to the relative time scales and absolute scales of submarine propulsion; how it was going with the deliverability of tactical weapons, what needed to be done here, what needed to be done there.[19]

Now, two years later, Oppenheimer intended to take a "deeper bite." The fighting in Korea, the bleak prospects for a thermonuclear weapon—these were the circumstances that surrounded the second conference. LeBaron, who put the committee together, asked Oppenheimer and his team to consider the present status of nuclear weapons research and the state of the nation's defense posture.

Wilbur Kelly, who was now president of Bell Telephone's laboratory in New York City, found Oppenheimer an able and fair chairman. Kelly thought that Oppenheimer's views by and large reflected those of the committee as a whole; where differences existed, they were no more than the differences that would exist between any two men. His chairmanship had been impartial and solicitous of everyone's view. Kelly signed the report of the panel without reservation.

Roscoe Wilson was not so impressed. He was, as he described himself, a "big-bomb man." As a member of the Air Force, he disliked

Oppenheimer's opposition to nuclear-powered aircraft and his support for nuclear-powered ships and submarines. While he realized that Oppenheimer's judgments stemmed from technical considerations, he believed they would be jeopardizing American defense.[20]

Oppenheimer had personally asked Alvarez to serve on the panel. "I would like to have you on this committee," he told Alvarez, "because I know you represent a point different from mine, and I think it would be healthy to have you on this committee." The two men diverged chiefly in their evaluations of the hydrogen bomb. Oppenheimer, backed by Lauritsen, expressed the fear that the small-weapons program at Los Alamos would suffer because of the hydrogen bomb program. Alvarez was surprised by one of Oppenheimer's comments: that "they"—the members of the committee—were in agreement that the hydrogen bomb program should be stopped, but that work had progressed so far that to stop the program now would only cause disruption in commission laboratories like Los Alamos. It was better, Alvarez remembers Oppenheimer saying, that "it die a natural death with the coming tests." Alvarez chose not to argue the point and even signed the report, thereby endorsing it, along with all of the other members of the group.

Oppenheimer sent the panel's findings to LeBaron on December 29, 1950. The report emphasized the role that small fission weapons could play in defense, even in an all-out war. The thermonuclear bomb was a "long-range" weapon, and only an explosion would prove its workability. The report was modified somewhat by the commission and the military liaison committee and endorsed by the General Advisory Committee.[21] A few months later Teller anxiously called Alvarez and asked why he had signed the long-range objectives report. Alvarez replied that he had not found anything wrong with it. Teller insisted, however, that a close reading suggested that the hydrogen bomb program was interfering with the small-weapons program at Los Alamos. "It is being used against our [thermonuclear] program," Teller said. "It is slowing it down and it could easily kill it." Alvarez reread the report and had to admit that he had missed those implications. Oppenheimer's reply was that the report had circulated among all the members as it had within the AEC, and was approved by all. There had been plenty of chances to seek clarification, modification, or simply to refuse to sign.

Undoubtedly, Oppenheimer's views on the hydrogen bomb were a source of great concern to some people. Teller and Lawrence were both outspoken proponents; the military leadership was equally supportive. To these individuals, Oppenheimer appeared unacceptably opposed to—or, at best, ambiguous about—a major program of development. It was true

---

*Oppenheimer, when confronted with this statement four years later at his hearing, said that he did not think he could have made such a generalization as "we all agree. . . ."

that the General Advisory Committee had recommended against an all-out program, and that Oppenheimer was the committee's guiding force. He continued to ask questions about the weapon's feasibility and to challenge the theoretical studies underway at institutions like Los Alamos and Princeton. To others, like his colleagues on the GAC, Oppenheimer was not so much opposed to the weapon as he was uncertain about its eventual success. Certainly, at the end of 1950, there was no firm evidence—theoretical or otherwise—that such a weapon could ever be made. He had spoken out against the unnecessary development of larger weapons as much as he had against the growing reliance by military planners on large weapons as the basis for national defense. Perhaps the collapse of discussions at the United Nations had convinced him of the need for the United States, as the leading nuclear power, to assume a moderate position in the world regarding such weapons.

Men close to the development of the hydrogen bomb were not all as certain as Edward Teller of its success. Bradbury, who favored continuing work on thermonuclear weapons, obviously waited for the results of theoretical and experimental studies to make a final judgment. Oppenheimer did not oppose study; in fact, his record since joining the GAC had been one of cautious but continuing support for exploration and study. Perhaps Oppenheimer only wished more loudly than others that the weapon would never succeed.

In December the General Advisory Committee approved the Army's bombing and gunnery range in Nevada as the nation's continental test site for experimental nuclear explosions. A series of tests, called Ranger, were scheduled for the first days of February 1951. Los Alamos would be testing its small fission weapons in Nevada—tests that would confirm their designs as much as Oppenheimer's arguments that limited weapons could be of use in the field. In one experiment, for example, a small atomic weapon would be fired as an artillery shell, with several thousand foot soldiers participating in the exercise.

As the Greenhouse tests in the Pacific neared, Los Alamos appeared no closer to solving the problems of creating and sustaining a thermonuclear reaction. Computer results, however, had confirmed Ulam's elaborate calculations. Teller, under enormous pressure to deliver a weapon, pushed himself and his staff harder. Morale deteriorated sharply and working relationships became strained. Bradbury, responsible for more than just a hydrogen bomb, had to make many decisions which some thought hampered the super program at the laboratory. In Washington, Gordon Dean, Oppenheimer, and most others received reports of the conditions at Los Alamos. Teller found himself forced to lobby for support in Washington, and ex-AEC member Lewis Strauss tried his hand at increasing support from the sidelines for the super program. More money, more staff, and more time were the demands most frequently heard. Teller also wanted administrative support from Los Alamos leadership. Increasingly, the charge was heard that Oppenheimer had failed to place his support behind the thermonuclear effort.

Though sometimes acerbic and often strained, the atmosphere at Los Alamos did generate an environment in which ideas, some imaginative but unrealistic, were tossed between individuals. After the tense months in late 1950 and early 1951, a new idea developed that sparked a major breakthrough. In February, Stan Ulam conceived a dramatic new approach to the design and construction of a thermonuclear weapon. Drawing on his experience during the past several years, Ulam suggested a completely different idea that evolved from a new means of addressing the problems that had beset all of Los Alamos. Interestingly, it was an approach that would not have been conceivable before Los Alamos had acquired important information about the behavior of nuclear explosives.

Ulam took the idea to Carson Mark and then to the laboratory's director, Norris Bradbury. Both realized that the concept had revolutionary implications, although Mark didn't know if it was the breakthrough they were all looking for.[22] The next day, Ulam discussed his idea with Teller, who, after some hesitation, suggested an alternative design, one that Ulam thought was "parallel" to his plan but "perhaps more convenient and generalized."[23] Frederick de Hoffman, a young mathematician, also offered ingenious mathematical support. The idea, generated by Ulam and reworked by Teller and de Hoffman, became the real "secret" of the H-bomb. They realized that when a fission bomb exploded, some of its radiation could be contained in the bomb design long enough to compress the thermonuclear material. This powerful compression, along with other phenomena, would cause the fuel to burn in a way necessary to cause an explosion.*

With new hope for the thermonuclear program, Bradbury took time to reorganize some aspects of the laboratory; he chose to strengthen the committee approach to working on the super. Teller would have his own group, but not a division. It was important, Bradbury thought, to be able to draw on the resources of many units within the lab. Darol Froman was put in charge of the overall effort. Teller, while not in personal disagreement with Froman, objected to the fractured nature of the laboratory. It should direct its energies, he felt, toward completion of the work necessary for the Greenhouse tests and on the work based on the new Teller-Ulam design. He wanted control of a separate division. To Bradbury

*In 1980 the Department of Energy (successor to the AEC) declassified a simplified statement of this principle: "In thermonuclear weapons, radiation from a fission explosive can be contained and used to transfer energy to compress and ignite a physically separate component containing TN [thermonuclear] fuel."[24]

he wrote: "I do not believe that the thermonuclear work can either be continued or directed on a part-time basis."[25] For Teller, the Bradbury reorganization only served to weaken the program at Los Alamos by failing to concentrate its energies. He decided to leave as soon as the Greenhouse test confirmed that a thermonuclear reaction could be achieved. In the meantime, Teller resisted urgings from people he considered "friends of Oppenheimer" to expand the Greenhouse tests to include larger experiments of thermonuclear principles. "It was my conviction that," Teller said, "this suggestion was made in the hope that the test would fail, thereby terminating the program altogether."[26]

Greenhouse was under the control of Joint Task Force 3. Los Alamos appointed Alvin Graves as scientific director. The firing team and VIPs, including Gordon Dean from the commission and Teller, located themselves in the control center at Parry Island. There were four shots altogether, but two were especially important. The first shot, nicknamed George, tested thermonuclear principles and was scheduled for May 8; the second shot, called Item, was scheduled for May 24. On May 8 the weapon exploded, taking in its searing explosion a three-hundred-foot tower and most of the island of Eberiru. The mushroom cloud rose to an altitude of seventy thousand feet; an unusual phenomenon occurred: Ice caps formed at different levels as the cloud rose. Suddenly visible at the explosion's peak was the translucent blue-violet nimbus of ionization. Temperatures exceeded 500,000° Kelvin, momentarily hotter than the center of the sun. Even the most preliminary evidence was enough to confirm that for a fraction of a second a thermonuclear reaction had taken place, using a mixture of deuterium and tritium. Teller cabled Los Alamos: "It's a boy!"* On May 24 the scientists exploded Item, which employed the booster principle; certain amounts of thermonuclear fuel were used to boost the explosive power of a fission weapon. It too exploded in a blinding flash, removing Engebi from the catalog of small Pacific islands.

Oppenheimer was asked to plan and chair a top-level conference at Princeton in early June. Its purpose would be to review the Greenhouse results, preliminary as they were, and to study the new developments at Los Alamos and make recommendations for the next year or two of work in the thermonuclear program. All of the commissioners attended, as did some military representatives, the AEC's general manager, as well as staff from Los Alamos under Bradbury, and individuals such as Fermi, Bacher, Kobi, von Neumann, and Cyril Smith. Teller also attended, although he

---

*Journalist Stanley Blumberg and Gwinn Owens, in *Energy and Conflict: The Life and Times of Edward Teller* (Putnam, 1976), argue that the Soviets were actually the first to test a full-scale thermonuclear weapon, earlier in 1952. This is disputed by the United States government.

planned to return to the University of Chicago, where he would remain a consultant to Los Alamos. Oppenheimer knew about the tension of Los Alamos and asked Bradbury to prepare a program of review for the upcoming meeting. Bradbury responded on the first of June: Carson Mark would review the recent Greenhouse tests; Darol Froman would speak of the proposed laboratory program, including, where possible, the projected dates for key events; and Bradbury would address the laboratory's philosophy on the development of both fission and thermonuclear weapons. Bradbury did not plan to discuss the differences of approach to thermonuclear research (e.g., Teller versus Bradbury), "unless the question of separate laboratories or separate division of Los Alamos is brought up by someone else."[27]

The meeting breathed new life and hope into the thermonuclear program. The results of Greenhouse at last offered the scientific proof necessary to continue work for a major bomb design. Teller's description of the new design, based on his and Ulam's work, was perhaps the high point of the two-day meeting; the sheer cleverness of the invention was enough to cause Oppenheimer to explain several times how "technically sweet" the concept was. Whatever the final implications of the weapon, the beauty of the idea was enough to overwhelm Oppenheimer's sense of distaste for superweapons. The idea had so much promise, in fact, that the so-called superbomb, on which Los Alamos had labored since 1945, was put lower in priority; top priority was given to the new hydrogen weapon.* For the first time, there was consensus that the weapon would work. Oppenheimer remembered that:

> The program we had in 1949 was a tortured thing that you could well argue did not make a great deal of technical sense. It was therefore possible to argue also that you didn't want it, even if you could have it. The program in 1951 was technically so sweet that you could not argue about that. It was purely the military, the political, and the humane problem of what you were going to do with it once you had it.[28]

Gordon Dean left the meeting quite pleased; he had noticed that even Oppenheimer had been "thrilled" at the Teller-Ulam breakthrough. The new weapon seemed so promising, in fact, that Dean authorized construction of a plant to produce critical materials, even though he had no money in the AEC budget to do so. Teller, who had come to Princeton meetings with misgivings, frankly expected Oppenheimer to oppose any further development. He was surprised and pleased that his colleague accepted the new possibility "so warmly."

---

*This new device carries no nickname such as "super"; the name given to it by scientists, in fact, is still classified.

Julius and Robert Oppenheimer. Julius Oppenheimer emigrated to the United States from Germany at age eighteen. Robert Oppenheimer is about two years old in this photograph. *(Courtesy of Oppenheimer Memorial Society)*

Oppenheimer as a young student. Oppenheimer attended the Ethical Culture School in New York City. *(Courtesy of Oppenheimer Memorial Society)*

Kitty Oppenheimer. Kitty was born Katherine Puening and was married to Stewart Harrison when she and Oppenheimer first met in 1939. Kitty and Oppenheimer were married in Nevada on November 1, 1940.
(Courtesy of Oppenheimer Memorial Society)

Major General Leslie R. Groves.
Groves was the overall director of the wartime Manhattan Project. He made Los Alamos the central laboratory for the design and production of the first atomic weapons. After the creation of the U.S. Atomic Energy Commission in 1947, he remained an advisor to the military on atomic energy affairs.
(Courtesy of Los Alamos Scientific Laboratory)

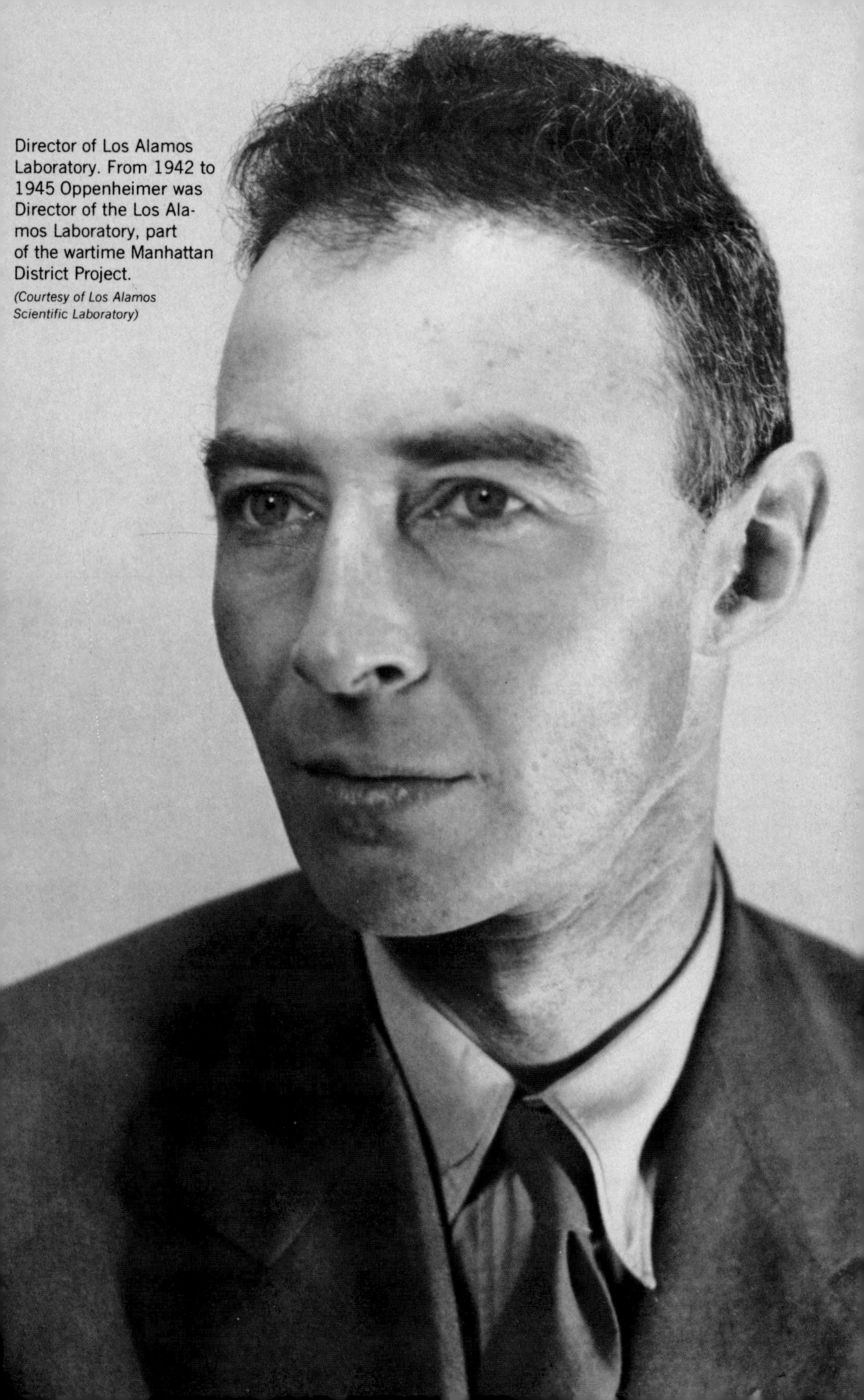

Director of Los Alamos Laboratory. From 1942 to 1945 Oppenheimer was Director of the Los Alamos Laboratory, part of the wartime Manhattan District Project.

(Courtesy of Los Alamos Scientific Laboratory)

Party at wartime Los Alamos. Left to right: Dorothy McKibbin, Robert Oppenheimer, and Victor Weisskopf. *(Courtesy of Los Alamos Scientific Laboratory)*

Inspection of Ground Zero. Groves and Oppenheimer (center of photograph) inspect the remains of the steel tower at the center of the first atomic bomb explosion at Trinity Site, New Mexico. The area was sufficiently radioactive to require visitors to the area to wear protective coverings on their shoes. *(Courtesy of White Sands Missile Range, New Mexico)*

Postwar meeting at Los Alamos. First row, left to right: Norris Bradbury, who assumed directorship of Los Alamos after Oppenheimer, John Manley, who became secretary to the General Advisory Committee of the Atomic Energy Commission, Enrico Fermi, and John Kellog. Second row, left to right: Oppenheimer, Richard Feymann, and Phil B. Porter. Third row, left to right: Gregory Breit (partially hidden), Arthur Hemmendinger, and Art Schelberg. *(Courtesy of Los Alamos Scientific Laboratory)*

Oppenheimer's resignation and awards ceremony. Groves (center) presents Oppenheimer and the Laboratory a Certificate of Appreciation from the Secretary of War on October 16, 1945. To the right of Groves is Gordon Sproul, President of the University of California.

(Courtesy of Los Alamos Scientific Laboratory)

Edward Teller. Teller and Oppenheimer first met in the 1930s, soon after Teller emigrated to the United States from Hungary. Teller devoted much of his energy at Los Alamos during the war to the study of the thermonuclear weapon. After the war, he became the weapon's leading advocate and with colleagues made an important discovery which led to the successful development of the first thermonuclear bomb. Teller revealed a lack of trust in Oppenheimer during Oppenheimer's government hearing in 1954. *(Courtesy of Los Alamos Scientific Laboratory)*

Testimony before Congress. On June 13, 1949, Oppenheimer testified before the Joint Congressional Committee on Atomic Energy. It was during this event that he ridiculed the importance of radioisotopes.
(Used by permission; United Press International Photo)

Oppenheimer receives Enrico Fermi Award. Despite opposition, President John Kennedy announced his intention to award Oppenheimer the government's Enrico Fermi Award on November 22, 1963, the day the President was assassinated. Lyndon Johnson personally presented the award on December 2. Edward Teller had received the same award the year before.
(Courtesy of Oppenheimer Memorial Society)

Lewis Strauss. A rear-admiral during WWII, Strauss served as a member of the first Atomic Energy Commission and later as its Chairman. It was during this latter period that Robert Oppenheimer had his infamous hearing in 1954.
(Used by permission of Wide World Photos)

Director of the Institute for Advanced Study. Oppenheimer accepted the directorship of Princeton University's prestigious Institute for Advanced Study in the spring of 1947; he formally began his tenure in October and remained director until 1966. Oppenheimer aged visibly after his hearing in 1954.
(Courtesy of Oppenheimer Memorial Society)

Oppenheimer shortly before his death. Oppenheimer died on February 18, 1967, in Princeton, New Jersey. Oppenheimer's wife had his body cremated and the ashes scattered in the sea near the Virgin Islands.
(Courtesy of Oppenheimer Memorial Society)

The positive atmosphere certainly encouraged an energetic program to develop and test the Teller-Ulam approach as soon as possible. Some projected that the new weapons would be ready by the fall of 1952. Oppenheimer, however, was not so sure. He remembered Teller and Bethe approaching him in 1943 with the enthusiastic assessment that "if we had the material [uranium and plutonium] now, we could have a bomb in three weeks." In actuality, they had had the bomb in two years, and even that occurred under conditions where the laboratory's size doubled every nine months. The thermonuclear weapon posed many unknowns, but at last there was a promising line of development to follow.

What the meeting did not achieve was a tempering of the ill will between scientists at Los Alamos. Teller had made up his mind not to return; he was already thinking of a new laboratory—supported by Air Force money, and perhaps located in Boulder, Colorado—with one hundred men, including fifty "top" men.[29] Others, like Wheeler and von Neumann, were convinced that Los Alamos was too sluggish. Certainly this was the perception of men like Strauss, who still monitored the developments as an ex-commissioner, and also of McMahon and many senior military leaders. Teller, in fact, appealed to Oppenheimer to return to Los Alamos; Bradbury, he argued, was not the man for the job. There were three men whom Teller believed could lead the thermonuclear effort: Oppenheimer, Fermi, and Bethe. When both Fermi and Bethe declined the role, Teller asked Oppenheimer if he would take it. Oppenheimer replied that it would depend on "whether I would be welcomed by Bradbury." He agreed to call the Los Alamos director, believing nevertheless that as the former director, it would not be a good idea to return. Oppenheimer later reported that he had talked with Bradbury, but that the man had given no indications of wanting Oppenheimer back: "Bradbury said he had confidence in the present director."[30] For Oppenheimer, it was just as well; later he confessed that even if he had returned, he wasn't sure that "I could have been on my toes."

The meeting at Princeton was the turning point in the development of the hydrogen bomb. While difficulties lay ahead, there was now a sure course to follow. Within a few months Los Alamos was able to project the general size and weight of a thermonuclear weapon for military planners. A deliverable hydrogen bomb would be enclosed within a case approximately twenty feet long and seventy-two inches in diameter. Its weight would be approximately fifty thousand pounds, pushing the limits of a B-36 or B-52.[31]

Despite the new optimism, however, Oppenheimer felt compelled to suggest that philosophical questions remained, and they were questions that not many chose to discuss or to answer.

14. Scorpions in a Bottle

The news from Los Alamos gave some political leaders new hope. It coincided with new demands from Senator McMahon and the Joint Committee on Atomic Energy for the production of more weapons. But an increase in demand for weapons meant a corresponding increase in production of fissionable materials. Simply increasing present American production by 50 percent meant spending an additional $2.8 billion in new construction and an additional $220 million a year in operating costs. Six new atomic reactors would be needed.[1]

In the midst of these considerations, Edward Teller resigned from Los Alamos. Oppenheimer tried to reassure the AEC commissioners that such a break was inevitable: Teller and Bradbury would never have an easy relationship. Oppenheimer's refusal to return to Los Alamos, along with similar refusals from Fermi and Bethe, only meant the break would occur sooner. Teller departed with considerable accomplishments to his credit and with promises to be available for consulting.

Teller's departure added fire to the demands by some that a second weapons laboratory be created, one that could help relieve Los Alamos of the load. As Dean and Oppenheimer were to argue, such a move would cause problems. It would obviously be another blow to Los Alamos morale; there would be a difficult question of deciding which work to take from Los Alamos to the new laboratory; and a division of staff could not be made simply on the basis of a head count. Henry Smyth believed that everyone qualified was already working on the thermonuclear program.

In late September the United States picked up evidence of another Soviet atomic detonation. Truman again delayed issuing a press release on the event. There were calls from the Joint Committee, similar to those made twenty-five months before, for increasing the American stockpile and producing the hydrogen bomb as soon as possible. From the floor of the House of Representatives, Congressman Henry Jackson called for an increase in federal expenditures in atomic energy. The nation, he argued, needed to increase its stockpile to cover enemy tactical targets, as well as major ones.

Oppenheimer and the General Advisory Committee met on October 11, 1951, to hear Bradbury's latest report from Los Alamos, as well as to consider proposals for a second weapons laboratory. Bradbury's plans for a systematic program and for tests in Nevada were also given approval.

Libby, a member of the GAC, strongly endorsed a second laboratory, but was countered by Rabi, who thought that such a move would mean dividing the scientific resources already at work. Bradbury concurred. The committee, despite Libby's protests, agreed as well: It could not recommend creating a second laboratory. The committee, however, would not take up the recent demands from the military and from Congress to expand current production. There was nevertheless the realization that whatever the degree of expansion, actual output of plutonium and uranium would not increase until 1956. If the period of national concern was for the present or for the immediate future, what purpose would be served by such an elaborate enlargement of current production capacity? The issue now seemed destined to be taken up by the National Security Council and the Departments of Defense and State.

These large matters inevitably raised again the question of another laboratory. Teller made a personal visit to Oppenheimer in early November. He felt that the GAC's failure to recommend a second laboratory was wrong, and he asked for a chance to personally make a presentation in favor of such an institution at the next GAC meeting in December. His argument was simple: Los Alamos scientists were excellent men, but the atmosphere for constructive research was hampered by the limited goals of the institution. A new laboratory would have thermonuclear weapons as the chief priority. There was, Teller added, reason to act quickly. After all, the Russians had by now detonated their third atomic weapon; who knew how far along they were in developing a hydrogen bomb? The GAC responded with the same concerns expressed before: staffing, duplication of effort, and low morale—but perhaps a compromise could be worked out. Los Alamos could create an entirely new division, one that would have responsibility for long-range goals and would be unfettered by day-to-day demands.[2] Would such a plan be acceptable to Bradbury? Could a suitable division director be found? Also, perhaps the reduction of the work load of present production tasks at Los Alamos would help. Kenneth Fields, director of the division of military applications, suggested that such a reduction in work would lessen the need for a second laboratory; Los Alamos would find it easier to concentrate on thermonuclear and fission work without its manufacturing duties. Oppenheimer agreed, as did his committee. With that recommendation, the commissioners voted 4–1 (Murray dissenting), to reject a second weapons laboratory. For the moment, Los Alamos was the nation's only weapons laboratory.

In May 1951, Oppenheimer was asked by his former GAC colleague Lee DuBridge to attend briefings from a study sponsored by the Air Force, Army, and Navy on ground and air tactical warfare. Called Project Vista, the study had been awarded as a contract to the California Institute of Technology. Most of the senior consultants were old friends of Oppenheimer's: Robert Bacher, Robert Christy, Charles Lauritsen, Clark Millikan, and William Fowler. The real concern of the study was the defense of Western Europe against Soviet aggression.

Oppenheimer flew to Pasadena to join the others in reviewing what was essentially the first draft of the report. One chapter—Chapter Five—related specifically to the use of nuclear weapons. Following discussions, Oppenheimer was asked to take the chapter and revise it to incorporate the thinking of the last few days. The report found that atomic weapons could be useful—even decisive—in limited tactical settings. The examples relevant to the times included the mass attacks by Russian troops during World War II and similar attacks by the Chinese in the Korean War. One recommendation was to divide the present stockpile of nuclear weapons so that some number of weapons would always be available for immediate, or near-immedate, use in a variety of settings and under differing weather conditions. Strategic weapons, such as the most powerful fission or thermonuclear weapons, had their place, but so did small weapons. While these limited tactical weapons did not yet exist—they were still under development at Los Alamos—they would be weapons that could be used with great accuracy against targets. They could be artillery shells or the tips of missiles, for example. Accuracy was a key, however; accurate weapons meant smaller weapons and therefore an economy of fissionable material. Low accuracy meant that more powerful weapons would be needed to compensate for the lack of precise targeting. These weapons would be used to support ground operations. Larger weapons had primarily strategic value, perhaps for retaliatory actions against an attack on the United States.

The Vista report, particularly Chapter Five, became a matter of considerable controversy for Oppenheimer. The Air Force, especially, took exception to the findings. Air Force Secretary Thomas Finletter thought he saw criticism for the role of the Strategic Air Force in the report, as did General Vandenberg. The defense establishment saw a refutation of the need for thermonuclear weapons. The great emphasis in the report on very precise, highly deliverable atomic bombs seemed to lessen the importance of hydrogen weapons as tactical weapons, if not suggesting that strategic weapons were peripheral at best. David Griggs, the chief scientist for the Air Force, reviewed the report in November and found it unfavorable, especially since it recommended a three-way split of fissionable materials: to the Strategic Air Command, to the developers of smaller tactical weapons, and to a reserve fund for future use in other weapons. The Strategic Air Command had been the primary recipient of nuclear materials for some years. Much of the current defense strategy called for the delivery of weapons by SAC against enemy targets. The suggestion that the H-bomb be used only as a retaliatory weapon further irritated the Air

Force. Oppenheimer, who was cited—inaccurately—as the principal author of Chapter Five, came under even more criticism from the military, but especially from the Air Force.

David Griggs was typical of those people within the military who found Oppenheimer's involvement with defense matters suspect. "Dr. Oppenheimer," he later said, "is the only one of my scientific acquaintances about whom I have ever felt there was any serious question as to their loyalty." His assessment was not from personal contact, but from colleagues who spoke of the scientist's past. He had been told that Oppenheimer had been considered a "calculated risk" during his Los Alamos days. Air Force Secretary Finletter had personally expressed his concern over Oppenheimer's loyalty after having read Oppenheimer's FBI files.[3]

Both Oppenheimer and DuBridge believed that the draft of the Vista report needed comment from those individuals charged with defending Western Europe. With the approval of Secretary of Defense Robert Lovett, Oppenheimer, DuBridge, Lauritsen, and Walt Whitman of the R & D Board left for Paris on December 3 for a conference with Dwight Eisenhower, the commander of Supreme Headquarters, Allied Powers in Europe (SHAPE). Although he and his colleagues refused to comment on the purpose of their trip, Oppenheimer soon became the center of the press attention, with headlines in America that ran "Oppenheimer Lands in Paris," and "Oppenheimer Visits with Eisenhower for Hour." They crossed Europe to meet with other Army and Air Force leaders, including General Lauris Norstad, who had been briefed earlier by Finletter so that he would be prepared to counter aspects of the Vista report when he met with Oppenheimer and the others. The general made what Oppenheimer considered to be a rather "formal" objection to the report, but he agreed that most of its contents were good. Oppenheimer offered to rewrite the report in order to correct some of the objections: "[It is perhaps] a matter of substance, and it may be a matter of language. Let us rewrite this in order to remove from it those phrases and those arrangements of ideas which appear to be bothering you and see if then this statement of the case is one which is satisfactory to you." The changes apparently pleased Norstad. A few days later he volunteered: "If I am asked, I will tell the Chief of Staff and the Secretary [of the Air Force] that I think this is a fine report and very valuable."[4] After additional comments, Oppenheimer drafted another version of Chapter Five, and the report was formally submitted. Even so, the new version failed to please Air Force officials: they remained convinced that the report suffered from Oppenheimer's excessive attempts to influence atomic policy.

Not everyone objected to Oppenheimer's role, however. Walter Whitman, who attended the military briefings on Vista in Europe, thought Oppenheimer had done a remarkably fair job: "I should say that he more than any other man served to educate the military to the potentialities of the atomic weapon for other than strategic bombing purposes; its use possibly in tactical situations or in bombing 500 miles back." Whitman remembered that deliverability was one factor Oppenheimer stressed. The smaller the weapon, the more easily it could be taken to its target, whether in a medium bomber, a fighter plane, or on the tip of a missile or rocket. "In my judgment, his advice and his arguments for a gamut of atomic weapons, extending over to the use of atomic weapons in air defense of the United States, has been more productive than any other one individual."[5]

Despite such support, Oppenheimer seemed destined to cross swords with the Air Force. During the same summer he agreed to be involved with the Lincoln Laboratory outside Boston, which concerned itself with early warning systems, radar, and other measures of continental defense. Its summer study program was a component of the Lincoln Project, which was largely funded by the Air Force to advise on air defense. Jerrold Zacharias, who was associate director of the program, recruited Oppenheimer as much for his knowledge on atomic weapons as for his name, believing that Oppenheimer's reputation would attract the interest of others. The idea of involving Oppenheimer, as well as Isidor Rabi and Charles Lauritsen, had originated earlier in the year in March. Meeting in Boston's Statler Hotel, Zacharias had approached Oppenheimer, Rabi, and Lauritsen with the idea of meeting in the summer, on a part-time basis, to assess the growing threat of newer enemy airplanes and the prospect of missile-developed weapons. The Lincoln group envisioned a multi-ring system of defense that ranged from the protection or defense of targets at home in a "last-ditch" effort to the destruction of enemy bases and fighting power by long-range aircraft. The final report, which carried Oppenheimer's name and which emphasized strengthening air defense, was perceived by some Air Force critics as an attempt to downplay the role of the Strategic Air Command. It became associated with what Air Force insiders considered a cabal of plotters: Oppenheimer, Zacharias, Rabi, and Lauritsen.

Oppenheimer was already under suspicion by David Griggs, Air Force Secretary Finletter, and his aides William Burden and Garrison Norton. In Griggs's words, there was "a pattern of activities all of which involved Dr. Oppenheimer." This pattern referred to his supposed opposition to the thermonuclear weapon, his objections to a second weapons laboratory, and the recommendations purportedly authored by him in the Vista project. His behavior, it seemed, had cast doubts on his loyalty. Griggs and Oppenheimer had had an unpleasant meeting on May 23, 1952, when Griggs had journeyed to Princeton for a meeting with the scientist. Part of Griggs's agenda was to ascertain the scientist's role in spreading a story involving Secretary Finletter. According to unknown sources, a story had been circulated in Washington and in military circles which quoted

Finletter as telling Edward Teller that "if only the United States had enough hydrogen bombs, we could rule the world." Oppenheimer, unfortunately, had been credited with spreading the tale. When questioned by Griggs, Oppenheimer admitted to having heard the story from a source "he could not question." Regarding thermonuclear weapons, Oppenheimer denied having tried to retard the program, volunteering as proof the October 29, 1949, letters written by the GAC to Lilienthal.

The meeting was exasperating for both men. Oppenheimer clearly sensed that his loyalty was in question. He abruptly asked Griggs if the man thought he was "pro-Russian" or merely confused. Griggs replied that he wished he knew. Oppenheimer then asked if Griggs had ever "impugned his loyalty to high officials of the Defense Department." Griggs responded that he had and that he had heard Oppenheimer's loyalty questioned by others in the department. Griggs was certainly thinking of Finletter and General Vandenberg, to mention only two. Oppenheimer, wearied from the tedious meeting, could only reply that he thought Griggs was paranoid.[6] Griggs left to return to Washington, where he prepared a memo for Finletter on the meeting. He labeled it "Eyes Only." Finletter was appalled that Oppenheimer was again going to be involved with an Air Force project. The notion of a summer study as an adjunct of Project Lincoln was enough to cause Finletter to order Griggs to check directly with the president of M.I.T., which sponsored the project. Griggs revealed the Air Force's anxiety over Oppenheimer's participation and the belief that a report stemming from the proposed summer study would be detrimental to the Air Force. James Killian, the president of M.I.T., was only barely aware of the summer meetings. His provost, Julius Stratton, conducted furtive investigation. Oppenheimer had been invited by Lincoln's director, but he assured Griggs that the summer study would be "kept in bounds."[7] Oppenheimer came to a sad realization, one he had suspected for so long: His much-vaunted position was the subject of the gravest sort of controversy, and that perhaps there would not be much more time left for him to serve as "the father of the atomic bomb."

On May 16, Oppenheimer received a disquieting call from Gordon Dean, who explained that the Justice Department planned to indict Joseph Weinberg for perjury within the week. Weinberg testified, contrary to other evidence, that he had never attended a Communist party meeting, especially one that was alleged to have taken place in Oppenheimer's home. Dean hoped the scientist could be kept out of it, although he could not be sure. On May 23, Weinberg's indictment made the newspapers, but fortunately without a mention of Oppenheimer's name.[8] Later in September two articles by Stewart Alsop appeared in the New York *Herald Tribune*, entitled "The Air War." They addressed the increased sophistication of Soviet air power and the country's ability to make a first strike against the United States that could cripple the nation's ability to retaliate. The articles encouraged long-range detection and sophisticated radar to precede such an attack. The information seemed authentic enough to cause some to believe that someone within the government had leaked the information. It was known that Oppenheimer was a good friend of Stewart's brother, Joseph.

The prospects for a second weapons laboratory improved with a meeting between Teller and Ernest Lawrence in February 1952. Visiting the site of Lawrence's new accelerator at Livermore, the elder scientist proposed that Teller leave Chicago and start a new laboratory in California. Teller agreed, but only under the condition that the work would include thermonuclear weapons research. Teller took the idea to Finletter a few days later. On March 19 he met with Secretary of Defense Lovett and the three service chiefs. By the first of April there was little doubt that a second laboratory would be created at Livermore. The first task of the new laboratory would be to concentrate on refining the new approach based on the Teller-Ulam breakthrough. By September there were 123 scientific and technical people at Livermore. For the moment, Livermore would be concerned only with research, leaving Los Alamos in charge of the first full test of the thermonuclear weapon on November 1.

The summer of 1952 was a period of recollection for Robert Oppenheimer. Since 1942 he had been actively engaged in the atomic energy program of the United States. For nearly six years he had chaired the General Advisory Committee of the Atomic Energy Commission. It had been a long and arduous road for a man who had just turned forty-eight. His influence, which had once placed him at the highest levels of the government, was now one primarily of service within the GAC. Massive weapons had become the cornerstone of foreign and military policy despite the endless arguments by Oppenheimer and others. He understood how his arguments and cautions had been so frequently misunderstood. There was a decided change in the atmosphere in Washington toward him, toward weapons, toward the role the United States would play as the world's great superpower. The attacks from the Air Force, from some members of the commission, and from old colleagues were finally taking their toll. The hearings being conducted by Senator Joseph McCarthy on Communist infiltration of the United States government were unsettling, as were the continuing investigations by the House Un-American Activities Committee. Oppenheimer had little reason to believe that his past would ever be fully behind him and that his perceptions of defense and weapons would ever be assessed without prejudice.

Oppenheimer had stayed on in the bureaucracy when many of his colleagues had left to return to their classrooms and laboratories. He was no longer a scientist but a policymaker. Even with its enormous potential, atomic energy no longer carried the excitement for him that it had before and during the war. The practice of atomic energy had matured, much like the bureaucracy that managed it.

To his brother, Frank, Oppenheimer wrote:

> By August 1 my six years on the Gen. Advisory Committee are over; they have seemed long. Physics is complicated & wondersome & much too hard for me except as a spectator; it will have to get easy again one of these days, but perhaps not soon.[9]

In May he decided to let his term on the General Advisory Committee end in July and not to accept any offer for reappointment. Gordon Dean was understanding and possibly even relieved. He wrote: "I am quite aware that there is no one who can adequately take your place."[10] Truman accepted the end of Oppenheimer's services with praise for his many contributions.

Oppenheimer believed that a report to the President on the work of the General Advisory Committee would be in order. With ideas from Conant, DuBridge, and Oliver Buckley, Oppenheimer prepared the first drafts of two reports. The first was a message for the President only; the second, to be released as a public statement, if desired. The draft reports were ready by the meeting of the GAC on June 13. Revised during the discussions, the statements revealed much of Oppenheimer's thinking. The first and privileged message to President Truman spoke to the considerable changes that had occurred over the previous years. The development of weapons and of "beautiful discoveries" in the basic sciences were substantial, he wrote, but still largely based on the discoveries made before or during the war. Certainly the nation could feel some comfort in the fact that the stockpile of weapons now could provide the security the United States needed. But what of the future? Weapons a thousand times more powerful than those of Hiroshima and Nagasaki were inevitable; already there was evidence of the workability of thermonuclear reactions. The fissionable material in weapons, however, could always be turned back into food for reactors and for scientific exploration. If this were not to occur, catastrophe seemed possible: "Thus atomic armament, which is now held to be the shield of the free world, may in a foreseeable time become the gravest threat to our welfare and security."[11]

The public statement, written in Oppenheimer's graceful style, reviewed the creation and growth of the General Advisory Committee. In six years the committee had met thirty times—in scheduled meetings and in Washington, Los Alamos, Berkeley, Princeton, Pasadena, Oak Ridge, and Argonne. Remarkably, with few exceptions, each meeting was attended by the full committee—a testament to the commitment of the members to their task. Full and frank discussions had taken place between the GAC and the members of the commission itself.

The commission had been the primary source of information for the committee, which had also chosen on occasion to speak first-hand with other scientists, especially those at Los Alamos, and with members of other AEC laboratories or plants. By and large, the committee had addressed problems identified by the commission.

> Our agenda has thus for the most part reflected the commission's current preoccupations. We believe that this procedure has perhaps led us to postpone too long the considerations of some technical problems, but that it had worked well in those cases where the commission or we were aware of a problem, and where the technical information in fact existed.[12]

There had been difficulties, perhaps with greater implications than anticipated: The creation of independent advisory bodies on raw materials, biology, and medicine had "often left us rather remote from the realities even of those decisions for which technical arguments were of the greatest importance." There was, Oppenheimer argued, a "critical interdependence" between technical and military evaluations. He wrote:

> . . . we have not thought it proper to discuss directly with representatives of the military establishment their assessments of military worth, or their establishment of military requirements. When we have talked directly with the Military Liaison Committee, it has been in an attempt to make available to that Committee facts and evaluations of which we were quite confident, and on the basis of which the Commission wished to proceed.

Importantly, the committee had sometimes found itself "forced to consider, or asked to advise on, matters which were not in any narrow sense scientific." The reasons for this were two: Technical developments could not prosper in the absence of policy or objectives, and the execution of technical policy depends on the arrangements made to carry out the policy.

> We have throughout tended to act as a committee, on almost all important points seeking, if not quite always achieving, unanimity. With a very few exceptions, our views have been unanimous.

On September 27, Truman wrote to Oppenheimer, accepting his resignation and thanking him for his service. Oppenheimer had made "a lasting and immensely valuable contribution to the national security and to atomic energy progress" in the United States. Regrettably, much of the scientist's work could not be disclosed fully.

> I shall always be personally grateful for the time and energy you have so unselfishly devoted to the work of the General Advisory

> Committee; for the conscientious and rewarding way in which you have brought your great talents to bear upon the scientific problems of atomic energy development, and for the notable part you have played in securing for the atomic energy program the understanding cooperation of the scientific community.[13]

Gordon Dean wrote a letter of appreciation as well, addressing the scientist affectionately as "Dear Oppy." Ironically referring to the great scientific and technological strides made by the nation, he said:

> I sincerely hope that some day, when the ills of the world are sufficiently diminished, the complete story of this progress can be told, so that the contribution of you and your colleagues may find its rightful place in the chronicle of our times.[14]

Dean appointed Oppenheimer as a consultant to the commission for one year, continuing his Q clearance and preserving his access to classified information. In December, Dean ordered three security officers to Oppenheimer's office at Princeton to catalog and remove the bulk of the scientist's classified papers and reports. In June 1953, Dean extended Oppenheimer's consultant contract with the AEC for one additional year.

The first full-scale test of a thermonuclear weapon was in Operation Ivy, which consisted of two explosions. The first, nicknamed Mike, was the test of the Teller-Ulam device; the second, called King, was a test of an enormously powerful fission weapon. Los Alamos was absorbed in the preparations for both tests. In June, in a move that surprised their colleagues, Oppenheimer and Bethe suggested that the Ivy tests be postponed; their suggestion centered on the fact that the presidential elections were scheduled for November 4, just three days after the Ivy experiments. It was possible, they argued, that the tests could be exploited for their propaganda value by unscrupulous individuals in the campaigns. Bradbury was startled by the proposition. He wrote Oppenheimer on June 11, expressing the considerable difficulties involved in postponing the tests. There were only a few days of good weather in November; even a delay of a few weeks might well mean that Ivy would have to conducted in 1953. The matter went back and forth between the Defense Department, the AEC, and the White House. Truman did not feel he could delay the tests, even by a few days, unless there was a technical reason to do so. No reason arose, and plans for the test proceeded. The Mike device was shipped to Enewitok aboard the U.S.S. *Curtis*; from there, it went by barge to Elugelab. The test was controlled from the U.S.S. *Curtis*, anchored off Enewitok Island, and monitored by television cameras. Once assembled, Mike weighed eighty tons. The liquid deuterium required a bulky cryogenic system that consumed a multistory building on an adjacent island. On

November 1, 1952—October 31, Pacific Ocean time—Mike exploded. It was the largest explosion ever devised by man to that date. The tiny Micronesian island of Elugelab disappeared in a blinding second in almost ten and a half million tons of explosive force. The crater left by Mike was a mile across, consuming pieces of two adjacent islands. Its yield of 10.4 megatons was 1,000 times the force of the Hiroshima blast. Unlike fission weapons, the ball of fire expanded quickly and rose, forming many ice caps.

As successful as the test was, the weapon, at eighty-seven tons, was hardly capable of being delivered, except as Oppenheimer had said, by "ox cart." The weapon, which was intentionally devised as an experimental model, utilized liquid deuterium, normally a gas unless refrigerated at −250°C to make it a liquid. A small island near Elugelab had been converted into a large refrigeration plant, with a central building several stories high constructed to house the cumbersome apparatus necessary to produce liquid deuterium.*

The second test involved an airdropped bomb designed to explode at fifteen hundred feet. King was an all-fission weapon which produced an explosive force of over five hundred thousand tons, more than twenty-five times the size of the most powerful weapon dropped on Japan during World War II. The escalation of explosive power had been made possible by new techniques and designs proven in the earlier Sandstone tests. The success of King proved Oppenheimer's argument that large weapons did not necessarily mean only thermonuclear ones. A weapon designed to produce five hundred kilotons of force could be further designed, in theory, to yield even more powerful explosions.

The success of King, however, was overshadowed by the vast power of Mike. Even the jaded scientists of Los Alamos were numbed by the sheer size and energy of the hydrogen bomb. Its fire and color had raged like the most blinding image of götterdämmerung. The atomic age of World War II had been replaced by an ominous and forbidding new era. Barely six months later, the United States would detonate a "deliverable" thermonuclear weapon.

In July 1952 the Republicans meeting in Chicago selected General Dwight D. Eisenhower as their presidential nominee and Senator Richard M. Nixon of California as his running mate. President Truman had announced in March that he would not be a candidate for reelection; he favored Governor Adlai E. Stevenson of Illinois as the Democrats' nominee. Meeting also in Chicago at the end of July, Stevenson won out

*Mike used liquid deuterium because its "burning" in a thermonuclear reaction was more straightforward and easier to calculate. Also, natural lithium contains less than 8 percent of the critical isotope Li 6, which is the isotope that produces tritium when reacting with neutrons. The alternative was to use solid lithium deuteride.

over Senator Estes Kefauver of Tennessee on the third ballot. Senator John Sparkman of Alabama was nominated as Vice-President. During the national election, Eisenhower scored a sweeping victory with 442 electoral votes to Stevenson's 89. Both the House of Representatives and the Senate gained slim Republican majorities. Eisenhower appointed John Foster Dulles, who had lost his New York Senate seat in the November election, as secretary of state. Charles E. Wilson, formerly the director of the Office of Defense Mobilization, was named the new secretary of defense.

Oppenheimer acknowledged the developments by commenting to close friends that the political climate did not augur well for him.

During the summer a series of magazine articles appeared in the public press. One was written by Oppenheimer and appeared in the journal *Foreign Affairs*. Two other articles, one in May and the other in August, appeared in *Fortune*; they were written by Charles Murphy, formerly with the U.S. Air Force.

Murphy's first article, which he chose not to sign, was entitled "The Hidden Struggle for the H-Bomb: The Story of Dr. Oppenheimer's Persistent Campaign to Reverse U.S. Military Strategy." National military policy, he wrote anonymously, was engaged in a "life and death" struggle between the defense establishment and certain influential scientists, led by Robert Oppenheimer. Murphy recreated the key events of the previous years: the October 29, 1949, recommendation against the hydrogen bomb, the Truman decision, the controversy over a second weapons laboratory, and the attempts to challenge the nation's strategic defense plans. The strong, and presumably correct, response from the Defense Department was said to be one of considerable concern. Fearing the failure of the Vista report, for example, Oppenheimer had led a group of scientists to Europe to speak with Eisenhower and others to solicit support for the report's recommendations. These same scientists, according to Murphy, had organized themselves into something they called ZORC, standing for Zacharias, Oppenheimer, Rabi, and Charles Lauritsen.* Their philosophy was to call for strong continental defense measures at the expense of long-range strategic bombing attacks. It was unacceptable that scientists would attempt to determine policies that they had no responsibility for carrying out.

Oppenheimer appeared hardly so manipulating when his own thoughts appeared in the July issue of *Foreign Affairs*. He had taken the precaution of submitting his article to President Truman for approval, and there had been no objections.

He began optimistically: "It is possible that in the large light of

---

*The "C" presumably referred to Lauritsen's first name, Charles.

history, if indeed there is to be history, the atomic bomb will appear not very different than in the bright light of the first atomic explosion." The bomb, he wrote, had been developed to end a "great and terrible war," as much as to end all wars. Efforts to control the atom internationally had been rejected by the Russians, whose "hostility," combined with the disharmony and disunity of the "free world," had prevented any such control from being achieved. The atom had therefore been turned to weapons under the argument, "Let us keep ahead. Let us be sure that we are ahead of the enemy."[15]

The race for weapons had placed the United States some "four years" ahead of the Soviets—a guess that was to be woefully inaccurate—and with the Soviets in possession of an arsenal only half as large as this nation's. "The very least we can say is that there will come a time when, even from the narrowest technical point of view, the art of delivery and the art of defense will have a much higher military relevance than supremacy in the atomic munitions field itself." Weapons at best would bring the two great powers to the uneasy edge of mutual destruction. Oppenheimer's view was that there was inevitably a long period of cold war in which tension and armaments would exist side by side. During this period,

> . . . the atomic clock ticks faster and faster. We may anticipate a state of affairs in which two great powers will each be in a position to put an end to the civilization and life of the other, though not without risking its own. We may be likened to two scorpions in a bottle, each capable of killing the other, but only at the risk of his own life. . . . This prospect does not make for serenity.

There were three things to remember. One could not forget the hostility and power of the Russians. Nor could one forget that some weakness was necessarily inherent in the mutual need of all nations for unity and stability. And certainly there was the growing "peril" of atomic energy. Oppenheimer proposed three reforms. The first was a new openness or candor on the part of the government about armaments and the arms race. What could the public make, for example, of a recent statement by an Air Force general who said that it was not the business of air defenses to protect the nation, for that would interfere with the nation's retaliatory capacities, but to protect the country's strike force? How, without adequate but not classified information, could an evaluation be made?

> The political vitality of our country largely derives from two sources: one is the interplay of opinion and debate in the diverse and complex legislative and executive agencies which contribute

to the making of policy. The other is a public opinion which is based on confidence that it knows the truth.

When the citizens of the United States were told by their leaders that "substantial progress" had been made in armament, they needed to know what that meant.

The second reform was to better—or to establish, where necessary—more cooperative relationships with the nation's allies. The United Kingdom and Canada were two prime examples; the members of NATO were another. Since war was perhaps most likely in Europe, then Europeans must be brought into the making of policy decisions. "What we do will affect the destiny of Europe; what is done there will affect ours."

The last reform addressed the urgent need for the defense of "our people, our lives, our institutions, our cities." If, as General Vandenberg recently said, we might with luck intercept only 20 or 30 percent of an attack by the enemy, there was need for strengthening America's defensive capability. Surely an arms agreement would be the best long-range protection for everyone. Candor, collaboration, and cooperation, and defense and long-term regulation, were the cornerstones of his argument. "We need," he wrote somberly, "to liberate our own great resources to shape our destiny."

The following month, in August, Charles Murphy responded in a signed article published in *Fortune*. While rejecting war, Murphy warned that the openness called for by Oppenheimer might well produce "terrible consequences" if the Russians did not respond in kind. There were, Murphy argued, secrets that could not be given away. If the *Fortune* article failed to generate anxiety in some segments of American society, news on August 12 by the Atomic Energy Commission did. The AEC verified that the Soviets had recently exploded a thermonuclear device which the commission was calling Joe 4. Oppenheimer's prediction of four years no doubt produced only laughter in defense circles and strengthened the belief that the scientist's judgment was not to be trusted.

On June 20, 1953, the Department of Defense implemented Reorganization Plan Number 6 and effected, among other changes, the dissolution of the Research and Development Board. Eisenhower's Defense Secretary Charles Wilson noted the "smooth" way in which they had been able to drop Oppenheimer's membership.[16]

Early in July, Walter Whitman, who had directed the now-defunct Research and Development Board, was approached by security officials with a report on Oppenheimer which they claimed contained "derogatory information." Under President Eisenhower's April directive, all cases involving government employees or consultants with backgrounds including derogatory data had to be reexamined and in effect cleared again or dropped. Although Whitman was preparing to leave the Pentagon, he said that he would review the report. "I said I would personally review the whole case and leave for my successor my recommendation in terms of whether or not Dr. Oppenheimer should be re-appointed for another year as a consultant in the Department of Defense." His successor, Donald Quarles, would be named assistant secretary of defense, research, and development, and would be the person most likely to make use of Oppenheimer's consultancy. After spending a Saturday reviewing the file several times (the report contained FBI summaries of Oppenheimer's background), Whitman found nothing that suggested the scientist was disloyal or untrustworthy. He prepared a memorandum for Quarles. Regarding Oppenheimer, he wrote

> I have known for some time the general nature and salient features of the information contained in this file. It discloses nothing which would cause me to modify my previous confidence in his loyalty. . . . I am convinced that he can be of great service as a consultant to the research and development work of the Department of Defense. . . . I unqualifiedly recommend his reappointment as a consultant.[17]

Despite Whitman's endorsement, Oppenheimer was not reappointed as a consultant to the Defense Department.

On July 3, Lewis Strauss returned to the Atomic Energy Commission as its chairman. His nomination by Eisenhower had been a response to the man's assistance during the campaign and to the urgings from members of Congress and the Defense Department. Earlier, in March, Strauss had been appointed special assistant to the President for atomic energy; in June he had been nominated to replace Gordon Dean as chairman. One of his first acts was to call for the security file on Oppenheimer. Word drifted down to the scientist that hard times might be ahead.[18] On July 7, Strauss ordered the removal of all classified documents that remained in Oppenheimer's Princeton files. Seven months before, the commission had removed some thirty-two linear feet of paper from Oppenheimer's vault, leaving only material immediately relevant to his work as a consultant. Strauss had been miffed that Dean, in one of his last acts before leaving the commission, had reappointed Oppenheimer to another year as consultant.

Strauss had little reason to be upset at Oppenheimer's continuing role as consultant. During the previous twelve months the scientist's services had been utilized only on six days, for which he had been paid $250. With the death of the Research and Development Board, and with the exception of his little-used consultant contract with AEC, Robert Oppenheimer no longer served the United States government in an official capacity.

Despite the internecine fighting in Washington, in 1953 Oppenheimer decided to deliver two lectures which revived him personally and awakened in new listeners a sense of awe and appreciation for the scientist's intellect and vision. To audiences in Brazil, where he talked to the members of the National Research Council, he spoke again of the beauty of physics and of its promise to humanity. A few months later, in November, he and Kitty left for England, where he was to deliver the Reith lectures. He had spent considerable time during the early fall preparing for what he regarded as one of the most important presentations of his life. Entitled "Science and the Common Understanding," his talk was composed of six lectures delivered in person and simultaneously broadcast over the radio by the British Broadcasting Corporation.*

He was received enthusiastically, although he was told that some thought him "hopelessly obscure." Some of the lectures were tough going for the nonscientist listener; some listeners seemed to be more taken with the eloquence of his delivery than the contents of his speech. In his last lecture he spoke directly and simply. Science was like a house, he said by way of analogy.

> It does not appear to have been built upon any plan but to have grown as a great city grows. There is no central chamber, no one corridor from which all others debouch. All about the periphery men are at work studying the vast reaches of space and the state of affairs billions of years ago; studying the intricate and subtle but wonderfully met mechanisms by which life proliferates, alters, and endures; studying the reach of the mind and its ways of learning; digging deep into the atoms within atoms and their unfathomed order.[19]

The house was only partly known, but "one thing we find throughout the house: there are no locks, there are no shut doors; wherever we go there are the signs and usually the words of welcome."

The art of science was complex: There was more than one way to describe and to measure. As well, men studying science were not in isolation; they were part of a community to which all humans belonged.

> The open society, the unrestricted access to knowledge, the unplanned and uninhibited association of men for its furtherance—these are what may make a vast, complex, ever-growing, ever-changing, ever more specialized and expert technological world, nevertheless a world of human community.[20]

---

*The Reith lectures included: "Newton, The Path of Light"; "Science as Action"; "Rutherford's World"; "A Science in Change"; "Atom in Void in the Third Millennium"; "Uncommon Sense"; and "The Science and Man's Community."

Robert and Kitty left for Paris, to spend an evening with Haakron Chevalier and his new wife, Carol. Chevalier prepared dinner for the four of them in the tiny Parisian apartment. They served the salad with a wooden bowl which had been a wedding gift from Robert and Kitty. Kitty insisted that the four of them write their names on a champagne cork. The following day Chevalier arranged for Oppenheimer to meet André Malraux. Speaking of Einstein, whom Malraux admired very much, Oppenheimer said that it was a pity that for the past twenty-five years Einstein "had done no science." Robert and Kitty left Paris that evening, They would never meet the Chevaliers again.

The Oppenheimers returned to the United States. Waiting for the scientist was an urgent message to call Lewis Strauss as soon as possible.

15. Our Science and Our Country

Oppenheimer agreed to meet with Strauss at 3:30 P.M., Monday, December 21, 1953. He arrived at AEC headquarters on time and went directly to Strauss's office, where the two men were joined by Kenneth Nichols, the commission's general manager. The room was large and octagonal in shape; it had been the scene of meetings of the Chiefs of Staff during World War II.

Strauss went directly to the point: The government had been forced to reassess Oppenheimer's background and the status of his access to government classified information, as a result of President Eisenhower's mandate for such action under Executive Order 10450 and a letter from William Borden to J. Edgar Hoover at the FBI. There was even the possibility of a Senate investigation into Oppenheimer's background, led by William Jenner. Strauss gave the scientist a copy of a letter prepared by the AEC stating the charges that brought Oppenheimer's status into question. What was at stake, at least superficially, was the matter of Oppenheimer's special Q clearance, which allowed him access to government secrets.

Oppenheimer was stunned. The eight-page letter contained references to his associations dating as far back as the 1930s, his brother's membership in the Communist party, his contributions to left-wing causes, and, perhaps most startling, the charge that he had tried to stop or delay the development of the hydrogen bomb. Oppenheimer agreed that some of the points were true; some, however, clearly were not.

Oppenheimer had two alternatives. He could resign, which would eliminate the question of continuing his clearance; if he did not, his security clearance would surely be suspended. The other alternative would be for him to appeal to the commission for a hearing; under AEC guidelines, a panel would be created to review the evidence in Oppenheimer's security file, and the scientist himself would have a chance to refute or challenge the information. It is not clear who first raised the question of resignation; Strauss and Nichols argued that it was Oppenheimer, while the scientist implied it was Strauss. Whatever the origin, it was clear that the chairman hoped Oppenheimer would resign. Oppenheimer was even shown a prepared letter from AEC headquarters to all contractors indicating that Oppenheimer had given up his clearance and was therefore no longer permitted access to commission projects or to information.

It was certainly a very complicated issue and, not surprisingly, Oppenheimer did not know what to do, but he agreed to contact Strauss the following day with his decision. The meeting lasted little more than half an hour. Oppenheimer left the AEC building—without a copy of the AEC letter—*and went directly to the law offices of Joseph Volpe, the AEC's former general counsel. They were joined by Herbert Marks, who had worked for the State Department. Oppenheimer related the conversation with Strauss and Nichols as best as he could. It was obvious to his listeners that Oppenheimer was deeply shaken. What should he do, he asked? Oppenheimer left with Marks for the attorney's home in Georgetown. The scientist was greatly distressed and confused; he paced back and forth, wondering aloud how this could happen to him. Despite all the suspicions that had been lodged against him over the years—by the Air Force, the FBI, the various congressional investigating committees—Oppenheimer was still shocked that his loyalty and his service had actually been brought into question, and on such a grand scale. Over drinks, Oppenheimer finally came to a decision: He would place himself, and his history, before a special AEC panel.

That night he prepared a letter which would be delivered to Lewis Strauss the following day. "You put to me," he wrote, "as a possibly desirable alternative that I request termination of my contract as a consultant to the Commission, and thereby avoid an explicit consideration of the charges on which the Commission's action would otherwise be based." This, he said, was something he just could not and would not do:

> I have thought most earnestly of the alternative suggested. Under the circumstances this course of action would mean that I accept and concur in the view that I am not fit to serve this government, that I have now served for some twelve years. This I cannot do. If I were thus unworthy I could hardly have served our country as I have tried, or been the Director of our Institute in Princeton†, or have spoken, as on more than one occasion I have found myself speaking, the name of our science and our country.[1]

With this letter Oppenheimer set into motion the mechanism for a hearing of considerable import and great personal cost.

The trigger for these unusual circumstances was an event that occurred a month and a half before, while Robert and Kitty were in

*Strauss wouldn't let him have a copy at that time.
†The reference to "our Institute" referred to the fact that Lewis Strauss was still on the Board of Trustees.

Europe. On November 7, 1953, William Liscum Borden sent a registered letter to J. Edgar Hoover and copies to the members of the House of Representatives-Senate Joint Committee on Atomic Energy. Borden was the former staff director for the Joint Committee and in that capacity had become intimately familiar with Robert Oppenheimer, his past, and his activities in Washington. Over the years Borden had developed the view that Oppenheimer was anything but a loyal citizen who merely had dissenting views on weapons and national defense. He was, in Borden's words, more probably than not "an agent of the Soviet Union."

Borden had since left the service of the Joint Committee to work for the atomic power division of Westinghouse Electric Corporation. During the month of October, Borden began to draft a long letter that summarized all those aspects of the scientist's past he felt were suspicious. Congressman Sterling Cole had given his approval for preparation of the letter, which used information made available to Borden during his service on the Joint Committee staff. If, as Borden did, one started with the belief that Oppenheimer was an agent—or, at best, untrustworthy—then the full scope of the scientist's work in government could be seen as truly appalling. The man, after all, had served on the most important and critical government bodies overseeing or determining policy for weapons and for national defense and diplomacy. Borden listed the organizations Oppenheimer had served on or consulted with: the Department of State, the Departments of War and now Defense, the National Security Council, the three military services, the Research and Development Board, the Central Intelligence Agency, the National Science Foundation, National Security Resources Board, the American delegation to the United Nations, and the Atomic Energy Commission. He had served on such critical study groups as Vista and Project Lincoln. His access, his technical and scientific knowledge, all left him in a pivotal position to "compromise more vital and detailed information affecting the national defense and security than any other individual in the United States."

Borden, quite simply, rejected Oppenheimer; he didn't even consider him to be a scientist of any significant stature. As far as Borden was concerned he had not even made any "major contributions," and was only in the "second rank" of American scientists; his official or unofficial membership on "thirty-five," according to Borden, important committees, panels, or projects was the real reason the scientist had had the unusual opportunity to influence national policy. Borden's letter reconstructed Oppenheimer's past, from his prewar teaching days to his involvement in the development of the hydrogen bomb.

Regarding the scientist's prewar or wartime past, Borden cited the following facts as he saw them:

> He contributed "substantial monthly sums" to the Communist party.

> His wife and younger brother were Communists. He had no close friends except Communists. He had had at least one "Communist mistress."*
> He had recruited Communists into the Berkeley wartime project.
> He had been in frequent "contact" with Soviet agents.
> He had given false information to General Groves, the Manhattan District, and the FBI.
> He had employed a "Communist" to write the official Los Alamos history.†
> He had supported Los Alamos until the end of the war, when he "immediately and outspokenly" argued that it be disbanded.

Regarding Oppenheimer's postwar activities, Borden was equally unequivocal in his charges. The "evidence," he wrote, indicated that:

> He had been "remarkably instrumental" in influencing the government, and especially the AEC, to "suspend" H-bomb development until January 31, 1950.
> From that date on he had worked "tirelessly" to retard the hydrogen bomb program.
> He had sought to retard the nation's capacity to produce "A-bomb material" as well preventing the obtaining of larger supplies of uranium ore.
> He had worked against efforts to develop nuclear-powered submarines and aircraft and similar atomic power projects.

What did all this mean? To Borden, it justified several major conclusions. First, as "a sufficiently hardened Communist . . . [Oppenheimer] either volunteered espionage information to the Soviets or complied with a request for such information." Therefore, he wrote, "More probably than not, he had since been functioning as an espionage agent; and . . . he had since acted under a Soviet directive in influencing United States military, atomic energy, intelligence, and diplomatic policy." For Borden, the evidence was "abundantly clear" that Oppenheimer was a Communist. What had prompted Borden to write such a derogatory letter?

> Having lived with the Oppenheimer case for years, having studied and restudied all data concerning him that your agency [the FBI] made available to the Atomic Energy Commission through May 1953, having endeavored to factor in a mass of additional data assembled from numerous sources, and looking back upon the case from a perspective in private life, I feel a duty simply to state to the responsible head of the security agency most concerned

*Presumably Borden meant Jean Tatlock.
†David Hawkins.

> the conclusions which I have painfully crystalized and which I believe any fairminded man thoroughly familiar with the evidence must also be driven to accept.[2]

Borden obviously sought more than just the suspension of Oppenheimer's security clearance; indeed, the nature of his charges, if proved, would put Oppenheimer in jail or on death row. However absurd or unfounded the charges were, a letter as severe as this from a man formerly but highly placed in the government who had access to secret data would inevitably cause a serious confrontation of some sort.

There was also another side to Borden's history on the Joint Committee. Only a month before, John Wheeler, working at Princeton, had prepared a chronology of major events in the thermonuclear program. This abbreviated history had been prepared for Borden's staff. Unfortunately, Wheeler left the only existing draft of the chronology on a train, and it was never recovered. When the news of this crucial loss eventually made its way to Eisenhower, he exploded with anger; he summoned AEC and congressional staff to chasten them for their carelessness and for the unnecessary spread of classified information. Borden, with his history of criticism for Oppenheimer's personal carelessness, left with a dark cloud over his own career.[3]

Borden's letter found its way to Herbert Brownell, the attorney general of the United States, who only a year before had played a major role in the Rosenberg spy trial. In fact, on November 6—the day before Borden mailed his letter—Brownell had been quoted as attacking former President Truman for promoting Harry Dexter White to a position within the Treasury Department despite alleged evidence that he was a Soviet spy. Brownell took Borden's letter to Eisenhower. The wave of anti-Communist hysteria was growing; if word on the charges against Oppenheimer were to leak, it could be a political nightmare for the administration. Whether it was true or not, the mass of detail on Oppenheimer's activities appeared to cast a cloud of suspicion on the scientist's character. With the FBI pursuing the charges, Eisenhower called Strauss to a special meeting on December 3 in his office to discuss the Oppenheimer matter with Defense Secretary Wilson and Herbert Brownell. A week before, the FBI had delivered a thirty-inch-thick report on Oppenheimer and stated that no formal hearing had ever been held to consider the man's background. This, however, was only partly true; the AEC, with Strauss in attendance, had reviewed Oppenheimer's dossier in 1948 and granted him clearance. While not a formal review, it had been as thorough as was possible at the time under the circumstances prevailing during the early days of the commission. What the AEC had not reviewed in 1948, however, were the serious charges that Oppenheimer had used his prestige and position to thwart the development of the hydrogen bomb.

Eisenhower dictated a memorandum to Brownell instructing him "to procure from the Director of the FBI an entire file in the case of Dr. Oppenheimer and to make of it a thorough study." Eisenhower wanted some recommendation of what action should be taken. To his diary, Eisenhower confessed:

> It is reported to me that this same information [the file on Oppenheimer's past, etc.], or at least the vast bulk of it, has been constantly reviewed and re-examined over a number of years, and that the over-all conclusion has always been that there is no evidence that implies disloyalty on the part of Dr. Oppenheimer. However, this does not mean that he might not be a security risk.[4]

For the moment, however, the President ordered that a "blank wall" be placed between Oppenheimer and all atomic secrets. Copies of the memorandum on the scientist made their way quickly to the Joint Chiefs of Staff, the CIA, and the Department of Defense. From these agencies word drifted out through more informal channels. Oppenheimer's friends who learned about the new inquest were Admiral William Parsons, from Los Alamos days, and Herbert Marks.

Strauss called a meeting of his fellow commissioners to consider the Oppenheimer matter for December 10. The commissioners met with the general manager, Kenneth Nichols; Nichols's deputy; and the AEC general counsel, William Mitchell. Ultimately, the commission voted to conduct a hearing to consider the truth or falsehood of the charges. A statement of charges was left to Mitchell, who later received permission to bring one of his staff, Harold P. Green, into the small circle of AEC staff knowledgeable about the proceedings. Green prepared the first draft of the charges.

Green had worked for three years in the AEC's Division of Security, and had prepared many similar drafts of "security charges." In just the few months that Strauss had been back in the AEC as its chairman, Green noticed an increased number of security cases resurrected for review. Inevitably, they were the cases of men who had once been granted clearances under the previous regimes, but now were subjects of controversy. Green had also heard that Strauss rarely fired anyone in the AEC; the chairman was more subtle, often finding new jobs in industry or private business for those individuals whom he wished to remove from the commission's employ. It was also rumored that Strauss had promised Hoover to "purge" the commission of several individuals, one of whom was Oppenheimer. It is hard to understand the reasons for the FBI director's antipathy toward the scientist. Hoover apparently regarded the man's left-wing associations as suspect and his character as less than moral.[5]

Strauss was concerned that, should a decision ultimately be

necessary from the commission itself, the decision might be in Oppenheimer's favor. Of the five commissioners, Strauss could count only on two votes: his own and Joseph Campbell's. The other voters were Thomas Murray, Eugene M. Zuckert, and Henry D. Smyth; and Strauss could not rely on them for support. In an attempt to circumvent this possibility, Strauss tried to obtain a ruling that under Eisenhower's Executive Order 10450, he would be considered the "head of the agency," and as such would be able to "revoke and deny" security clearances regardless of the opinions of his fellow commissioners. When General Counsel Mitchell indicated that the executive order specifically referred to "the Atomic Energy Commission" instead of a specific agency head such as the secretary of state or secretary of defense, Strauss went over Mitchell's head to Brownell, hoping for a favorable decision. Strauss didn't bother to tell Mitchell he was seeking this ruling, and when the news drifted back to Mitchell through informal sources, he complained to Green that there was "nothing [he] can do about it." This behind-the-scenes maneuvering was an example of just how seriously Strauss was taking the Oppenheimer matter. Green was also startled when an FBI agent called him to offer the services of the bureau; in three years Green had never received more than what he considered "grudging compliance" from them. Quite by accident, Green saw a transcript of a conversation between Oppenheimer and his attorneys, and it had clearly been electronically monitored in secret by FBI agents.[6] In fact, later evidence revealed that many of Oppenheimer's "privileged" conversations with his lawyers had been secretly taped.

Mitchell left Green to prepare the draft, instructing him not to include charges against Oppenheimer on the hydrogen bomb matter, and to say nothing of his work to anyone. Only one secretary was cleared to type Green's draft. The commission, Mitchell said, believed that secrecy was the only way to minimize the adverse publicity that would surely arise from the hearing should it leak. Moreover, there was also the chance, he felt, that if the charges against Oppenheimer were true and he was a Soviet spy, he might very well try to escape to Russia.[7]

Green spent the entire weekend preparing his draft letter; under AEC guidelines, the finished letter would be signed by General Manager Nichols and delivered to Oppenheimer. Much of the material in Oppenheimer's file was old and repetitive. One new item, however—a recent interview with Edward Teller in which the scientist blamed Oppenheimer for delays in the thermonuclear program—offered Green an idea. On Sunday, Green added—contrary to his instruction—charges designed to test Oppenheimer's veracity on circumstances involving the development of the hydrogen bomb. The wording prepared by Green suggested that Oppenheimer had made conflicting statements regarding the thermonuclear weapon and, after 1950, had continued to oppose it and had also been instrumental in persuading other scientists not to work on it. On

Monday the draft was accepted by Nichols and the five commissioners. Strauss then waited for Oppenheimer to return from Europe for a confrontation. Ironically, on the morning of the meeting Herbert Marks met with Strauss with confidential news that Senator Jenner proposed a Senate investigation of Oppenheimer, an investigation he pleaded with Strauss to kill in some way. Strauss, however, seemed to have other things on his mind.

The formal letter from Nichols to Oppenheimer arrived on December 23. "As a result," Nichols wrote,

> . . . of additional information as to your character, associations and loyalty, and review of your personnel security file in the light of the requirements of the Atomic Energy Act and the requirements of Executive Order 10450, there has developed considerable question whether your continued employment on Atomic Energy Commission work will endanger the common defense and security and whether such continued employment is clearly consistent with the interests of the national security.

What followed, in eight single-spaced pages, was a catalog of charges, each prefaced with the phrase, "It was reported . . ." and, beginning on page 7, information on what steps would be taken and what alternatives Oppenheimer had available to him under the hearing procedures. The first twenty-eight charges concerned Oppenheimer's past, his associations, and his discrepant stories to security officials and the FBI regarding Chevalier. The last five charges related to Oppenheimer's behavior regarding the development of the hydrogen bomb.

> It was further reported that in the Autumn of 1949, and subsequently, you strongly opposed the development of the hydrogen bomb: (1) on moral grounds, (2) by claiming that it was not feasible, (3) by claiming that there were insufficient facilities and scientific personnel to carry on the development, and (4) that it was not politically desirable. It was further reported that even after it was determined, as a matter of national policy, to proceed with the development of a hydrogen bomb, you continued to oppose the project and declined to cooperate fully in the project.

Additionally, the scientist had been "instrumental" in persuading other "outstanding scientists" not to work on the project, and thereby "definitely slowed down" its development.[8]

Nichols concluded the letter with the procedures Oppenheimer should follow. The scientist could request an appearance before an Atomic Energy Commission personnel security board; in order to do this, Oppenheimer had to respond to the charges within thirty days and request a formal hearing. Members of the board could be challenged by Oppenheimer for cause. If no challenge was raised, Oppenheimer would be notified, no less than forty-eight hours before the hearing, of its date and time. Also, Oppenheimer could choose counsel to represent him. Nichols added an ironic line: "In view of your access to highly sensitive classified information, *and in view of these allegations which, until disproved* [emphasis added], raise questions as to your veracity, conduct and even your loyalty, the Commission has no other recourse . . . but to suspend your clearance until the matter is settled." Apparently the commission would not be put in the position of proving the allegations; instead, Oppenheimer would have to prove he was innocent. The so-called blank pad rule—known legally as the exclusivity of the record—would not apply. Instead of entering into the hearing with no evidence introduced, the members of the board and the prosecution team would have the evidence already in hand as part of the charges against the defendant. Unfortunately, security-risk cases were not included under the 1946 Administrative Procedure Act, which guaranteed protection under the blank pad rule.

Arriving the same day as Nichols's eight-page letter was a second letter from the general manager notifying Oppenheimer to deliver to a security representative of the AEC "all paper, documents, records and files in your possession or under your control which contain any Restricted Data, and all [material] which came to you from the Atomic Energy Commission or any of its offices, employees or contractors." This action would remove Oppenheimer entirely from his connection with the commission. His secretary, Katherine Russell, spent nearly a week cataloging and boxing material to be returned.* Oppenheimer especially regretted this last action; undoubtedly, his files contained memoranda or copies of correspondence that would have been helpful in preparing his defense before the Personnel Security Board.[9]

On December 23 a confidential letter from Nichols was sent to all AEC installations advising them of the "blank wall" ruling:

> The clearance of Dr. J. Robert Oppenheimer for access to Restricted Data and other classified information has been suspended. The *fact* that his clearance has been suspended is presently classified information.[10]

In mid-January, Oppenheimer received a telephone call from James Reston, a reporter from *The New York Times*. Through a myriad of connections in Washington, Reston had learned of the commission's recent action and of Nichols's letter to Oppenheimer. He wanted the

*Five and a half years later Oppenheimer received a request for information on his consultantcy with the Naval Research Advisory Committee. To the author, Oppenheimer returned the original letter with a handwritten note, which read: "My files have been confiscated."

scientist's side of the story. Oppenheimer demurred, feeling it was inappropriate to release the story until the government made the events public. A week later Reston talked with Oppenheimer's attorney; he rightly guessed that the AEC letter would become public without any response from Oppenheimer himself. Reston suggested that both the AEC letter and Oppenheimer's response be given to the *Times*, with the understanding that neither would be published except together and only when it was appropriate. Reston was forced to sit on the story until April.

Oppenheimer's first task in preparing for the hearing was to choose suitable legal counsel to represent him. Herbert Marks and Joseph Volpe had been involved since Oppenheimer's first meeting with Strauss on December 21. Both, however, believed they could not represent Oppenheimer because of their past affiliations with the Atomic Energy Commission. On the advice of Marks and Volpe, Oppenheimer asked Lloyd K. Garrison to assist him. Garrison practiced in New York but was well known in Washington, where he was highly respected. Among other activities, Garrison served on the board of trustees for the Institute of Advanced Study and had been dean of the University of Wisconsin Law School. He also had a solid reputation for public service through his work for the American Civil Liberties Union. At first Garrison hesitated, but agreed for the moment to assist Oppenheimer in preparing a reply to the Nichols letter. Garrison suggested several other attorneys, but all were unable to accept the case because of the obvious necessity of working full time on the matter for a period of perhaps six months. Inevitably, Garrison came to serve as Oppenheimer's counsel, with Marks assisting part-time.

The information that Lloyd Garrison would likely serve as Oppenheimer's attorney greatly concerned Strauss. Garrison had a very good reputation, and Commission officials believed that no one on their legal or security staff could be a match for the man. While the commission's legal staff was aware of personnel security matters, it was not thought to be Garrison's match as a legal tactician. The commission eventually took the unprecedented step of hiring a lawyer from the outside—someone with little security expertise, but with considerable courtroom and prosecution experience. His name was Roger Robb, an assistant United States attorney with seven years of experience, including twenty-three murder trials and a famous libel case involving Drew Pearson.*[11] Robb was young, tough, and had a strong reputation as a prosecutor.

The commission also needed to assemble a three-man board to hear the evidence for and against Oppenheimer and to make a ruling. With some help from Eisenhower, the commission selected Gordon Gray, the forty-five-year-old president of the University of North Carolina, as

*Robb represented the individual suing Pearson.

the first member and chairman. Like Oppenheimer, Gray had been born wealthy and was well educated. He had joined the Army as a private during World War II and later became assistant secretary of the Army. Gray would bring the board experience in the government and a familiarity with national security concerns. While a Democrat, Gray did not consider himself a liberal.

The second member of the board was Ward V. Evans, the chairman of the department of chemistry at Northwestern University. Ward's background included work for the United States Bureau of Mines as an expert on explosive effects and as a consultant to industry. A lifelong Republican, Ward was politically a conservative.

The final member of the board was Thomas A. Morgan, a retired businessman and industrialist. Morgan, unlike the financially comfortable Oppenheimer, had grown up in North Carolina, where his parents were tobacco famers. He had joined the Sperry Company, manufacturers of gyroscopes and other precision equipment, and eventually became its president. Although retired from active business, Morgan spent a considerable amount of time on civic cases. Morgan was also a conservative Republican.

The hearing was set for April 12, 1954.

For Oppenheimer and his lawyers, the months before the hearing were spent in frantic preparation. Without access to any of Oppenheimer's government files or to any of the material certainly available to Robb, the team needed to carefully reconstruct the last twenty years or so of the scientist's personal and public life. Names, dates, committee memberships, associations, political contributions—all had to be extracted from the past and put into sequence. By now the legal staff included Garrison, Marks, Samuel Silverman, and Allan B. Ecker.

Oppenheimer and Garrison were disheartened to learn that the three-member board presently being assembled by Strauss and the commission would spend one entire week *before* the hearing being briefed on the case, Oppenheimer's background, and various other scientific and technical developments. Roger Robb would be part of these proceedings. Garrison immediately asked Nichols to permit him to attend the week-long sessions, urging that it would only be fair. Nichols declined, claiming that the nature of the material to be reviewed was confidential. Garrison then asked to spend the opening day with the board in order to discuss the procedures to be followed, a request that was also rejected by Nichols.

Oppenheimer and Garrison had to grapple with the option of seeking a security clearance—the same Q clearance held by Oppenheimer but now in suspension—for Garrison and perhaps another member of the legal team. The Q clearance would mean that Oppenheimer and his counsel would have access to classified material, including some of the minutes of the pivotal October 1949 General Advisory Committee meetings involving discussions on the thermonuclear weapon. Without this clearance, Garrison might not even know the full nature of a charge against his client. There were, however, several complications: For one thing, the normal time for processing an application and conducting a background check could take three or four months. Also, if both teams had access to secret material, it was possible that the hearing might dwell unnecessarily on the technical developments of weapons, rather than on policy issues. Too much classified information might inhibit an effective appeal of the board's decision in the future.

On January 28, Garrison met with Strauss, Nichols, and Mitchell to discuss the matter of clearances. The AEC offered to expedite Garrison's application should he choose to submit an application; there was a provision in the security code that permitted an emergency and temporary Q clearance to be issued on the basis of a brief background check. A permanent clearance would need a full background check, which could take months. Garrison asked that Marks be granted a clearance as well, as he would be deeply involved in the proceedings. A few days later Garrison also asked that Silverman be granted a clearance. Nichols replied that only Garrison's application would be considered; he gave no reason for rejecting the others. Robb's request, meanwhile, had been processed in a record eight days.[12]

Garrison and his associates deliberated the matter of clearances for a week. Finally, on February 3, Garrison wrote a letter to Strauss rejecting the possibility of obtaining clearance for himself. Even if clearances could be obtained for all three lawyers, he wrote, "the delays incident to clearance by the regular process of full field investigation would impair the usefulness of clearance when it was finally granted." Even expedition of the application process would not leave sufficient time. Because of these uncertainties, the initial preparation of the case on a non-classified basis becomes essential whether clearance is sought or not." Strauss had already made it plain to Garrison that the commission itself would decide which documents were relevant and what portions of the material Garrison could examine. Therefore, even with a security clearance, Garrison would not have the "privilege" of "knowing the facts in the possession of the Personnel Security Board which will be used in the Board's final judgment of Dr. Oppenheimer's case." Garrison at least hoped that he would be able to count on the commission's cooperation in declassifying the material as could be declassified consistent with national interests. He would submit a list of documents thought necessary to Oppenheimer's defense; by name, he specifically mentioned the "greatly needed" General Advisory Committee report of October 29, 1949.[13]

Very quickly, this move proved to be a mistake. Nichols turned down all requests for declassification but two. One document would remain classified and therefore unavailable to Garrison, but Oppenheimer could see it *if* he came personally to the AEC headquarters and requested the document. This Oppenheimer refused to do; it was ignominious enough to be "on trial" before his colleagues, and he simply would not endure further humiliation by visiting the AEC to review one document. Garrison and his team reconsidered the matter of clearance; they were increasingly concerned that the introduction of classified information during the hearing would necessitate their removal, temporarily, from the proceedings. This would leave their client "without representation." On March 26, Garrison wrote Nichols requesting clearance for himself. However, by April 12, the first day of the hearing, Garrison's application had not yet been fully processed; in fact, by the end of the hearing it was still not available to him.

Garrison's failure to apply for clearance in January also proved to be a mistake. True, he and Marks and the others had reasoned that with no clearance the AEC might be forced to limit the amount of the classified material they used, thus making appeal easier and limiting discussion to motives and not to technical matters.[14] The circumstances surrounding the hearing were exceptional, however. Garrison would be facing the combined forces of the Atomic Energy Commission, the Federal Bureau of Investigation, and the general antipathy of the highest echelons of government. The rejection of requests for participation in the pretrial preparations and the failure to supply critical reports and correspondence were other ominous signs. It is likely that not even Oppenheimer, with his years of government service, realized just how inexorably the bureaucracy moved once it was set into motion. The government believed it had to win, whether they achieved a victory through fair or unfair tactics.

Garrison's only defense was to rebut the charges made by the AEC by exposing what he called the "whole man concept." He felt that no one would be able to make a proper evaluation of Oppenheimer without an understanding of the scientist's life, the times he lived in, and the context of his actions. What emerged was a forty-two-page "biography" of Oppenheimer's life. Embedded in the lengthy letter of March 4 were Oppenheimer's responses to the charges formulated in Nichols's December 23 letter. In a preliminary statement, Oppenheimer wrote that though he would have no desire to remain a consultant if not needed, he could not "ignore the question you have raised, nor accept the suggestion that I am unfit for public service." To explain the nature of his response he said:

> The items of so-called derogatory information set forth in your letter cannot be fairly understood except in the context of my life and work. This answer is in the form of a summary account of

> relevant aspects of my life in more or less chronological order, in the course of which I shall comment on the specific items in your letter. Through this answer, and through the hearings before the personnel security board, which I hereby request, I hope to provide a fair basis upon which the questions posed by your letter may be resolved.

His letter was divided into the three adult phases of Oppenheimer's life: his years as a student and teacher; the advent of war and his directorship of Los Alamos; and his multifaceted career through the last half of the 1940s and until 1954.

The later half of the 1930s had had a profound effect upon him, he wrote. His awareness of the oppression of Jews in Germany left him with a "smouldering fury"; the economic devastation of the Depression had taken its toll most graphically on those immediately around him—his students. His sense of political and social forces grew as well. The so-called Communist United Front embraced many organizations—some political, some humanitarian—including organizations of interest to Oppenheimer. He contributed money to various causes, including the Spanish Loyalist cause. His statement, quoted in the Nichols letter, that he belonged to every Communist front organization on the West Coast had been made, if at all, as a joke. Through the Spanish Loyalist cause he had met men like Thomas Addis, Rudy Lambert, and Isaac Folkoff. His interests and his contributions ended largely with the Pearl Harbor attack. His brother Frank had told him that he was no longer a member of the Communist party. About himself he said, "I was never a member of the [Communist] party, concealed or open."

His involvement with the wartime fission work had begun with his consultation with the Berkeley radiation project. His first security questionnaire had been filled out when he joined the metallurgical staff in early 1943; Groves had formalized the clearance with a letter in the summer. Men now under suspicion, such as Weinberg and Lomanitz, had never been employed at Los Alamos. Regarding the Chevalier incident, he wrote:

> It has long been clear to me that I should have reported the incident at once. The events that led me to report it—which I doubt ever would have become known without my report—were unconnected with it. . . . When General Groves urged me to give the details, I told him of my conversations with Chevalier. I still think of Chevalier as a friend.[15]

Regarding the more immediate past, and especially the emergence of Soviet hostility, scientists "had more and more to devote ourselves to findings ways of adapting our atomic potential to offset the

Soviet threat." As chairman and member of the General Advisory Committee, Oppenheimer had agreed with colleagues that atomic weapons were the first priority of the Atomic Energy Commission. The committee had recommended strengthening Los Alamos, diversifying its weapons program, creating the laboratory at Sandia, establishing a program of nuclear weapons testing, expanding production capability, and so forth. Regarding the crucial October 1949 meeting of the GAC, Oppenheimer recaptured the moment:

> It would have been surprising if eight men considering a problem of extreme difficulty had each had precisely the same reasons for the conclusion in which we joined. But I think I am correct in asserting that the unanimous opposition we expressed to the crash program [on the thermonuclear weapon] was based on the conviction, to which technical considerations as well as others contributed, that because of our overall situation at that time such a program might weaken rather than strengthen the position of the United States.[16]

Summing up, Oppenheimer admitted to instances where he acted "unwisely." "What I have hoped was, not that I could wholly avoid error, but that I might learn from it. What I have learned has, I think, made me more fit to serve my country."

Oppenheimer did not refer to Project Vista in his lengthy letter, although he realized that some of the strong antagonism toward him stemmed from his participation in this influential project. In trying to formulate a defense, especially against a setting of secrecy promulgated by the commission, it was important to understand what individuals or forces might have participated in, or contributed to, the personal and vociferous opposition to Oppenheimer exemplified by the William Borden letter. Those associated with Vista were likely candidates. In a meeting with Garrison and others on January 19, Oppenheimer wrote in his personal notes, for use by his counsel, that "the attacks on Oppenheimer in relation to the hydrogen bomb did not occur at this point [the October, 1949 GAC meeting] but much later and seemed to have grown out of his association with Project Vista." The scientist's visit to then NATO chief Eisenhower was perhaps the turning point.

> The visit . . . marked the beginning of an attack by certain people identified with strategic air operations and it was believed by some that these attacks may have been motivated by fear that if a program for tactical use of atomic weapons was adopted this would mean that money essential for strategic air would be diverted to other purposes.[17]

Oppenheimer tried to explain his activities after the war. There was, he said, a "connecting link" between his work on the many panels, conferences, and committees he had participated in. The link was Oppenheimer's belief that the nation needed to reduce the chance of all-out nuclear war while remaining strong, in part by adapting atomic weapons for many purposes, not simply for use in single, massive weapons. In sum, the "link" was his long-held belief in the diversification of weapons for both field and strategic use. This philosophy had been evident in his influence on the Acheson-Lilienthal report for the State Department, the Los Alamos thermonuclear program, Project Vista, and Project Lincoln.

For Garrison and his other legal staff, Oppenheimer listed what he believed to be major recommendations made by the General Advisory Committee *in support of* America's weapons program:

> Recommending as the highest priority of the Atomic Energy Commission the further development of atomic weapons at a revitalized Los Alamos (made at the GAC's *second* meeting in 1947).
> Recommending a strong program of weapons testing, first in the Pacific and then in the Nevada Proving Ground.
> The broadening of the weapons program *beyond* that recommended by the Joint Chiefs of Staff, who based their requirements only on existing production rates of uranium and plutonium.
> Urging the "marriage" between tactical weapons and the guided missile program.
> Recommending that weapons be designed for use in smaller, high-performance airplanes.
> Assisting the thermonuclear program of Los Alamos by recommending additional support in personnel and material areas.

Defending Oppenheimer's role in the nation's weapons program would normally have presented no problems: After all, the sheer number of committees and panels in which he participated and the very success of the program certainly provided enough evidence of his value. But the nature of the charges—his "moral opposition," his failure to "cooperate fully" after the 1950 Truman decision—were vague, without mention of specific incidents. Moreover, his lack of access to confidential reports and the minutes of key meetings was a severe handicap. Oppenheimer's team would have to reconstruct the chronology of events as best they could and hope to receive support through the testimony of supporting colleagues.

To help prepare a defense against charges of Oppenheimer's earlier associations, Garrison ordered a heavy background search on the organizations and individuals involved. Garrison wanted to know, for example, what the professional aims had been and who the officers and board members were of organizations such as the Friends of the Chinese People, the American Committee for Democracy and Intellectual Freedom, and the Independent Citizens Committee of the Arts, Sciences and Professions. What "non-left-wing" organizations had the scientist belonged to in the 1930s and early 1940s? What was the public program or platform of the Communist party in the 1930s? Background on men like Isaac Folkoff, Steve Nelson, Rudy Lambert, Kenneth May, Joseph Weinberg, and Haakron Chevalier were needed. Those involved with Los Alamos or with the radiation lab were other candidates: Giovanni Rossi Lomanitz, David Bohm, Bernard Friedman, and David Hawkins. What would a background investigation of Kitty Oppenheimer reveal? Anything that might show her disengagement from politics or from the Communist party?

Oppenheimer had been charged with subscribing to the *Daily Peoples World*. What other magazines or journals did Oppenheimer subscribe to? Was it not possible to show that Oppenheimer's professional reading far outweighed his political? And what of his students? Had not many of them gone on to major positions in other universities or into government work? What was the role of the department of physics at Berkeley and Cal Tech in contributing to the early stages of the atomic bomb project? Was not Oppenheimer's role significant? What of his friends and his work at Los Alamos?

If they were to be successful in defending Robert Oppenheimer, Garrison and Marks would have to develop the broad perspective on the scientist's life that they spoke of earlier as the "whole man." The stupidity of the Chevalier incident could not be denied, but was it not softened by the fact that Oppenheimer brought the troubles upon himself by reporting the incident to the security officials at the time? Were his associations with Folkoff and the others of a political nature, and were they evidence of some sinister plan, as suggested by the AEC, or merely the result of living and working in the intellectual atmosphere of a university in a time of pronounced political and economic changes? Was his record during the war one of carelessness, either with regard to his work or to his understanding of the need for security? Was the sum of his postwar experiences evidence of someone seeking to thwart American security, or merely an example of an individual with views different from some of his colleagues and contemporaries?

How well this argument could be played depended on many factors during the hearing, not the least of which was whether or not the commission and its prosecutor, Robert Robb, would allow an atmosphere in which the charges could be fairly and openly discussed. As the day of the hearing neared, there was a sense of anxiety; too much had occurred, from Garrison's perspective, to allow him to feel comfortable with the approaching proceedings. But, as he assured Oppenheimer, they would do the best they could under the circumstances.

Shortly before the trial in January 1954, Oppenheimer ran into John Manley on a street in Washington, D.C. Manley quickly sensed that the anxiety produced by the impending hearing was clearly dominating Oppenheimer's attention. Referring to himself and Kitty, Oppenheimer ominously confessed to Manley that they were "in real trouble."

16. The Hearing

The hearing began at 10 A.M. on April 12, 1954, in Room 2022 of Building T-3, one of the Atomic Energy Commission's "temporary" two-story buildings near the Washington Monument. The room was long and sparse: Three tables had been arranged in a T formation, with Gray, Ward, and Evans sitting at the short table, facing two perpendicular tables joined together. At the end of the T was a single chair for witnesses. The opposing legal teams were to sit on either side of the two joined tables. The only wall of windows looked out across Constitution Avenue.

By 10 A.M. the cast had assembled: The three judges were at their table, and Gordon Gray, the chairman, sat in the center. Roger Robb was joined by his assistant, Arthur Rolander, Jr.; both sat on one side. Garrison was with his team, Sam Silverman and Allen Ecker, who were sitting opposite Robb. Robert Oppenheimer took the witness chair and Kitty sat on a small sofa against the wall facing the windows.

Gray began the proceedings with a formal statement:

> An investigation of Dr. J. Robert Oppenheimer conducted under the provisions of section 10 (b) (5) (i-iii) of the Atomic Energy Act of 1946 has revealed certain information which casts doubt upon the eligibility of Dr. Oppenheimer for clearance for access to restricted data. . . .[1]

Gray then launched into a laborious reading of the Nichols letter, with its multiple charges. He followed it with Oppenheimer's response of March 4. "This proceeding," Gray intoned, "is an inquiry and not in the nature of a trial. We shall approach our duties in that atmosphere and in that spirit." In fact, the proceedings were to be regarded as "strictly confidential" between the AEC and Oppenheimer and his counsel. "The Atomic Energy Commission will not take the initiative in public release of any information relating to the proceeding before this board." Oppenheimer was then sworn in and advised that if restricted data were to be mentioned, advance warning should be given in order that unauthorized persons could be removed from the hearing room. This would occur on many occasions.

Garrison's opening remarks were polite and deferential. The board, he said, had taken on an "exacting and onerous job." For the past week "members of the board have been examining a file containing various items about Dr. Oppenheimer to which we have had, and to which we shall have no access at all. . . . I am sure that it goes without saying that we are confident that the minds of the members of the board are open to receive the testimony that we shall submit." No doubt Oppenheimer wondered if that would be true.

Garrison attempted to explain to the board the concept of his defense for Robert Oppenheimer; it was not an attempt to hold onto Oppenheimer's job, but instead, an attempt to establish the truth of his character and to dispel the "derogatory" charges against him. All of Oppenheimer's colleagues interviewed had spoken favorably to Garrison without reservation about the scientist's character and about the nature of his services. As well, most of the charges dated from twelve to fifteen years in the past. His contemporary work, including his association with the hydrogen bomb, had been conducted "in a blaze of light," and obviously subject to criticism and review at all times. It was important, Garrison continued, to conduct the case on nontechnical merits. He was not a scientist; two of the three board members were also not scientists. "The real question," stated Garrison, "is, was his judgment an honest judgment; did he do the best he could for his government." To assist in that determination, Garrison hoped to call some twenty-seven witnesses.* The first session was then adjourned for lunch.

The afternoon session resumed at 2:15 P.M. It was Oppenheimer's first opportunity to be questioned by his own counsel, Lloyd Garrison. The questioning, which took all afternoon, sought to amplify Oppenheimer's history of involvement in atomic energy: his attendance at a late 1941 meeting in Chicago called by Arthur Compton to discuss fission developments, his leadership at Los Alamos, and subsequent events including the invitation to accept his present position—that of director of the Institute of Advanced Study—from Lewis Strauss. Complimentary letters from Franklin Roosevelt, Leslie Groves, and Harry Truman were read into the record. Oppenheimer explained that at the end of the war neither he nor Groves were certain that the wartime directive to develop an atomic weapon necessarily extended to include the development of a super, or hydrogen bomb. It was also pointed out that despite heavy criticism from fellow scientists, Oppenheimer had supported the May-Johnson Bill, whose measures for security were so strict that they were considered "repressive" by some. In part to answer later criticism about Oppenheimer's role in weapons development, Garrison read an extract from one of the scientist's reports on international control prepared for the State Department:

> It therefore becomes absolutely essential that any international agency seeking to safeguard the security of the world against warlike uses of atomic energy should be in the very forefront of

*Ultimately, it was thirty-one.

> technical competence in the field. If the international agency is simply a police activity for only negative and repressive functions, inevitably and within a very short period of time the enforcement agency will not know enough to be able to recognize new elements of danger, new possibilities of evasion, or the beginning of a course of development having dangerous and warlike ends in view.[2]

Garrison introduced a variety of examples of Oppenheimer's thinking on the complex matters of international accord and national defense. At 5:13 P.M. the first day of the four weeks of testimony and questioning came to an end.

Gray reopened the proceedings the following day with news from Garrison that James Reston of *The New York Times* was in possession of both the Nichols letter and Oppenheimer's reply. Garrison and Oppenheimer had been pressured by Reston to give him both documents, with a warning that news of the hearing was already out and that it would be beneficial to have both documents available when the news media broke the story. Gray was greatly displeased, especially at what he perceived as an attempt by Garrison and Oppenheimer to lead him and his colleagues to believe that efforts were being made to withhold the story from the papers. Gray dryly quoted Garrison as trying to keep "fingers in the dike." Who else on Oppenheimer's team, demanded Gray, was talking to the press? Garrison revealed that Reston had learned of the charges against Oppenheimer and the impending hearing in early January. Oppenheimer jumped in and said that Reston had first contacted him directly. "I said I thought it contrary to the national interest that the story should be published, that I did not propose to discuss it with him, but if the time came when it was a public story, I would be glad to discuss it with him." Oppenheimer added that Reston had learned that the scientist's clearance had been revoked; in fact, it had been broadcast to "submarine commanders throughout the fleet and Army posts throughout the world."

But Reston was not the only member of the press interested in the story, Oppenheimer revealed. Stewart Alsop had called with "frantic" pleas to publish the story, urging Oppenheimer to talk with his brother, Joseph. Again, Oppenheimer repeated to Joseph Alsop that he thought prehearing publicity would be harmful. Oppenheimer was afraid that a wrong impression would be created: "Either I was a traitor and very, very important secrets had been in jeopardy over the last twelve years, or the government was acting in a most peculiar way to take proceedings against me at this moment." Alsop retorted that he feared McCarthy, who knew of the hearings, would make a mess of the matter.

Gray was startled to learn that Garrison had given Nichols's letter and Oppenheimer's reply to James Reston four days earlier with the understanding that the reporter would sit on them until the story couldn't be contained any longer:

Gray: So you knew when you made the statement here yesterday morning that you were keeping the finger in the dike, that these documents . . . were already in the possession of *The New York Times*.

Oppenheimer: Indeed we did.[3]

Gray was disgruntled. He thought the release to the press was an act tantamount to conducting the hearing in the press. "I think these stories are very prejudicial to the spirit of inquiry. . . ." Evans and Gray, however, had to admit that both had been called by the press the evening before; Garrison stressed that no one on Oppenheimer's side had revealed the *names* of the board. Obviously, there were leaks on all sides. Unhappy, the board returned to the business at hand, agreeing to hear the first witness called by Oppenheimer, who was available only that day: Mervin J. Kelly.

Kelly had served with Oppenheimer on the Research and Development Board from 1950 to 1951 and was now president of the Bell Telephone Laboratory in New York. From Kelly's testimony Garrison hoped to develop some sense of Oppenheimer's leadership capabilities and his contributions to national defense. Their work together on the R & D Board had touched on a variety of topics, largely dealing with nuclear weapons and recommendations for meeting military needs. Certainly, to Kelly, Oppenheimer was fair and able; he was known among his peers "for his accuracy of thought and cleanness of expression." Kelly believed his reports reflected the thinking of his committee members as well. Oppenheimer's absence from further government service "would be," he claimed, "a distinct loss."

When Robb took over the questioning, the board first sensed that the prosecutor's intended approach to the hearings would be one of thinly disguised antagonism rather than civil, even-tempered inquiry. He sought quickly to establish that Kelly was not, by admission, a nuclear physicist; and weren't the leading authorities on the hydrogen weapon Oppenheimer, Teller, Bradbury, and von Neumann? Asked if a particular report which Kelly, Oppenheimer, and others had written on December 29, 1950, contained a reference to thermonuclear weapons, Kelly replied he didn't think so. Robb then asked to enter into the records an excerpt from the specific report mentioning the new weapon. In order to discuss it, however, Garrison and his colleagues had to leave the room. But first Garrison appealed to the board:

> Mr. Chairman, we hoped that this might not arise, but if it is the feeling of the Board that it is important to its own understanding of the case to put this kind of question, of course it is entirely acceptable to us, and we shall withdraw.[4]

Gray concurred, and the three men left the room briefly. It was the first of many instances where Robb was able to use his special access to materials held by the commission and other agencies, to the detriment of Oppenheimer's defense. Should Garrison have protested more vigorously? Was his "cooperative spirit" perhaps more harmful than not? It was a reasonable criticism leveled later at Oppenheimer's defense counsel.

The hearings resumed, and Gray suggested that perhaps the report failed to reflect *all* the discussions conducted at the time. Kelly disagreed, saying that he would not have been likely to sign a document unless it reflected all the discussions and conclusions accurately. Kelly left and Garrison resumed his direct examination of Oppenheimer. The scientist protested the suggestion that the report—or any report with which he may have had a connection—would deliberately fail to reflect all the committee thinking:

> Any judgement that was expressed about the thermonuclear program could have been expressed only with the consensus, the complete agreement of all members of that committee who knew about it and the undertaking on the part of those who didn't.

Robb did not challenge this statement—at least, not yet. Garrison went on to establish, through direct questioning, Oppenheimer's role in the General Advisory Committee.

To help answer the allegation that Oppenheimer had exercised more influence than might have been proper, Garrison directed a question to the scientist on the mechanics of the General Advisory Committee in making a recommendation. Oppenheimer explained:

> The meeting was generally opened by a meeting with the Commission, sometimes with the military liaison committee, in which the Commission would discuss with us what was on its mind, what advice it wanted. There would be a period of briefings. . . . We would then go into executive session, go over the program aloud and begin to talk about questions. Sometimes it was clear that the answer was obvious. Sometimes it was very tough. . . . When we were clear as to what we had to say, we would meet again with the Commission . . . and at that point I would usually summarize out loud what our thoughts were and a record would be made of that. If I knew of differences of opinion, I would call on those who had any divergent opinion to express their differences. This oral report I then made the basis of a letter to the Commission. . . . This was circulated to the members of the (General Advisory) committee who could approve it.[5]

Garrison also probed into the evolution of the thermonuclear program. Discussing the October 29, 1949, meeting, Oppenheimer spoke of the GAC's executive session. Regarding the feeling of the GAC on the question of the hydrogen bomb, he said: "There was surprising unanimity—to me very surprising—that the United States ought not to take the initiative at that time in all-out program for the development of thermonuclear weapons." Oppenheimer was forced to ask for a copy of the crucial GAC letter resulting from that meeting, and its two annexes. It was necessary for the hearing to adjourn so that Oppenheimer could review the letter—still classified—and extract salient portions. In the afternoon, Oppenheimer read one of several key passages from the letter, including the sentence "We are all agreed that it would be wrong at the present moment to commit ourselves to an all-out effort towards its development." Robb had no comment except to say that "later on we might want to come back to this report."

Oppenheimer and Garrison attempted to link the eventual success of the hydrogen weapon to various theoretical and developmental steps that occurred between 1945 and 1951. As Oppenheimer said, "If we had not had good ideas in 1951, I do not think we would have it [the hydrogen bomb] today." In light of this evolution, it was believed that one could question whether or not such weapons needed to be developed in the first place. Certainly, he argued, the world would be safer today without Russian and American hydrogen bombs. Oppenheimer probably perplexed his judges when he offered a seemingly contradictory thought:

> However, it is my judgment in these things that when you see something that is technically sweet, you go ahead and do it and you argue what to do about it only after you have had your technical success. That is the way it was with the atomic bomb. I do not think anybody opposed making it; there were some debates about what to do with it after it was made.[6]

With success in hand, it was believed that the sheer terror of these weapons might put an end to major wars. What frightened and bothered Oppenheimer was that these weapons would actually be used. "I suppose that bother is part of the freight I took into the General Advisory Committee, and into the meetings that discussed the hydrogen bomb."

Garrison now read into the proceedings a lengthy letter from John Manley, Oppenheimer's former colleague at Los Alamos and on the GAC, and associate director of Los Alamos. From 1946 until his resignation from the GAC in 1951, Manley knew of "no circumstances in which Dr. Oppenheimer attempted to influence in a direct personal way the course of events at Los Alamos as distinct from the effect that the recommendations of the GAC might, in normal course, have on the work of the laboratory." Manley also clarified the circumstances surrounding the alleged "release" of secret documents by Oppenheimer to members of the laboratory staff in November 1949. Manley personally had made the

October 29, 1949, report by the GAC available to fellow staff members under a request from Carroll Wilson, the AEC's general manager. Oppenheimer had absolutely no role in the matter. Manley addressed the issue of loyalty in his own direct style: "I am absolutely clear that he [Oppenheimer] is in no sense a security risk."

Tuesday's session ended quietly at 4:20 P.M.

Occurring as it did amid preparation for the McCarthy-Army hearings, Oppenheimer's security review at first stunned the nation, and then drifted into the day's news as a less-than-headline story.* Since the hearing itself was privileged, the transcript was neither released nor covered by newsmen. Word did drift out informally as reporters took note of the scientific luminaries who were called to testify. On April 13 the Atomic Energy Commission issued a statement on the hearing, citing as the origins of the case the President's April 27 Executive Order to investigate anyone who might be a security risk. "Because there was such material in the file of Dr. Oppenheimer, it was subject to review." The only reference in the statement to Borden's letter was so vague that only insiders could interpret it: "Because of the material therein [in Oppenheimer's file] which had been brought to the attention of the President by the Department of Justice, the President . . . directed that pending a security review of the material in the file, a blank wall be placed between Dr. Oppenheimer and any secret data. . . ." Representative Sterling Cole and Senator Bourke Hickenlooper took pains to speak for the Joint Committee on Atomic Energy: "We do not believe it necessary for further Congressional action at this time." Drew Pearson, in his syndicated column, attributed the present hearing to Oppenheimer's testimony on isotopes in 1949. Pearson had learned that Strauss had taken great offense at the manner in which Oppenheimer had rejected the commissioner's strongly held beliefs that isotopes should not be made available because of their potential for use in weapons. Senator McCarthy garnered even more press publicly joining the anti-Oppenheimer forces; he blamed the scientist for delaying the development of the hydrogen bomb by eighteen months.

Secretary of Defense Charles Wilson held a press conference at the Pentagon. The first question related to Oppenheimer's hearing. The secretary would not comment directly on the matter, but did volunteer that as a bank president you didn't wait until a teller with a history of theft convictions stole money in order to take action. Oppenheimer, he said later, had been dropped from the consultant roles of the Air Force by eliminating the entire advisory on which he served.[7]

---

*The hearings were so-named because they were conducted by freshman Wisconsin Senator Joseph R. McCarthy and concerned subversion in the military. The thirty-five-day hearing was conducted with great emotion and broadcast over nationwide television.

Old friends rose to support Oppenheimer, however. John Manley cabled from Los Alamos: "Deeply regret news break. Continuing support. Concern and love assured." Hans Bethe cabled: "You know that we believe in you and will do all we can to help." Norman Ramsey, contacted at Harvard by Garrison for a letter testifying to Oppenheimer's loyalty and contributions, wrote: "I [am] glad to write him a statement. My only regret was that such a statement should ever be considered necessary." Victor Weiskopf, a friend from California teaching days, wrote: "I would like you to know that I and everybody who feels as I do are fully aware of the fact that you are fighting here our own fight. All our feelings are with you, and we hope that you will have the strength and forcefulness which you always had before, in order to get the situation rectified." Other friends and colleagues submitted letters to the Security Board on Oppenheimer's behalf. John von Neumann, a man closely identified with support of the thermonuclear program, wrote that he was convinced of Oppenheimer's integrity and loyalty. Referring to the issue of Oppenheimer's involvement with the H-bomb, von Neumann wrote:

> Dr. Oppenheimer soon became a leading figure of the latter group [opposing an accelerated thermonuclear program]—my impression was, that he took this position after some hesitation. . . . I consider it entirely unjustified to attribute the *opposition to the acceleration program* [emphasis added] to a desire to help Russia. The opposition involved many people, covering a wide spectrum of backgrounds and convictions, including several political conservatives.

Norris Bradbury, in a statement from Los Alamos, expressed his belief that Oppenheimer and the General Advisory Committee had been completely cooperative to the laboratory both before *and* after the presidential decision of January 1950. "I have the firm personal opinion that he always displayed a strong interest in the technical status of the projects and never, in my presence, acted other than deeply and sincerely interested in the progress of the program." Bradbury knew of no scientist, senior or junior, whose convictions regarding the hydrogen weapon were changed as a result of Oppenheimer's thinking or of his persuasion.[8]

Some colleagues took more public action. Kenneth Bainbridge, the test director at Trinity; George Kistiakowsky, the leader of the Los Alamos Fat Man project group; and Robert Williams, another Los Alamos alumnus, joined several others in signing a letter written to the editor of *The New York Times*. Printed on June 18, the letter stressed Oppenheimer's great achievements at Los Alamos. "His exceptional contributions to the welfare and security of our country are now a matter of historical record. Dr. Oppenheimer does not need any public recognition of his achievements, but America can ill afford to dispense with the services of such a man."*

The AEC's letter and Oppenheimer's response, released by *The New York Times*, then picked up by other newspapers, gave the public a unique portrait of the scientist's influence and activities over a decade and a half. There were few individuals whose past was as well known as Robert Oppenheimer's was now. The press rediscovered him. Now, more than ever, they tried to get an interview, followed him and Kitty as they came and went from the hearing, and dug deep into their newspaper files for background information to add to sketches for their daily reporting. One newspaperman found himself on the same train with Oppenheimer and Kitty between Washington and Princeton. Stuck with the reporter over dinner, Oppenheimer gently refused to comment while the hearing was still continuing. The man was surprised to see two security "shadows" following Oppenheimer's every move on the train. The only scoop the reporter gained was useless: Oppenheimer revealed that he often received mail addressed to mystery writer E. Phillips Oppenheim.

The hearing began again on Wednesday, with Oppenheimer continuing as the witness. Garrison tried to explore the history of Robert's brother, Frank. The only thing approaching Robert's attendance at a Communist party meeting was with Frank sometime in the late 1930s. The meeting, which anyone could attend, was of little interest to Oppenheimer. Garrison also ascertained that Frank Oppenheimer had had nothing to do with the Chevalier incident. As well, he made it known that Robert had clearly disassociated himself from the Independent Citizens Committee of the Arts, Sciences and Professions. At mid-morning, Roger Robb took over the examination of the witness.

Robb's skill at interrogation quickly emerged. He directed questions at the compatibility of the "Communist movement" and weapons work. Why, for example, did Oppenheimer believe that membership or close association with the party was incompatible with what Robb called "secret war work"? Oppenheimer responded that there was hostility from the Soviet government as well as the possibility of espionage. One difference he attempted to articulate was that membership or association with the Communist party in the late 1930s or early 1940s was one thing; since 1943, membership was something else—absolutely unacceptable.[9]

Robb: Doctor, let me ask you a blunt question. Don't you know and didn't you know certainly by 1943 that the Communist Party was an instrument or a vehicle of espionage in this country?

---

*The letter was also signed by Herbert S. Bridge, David H. Frisch, Bruno B. Rossi, Victor Weisskopf, and Jerome Weisner.

Oppenheimer: I was not clear about it.

Robb: Didn't you suspect it?

Oppenheimer: No.

When asked if he had been a "fellow traveler"—a term that Oppenheimer himself had used earlier—he responded that he had been.

Robb: When?

Oppenheimer: From late 1936 or early 1937, and then it tapered off, and I would say I traveled much less as a fellow after 1939 and very much less after 1942.

Robb: How long after 1942 did you continue as a fellow traveler?

Oppenheimer: After 1942 I would say not at all.

Robb: But you did continue as a fellow traveler until 1942?

Oppenheimer: Well, now, let us be careful.

Robb: I want you to be, Doctor.

Oppenheimer: I had no sympathy with the Communist line about the war between the spring of 1940 and when they changed. I did not admire the fashion of their change.

Robb: Did you cease to be a fellow traveler at the time of the Nazi-Russian Pact in 1939?

Oppenheimer: I think I did, yes.

Robb: Now, you are changing—

Oppenheimer: Though there were some things that the Communists were doing which I still had no interest in.

Robb: Are you now amending your previous answer that you were more or less a fellow traveler until 1942?

Oppenheimer: I think I am.

Garrison: Mr. Chairman, I think Oppenheimer testified that he tapered off; did he not?

Garrison had been forced to interrupt in order to stop the relentless questioning by Robb. The commission's counsel, however, did not ease up. He turned to the implications of Communist party membership and quizzed Oppenheimer on wartime figures like Rossi Lomanitz, David Bohm, and Joseph Weinberg. There was even a brief exchange when Garrison attempted to read into the record a telegram sent by Oppenheimer to Colonel James Marshall of the Manhattan Project in 1943 concerning Lomanitz. The telegram had been acquired as documentary evidence by Herbert Marks. Robb quickly stepped in, apparently startled that Oppenheimer was in possession of the telegram.

Robb: Mr. Chairman, may I inquire what other official papers that Mr. Marks had that he turned over to counsel for Dr. Oppenheimer?

Garrison: This is an official paper?

Robb: It certainly is.

Gray: I believe this is an official paper. . . .

Robb: I have the original here. It is stamped confidential. It came from the records of the Manhattan District. I am slightly curious to know what Mr. Marks, a lawyer in private practice, is doing with parts of the file of the Manhattan Engineering District.

Robb refused to let go, directing another battery of questions to Oppenheimer about what other records he might have, and, if he had any, whether they were commission or some other government agency property. Robb returned briefly to Lomanitz before he raised, for the first time, the Chevalier incident.

Oppenheimer recreated the circumstances and the simple facts of the incident: Chevalier had approached him, indicating that George Eltenton, a British scientist, had suggested that a means existed to pass information to the Russians. Oppenheimer had replied that it was treasonable and Chevalier had agreed. "It was a very brief conversation," Oppenheimer added. After a break for lunch, Robb picked up the story on Chevalier and Eltenton. Robb asked if Oppenheimer, on any occasion other than the one meeting at his Eagle Hill house, had Eltenton in his house:

Oppenheimer: I am quite sure not.

Robb: Did he come to your house in 1942 on one occasion to discuss certain awards which the Soviet government was going to make to certain scientists?

Oppenheimer: If so, it is news to me. I assume you know that this is true, but I certainly have no recollection of it.

Robb: You have no recollection of it?

Oppenheimer: No.

Robb: Let me see if I can refresh your recollection, Doctor. Do you recall him coming to your house to discuss awards to be made to certain scientists by the Soviet government and you suggesting the names of Bush, Morgan, and perhaps one of the Comptons?

Oppenheimer: There is nothing unreasonable in the suggestion.

Both Oppenheimer and Garrison must have guessed by now that the pinpoint accuracy of Robb's questions left only one explanation: that he had obtained access to a secret recording of the events at Oppenheimer's house during that visit. Both could wonder, with some alarm, just what else Robb had culled from the files and what he would use. Robb chose to continue with the events following the Chevalier incident.

Lieutenant Charles Johnson was the first security officer to whom Oppenheimer had reported the Chevalier incident.

Robb: What did you tell Lieutenant Johnson about this when you first mentioned Eltenton to him?

Oppenheimer: I had two interviews, and therefore I am not clear as to which was which.

Robb: May I help you?

Oppenheimer: Please.

Robb: I think your first interview with Johnson was quite brief, was it not?

Oppenheimer: That is right. I think I said little more than Eltenton was somebody to worry about.

Robb: Yes?

Oppenheimer: Then I was asked, why did I say this. Then I invented a cock-and-bull story.

Robb: Then you were interviewed the next day by Colonel Pash, were you not?

Oppenheimer: That is right. . . .

Robb: Now let us go back to your interview with Colonel Pash. Did you tell Pash the truth about this thing?

Oppenheimer: No.

Robb: You lied to him?

Oppenheimer: Yes.

What Oppenheimer had lied about was the number of people on the project at Berkeley whom Eltenton had purportedly approached. Oppenheimer at first had said three—that was the cock-and-bull story to which he referred—and later had changed his story, saying that Eltenton only approached him through Chevalier. He also admitted that he had not revealed to Johnson, to Pash, or even to Landsdale, that Haakron Chevalier was the mysterious "intermediary" between himself and Eltenton. It was here that Robert Oppenheimer offered his infamous explanation for his behavior—an explanation totally unlike the sophisticated and brilliant man who had dazzled his contemporaries on so many occasions during the last twelve years:

Robb: Why did you do that, Doctor?

Oppenheimer: Because I was an idiot.

It was a devastating moment for the intellectual and sensitive Oppenheimer. But Robb was relentless.

Robb: And didn't you know, Doctor, that by refusing to give the name of X [Chevalier] you were impeding the investigation?

Oppenheimer: I must have known.

The scientist then further admitted that he had lied to Landsdale the following month.

Robb returned to the interview with Pash in August 1943. He read portion after portion of selected dialogue between the two men. Once, when Oppenheimer indicated some hesitancy, Robb added that the government had a voice recording of the conversation. Oppenheimer again admitted that the story he had concocted about Eltenton and the three contacts was pure "fabrication."

Garrison was forced to interject, requesting Robb to furnish Oppenheimer and his counsel with a copy of any transcript he proposed to read from because it might contain information which would put the incidents into a broader perspective. Robb objected, indicating that the very transcript he was reading from was marked secret and, therefore, unavailable to Garrison. It was Oppenheimer who ironically pointed out that the text was already being read into the record by Robb himself. Robb could only reply, "That is right," and continued, unaffected by the stupidity of the situation.

Robb: Why did you go into such great circumstantial detail about this thing if you were telling a cock-and-bull story?

Oppenheimer: I fear this whole thing is a piece of idiocy. I am afraid I can't explain why there was a consul, why there was microfilm, why there were three people on the project, why two of them were at Los Alamos. All of this seems wholly false to me.

Robb: You will agree, would you not, sir, that if the story you told to Colonel Pash was true, it made things look very bad for Mr. Chevalier?

Oppenheimer: For anyone involved in it, yes sir.

Robb: Including you?

Oppenheimer: Right.

Robb: Isn't it a fair statement today, Dr. Oppenheimer, that according to your testimony now you told not one lie to Colonel Pash, but a whole fabrication and tissue of lies?

Oppenheimer: Right.

When Oppenheimer finally confessed to General Groves in December 1943 that the mysterious "X" intermediary was really Chevalier, he recalled also having told Groves that there were no other "three persons" contacted. When recounting this incident to Robb, the counsel produced a copy of a memorandum from then Colonel Kenneth Nichols to security officers in other Manhattan laboratories revealing Chevalier as the intermediary, adding: "Oppenheimer states that in his opinion Chevalier engaged in no further activity other than three original attempts."[10] This memorandum seemed to discredit Oppenheimer's story that he had finally "confessed" all to Groves. Robb let the matter drop for the moment in order to examine Oppenheimer's relationship with the late Jean Tatlock. Oppenheimer admitted that he had last seen Tatlock in June or July of 1943. She had been undergoing psychiatric treatment and was very unhappy. She had asked to see Oppenheimer.

Robb: Did you find out why she had to see you?

Oppenheimer: Because she was still in love with me. . . .

Robb: You spent the night with her, didn't you?

Oppenheimer: Yes. . . .

Robb: You didn't think that spending the night with a dedicated Communist—

Oppenheimer: I don't believe she was a dedicated Communist.

Shortly after this exchange, the questioning ended for the day. The next day General Leslie Groves would be called to testify.

If Oppenheimer appeared beaten and hesitant, Leslie Groves did not. He was forceful and could not be bullied by Robb's inquisitive style. He spoke extensively about Oppenheimer's work at Los Alamos. In Groves's words, Oppenheimer "had done a magnificient job," although he added that this "job" had been done under his control until the end of the war. The scientist's hard work, in fact, had made Groves worried that Oppenheimer's health might not withstand the terrible strain of directing Los Alamos. Groves also tried to explain the Chevalier incident to the board:

> When I learned about it [the Chevalier incident], and throughout, that he was always under the influence of what I termed the typical American schoolboy attitude that there is something wicked about telling on a friend. . . . I did know this: That he was doing what he thought was essential, which was to disclose to me the dangers of this particular attempt to enter the project. . . . I always had the very definite impression that Dr. Oppenheimer wanted to protect his friends of long standing, possibly his brother. It was always my impression that he wanted to protect his brother, and that his brother might be involved in having been in this chain. . . .[11]

Groves clearly did not find the Chevalier incident as damaging an item in Oppenheimer's background as the AEC and Robb did. Under pressure from Robb, however, he admitted that he had "cleared" Oppenheimer because he was "essential" to the Manhattan Project.

Robb: General, in light of your experience with security matters, and in the light of your knowledge of the file pertaining to Dr. Oppenheimer, would you clear Dr. Oppenheimer today? . . .

Groves: [after some intervening conversation] I would not clear Dr. Oppenheimer today if I were a member of the Commission on the basis of this interpretation.

Groves had hardly done any favor for Oppenheimer. The General had provided an interesting insight into the problems of managing the Manhattan effort and the efforts to remove security risks. One such case involved asking General Lewis Hershey to personally revoke a young scientist's draft deferment.

Another important fact that emerged from Groves's testimony was that American predictions of eventual Soviet atomic bomb success were based in part on knowledge of Russian access to uranium ore. Intelligence sources indicated that this access was limited; it wasn't until *after* the first Soviet detonation that government intelligence realized that the Soviets had had the rich mines of Saxony in East Germany to draw upon.

Once again Oppenheimer resumed his seat in the witness chair. In quizzing Oppenheimer on his contributions to various causes, Robb revealed that he had access to the scientist's state income tax form for 1942. Again, that sort of revelation suggested that Robb had been able to draw from a seemingly inexhaustible well of information which neither Oppenheimer nor Garrison could use. The effect was more than unsettling. The usually calm and possessed Oppenheimer sat in his chair, tensed, leaning forward, and often wringing his hands. As others testified, he sat stooped on the small sofa against the wall, smoking incessantly.

Robb continued to ply Oppenheimer with questions about his acquaintance with David Hawkins, Philip Morrison, Joseph Weinberg, and several others. At one point, in an effort to jog Oppenheimer's memory, Robb read selected portions from a transcript of an interview with security officers. Marks interrupted to inquire as to the nature of the document.

Marks: May I inquire, Mr. Chairman, if transcripts are taken from recordings, just so we can understand what is being read?

Robb: Yes. I have every reason to believe it is accurate.

Marks: I don't question that, I just wondered what the origin was.

Robb: I don't think that is necessarily a question counsel should have to answer.

Robb continued to read from the transcript, and once again Oppenheimer's lawyers—this time Garrison—interrupted to ask for a full copy of the transcript. Gary responded that it would be given to them, but only at the end of the questioning, which was obviously too late to assist in the present dialogue. A few minutes later Garrison objected again. Reading "bits and pieces" from an old transcript to a man whose memory had been taxed by so many revelations was unfair. Robb sharply replied: "I resent counsel's statement that I am trying to be unfair with this witness because I assure you that I made every attempt to be fair with him." In fact, Robb said:

> Were I trying to be unfair, I would not ask this witness any of these questions, but would leave it in the file for the Board to read. I am giving the witness a chance to make whatever explanation he wishes to make.[12]

Fair or unfair, the situation typified the proceedings. Robb had amassed an incredible amount of background material. He was able to mention names and incidents that Oppenheimer had all but forgotten. Despite Oppenheimer's responses to situations he remembered clearly or not, the board would still have before it the full transcripts, unsigned memoranda, reports, affidavits, and similar information which would inevitably affect its final judgment. Oppenheimer, no matter how carefully or craftily he responded, would always have a disadvantage. Garrison's only hope was to press for the argument that what was acceptable in trial law would also be acceptable here. Gray conceded the immediate point, and gave to Garrison and Marks a transcript of Oppenheimer's interview with Colonel Landsdale.

Robb then quizzed Oppenheimer about his 1950 testimony before the House Un-American Activities Committee hearings on Bernard Peters. During the course of his testimony—which was supposed to have been privileged under executive session proceedings—he revealed that he knew Peters to be "quite Red" and that Peters himself had said this to Oppenheimer some years before. Shortly after his testimony, the story had leaked to a newspaper in Rochester and Oppenheimer was forced to recant his comments after some bitter attacks by colleagues like Hans Bethe and Edward Condon, who felt Oppenheimer had betrayed a colleague. His "reformed" statement indicated that Peters had been a Communist while in Nazi Germany, but not in America.* Robb sought to exploit this incident as evidence of Oppenheimer's susceptibility to pressure from colleagues; such wavering suggested that Oppenheimer would put personal loyalty over loyalty to national interests. The day's session ended with Robb asking questions about Oppenheimer's alleged attendance at a Communist party meeting in his own house, which Paul and Sylvia Crouch attended.

Friday's session focused by and large on the thermonuclear program. Asked why he regarded the hydrogen bomb as dreadful, he replied: "Because I have always thought it was a dreadful weapon. Even from a technical point of view it was a sweet and lovely and beautiful job, and I have still thought it was a dreadful weapon."[13] Robb tried to get Oppenheimer to admit that his attitude greatly influenced other scientists:

Robb: . . . Wouldn't you agree that anything said by you would have great weight with a great number of nuclear physicists?

Oppenheimer: Would have some weight with quite a few people, physicists and non-physicists.

Robb: Doctor, let me ask you, sir, do you think that public statements which you have told us about and which you have summarized, tended to encourage other physicists to work on the hydrogen bomb?

Oppenheimer: I should think that they were essentially neutral. I coupled the hydrogen bomb and the decision to seek international control of atomic energy first, so that there was no substantive criticism of the decision.

Later, Robb carefully broached the subject of the October 29, 1949, meeting in which the General Advisory Committee had "unanimously" recommended against crash development of the thermonuclear bomb.

Robb: Now, I have a note here, Doctor, that you testified that there was a surprising unanimity—I believe that was your expression—at the GAC meeting of October 29, 1949, that the United States ought not to take

---

*See Chapter Eleven.

the initiative at that time in an all-out thermonuclear program. Am I correct in my understanding of your testimony?

Oppenheimer: Right.

Robb: In other words, everybody on the committee felt that way about it?

Oppenheimer: Everybody on the committee expressed themselves that way.

Robb: Beg pardon?

Oppenheimer: Everybody on the committee expressed themselves that way.

Robb: How many people were on the committee?

Oppenheimer: There were 9 on the committee; 1 man was absent in Sweden.

Robb: Who was that?

Oppenheimer: Seaborg.

Robb had laid the trap. He asked if the committee had known how Seaborg felt about the matter:

Oppenheimer: We did not. . . . He was in Sweden, and there was no communication with him.

Robb: Beg pardon?

Oppenheimer: He was in Sweden, and there was no communication with him.

Robb: You didn't poll him by mail or anything?

Oppenheimer: This was not a convenient thing to do.

During the precise questioning, with Robb several times asking the scientist to repeat certain answers, Oppenheimer failed to mention the letter from Seaborg, written on October 14. Robb did not immediately reveal that he knew of the Seaborg letter; instead he spent some fifteen minutes reviewing Oppenheimer's "moral" views on the thermonuclear weapon, at one point asking the man if he had had "moral scruples" about the bombing of Hiroshima. Oppenheimer quietly replied, "Terrible ones."

Robb finally produced the Seaborg letter.

Robb: So, Doctor, isn't it clear to you now that Dr. Seaborg did express himself on this matter before the meeting?

Oppenheimer: Yes, it is clear now. Not in unequivocal terms, except on one point, and on that point the General Advisory Committee I think made the recommendation that he desired.[14]

Robb then revealed that Oppenheimer had failed to mention Seaborg's letter in testimony before the Joint Committee on Atomic Energy on January 29, 1950, just two months after the October meeting. Oppenheimer replied that he would have to see the transcript.

Robb: If you did make that statement, it was not true, was it?

Oppenheimer: It is clear that we had an expression, not unequivocal, from Seaborg, before the meeting of October 29.

Robb: Did you hear my question?

Oppenheimer: I heard it, but I have heard that kind of question too often.

Robb: I am sure of that, Doctor, but would you answer it, nevertheless?

Marks: Isn't Dr. Oppenheimer entitled to see the testimony which is being referred to, instead of answering a hypothetical question?

Robb: It is not a hypothetical question.[15]

Garrison was unable to secure a copy of the transcript of the Joint Committee hearings. The actual question and answer could make a considerable difference, since Oppenheimer's reply might have been to a question other than "Did *all* members of the GAC agree with the final decisions?" Powerless to obtain the material to which Robb referred, the board was left with the clear impression that Oppenheimer might well have lied—to themselves and to the Joint Committee four years ago.

Oppenheimer became exasperated. He said he wanted to make "a general protest":

> I am told I have said certain things. I don't recall it. I am asked if I said these, what would that be. This is an extremely difficult form for me to face the question. I don't know what I've said. It is of record. I had it in my own vault for many years. . . . Having no recollection of the Seaborg letter, I cannot say that I did [read the letter to the GAC]. But it would have been normal practice for me at one of the meetings with the Commission not merely to read the letter . . . but to read parts of it relevant to our discussion. . . .[16]

Robb concluded his questioning by asking Oppenheimer if he remembered taking an oath to tell the truth. Garrison objected immediately and Gray concurred; there was no reason to raise the question again. Exhausted, Oppenheimer prepared to take a quick break, but Gray moved to ask some questions; Oppenheimer, drained by the earlier interrogation, replied: "Let us get that over with."

Oppenheimer left the witness chair and was replaced by two old colleagues—Thomas Keith Glennan, who was now president of Case Institute in Cleveland, and, shortly later, Karl T. Compton, formerly the president of the Massachusetts Institute of Technology and a member of the wartime National Defense Research Council. Glennan also had been an AEC commissioner from 1950 to 1952, during the critical times of the thermonuclear program. Glennan read from a prepared statement until abruptly stopped by Robb, who protested that he "apprehended" that Glennan was about to make an argument from the witness chair—a practice not permitted by the AEC procedures. Garrison also interrupted to say that all witnesses called by the defense had been asked to speak about their relationship to Oppenheimer, their views of him and his loyalty, and the contributions he may have made. Robb persisted, framing his comments in polite terms. Garrison, exasperated, said: "Mr. Chairman, I am amazed that this question should be raised." Glennan returned to his text, which was less than a paragraph in length. Robb had no questions and Karl Compton took the stand. Both Glennan and Compton expressed their belief that Oppenheimer was indeed loyal and that he should continue in government service. Again, Robb had no questions. After lunch John Landsdale took the witness chair.

Landsdale, an attorney himself, proved to be a match for Robb. Under Garrison's questioning, Landsdale revealed that Oppenheimer had been watched at all times and his mail opened while at Los Alamos. Landsdale did not believe that Oppenheimer was a "calculated risk," nor that any information had ever leaked because of an indiscretion or action on his part. After two and a half hours of questioning, Landsdale offered one of the more lucid comments on the nature of using one's past associations to judge a man's worth in the present:

> It would be a terrible mistake to assume that, once having had sinister associations, a man was forever thereafter damned. Yet, once you uncover those, you must always exercise judgment. That judgment is always made up of a large body of intangibles. It is seldom you get anything concrete.[17]

With the conclusion of Landsdale's testimony, the proceeding adjourned its first full week. The hearing would last three more weeks.

The second week began with a comparison of the recording of Colonel Pash's interview with Oppenheimer on August 26, 1943, and the transcription used by Robb the previous week. As Garrison expected, there were discrepancies, but none which Gray or his colleagues on the board thought sufficiently important to rule on the admissibility of earlier questioning by Robb.

Gordon Dean, the former AEC commissioner, was the first witness on Monday morning. He described, among other events, his recollection of the Crouch testimony before an investigative body which implicated Oppenheimer as being the host of a Communist cell meeting in the 1940s. It was Dean's first occasion to read Oppenheimer's voluminous security file: "There was never any doubt in my mind after I examined the file and based partly on my knowledge of Dr. Oppenheimer, which was very close, there was never any doubt as to his loyalty in my opinion. None."[18] Robb began his questioning and carelessly—or intentionally—inserted his own words into Oppenheimer's earlier testimony:

Robb: He has further testified that when interviewed about this matter by intelligence officers of the United States Army, he told these officers a fabrication and tissue of lies. He has also testified—

Dean: May I ask, are you quoting some testimony?

Gray: Just a minute, please.

Garrison: Mr. Chairman, I want to object in the strongest terms to the form of the question which counsel has put.

Indeed, Garrison had reason to object! Robb's wording left the unmistakable impression with Dean—or anyone else who had not heard Oppenheimer's own testimony—that Oppenheimer had in effect branded his interviews as untruths. Gray only made Robb rephrase his question for Dean. Shortly thereafter, Garrison, Silverman, Ecker, and Marks were required to leave the room so that Dean could answer questions about the government's long-range detection system for atomic explosives. This was the second time it was necessary to leave Oppenheimer without benefit of counsel.

Immediately after lunch Nobel prizewinner Hans Bethe was the witness. Marks replaced Garrison as Oppenheimer's counsel for the afternoon session. Bethe was able to cast some additional light on the character and talents of Edward Teller, whose complaints about Oppenheimer's lack of support for the thermonuclear weapon were well known and had been cited often during the previous six days. During the war, at Los Alamos, Teller had been part of Bethe's staff; to Bethe's thinking, at least, he had not been particularly cooperative:

> He did not want to work on the agreed line of research that everybody else in the laboratory had agreed to as the fruitful line. He always suggested new things, new deviations. He did not do the work which he and his group was supposed to do in the framework of the theoretical division. So that in the end there was no choice but to relieve him of any work in the general line of development . . . and to permit him to pursue his own ideas entirely unrelated to the World War II work. . . . This was quite a blow to us because there were very few qualified men who could carry on that work.[19]

Bethe was also able to support Oppenheimer's defense that he had been at his New Mexico ranch during most of July and early August 1941—the period called into question by the Crouch testimony. Bethe remembered visiting the ranch because he remembered it as an occasion during which Oppenheimer was kicked by a horse.

Bethe was followed by James B. Fisk, a present member of the General Advisory Committee and formerly the director of the AEC's Division of Research. Fisk's questioning was the briefest so far. After stating that there was no "more devoted citizen in this country," he was excused and replaced by General Frederick Osborn, the former American deputy representative to the United Nations Atomic Energy Commission. Osborn's testimony lasted less than half an hour.

Tuesday's session was the longest and most arduous so far. George Kennan, from the Institute for Advanced Studies at Princeton and one of the country's experts on Russia, was the first witness. Kennan's comments were low-key, but reflected the considerable breadth of his experience and understanding. Gifted men and women, he replied to one question put to him by Gray, were less apt to have "conventional" backgrounds, but that alone was not nor should be grounds for excluding their services to the nation. Evans, a member of the board, almost seemed to plead with Kennan to understand that it was the board's task to judge a man's character, the import of his past associations, and his loyalty. Evans repeated several times that it was a job that nobody on the board wanted. Evans later offered the following quote, which brought a smile from Oppenheimer: "Great wits are near to madness, closely allied and thin partitions do their bounds divide."[20] Given Oppenheimer's familiarity with literary allusions, he just may have smiled at the fact that Evans quoted incorrectly. The lines John Dryden actually wrote read: "Great wits to madness sure are near allied, and thin partitions do their bounds divide."

David Lilienthal was the next witness, followed by James Conant, who at that time was the U.S. high commissioner for Germany. Conant was direct: Opposition, per se, to the hydrogen bomb—a key element of the allegations against Oppenheimer—could not make a man disloyal. "If it did, it would apply to me because I opposed it as strongly, as strongly as anybody else on that Committee [GAC]."[21] Sumner Pike and Norman Ramsey also spoke on behalf of Oppenheimer, as did Isidor Rabi, the final witness on Wednesday.

Rabi was the present chairman of the GAC, and someone who had served since the earliest days of the AEC. He quickly cleared up an error in a recent issue of *Time* which credited Livermore with the development of the hydrogen bomb. To Robb he confessed that he had grave misgivings about the hearing, both for his friend and for the security of the United States. The Chevalier incident was not untypical of Oppenheimer at the time; today, said Rabi, approached like that, Oppenheimer would no doubt have the man "put in jail." Oppenheimer, he thought, had changed with the times:

> I think he was always a loyal American. There was no doubt in my mind as to that. But he has learned more the way you have to live in the world as it is now. We hope at some future time that the carefree prewar days will return.[22]

Suspending Oppenheimer's clearance was unfortunate, Rabi argued. As a consultant, he did not need to be called.

> So it didn't seem to me the sort of thing that called for this kind of proceeding at all against a man who had accomplished what

> Dr. Oppenheimer had accomplished. There is a real positive record, the way I expressed it to a friend of mine. We have an A-bomb and a whole series of it, and what more do you want, mermaids? This is just a tremendous achievement. If the end of that road is this kind of hearing, which can't help but be humiliating, I thought it was a pretty bad show.[23]

The following day Norris Bradbury was the first witness. Bradbury was able to say confidently that Oppenheimer's opinions had not slowed down work on the hydrogen bomb. Personally, Bradbury was shocked with Oppenheimer's appearance; to Bradbury he looked like he had been struck by the "wrath of God." During the day, three more men testified: Walter Whitman, a current member of the General Advisory Committee; Hartley Rowe, who had served under Bush during the war at OSRD and one of the first members of the General Advisory Committee; and Lee Alvin DuBridge, another member of the first GAC. Whitman reaffirmed that his study of Oppenheimer's security folder had still permitted him "prayerfully" to reach the conclusion that Oppenheimer posed no threat and that Whitman's own experience with the scientist during 1950 gave him no cause to believe that the scientist had attempted to stall development of the H-bomb. Rowe believed that Oppenheimer was even more trustworthy now because of his mistakes in the past: "I think a man of Dr. Oppenheimer's character is not going to make the same mistake twice. I would say he was all the more trustworthy for the mistakes he made."[24]

On Friday, the tenth day of the hearing, the board heard from only two witnesses: Harry Winne, a former member, along with Oppenheimer, of the Department of Defense's Research and Development Board; and Vannevar Bush, the wartime director of the Office of Scientific Research and Development and now the president of Carnegie Institution. Bush was by far the most criticial of the hearing to date. The hearing and the General Nichols letter could well be interpreted as putting "a man on trial because he held opinions," and this was contrary to the American system. From conversations with other colleagues, Bush had the sense that Oppenheimer was being "pilloried" because he had strong opinions. "If this country ever gets to the point where we come that near to the Russian system, we are certainly not in any condition to attempt to lead the free world toward the benefits of democracy."[25] Even more strongly, Bush said that the hearing was wrong even if it had been kept secret.

On Monday morning Kitty Oppenheimer testified before the board. Most of the questioning referred to her early adult life, her first marriage, and her involvement with communism. She was followed by Charles Lauritsen, Jerrold Zacharias, Oliver E. Buckley, and Robert Bacher. Buckley had joined the General Advisory Committee in 1948 and was still a member. He, too, clarified the circumstances of the October 1949 GAC meeting. He had, almost five years before, opposed an "all-out" program to develop a super. Bacher revealed that he did not concern himself with security background checks during the war; judgments were made about a man's scientific or technical experience, and security concerns were left to security officials.

On Tuesday morning General James McCormack testified, followed by John von Neumann. Quizzed about the Chevalier incident—like most of the witnesses before him—von Neumann observed that action in 1943 might be one thing; action today was another. "I know that neither of us [presumably Oppenheimer and von Neumann] were adolescents at that time, but of course we were all little children with respect to the situation which developed, namely that we suddenly were dealing with something with which one could blow up the world."[26]

In the afternoon Robb introduced the government's first witness, Wendell Latimer, the associate director of Berkeley's Radiation Laboratory. For Latimer, Oppenheimer had been the central voice opposing the thermonuclear weapon. "You know," he said to Robb, "he is one of the most amazing men that the country has ever produced in his ability to influence people. It is just astounding the influence that he has upon a group. It is an amazing thing." Latimer further volunteered that he would find it "difficult" to trust the scientist in matters of security. Samuel Silverman, who questioned on Oppenheimer's behalf, asked for a brief recess. He and Garrison had had no time to prepare for this witness; after all, Robb had never revealed his list of witnesses. Gray refused, and the hearing proceeded.

Silverman tried as best he could to attack the basis for Latimer's assumptions and beliefs. The dialogue quickly revealed that Latimer had not been involved in the weapons program of the government since the end of the war. Despite this, Latimer continued to stress Oppenheimer's considerable influence over other men: Groves, for example, was "very definitely" under the scientist's influence, as was Seaborg, who worked at Berkeley with Latimer and Conant. Asked by Silverman why he thought this was true of Conant, he replied, "The fact that he followed along so consistently." Latimer also claimed that many young men had returned to college campuses as pacifists as a result of Oppenheimer's influence and perhaps a bit of "indoctrination."[27] After over an hour of questioning, Latimer was excused. Garrison ended the day's proceedings by reading a letter from John H. Manley.

General Roscoe Wilson was the first witness on Wednesday, April 28. Wilson had served as a liaison officer to General Groves during the war; afterward he represented the military in weapons concerns. He had served on the Military Liaison Committee until 1951. Robb tried to draw out Wilson's considerable dislike of Oppenheimer's desire to (as Wilson called it) "internationalize" atomic energy by sharing it with the world. Also, Wilson objected to Oppenheimer's opposition to several warning devices for atomic explosions, as well as atomic-powered aircraft. Despite Oppenheimer's intelligence, prestige, and powers of persuasion, Wilson felt uncomfortable with his judgment in defense matters. Silverman was able to extract concessions from Wilson, including an acknowledgment that Oppenheimer's objection to certain "detection" devises was based purely on technical grounds. Wilson also revealed that he was uninformed on Oppenheimer's role in the Baruch plan for atomic energy control in the United Nations. In fact, he was surprised to learn that it was Oppenheimer who had said that inspection "was not enough."

Kenneth Pitzer, the AEC's former director of research from 1949 to 1951, was the next witness. Under Robb's questioning, Pitzer stated his belief that Oppenheimer had not done everything he could have done to promote the H-bomb program after the President's decision in January 1950. His considerable "influence" in scientific circles had no doubt left implications that affected the actions of others who were considering working on the program. According to Pitzer, Dr. Oppenheimer was not indispensable "in the policy area." He had come to the hearing, he added, only at "the very specific and urgent request of the general manager [Kenneth Nichols]."[28] During the redirect examination, Robb asked Pitzer what Robb thought was, perhaps, at the heart of the commission's charge against Oppenheimer's conduct in the development of thermonuclear weapons:

Robb: Doctor [Pitzer], is it or is it not true in your opinion that in the case of a scientist as influential as Dr. Oppenheimer, a failure to lend enthusiasm and vigorous support to a program might constitute hindrance to the program or opposition to the program?

Pitzer: There is a certain element of semantics in that question, but I would say yes.

Robb: Thank you.

Thus far, Robb had not been able to cajole or exact any *specific* proof that Oppenheimer had acted wrongfully when he tried to stop or deter the thermonuclear program. What Robb was creating was, in fact, a portrait of a man who had merely failed to react along with most Americans to the hysterics of the Russian weapon successes and to sudden military demands for weapons of unlimited size and destructive force. Very simply, Oppenheimer had chosen to disagree.

By far the most controversial witness of the proceedings was now to take the stand. Near the end of the afternoon Edward Teller was sworn in as a witness appearing only, he said, because he had been asked and because it was his duty to do so. Clearly he was uncomfortable: "I would have preferred not to appear." Just six days earlier, in a conversation with

AEC staff member Chester Heslep, Teller had stated that he really did not think Oppenheimer was disloyal. What he did think, however, was that since the hearing would be listened to on the basis of national security, the government should document the "consistently bad advice" Oppenheimer had given since the end of World War II. Oppenheimer, to Teller at least, was not so much a menace as he was no longer a valuable asset to the government. To scientists, however, Oppenheimer was politically powerful, and it would be hard to prove the conditions of his bad advice.[29] Whatever his personal feelings or anxieties, Teller made this point in the first few minutes of Robb's questioning:

Robb: Is it your intention in anything that you are about to testify to, to suggest that Dr. Oppenheimer is disloyal to the United States?

Teller: I do not want to suggest anything of the kind. . . . But I have always assumed, and I now assume that he is loyal to the United States. I believe this, and I shall believe it until I see very conclusive proof to the opposite.

Robb: Now, a question which is the corollary of that. Do you or do you not believe that Dr. Oppenheimer is a security risk?

Teller: In a great number of cases I have seen Dr. Oppenheimer act—I understand that Dr. Oppenheimer acted—in a way which for me was exceedingly hard to understand. I thoroughly disagreed with him in numerous issues and his actions frankly appeared to me confused and complicated. *To this extent I feel that I would like to see the vital issues of the country in hands which I understand better, and therefore trust more* [emphasis added].[30]

From Teller, the acknowledged leader of the hydrogen bomb developers, such a statement was devastating. It was a statement that affected both men badly: Oppenheimer, because the highly regarded Teller could not fail to make a stinging impression on the board members; and Teller, since soon enough the "confidential" proceedings would be made public and his friends and colleagues would divide sharply over the propriety and decency of his remarks. To Teller's credit, he seemed genuinely uncomfortable with the very notion of a hearing—any hearing—that would involve such questions as "loyalty." Also, he seemed unhappy that their old friendship, despite its problems during the past eight or nine years, would be damaged. But in the end, he spoke his mind.

To Teller, Oppenheimer's opposition to the thermonuclear weapon seemed to waver. In 1942, when the concept of the thermonuclear weapon was new, although still theoretical, Oppenheimer had seemed quite interested. In mid-1945 he still seemed interested. But as that year ended, the director of the Los Alamos Laboratory seemed—to Teller, at least—to shift his thinking; he began to argue that the weapons should not be pursued any further. From September 1945 on, Oppenheimer never again seemed to reassert a strong belief in the thermonuclear program. Teller did remember one of Oppenheimer's comments clearly enough: Informed of the first Russian atomic bomb success, Teller urgently called Oppenheimer to ask his advice on what steps to take. Oppenheimer's reply was blunt: "Keep your shirt on." Teller also remembered visiting Oppenheimer early in 1950 to ask for help in recruiting people to work on the hydrogen bomb program. Oppenheimer responded, as Teller recollected, with "You know in this matter I am neutral." Oppenheimer finally agreed to provide a list of individuals whom Teller could contact and invite to Los Alamos. Of those names, however, Teller noted that not one agreed to work on the H-bomb.

At the close of the questioning, Gordon Gray put a question to the witness:

Gray: Do you feel that it would endanger the common defense and security to grant clearance to Dr. Oppenheimer?

Teller: I believe . . . that Dr. Oppenheimer's character is such that he would not knowingly and willingly do anything that is designed to endanger the safety of this country. To the extent, therefore, that your question is directed toward intent, I would say I do not see any reason to deny clearance.

If it is a question of wisdom and judgment, as demonstrated by actions since 1945, then I would say one would be wiser not to grant clearance. I must say that I am myself a little bit confused on this issue, particularly as it refers to a person of Oppenheimer's prestige and influence.

Silverman explored the issue a bit further: Would there be any danger to national security if Oppenheimer had access to classified information "without regard to the wisdom of his advice"? In other words, if Oppenheimer kept his opinions about policy to himself, would mere possession of data constitute danger? Teller responded: "I believe there is no danger." Edward Teller, Oppenheimer's long-time friend and colleague, had virtually advised against continuing clearance. As he left, Teller turned around to Oppenheimer and offered his hand. The scientist took it, but there was pain on his face.

From his seat on the couch, Oppenheimer made notes of the proceedings, indicating, where he could, counterarguments or other facts that might support or attack a witness's testimony. Hearing Teller, he noted on his yellow pad:

Teller—aggressive
had conscience
hysterical
two sides on H-bomb

Later in the proceedings, Oppenheimer recalled a statement once made by Teller which he wrote down on his note pad to have checked out: "Since I cannot work w. the appeasers, I will work with the Fascists.

Lauritsen knows E.T. has done this, in fact. Someone heard E.T. say this. Who?"[31]

On Thursday, before Robb continued calling government witnesses, John J. McCloy was sworn in. He had been asked to testify by Garrison and was only available on this date. McCloy had a long history in government service; he had first met Oppenheimer during the war while serving under Stimson. To McCloy, "security" meant having the "best brains and best reach of mind" in any field; this sense of security was certainly applicable to atomic energy. McCloy called the concept "affirmative security":

> I would say that even if Dr. Oppenheimer had some connections that were somewhat suspicious or made one fairly uneasy, you have to balance his affirmative aspect against that, before you can finally conclude in your own mind that he is a reasonable security risk, because there is a balance of interest there.[32]

Robb, upon questioning McCloy, found the concept of affirmative security too loose. Instead, he chose to cast the question of security risk and the Chevalier incident in terms of banks and bank robbers.* Gray asked McCloy if he would place someone in charge of the bank's vaults if he had doubts about his loyalty? McCloy replied that he probably wouldn't. McCloy further illuminated his idea of security; as one of the commissioners in Germany after the war, McCloy had been instrumental in arranging for German scientists to come to America to continue their work. Their contributions, McCloy suggested, balanced their risks.

McCloy was followed by David Griggs, who served as the chief scientist to the Air Force. Griggs reflected, more strongly than General Wilson, the antipathy of the Air Force toward Oppenheimer. Griggs recounted three stories for the board. The first was an occasion in which Griggs witnessed Zacharias write the initials ZORC on a blackboard at a meeting in 1952 when he was presenting the results of the Lincoln Summer Study. The second incident was a meeting between himself, William Burden, Garrison Norton, I.I. Rabi, and Lee DuBridge in Washington in 1952, an occasion on which Griggs expressed his displeasure with the General Advisory Committee's slow handling of the thermonuclear program. The GAC was not doing enough, he said during the luncheon meeting. Rabi had disagreed and later offered to set up a meeting between Griggs and Oppenheimer. This ultimately led to the third incident: the infamous meeting at Princeton at which Oppenheimer called Griggs "paranoid." Silverman, who took up the questioning, attempted to clarify the issue of Oppenheimer's involvement in such studies as Lincoln and

*McCloy was at the time the president of the Chase National Bank, the third largest in the nation.

Vista. Without access to government classified material, he was at a disadvantage. Both Silverman and Garrison had to rely on jogging the witness's memory. At one point Gray admonished Silverman for taking so many notes during the questioning, claiming that "it was one reason he missed some of the questions." Despite this handicap, when pressed by Silverman, Griggs became less categorical in his assertions that Oppenheimer had been able to negatively influence or jeopardize national defense objectives. The dialogue revealed more concern for Air Force objectives than for national ones. Griggs did offer one interesting insight: Speaking about having been on the "opposite side" of the controversy of whether or not there should be a quick development of the hydrogen bomb, he said:

> I think it is a fair general observation that when you get involved in a hot enough controversy, it is awfully hard not to question the motives of people who oppose you.

But then he added, ironically, "If it ever comes to the day when we can't disagree and disagree violently in public and on national policy, then of course I feel that it will be a calamity for our democracy."[33]

The final witness of the day was Luis Alvarez, who was able to add to the board's understanding of the events leading to the President's decision in January 1950 to proceed with the development of the H-bomb. He brought with him his diary of the events that occurred over a three-week period in October 1949. The diary focused on his and Ernest Lawrence's* attempt to garner support for the thermonuclear weapon and traced their lobbying activities in the days immediately following the announcement of the first Russian atomic bomb. One of the diary entries read: "Felt Oppie was lukewarm to our project and Conant was definitely opposed." Another insight offered by Alvarez related to the "climate" in which "brilliant inventions" could be made. Alvarez recalled that when he first arrived at Los Alamos in 1944, George Kistiakowsky believed Oppenheimer was "mad" to believe that the implosion bomb would work. "Dr. Oppenheimer was absolutely right, and he was right because he set up a group of people that put a concentrated effort on the program and 2 or 3 brilliant inventions did come out which made this thing possible." The implication, of course, was that the climate had not been right for the hydrogen bomb for many years after the war.

Ward Evans, who had been quiet for most of the hearing, ventured to ask Alvarez what was meant, if anything, by Oppenheimer's supposed opposition to the hydrogen bomb. Alvarez replied, "By itself it means absolutely nothing because I have many friends in the scientific

*Ernest Lawrence had been asked to testify as a government witness. Originally, he planned to do so and encouraged Alvarez to testify as well. Early in the hearing, however, he became sick and did not appear.

world who feel precisely this way." Oppenheimer was not disloyal, he explained, but had perhaps shown "exceedingly poor judgment" in opposing the new weapon's development. Alvarez had been surprised by Oppenheimer's objections, especially since the scientist had used the possibility of the super to lure Alvarez to Los Alamos in 1943.

Boris T. Pash, the original Army officer assigned to the San Francisco area for Manhattan District security, was the next witness. With the assistance of documents procured by Robb, Pash was quizzed on Oppenheimer's background, using information collected over a period of almost two years by the Army's G-2 Section and the FBI. Pash made it clear that he still believed Oppenheimer was connected with the Communist party.

The final government witness was William Borden, the author of the infamous letter to FBI Director J. Edgar Hoover regarding Robert Oppenheimer. Borden asserted that he was at the hearing under a subpoena, "commanding" him to appear. Robb began to read Borden's letter into the record when Garrison protested: To do so would enlarge the nature of the inquiry. Borden's charges, such as they were, rambled across many subjects and events. Gray disavowed the objection, indicating that the letter had been before the board from the beginning. The letter was then read into the record. Curiously, when the reading was finished, Gray made a statement on behalf of his colleagues. The board, he said, had no evidence before it that Oppenheimer was a Soviet agent, nor that he had supplied information to the Soviets, nor that he was operating under directives from the Soviets. After a few questions from Robb, the hearing was adjourned for the weekend. Borden was to return Monday for questioning by Garrison.

Over the weekend Garrison, Marks, and Silverman decided that questioning Borden would gain them nothing. Since Gray had renunciated most of Borden's charges late Friday afternoon, then what would be served by questioning Borden? Robb still had access to documentation that was not available to Garrison and his colleagues. Garrison announced their decision at the start of the final week's proceedings. With that business out of the way, the August 27, 1943, interview between Boris Pash and Robert Oppenheimer and the interview between John Landsdale and Oppenheimer on September 12, 1943, were read into the record. Following that, Robert Oppenheimer again took the witness chair.

Gray led the questioning. He returned to the Chevalier affair.

Gray: Now here is my question: If Chevalier was your friend and you believed him to be innocent and wanted to protect him, then why did you tell a complicated false story that on the face of it would show that the individual was not innocent but on the contrary, was rather deeply involved with several people in what might have been a criminal espionage ring?

Oppenheimer: . . . Now, when you ask for a more persuasive argument as to why I did this than that I was an idiot, I am going to have more trouble being understandable. . . . I think I was impelled by 2 or 3 concerns at that time. One was the feeling that I must get across the fact that if there was, as Landsdale indicated, trouble at the Radiation Laboratory, Eltenton was the guy that might very well be involved and it was serious. Whether I embroidered the story in order to underline that seriousness or whether I embroidered it to make it more tolerable that I would not tell the simple facts, namely, Chevalier had talked to me about it, I don't know. There were no other people involved, the conversation with Chevalier was brief, it was in the nature of things not utterly casual, but I think the tone of it and his own sense of not wishing to have anything to do with it, I have correctly communicated.[34]

Gray then sought further clarification of Oppenheimer's perception of his role in Vista and Project Lincoln. Quizzed about the October 1949 GAC report, specifically the paragraph in the first signed annex that begins, "We believe a super bomb should never be produced," Oppenheimer replied:

> But look at what that means. If we had had indication that we could not prevent the enemy from doing it, then it was clear that a super bomb would be produced. Then our arguments would be clearly of no avail. This was an exhortation—I will not comment on its wisdom or folly—to the Government of the United States to seek to prevent the production of super bombs by anyone.[35]

On Tuesday, Vannevar Bush again took the witness chair. He rejected Alvarez's statement that Oppenheimer was not made chairman of the committee to study the first Russian atomic bomb because Truman didn't trust him. Kitty Oppenheimer was again called to testify, followed by Jerrold Zacharias, who denied having written the initials ZORC on a blackboard in 1952. Albert Hill, the director of the Lincoln Laboratory, was sworn in Tuesday afternoon. Hill also disputed Griggs's story that Zacharias wrote ZORC on any blackboard: "I know Zacharias well enough to know that I would have been quite angry with him had he done it [written such a thing on a blackboard in a formal setting]."[36]

On Wednesday morning Oppenheimer took the chair for the last time. Robb again touched on one of the major themes of the hearing, which was Oppenheimer's influence on other individuals and on decision making:

Robb: Doctor, I am a little curious and I wish you would tell us why you felt it was your function as a scientist to express views on military strategy and tactics?

Oppenheimer: I felt, perhaps quite strongly, that having played an active part in promoting a revolution in warfare, I needed to be as responsible as I could with regard to what came of this revolution.[37]

Garrison finally asked the board to permit him to make his summation on Thursday, the following day. Gray grudgingly complied, but asked that Garrison be through by 1 P.M.

On Thursday, May 6, after a few preliminaries, Lloyd Garrison made his final statement on behalf of Robert Oppenheimer. "It is the man himself to be considered," he argued. The basic question before the board was whether or not Oppenheimer could be trusted with restricted data. "That, it seems to me, is what confronts this Board, that bare, blunt question." Garrison reviewed security criteria in light of that question.

> It seems to me that . . . the most impelling single fact that has been established here is that for more than a decade Dr. Oppenheimer has created and has shared secrets of the atomic energy program and has held them inviolable. Not a suggestion of any improper use by him of the restricted data which has been his in the performance of his distinguished and very remarkable public service.

The primary elements of the government's long scrutiny of Robert Oppenheimer were his opposition to the H-bomb development, notably to his role in the October 1949 GAC report; and his "left-wing and related incidents" through 1943. The Chevalier incident, argued Garrison, had "assumed undue importance, and must be judged in perspective."

In all of his remarkable and extemporaneous summation, Garrison was perhaps the most eloquent in his final comments:

> There is more than Dr. Oppenheimer on trial in this room. . . . the Government of the United States is here on trial also. Our whole security process is on trial here, and is in your keeping as is his life—the two things together. There is an anxiety abroad that these security procedures will be applied artificially, rigidly, like some monolithic kind of machine that will result in the destruction of men of great gifts and of great usefulness to the country by the application of rigid and mechanical tests. America must not devour her own children. . . . You have in Dr. Oppenheimer an extraordinary individual . . . a gifted man beyond what nature can ordinarily do more than once in a very great while. . . . Does this mean that you should apply different standards to him than you would to somebody like me or somebody else that is just ordinary? No, I say not. . . . But this man bears the closest kind of examination of what he really is, and what he stands for, and what he means to the country.[38]

Gray thanked Garrison and closed the proceedings. It was May 6, 1954. The decision of the Personnel Security Board would appear in twenty-one days.

17. A Failure to Enthuse

The board was left with three thousand pages of testimony, as well as all the assembled material that comprised the voluminous Oppenheimer file. After four weeks of proceedings, Gray, Morgan, and Evans left for a brief vacation. When they reconvened in Washington, they spent nearly two weeks composing their answer. It was not a unanimous decision: Gordon Gray and Thomas Morgan formed the majority and voted not to reinstate Oppenheimer's clearance. Ward Evans was the single dissenter. Their response—a majority and minority report—was prepared in the form of an extensive letter to Kenneth Nichols, the general manager of the AEC.

Their introduction set the stage for the report. "We believe," they wrote, "that it has been demonstrated that the Government can search its own soul and the soul of an individual whose relationship to his Government is in question and security can be examined within the frameworks of the traditional and inviolable principles of American justice." Their response was formed around the twenty-four allegations contained in the Nichols letter of December 23, 1953. The first twenty-three allegations dealt with Oppenheimer's past activities and associations. The twenty-fourth and final allegation dealt with Oppenheimer's role in the development of the hydrogen bomb. Regarding Oppenheimer's past, the allegations ranged from his membership in left-wing organizations such as the Friends of the Chinese People; his contributions to the Communist party; his associations with Jean Tatlock, Kenneth and Ruth May; and the Chevalier incident; to the membership of his brother and sister-in-law in the Communist party. In all cases but one, the board found the allegations "true," "substantively true," or "probable." The exception was allegation seventeen (raised by the Crouches), which charged that Oppenheimer had attended a closed meeting of the Communist party in his house in August 1941; the evidence on this was "inconclusive."

The final allegation—regarding the hydrogen bomb program—was also upheld. From the autumn of 1949 on, the majority board found that Oppenheimer

> . . . strongly opposed the development of the hydrogen bomb on moral grounds; on grounds that it was not politically desirable; he expressed the view that there were insufficient facilities and scientific personnel to carry on the development without seriously interfering with the orderly development of the program for

> fission bombs; and until the late spring of 1951, he questioned the feasibility of the hydrogen bomb efforts then in progress.

The board also found the thermonuclear program would have been pursued with more vigor in the nation's scientific communities if he had enthusiastically supported the program. His influence had delayed the "initiation of concerted effort." The board had also found Oppenheimer less than candid in making the distinction between a continuing program of thermonuclear development and an all-out crash program.

With this response to the list of allegations, the board proceeded to a discussion of "general considerations." Ironically, they found no evidence of disloyalty:

> Indeed, we have before us much responsible and positive evidence of the loyalty and love of country of the individual concerned.

But, on the other hand, "we do not believe that it has been demonstrated that Dr. Oppenheimer has been blameless in the matter of conduct, character, and association." The general considerations included discussions of the meaning of loyalty, the relationship of loyalty and risk, the right of a citizen to continued employment because of loyal and distinguished service to the country, and the role of scientific advisers. The board had taken note, for example, of the background of "pervasive disillusionment" that had permeated the 1930s—the sort of environment in which Oppenheimer had become actively involved in political causes and events. They also noted that past contributions and professional capabilities were alone insufficient causes to warrant continued government employment. They chose, in fact, to quote Oliver Wendell Holmes: "The petitioner may have a constitutional right to talk politics, but he has no constitutional right to be a policeman." Regarding moral convictions, the board expressed their belief that personal doubts and concerns must yield to the security of the nation.

In essence, Robert Oppenheimer was found to be a loyal citizen. His earlier activities and associations were a matter of poor judgment, but they hardly made him a disloyal citizen. It was true, however, that his lack of support and his lack of belief in the thermonuclear program had delayed the start of a concerted effort to build the hydrogen bomb, and that his considerable influence had had a negative effect on the enthusiasm of his colleagues. Both Gray and Morgan believed that Oppenheimer's "lack of candor" was less than desirable regarding his attitude and position "in the entire chronology of the hydrogen-bomb problem." Their conclusions, therefore, were as follows:

> 1. That Oppenheimer's continuing conduct and associations have reflected a serious disregard for the requirements of the security system.

2. Oppenheimer's susceptibility to influence could have serious implications for security interests.
3. His conduct in the thermonuclear program raised doubts as to his concern for the national interests of the nation.
4. Oppenheimer had been less than candid in his testimony.

Because of these conclusions, they could not recommend reinstatement of his clearance.

While Evans agreed with the findings of the board regarding the twenty-four allegations, he did not find Oppenheimer's character lacking, but found instead that some of the scientist's testimony was merely naive and that he had simply forgotten some matters, such as the Seaborg letter written before the October, 1949, GAC meeting. And regarding his influence, Evans wrote: "If his opposition to the H-bomb caused any people not to work on it, it was because of his intellectual prominence and influence over scientific people and not because of any subversive tendencies." He believed that the failure to restore Oppenheimer's clearance would have a deleterious effect on the scientific community in America. Moreover, having been cleared in 1947, Oppenheimer had been even more careful in his activities and associations. "To deny him clearance now for what he was cleared for in 1947, when we must know he is less of a security risk now than he was then, seems to be hardly the procedure to be adopted in a free country."

The most obvious characteristic of the majority report was the paradox of finding Oppenheimer loyal and discreet and yet unworthy of continued service to a country to which Gray and Morgan both admitted he had made incredible contributions. The difficulty of their opinion lay in its lack of assessment and balance of difficult and sometimes contradictory evidence. Oppenheimer's continuing conduct and associations reportedly reflected a lack of regard for security requirements and yet, in the case of his continuing friendship with Haakron Chevalier, for example, no violation of security had occurred. His lack of candor during the hearing was not evidenced in any deliberate lie, but was reflected at worst in the subtle shading of Oppenheimer's recall of crucial events such as the debate over continued development versus crash development of the hydrogen bomb. His "susceptibility to influence" seemed centered in his wartime support of Rossi Lomanitz and his public recanting of testimony regarding Bernard Peters. Yet in both these cases, no violation of national interest had occurred. In fact, the board did not associate Oppenheimer's support of Lomanitz with any subversive intent. The final conclusion appears equally unjustified. Others had opposed the development of the thermonuclear weapon. James Conant and Vannevar Bush were only two who testified to this fact before the board during the hearing. Was Oppenheimer's considerable influence on others the key irritant, or was it merely the fact that he was more visible during that period? Could, in fact, the government encourage dissent on the one hand, and yet demand that government service be divorced from conviction on the other? Granting Oppenheimer's influence, what evidence had been produced that proved his conduct was detrimental to either the development of the weapon or the dedication of others to work on it? Ward Evans, whose conservatism had appeared a bad omen in the beginning, seemed to have been one of the few who had sensed these difficulties.

Both Gray and Morgan suggest that they could have decided otherwise, but for the constrictive nature of the requirements of the Atomic Energy Act:

> It seemed to us that an alternative recommendation would be possible, if we were allowed to exercise mature practical judgment without the rigid circumscription of regulations and criteria established for us.[1]

But did that not go directly against the very language of the AEC criteria for clearance: "The decision as to security clearance is an overall common-sense judgment . . ." The same criteria also specified that individual cases "must be carefully weighed in the light of all information, and a determination must be reached which gives due recognition to the favorable as well as unfavorable information concerning the individual." This had been in large part Lloyd Garrison's argument in the defense of J. Robert Oppenheimer.[2]

The majority and minority reports were given to Kenneth Nichols on May 27. Nichols in turn sent them to Oppenheimer on the following day, with copies to Garrison in New York. Nichols's letter was brief: "A majority of the Board recommends that your clearance not be reinstated." The final arbiter of the matter would be the Atomic Energy Commission. Oppenheimer had the right to request a review of his case by the Personnel Security Review Board. Should he request that review, the decision, along with Nichols's own recommendation, would be sent to the commissioners. Despite the ominous character of the hearing, and the warnings from Garrison that the case was an "uphill battle," Oppenheimer was greatly distressed with the majority finding, alternating between agitation and numbness. Garrison advised against a review by the personnel board. Since the commissioners would finally determine the matter, an appeal would only unnecessarily lengthen the proceedings. Oppenheimer's consultant contract with the AEC ended in little more than a month anyway. To delay the commission's decision unduly might very well extend the entire matter beyond June 30. At that time Oppenheimer's clearance would be moot, and in Garrison's words, the question would be "left in a state of confusion and uncertainty."

On June 1, Garrison responded to Nichols's letter on behalf of

Oppenheimer, stating that the scientist would waive his privilege to a review before the Personnel Security Review Board. Instead, Garrison requested that the matter be given the immediate attention of the commission itself. He requested permission to file a written brief and to make an oral argument before them. Garrison then identified key issues to be brought to the attention of the commission. Most significantly, it was astounding that the board arrived at its majority opinion while still finding Oppenheimer loyal and discreet. He noted the board's finding that here was an individual who had made considerable contributions to the nation, a man whose critics even found him to be loyal. Despite the findings of the board that his opposition to the H-bomb did not stem from disloyalty or subversive intent, the primary reason for the decision seemed to lie, according to Garrison, entirely in Oppenheimer's lack of enthusiasm for the weapon. He wrote:

> We submit that the injection into a security case of a scientist's alleged lack of enthusiasm for a particular program is fraught with grave consequences to this country. How can a scientist risk advising the Government if he is told that at some later date a security board may weigh in the balance the degree of his enthusiasm for some official program? On that he may be held accountable for a failure to communicate to the scientific community this full acceptance of such a program.[3]

No system, Garrison argued, could bar a loyal scientist whose advice "did not necessarily reflect a bare technical judgment, or which did not accord with strategical considerations of a particular kind." To do so would be to condemn the individual for personal opinion. "Surely our security requires that expert views, so long as they are honest, be weighed and debated and not that they be barred."

The same day, Garrison provided the press with copies of his letter as well as the majority and minority board opinions. This had been a defensive action. If the board's decision was made public without Garrison's letter, the reader would have a biased assessment of the hearing. The majority report, for example, contained no mention of the many individuals who had testified in favor of Oppenheimer's loyalty and for the reinstatement of his clearance. On Wednesday morning, June 2, the story broke in the newspapers. Predictably, there was a mixed reaction. *The New York Times* noticed immediately the inherent discrepancy between the Gray board's findings that Oppenheimer was loyal yet still considered a risk. President Eisenhower, while declining to comment on the Oppenheimer case, did indicate that the matter was not closed. At his June 2 press conference, he said that the case was going through a "quasi-judicial" process. Oppenheimer himself, contacted at Princeton, also refused to comment until the matter was fully adjudicated. Reporters did weasel out of his secretary, Katherine Russell, the fact that with the release of the board's decision and the Garrison letter, Oppenheimer believed the next move to be up to the commission. For the press, at least, Oppenheimer seemed calm, even producing a smile for some reporters. That same day Albert Einstein, who shared the faculty of the institute at Princeton, paid Oppenheimer a supporting visit before the intent eye of the press cameras.[4]

The Alsop brothers, in their syndicated column, raised the basic question, "What is national security?" They quoted the findings of the Gray board, which noted Oppenheimer's contributions and loyalty. Their assessment was that the threat posed to the national security by Soviet weapon advances was at the heart of the board's decision; in this context, a failure of "enthusiasm" would be suspect behavior. They wrote, "What imperils this country more greatly: Dr. Oppenheimer's regrettable tendency to be contemptuous of government flatfeet, or the loss to the Soviet Union of our lead in weapons development?"[5] The Alsops attributed the hearing, and ultimately the decision, to the "personal spite" of Lewis Strauss.

The reaction among scientists was, with some exceptions, one of alarm and outrage. Hans Bethe, speaking at Los Alamos, found the decision disturbing, especially when Oppenheimer had been found both loyal and a risk. At the same time, couldn't a scientist give nontechnical advice as long as it was not based on inaccurate technical information, he argued before colleagues. On July 8, in fact, 282 scientists at Los Alamos signed a petition protesting the majority opinion and telegraphed it to Eisenhower, Rep. Sterling Cole, the chairman of the Joint Committee on Atomic Energy, and the five AEC commissioners. David Hill, the retiring president of the Federation of American Scientists, similarly criticized the decision in a public release. Many who knew Robert Oppenheimer, Hill said, could only doubt the judgment of the board. Hill no doubt spoke for many when he said that Oppenheimer's contributions far outweighed those of the bureaucrats who administered the nation's atomic energy program and who now judged him. Strauss and Eisenhower came under fire as well.

Individual scientists took their own steps. Robert Bacher, who had testified at the hearing, wrote to Strauss. The board's decision had come as a "great surprise" to him, especially since the board had reaffirmed Oppenheimer's loyalty. "In my opinion, that the Board has made it so clear that his contributions have been great, and so clear that he is loyal and discreet, that to deny his clearance on the grounds presented would be both unjust and an estimation . . . that his future contributions would be of negligible proportions." Norman Ramsey, who had also testified, wrote Oppenheimer directly; speaking to the "susceptibility of influence" conclusion, Ramsey wrote that if anything, his friend "had been too hard instead of too easy to influence." Other writers were not so kind.

Oppenheimer received the ghoulish as well: "Are you a Communist? So I'm nosy, so what?"[6] And, "If you are a Communist, why don't you admit it and get it over with?"

The release of the three-thousand-page proceedings only exacerbated the public's reaction. To many scientists, Edward Teller's testimony came as a shock. Though most knew of Teller's strong feelings on the hydrogen bomb, and of his differences with Oppenheimer over the years, no one believed that Teller ever would flatly state that Oppenheimer was not to be trusted. Teller soon painfully learned the depths of his colleagues' feelings. Not only did he receive letters and phone calls of protest, but he experienced the worst sort of reprisal: He was shunned by old friends who even refused to shake his hand or talk with him at meetings. On the other hand, critics of Oppenheimer could take considerable comfort in the revelations of the scientist's personal past and of the methodical way in which Robb had been able to reduce the once proud Oppenheimer to a self-proclaimed "idiot." There were those who delighted in the scandalous reports about the man with his "Communist mistress," Jean Tatlock. While the prodigious hearings were hardly light reading, the more tantalizing portions were quickly extracted and reported in the press. In Europe, both the board's decision and the hearings were given more dramatic attention. Haakron Chevalier for one was shocked to learn of the findings as well as to see that his own name had figured prominently in the four-week proceedings.

Lee DuBridge put his own reputation on line with a letter to Lewis Strauss. Writing as chairman of the Science Advisory Committee of the Office of Defense Mobilization, DuBridge requested that Oppenheimer's Q clearance be restored, and that he should continue as a consultant to the advisory committee, with full access to all materials and documentation. DuBridge wrote that "Dr. Oppenheimer's knowledge and counsel will be of very critical importance" to the committee during the next few months on defense matters. While grateful for the board's finding that the scientist was indeed loyal, DuBridge noted that the board had failed to consider the "great value which Dr. Oppenheimer's services have been and will continue to be to the national welfare and security."[7]

In the middle of the public response, Nichols responded to Garrison's June 1 letter. At first he defended the procedural steps which had been taken, including the exclusion of classified material. Nichols indicated that no further presentation, either oral or written, would be entertained by the Personnel Security Review Board. The written brief mentioned by Garrison would be given attention, but "The Commission does not feel that it can accede to your suggestion that there be oral argument as well." The brief was due four days later. On June 7, for the first time, the AEC commissioners discussed the possibility of releasing the full transcript of the hearing. In part, this suggestion was prompted by Oppenheimer's release of the board's decision and Garrison's letter of reply.

There was some hesitation, seeing as each witness had been promised that his testimony would remain fully confidential. For the moment the AEC tabled the discussion. Four days later, on June 11, Commissioner Eugene Zuckert was on the train between Washington and Stamford, Connecticut. He had with him for study a summary of the investigative file on Oppenheimer, as well as significant portions of the proceedings of the hearing. Thinking he had the material with him in his briefcase, Zuckert deboarded the train and went home. It wasn't until the next day that he realized he had somehow left the material on the train. Strauss was immediately notified, and a special emergency meeting of the AEC was called for Saturday night. There seemed to be little choice but to release the massive transcript.* All 3,000 pages were sent to the Government Printing Office, which typeset and printed the document in a record two days. The final report was 993 pages long; it became available on June 15. Oppenheimer and Garrison, contacted on Sunday about the imminent release of the proceedings, refused to prerelease their own typed transcript in advance of the AEC's official release. In the final vote among commissioners on the matter of releasing the transcript, only Henry DeWolf Smyth voted against the idea.†[8]

On behalf of Oppenheimer, Garrison released a memorandum for the press on June 15. He hoped to mediate the effect of releasing almost one thousand pages of testimony in which only selected portions would ever be printed. "Dr. Oppenheimer has believed that it would not be appropriate for him to make the transcript public while the matter was still under consideration by the commission." Therefore, copies of the briefs filed with the board were released by Garrison. Both Oppenheimer and his counsel now waited for Nichols to make his recommendation to the commissioners.

Nichols had already drafted his decision in a letter to the five commissioners on June 12. Nichols carefully prefaced his decision with an acknowledgment of the "factors" considered in making his decision, including Oppenheimer's contributions to the nation's weapons program and the possible effects of denying his clearance. Whether or not the common defense would be endangered, Nichols wrote, would be based on a determination of character, associations, and loyalty. "To reinstate the security clearance of Dr. Oppenheimer," he wrote the commissioners, "would not be clearly consistent with the interests of national security and would endanger the common defense and security."

Nichols found the record to contain no direct evidence of Oppenheimer giving secrets to a foreign power or acting disloyally. He did find

---

*The material was later located in the lost and found office of the railroad. There was time to cancel the printing, but Strauss chose not to.

†Stern notes that while the testifying witnesses were each contacted, they were not asked for permission to publicly issue the document; instead, they were "informed" of the AEC's decision to do so.

the scientist to have had strong associations with Communist individuals, and he continued to maintain these relationships beyond the late 1930s or early 1940s. The Chevalier incident was evidence of untrustworthiness; to Nichols, his misrepresentations of the incident constituted "criminal conduct." Oppenheimer's behavior with security and FBI officials, as well as before the board, revealed some considerable doubts as to his veracity. In fact, Nichols found Oppenheimer's actions since World War II to show "a consistent disregard of a reasonable security system." Another "obstructionist" tactic revealed by Oppenheimer was that he had "repeatedly exercised an arrogance of his own judgement with respect to the loyalty and reliability of his associates and his own conduct which is wholly inconsistent with the obligations necessarily imposed by an adequate security system on those who occupy high positions of trust and responsibility in the Government."

Nichols agreed with the majority opinion that Oppenheimer's lack of "enthusiasm" had delayed a concentrated start on the thermonuclear weapon. Whatever the man's commitment or lack of it, it did not stem, Nichols felt, from "sinister motives."

As to Oppenheimer's value to the government, Nichols believed it to be of little importance at the moment. He was willing, however, to concede that Oppenheimer's value during the war had been considerable, if not absolutely essential. Digging into recent AEC files, however, Nichols had learned that Oppenheimer's services had consisted of no more than six days during the last two years. DuBridge's request for reinstatement was dismissed. Despite a consideration of Oppenheimer's "whole life," the prospect for devastating war was enough to "eliminate from classified work any individuals who might endanger the common defense or whose retention is not clearly consistent with the interests of national security."[9]

In many respects the Nichols letter was more devastating than the board's lengthy majority decision two weeks before. Nichols struck at the heart of Oppenheimer's character—apparently the basis for his recommendation that the clearance not be reinstated—when he charged that the Chevalier incident was evidence of "misrepresentations and falsifications" which constituted "criminal, dishonest conduct." Nichols's assessment ranged far beyond the scope of the Personnel Security Review Board in attacking Oppenheimer's veracity and character. Nichols, as one historian observed,[10] added to Oppenheimer's security considerations a new dimension—character, veracity, and perjury—without giving Garrison any chance to respond. Strauss and the other commissioners would now have to consider the charges added by Nichols in addition to the findings by the Gray board itself. The commissioners had already to hear further oral arguments from Garrison; Oppenheimer and his counsel would not have a chance to argue or defend against the broadened charges of the Nichols letter. It was hardly the simple "recommendation" that Nichols had promised Garrison on June 1.

In addition to Lewis Strauss, the commission included Henry DeWolf Smyth, the only scientist on the AEC; Joseph Campbell, an accountant; Thomas Murray, an engineer; and Eugene Zuckert, an attorney. Smyth, Murray, and Zuckert had been appointed by Harry Truman, a sign that was viewed as hopeful by Oppenheimer and his attorneys as the commission made its final decision. Presumably, as Truman appointees, they would be less susceptible to Republican or conservative influence. The Nichols letter had been formally submitted, meaning that the final act was now in the hands of the five commissioners. On June 16 a letter arrived from Norris Bradbury, addressed to Lewis Strauss. Bradbury urged that the commission make its final decision "*independently* of the whole hydrogen bomb issue and so state publicly." Bradbury noted that he and Strauss differed on the findings of the Gray board on this matter; it was unfortunate, he felt, that the Gray board had not been briefed more thoroughly on the scientific and production aspects of the thermonuclear program from its inception. "Had the board more information, however, they would have possibly appreciated 'the dangers of crash programs.' "[11] The letter failed to move Strauss and the other members of the commission.

On June 22, Smyth learned that each of his four colleagues on the commission were planning to vote against Oppenheimer; Smyth found himself the only one who had decided to vote for reinstatement. A week later, with a draft of majority opinion (largely written by Strauss) on his desk, Smyth redrafted his dissenting opinion with the help of AEC lawyers Philip Farley and Clark Vogel. At four o'clock in the afternoon of June 28, the Atomic Energy Commission released its final opinion "on the matter of J. Robert Oppenheimer."

In the majority opinion, signed by Strauss, Murray, and Campbell, the three men gave their decision:

> On the basis of the record before the Commission, comprising the transcript of the hearing before the Gray Board as well as reports of military intelligence and the Federal Bureau of Investigation, we find Dr. Oppenheimer is not entitled to the continued confidence of the Government and of this Commission because of the proof of fundamental defects in his "character."

Oppenheimer had "fallen short" of "acceptable standards":

> The record shows that Dr. Oppenheimer has consistently placed himself outside the rules which govern others. He has falsified in matters wherein he was charged with grave responsibilities in the national interest. In his associations he had repeatedly exhibited a willful disregard of the normal and proper obligations of security.[12]

This decision was supported by evidence of unacceptable behavior in "character" and in his "associations."

The majority opinion, largely in the words of Strauss, went beyond the course of considerations addressed by Kenneth Nichols. The opinion dealt with criteria different from those given to the Gray board months before. For example, the whole matter of the hydrogen bomb program had been dropped by the AEC commissioners. The findings of loyalty seemed muddled in the new findings of character and associated defects. Oppenheimer's "unusual discretion" went unmentioned. The final, damning assessment of Oppenheimer arose from six incidents which Strauss and the majority described in some detail:

1. Oppenheimer had told a "fabrication of lies" to Pash and to others regarding the Chevalier incident.
2. Oppenheimer had lied to the Gray board about his knowledge and actions regarding Giovanni Rossi Lomanitz.
3. Oppenheimer had lied about his knowledge of and association with Rudy Lambert.
4. Oppenheimer had testified before the House Un-American Activities Committee on Bernard Peters and later changed his story in a public recanting.
5. Oppenheimer had represented the October 29, 1949, GAC meeting as unanimously opposing an initiative in a thermonuclear program, when in fact Seaborg had written a letter offering some support for such a program.
6. Oppenheimer had lied to officials about his knowledge of Joseph Weinberg's membership in the Communist party.

While Campbell, Murray, and Zuckert agreed with Strauss, each prepared his own statement. Campbell believed that Oppenheimer had failed to adequately refute the charges made against him by the original AEC Nichols letter. Murray strongly defended Oppenheimer's right to dissent. Oppenheimer's objections to, or rather his failure to enthusiastically support, the thermonuclear weapon were not disloyal acts or acts that warranted denial of a security clearance. Oppenheimer's failure to abide by the regulations of security, however, had made him a risk. Zuckert found many of Oppenheimer's actions "disturbing" and, although his opinion was vague, he apparently felt these reasons were sufficient to warrant judging him a security risk.

Smyth, on the other hand, chose to agree with the Gray board's original finding that Robert Oppenheimer was a loyal and discreet citizen: He displayed a "high degree of discretion reflecting an unusual ability to keep to himself vital secrets." As well, he felt that too much significance had been read into the Chevalier incident. Similar overreactions had been made regarding Oppenheimer's associations both before and after the war, despite the fact that his repeated interrogations since 1943 indicated an amazing consistency, with the exception of the Chevalier matter. Smyth also dismissed other incidents: Bernard Peters, the Lomanitz deferment, his interviews by security officials, and the October 1949 Seaborg letter. He wrote:

> Application of this standard of overall common sense judgement (as proscribed by the AEC criteria) to the whole record destroys any pattern of suspicious conduct or catalog of falsehoods and evasions, and leaves a picture of Dr. Oppenheimer as an able, imaginative human being with normal human weaknesses and failings. In my opinion that conclusion drawn by the majority from the evidence is so extreme as to endanger the security system.

Smyth hit at the heart of the matter when he suggested that if one "starts with the assumption that Dr. Oppenheimer is disloyal, the incidents . . . arouse suspicion." However, read objectively,

> Dr. Oppenheimer's loyalty and trustworthiness emerge clearly and the various disturbing incidents are shown in their proper light as understandable and unimportant. . . . I would suggest that the system itself is nothing to worship. It is a necessary means to an end. Its sole purpose, apart from the prevention of sabotage, is to protect secrets. If a man protects the secrets he had in his hands and his head, he has shown essential regard for the security system.[13]

News of the decision was formally announced on Tuesday afternoon, June 29, although word already leaked out in the morning. Oppenheimer first learned of the decision when he was asked at midday for a comment from a reporter as he waited for formal notification from Nichols. Word came at 4 P.M., just thirty-two hours before his contract as a consultant to the Atomic Energy Commission was due to expire. Later in the evening, Oppenheimer issued a statement to the press; Smyth's dissenting decision spoke eloquently for his own feelings on the matter. With quiet resolve, he urged his colleagues not to be discouraged by the government's action, and encouraged them to stay on their jobs. "I hope," Oppenheimer said, "that the fruit of their work will be used with humanity, with wisdom, and with courage."

Public reaction was mixed, as it had been when Oppenheimer's security hearing was first announced earlier in April. Conservative newspapers and reporters were reassured by the decision; others were not. The Washington *Post* wrote that no one could "take pleasure" in the 4–1 decision. The Chevalier incident, which had seemed to take on such importance, was disturbing, the *Post* noted, but hardly worth more than a stern reprimand. The newspaper had been moved by Smyth's perception that thinking guilty produced a guilty verdict. But fundamentally, two questions remained:

> In light of the exhaustive scrutiny of his personal life to which Dr. Oppenheimer has been subjected, can anyone with originality and ideas fully satisfy the standards of character and associations which the AEC has prescribed? And, most important and most profound of all, will the security of the country really be stronger because Dr. Oppenheimer has been excluded from the program to which he has contributed so much?*[14]

For all practical purposes, the matter was now closed. Oppenheimer dismissed any appeal to the President or any kind of public campaign for vindication. Although Garrison, Marks, and others had accepted either little or no fees for the case, his legal expenses still ran over $25,000.† To his surprise, Oppenheimer received donations for legal costs from friends, and even from individuals he had never heard of. He was reassured to learn, on October 1, that the trustees of the Institute for Advanced Studies had unanimously voted to reelect Robert Oppenheimer as the institute's director. This was quite amazing to some, since Lewis Strauss still sat on the board of trustees. On July 19, Robert, Kitty, Peter, and Toni left for a month's vacation in the Virgin Islands.

As he noted to close friends, he was not likely to be in public service again.

---

*The *Post* also pointed out that Teller could be considered a security risk because of relatives in Communist countries.

†Stern estimates that the actual expenses, in 1954 dollars, totalled closer to $100,000.

18. End of the Journey

For the moment at least, Robert Oppenheimer and his family found peace in the recuperative setting of their summer home in the Virgin Islands. Elsewhere, however, the storm over the AEC's final decision still raged. Scientists were divided over support for Oppenheimer and support for the government's handling of the touchy question of security and loyalty. The division had emerged three months earlier at the annual meeting of the American Physical Society, where different points of view could be heard. Many scientists found themselves in the middle: While rejecting Oppenheimer's stance on the hydrogen bomb, or at least rejecting what they knew of it, they nevertheless disliked the crude manner in which the government had dealt with Oppenheimer. Newspapers were by and large supportive of the commission. While the Washington *Post* had found the decision distressing, the Chicago *Daily News* had agreed with the majority of the commissioners that the evidence of Oppenheimer's contradictory statements could not be overlooked. The Chicago *Sun-Times* had stated flatly that the nation's security could not be trusted with anyone guilty of "monumental" falsehoods and carelessness. The Detroit *Free Press* had found Oppenheimer a man "much too fallible in his judgments and breadth of understanding to be trusted with important matters."

But it was among scientists that the decision had the greatest effect. There were letters written in support of Oppenheimer, protests lodged at all levels of government, and small private protests like that of Cal Tech's president, Lee DuBridge, who quietly wrote to Lewis Strauss urging reinstatement of Oppenheimer's clearance so that the nation might continue to use his services. *The New York Times* reported efforts by some scientists within the government who asked Congress to appropriate money for Oppenheimer to pay his legal fees.[1] Word also drifted out to the news media that scientists, as a form of protest, were resigning their positions on government projects. Lewis Strauss made urgent trips to Los Alamos, Livermore, and Berkeley to assess the reactions by scientists. By September he was able to report that scientists were not leaving in unusual numbers. Carson Mark, head of the Theoretical Division at Los Alamos, spoke for many of his colleagues when he said that it was no surprise that scientists were still maintaining jobs critical to the nation's security, a fact which, he explained, did not mean that scientists were happy with the AEC's decision. David L. Hill, the past president of the

Federation of American Scientists, added in a newspaper interview that Strauss was in error "if he thinks indignation in the scientific community has abated regarding the decision to classify Oppenheimer as a security risk."[2] Alvin C. Graves, another Los Alamos scientist, returned from Europe with word that European scientists were aghast over what they regarded as the "public airing" of Oppenheimer's policy differences in the press.

Hans Bethe, president of the ten-thousand-member American Physical Society, compared criticisms of Oppenheimer's "lack of enthusiasm" for the hydrogen bomb to the similarly restrictive attitudes toward deviant opinion in Russia. Bethe released a formal statement on behalf of the society which criticized the government's withdrawal of Oppenheimer's clearance even though they had found the man loyal and discreet. The statement also made the point that opinions differed widely on the hydrogen bomb:

> If a man whose advice is sought must fear that his potential utility to the Government may be challenged because his reasoned recommendations later become politically unpopular, he may be tempted to give advice that is politically safe rather than technically safe.

For many scientists, many of whom knew little of Oppenheimer personally, this was the key issue of the hearing and of the entire security system.

Two literary events occurred in the fall that continued the debate over Oppenheimer and his hearing. The first was a book written by two journalists, entitled *The Hydrogen Bomb: The Men. The Menace. The Mechanism.** Compiled from interviews and unclassified information, James Shepley and Clay Blair, Jr., recreated the developments leading to the hydrogen bomb. In the book, Edward Teller emerged as the valiant champion of the new weapon, and not surprisingly, Robert Oppenheimer was portrayed as having seriously delayed its progress. The authors appeared to charge that Oppenheimer almost single-handedly had been able to stop developments from his key position in the General Advisory Committee. As a result, the Soviet Union had been able to perfect its thermonuclear weapon some seven months earlier than the United States. This incorrect conclusion served to put both Oppenheimer and the AEC in the poorest of lights. While the book elicited praise from some, it deeply angered others. Former AEC Chairman Gordon Dean called the book "vicious." Enrico Fermi issued a public statement from Chicago defending the role of Los Alamos in developing the H-bomb. Even Lewis Strauss was embarrassed by the book; he personally contacted the authors in an attempt to buy rights to the book to prevent its publication. Norris Bradbury was forced to admit, in a statement as close to a revelation of classified data as possible,

*New York, McKay, 1954. 244 pages.

that the *only* successful hydrogen bombs developed were those developed by Los Alamos. Bradbury was revealing the fact that one bomb tested by Livermore and designed by Teller had been a dud.

In late September Gordon Dean wrote to Oppenheimer regarding the book. Oppenheimer replied that there was little that could be done. "I have, as you must know, never seen any effective means to fight my way out of the tails of this yarn [his purported opposition to the H-bomb], in part because on so many specific points a rebuttal would take me closer to properly secret things than it has seemed right to go."[3]

The second event was an extensive article in *Harper's* magazine written by Joseph and Stewart Alsop, entitled "We Accuse!"[4] The article was a careful analysis of the events that led up to and occurred during the hearings. Both Alsops were friends of Oppenheimer, but the article was not concerned only with the scientist's side of the story; rather, it was a balanced criticism of the government's handling of security matters. The article was hard-hitting enough to produce results within the AEC; General Manager Kenneth Nichols ordered Arthur Rolander, who had served under Roger Robb and the Gray board, to compile a line-by-line rebuttal of the Alsops' article.

Oppenheimer returned from his month-long vacation and settled into a quiet life as the director of the Institute for Advanced Studies. To a newspaperman, he repeated the story of his political indifference in the 1930s, characterized perhaps by the fact that he never read newspapers. He had learned his lesson, however. "I should think that you wouldn't step twice in the same river. History doesn't repeat itself that way. At least, I've learned to read newspapers since then." He also denied any intention of leaving the United States to live and work elsewhere, perhaps in Europe or India. Regarding his future, he replied that his government career, at least, was over. Before the war he had been a physics teacher; during the war he had run Los Alamos; and for almost ten years he had worried over the direction of scientific research and development and over the quality of his counsel to the government. "This phase of my life is now concluded," he said. In response to the perception of him as a tragic character in a Greek drama, he replied, "In some dramas, a sense of the drama comes from the chorus."[5] Frank Oppenheimer sensed that his brother felt defeated by his enemies. Where once Robert had used words to express his feelings, Frank saw that his brother now hid behind words.

Oppenheimer made his first formal speech since the hearing on December 26, 1954. He participated in a series of talks that were broadcast over the radio marking the two hundredth anniversary of Columbia University. Oppenheimer's talk was entitled "Prospects in the Arts and Sciences," and he chose to prerecord the speech a month beforehand. "What do we see when we look at the world today and compare it with the past?" he asked his listeners.

> In an important sense, this world of ours is a new world, in which the unity of knowledge, the nature of human communities, the order of society, the order of ideas, the very notions of society and culture have changed, and will not return to what they have been in the past. What is new is new not because it has never been there before, but because it has changed in quality.[6]

He argued that the sheer prevalence of newness was a major force in the contemporary world. Knowledge of the physical world was growing dramatically, as was the nature of revelations between men in the global community. Communication itself was different. Dealing successfully with the world meant the necessity of having a broader understanding of the forces of change—this was a theme he would talk of often during the next few years. Both the artist and scientist, each in different ways, could bring a "special hope" to solutions. He closed with gentleness:

> This cannot be an easy life. We shall have a rugged time of it to keep our minds open and to keep them deep, to keep our sense of beauty and our ability to make it, and our occasional ability to see it, in places remote and strange and unfamiliar; we shall have a rugged time of it, all of us, in keeping these gardens in our villages, in keeping open the manifold, intricate, casual paths, to keep these flourishing in a great open windy world; but this is, as I see it, the condition of man; and in this condition we can help, because we can love, one another.

He seemed to echo Teilhard de Chardin's concept of "in-furling," the process by which mankind moves slowly and irregularly toward unity. Teilhard, perhaps like Oppenheimer, saw love and knowledge as the major elements of progress.

Oppenheimer could speak with some authority, since he had himself been a major contributor to the profound changes he described so eloquently. His contributions now were quiet ones: a firmer hand at the helm of the Institute for Advanced Study; a return to the professional meetings and colloquiums of scientists; more time for his students and colleagues and their problems. In early 1955 there was a moment of unplanned justice. Almost a year before, Oppenheimer had been invited to participate in a symposium at the University of Washington on the molecular basis of enzyme action. Shortly after the AEC's verdict, the university's president, Henry Schmitz, had withdrawn the invitation under pressure on the basis of Oppenheimer's "governmental relations." When this became known, the remaining eight speakers refused to participate in protest.* In January the university was forced to announce that it had cancelled the conference.

*The eight scientists were Robert A. Alberty, Konrad Bloch, David E. Green, Charles S. Hanes, Arthur Kornberg, Henry A. Lardy, William H. Stein, and Bert L. Vallee.

Perhaps no other episode concerning Robert Oppenheimer was as widely seen and heard as his televised interview with Edward R. Murrow. Millions watched the articulate Oppenheimer on this single thirty-minute program on *See It Now.* His mannerisms were familiar: the slightly slumped-forward posture, the omnipresent cigarette. Millions saw the flat, two-dimensional Oppy of newspaper and magazine photographs take on human depth and heard his eloquent, articulate voice for the first time. There was all of the quickness of his mind and none of the abrasiveness. There was, however, little humor in his words.

Shortly after the AEC's decision, Oppenheimer received a letter from Haakron Chevalier in Paris. It was the first correspondence since their dinner in Paris in December 1953. Chevalier had learned of the hearing and of Oppenheimer's testimony from the French newspaper *Paris-Presse.* Reading the newspaper, he learned of the content of Oppenheimer's 1943 interviews with Johnson and Pash for the first time. Chevalier wrote on July 7, indicating that he had been "shattered" by the disclosure. Within the week Oppenheimer responded with copies of the transcript and various legal briefs filed on his behalf by Lloyd Garrison. Chevalier was stunned with the content. He wrote another letter to his friend, cited the length and depth of their friendship, and asked for an explanation of Oppenheimer's behavior in what was now publicly called the "Chevalier incident." The letter arrived during the course of Oppenheimer's retreat in the Virgin Islands with his family. Katherine Russell, Oppenheimer's secretary at Princeton, noted the nature of the letter and forwarded it to Garrison in New York. Garrison responded to Chevalier with word that Oppenheimer was on a much-needed vacation and would undoubtedly respond as soon as he returned. In the meantime, however, Garrison drew Chevalier's attention to several passages in the transcript. Garrison sent his advice along with a copy of Chevalier's letter to Oppenheimer in St. Croix: "Obviously, you must write him yourself but I think you need be in no great rush about it."[7]

On September 3, Oppenheimer wrote his own letter to Chevalier.

> As for matters of fact having to do with what I suppose we shall have to call the Chevalier incident, there is probably nothing that I can add. I was scooped empty of knowledge and recollection during the hearings, and did as well to reconstruct the mood and motive of my actions as I could.

Nothing he had ever done, he added, had been done with the intention of hurting his friend or of making things difficult. "I think I have known something of the depth of your affection, and that this knowledge has been a part of the affection that Kitty and I bear you and have always borne you." What was not clear to Oppenheimer, however, was the degree to which "the shadow of my cock and bull story lies over you."[8]

The letter was apparently insufficient to quell Chevalier's sense of betrayal. On December 2 the French weekly newsmagazine, *France-Observateur,* published an open letter from Chevalier to Oppenheimer asking the question, "Why Did You Lie?" A week later, Chevalier wrote to Oppenheimer directly. He was no longer angry, he wrote, and it appeared that the two of them would be inextricably linked in a legend. Chevalier furthered the legend by writing two books. The first, a novel called *The Man Who Would be God,* was a fictional re-creation of scientists and the development of the atomic bomb. The two men would have no further contact until 1964, when Chevalier wrote to Oppenheimer to apprise him of the second book. This time, there was no response from Oppenheimer. The second book was a nonfiction semi-biography entitled, *Oppenheimer: The Story of a Friendship.* This book, published in 1965, was a detailed analysis of the events surrounding the Chevalier incident and of Chevalier's insights into Oppenheimer's character. Oppenheimer refused to comment on the book to anyone. The friendship, from which the ill-fated "incident" had sprung, was now over.

The hearing and the aftermath had taken its toll. Oppenheimer admitted that he had lost sleep and "a few pounds." Kitty Oppenheimer could not discuss the matter without anger. Oppenheimer himself did not regard the events so much as a tragedy as a farce. Whatever his views, he was remarkably constrained in public. He had been barred from further government work, but not from assuming a public role as spokesman for science and society. In February 1956 he gave a speech at the twenty-fifth anniversary meeting of the American Institute of Physics. He only had to walk into the auditorium to receive a standing ovation. He spoke of the discovery of a new scientific principle that was on the horizon, one that had "immense sweep and simplicity." It would be comparable to the work of Albert Einstein and Max Planck, and would most likely be the work of a young man. The "principle" he spoke of would explain cosmic rays in the nucleus of atoms. He also spoke to a theme that was increasingly present in much of his public speaking: the failure of scientists to impart or share with students a sense of the beauty of science.

Three months later, in May, he was honored along with singer Marian Anderson by Roosevelt University in Chicago for "services to the principles of American democracy." It was a more somber Oppenheimer that spoke that night.

> The threat of the apocalypse may be with us a long time. We can see perhaps only the dimmest outline of a course that in the long term may be hopeful: the creation of honest and viable international communities with increasing common knowledge and understanding.[9]

The community of science had the greatest mixture of hope and danger, he said, but certainly contained the greatest hope for the future. Weapons, however, were not the gravest danger.

> In the great strides in the biological sciences, and far more still in the early beginnings of an understanding of man's psyche, of his beliefs, his learning, his memory and his probable action, one can see the origin of still graver problems of good and evil.

To be a part of the community, rather than of chaos, the individual needed "to learn of the virtues, of the restraint and tolerance, and of the sense of fraternity that will be asked of us."

Oppenheimer continued his examination of science and of the role of science in human life in speeches and talks around the country. At Dartmouth College in April 1959 he spoke on the growth and development of science in a talk entitled "Freedom and Necessity in the Sciences." He asked to what extent the growth of science was a free thing and to what extent it was determined. On the one hand, growth came from the human quality of wanting to understand—or perhaps, he suggested, by a desire "to be impertinent." On the other hand, scientific discovery could occur because "somebody wants a product."

> Knowledge has a disconcerting tendency to turn out, if not itself useful, contiguous to and continuous with knowledge which is useful; if the knowledge is not useful, the gadgetry used in obtaining it is useful; if the theory is not useful, the mathematical framework in which you cast it is useful.

Just a few months later Oppenheimer received word through Lloyd Garrison that Senator Clinton Anderson was eager to initiate a senatorial investigation of Lewis Strauss and the role he had played in forcing Oppenheimer's hearing. Anderson had been provoked by an editorial in a Washington, D.C., newspaper which he believed whitewashed the Strauss role in the inquiry. Garrison, however, was far from encouraging. A rehash, as Garrison called it, might bring to the surface some of the political and personal motives behind the hearing, but it would also reopen "old wounds." Garrison wrote to Oppenheimer at his home on St. John in the Virgin Islands. Between them, they dissuaded Anderson from any immediate action. Garrison, in fact, believed Anderson's true motive was to embarrass Strauss, although it was clear that the senator thought highly of Oppenheimer.[10] From time to time, in fact, there were calls from public officials or Oppenheimer friends to reopen the case; none, however, was ever successful.

Ironically, Lewis Strauss suffered his own defeat that same month. With his retirement from the Atomic Energy Commission earlier in the year, he had been nominated by President Eisenhower to become the secretary of commerce. It was, as many thought, a position to which Strauss could easily bring considerable experience. His years on the commission, with its vast complex of laboratories and plants, certainly made him an experienced manager, one familiar with many aspects of business and industry. But Strauss had made his own enemies over the years. On June 18 the Senate refused to approve his appointment. For a proud man like Strauss it was a bitter moment, no doubt exacerbated by public comparison with his former colleague Robert Oppenheimer.

Oppenheimer had little time to gloat, however, even if he had the will. He was regularly asked to speak, to endorse, to correspond. In the fall of 1960 he accepted an invitation to visit Japan as the guest of the Japan Committee for Intellectual Interchange. Despite advice to the contrary, he accepted, arriving amid a gaggle of relentless Japanese reporters. Asked immediately if he regretted making the atomic bomb, he replied negatively. It was not, he said, that he didn't feel bad; it was just that he didn't feel any worse that day than the day before.[11]

When he returned to America, Oppenheimer wrote a nostalgic letter to Norris Bradbury, who was still director of the Los Alamos Scientific Laboratory. He reminisced about Bradbury's first visit to Los Alamos. "More than anyone else who came to Los Alamos, you expressed, with force and eloquence, your misgivings about what we were up to, and your reluctance to be involved in it." And after fifteen years as director, Oppenheimer wished Bradbury to know of the respect and affection he had earned.

In June 1961 Oppenheimer left for a tour of Latin and South America under the auspices of the Organization for American States. Wherever he went he was enthusiastically received, even if his career and contributions were seen as no more than as "el padre de la bomba atómica." This was a title he hardly coveted, but friends quietly enjoyed the black irony and humor of Edward Teller's new nickname, "Father of the Hydrogen Bomb."

His public appearances were frequent and varied. He spoke before scientists, educators, architects, publishers, students, and other groups. His major themes were science and physics; but often enough he spoke of society and change and the need for hope. Almost a decade had elapsed since Oppenheimer had been first notified by Lewis Strauss of the government's intent to remove his clearance. In that time he had seen the political climate change more to his liking. The Atomic Energy Commission had created the Enrico Fermi Award in 1955, intended to honor those who had made "especially meritorious contributions to the development, use, or control of atomic energy." The first recipient in 1956 had been John von Neumann; in 1961 and 1962, the recipients had been Hans Bethe and Edward Teller. The award consisted of a citation, a gold medal, and a check from the government for fifty thousand dollars.

In 1963, after several nominations in previous years by friends, the General Advisory Committee, and later the commission itself, the AEC, unanimously approved awarding the Fermi Award to Robert Oppenheimer. On April 5 the White House released news of the award to the public. Oppenheimer himself was pleased, as were his family and friends. There was momentary talk about restoring his clearance, more as a symbolic gesture than as a measure of involving him again in government work. There was, however, also some opposition to the award. Senator Bourke Hickenlooper, still involved in congressional atomic energy matters, announced his intention to boycott the awards ceremony. Letters of congratulations arrived at Princeton from all corners of the globe; there was even a congratulatory letter from Edward Teller. On November 22, the White House announced President Kennedy's intention to personally present the award to Oppenheimer on December 2. The month and the day were significant: Exactly twenty-one years before, Enrico Fermi and his colleagues at Stagg Field in Chicago had created and sustained the world's first chain reaction.

Sadly, twelve hours after the announcement, Kennedy was assassinated in Dallas, Texas. With the world in shock and grief, the question of Oppenheimer's award seemed insignificant. In another courageous act, the newly sworn-in Lyndon Johnson announced that he would make the award to Oppenheimer in Kennedy's place. Johnson had been advised that the Atomic Energy Commission itself could make the award, perhaps saving the new President any political embarrassment from conservatives who still opposed Oppenheimer. Johnson refused; he told Oppenheimer during the ceremony that it had been very important to the late President to make the award personally. Less important, he added, was the check for fifty thousand dollars.

Oppenheimer was visibly moved by the moment, and no doubt by the memory of all that had passed in the last two decades. His first visit to the White House with President Truman had not necessarily been a happy one. He accepted the award, speaking softly but quickly. "In his later years, Jefferson often wrote of 'the brotherly spirit of science which unites into a family all its votaries.' ... We have not, I know, always given evidence of that brotherly spirit of science." In part, he said, it was because mankind was attempting, in the "great enterprise of our time," to see if society could survive without war. Oppenheimer alluded to other events as well.

> I think it just possible, Mr. President, that it has taken some charity and some courage for you to make this award today. These words I wrote down almost a fortnight ago. In a somber time I gratefully and gladly speak them to you.

There was a round of applause and handshaking. After an awkward moment, Oppenheimer and Teller shook hands as family and friends looked anxiously on.

In March 1964, after just recovering from a severe case of pneumonia, Oppenheimer accepted an invitation from Norris Bradbury to return to Los Alamos as a guest of the laboratory. Most of Oppenheimer's close friends knew he was not in good health. Bradbury was struck by Oppenheimer's poor physical condition and the great look of sadness that seemed to grip his face. The once-elegant and rich voice was now only a loud whisper. His return to Los Alamos was particularly poignant. Combined with the recent Fermi Award, the event seemed to some a bittersweet victory—too late, perhaps, but welcomed nonetheless. Robert and Kitty declined to stay on the Hill, but accepted their old and close friend Dorothy McKibbin's offer to stay in Santa Fe. Except for a blackboard, Oppenheimer declined all props for his speech. If that were not available, he wrote from Princeton, he would "gesticulate." The speech was set for June 16 in the laboratory's largest auditorium. Afterward, a private lunch was held with old friends and colleagues.

Oppenheimer's talk was on the subject of Niels Bohr, who had joined the laboratory's staff for a brief time during the war. When Oppenheimer was a young man, Bohr had been as close to a mentor to him as anyone, and was very much Oppenheimer's symbol of the classic scientist and humanitarian. Quoting Bohr frequently in his speech, Oppenhimer recreated the efforts at the end of World War II, and immediately thereafter, to put atomic weapons into perspective and to create an international mechanism by which mankind could coexist safely with the new power. Toward the end, speaking of Bohr's sense of mortality, Oppenheimer could very well have been speaking his own thoughts.

> Bohr often spoke with a deep appreciation of mortality; mortality that screens out the mistakes, the failures, and the follies that would otherwise encumber our future, and that makes it possible that what we have learned, and what has proved itself is transmitted for the next generations.

The talk ended with an anecdote about Henry Stimson, the late secretary of war. It was in late September 1945, Stimson's last day before retirement. That very day he had advocated at the President's Cabinet meeting an international approach to the atom which included inviting the Soviet Union as a partner. Oppenheimer met briefly with Stimson as the secretary was having his hair cut. "When it was time for him [Stimson] to go, he said, 'Now it is in your hands.' Bohr never said anything like that to us. He did not need to."[12]

Oppenheimer spoke in a soft, husky voice that betrayed the illness besetting him. When he finished, the entire audience rose to their feet in loud and sustained applause. After almost ten minutes of applause,

Oppenheimer came back to the podium and bade them quiet down. "I can say no more than beg you to leave." He never returned to Los Alamos again.

Early in 1966 doctors discovered that he had cancer of the throat. He had announced a few months before his intention to retire as director of the Institute for Advanced Studies. His illness had even made it impossible for him to read the papers brought to him by members of the institute. In June, in an interview with *Newsweek* magazine, he denied that he was planning to write his memoirs. Instead, he said, he was giving a "hideously complete archive" dating back to 1945 to the Library of Congress. Earlier in the month he had received an honorary degree from Princeton University; he could stand during the ceremony only with the aid of a cane. To the *Newsweek* reporter he confessed that the cane was there only to remind him not to fall. His hope for retirement, he revealed, was to be able to write a history of modern physics. That little bit of news was enough to bring a dozen publishers rushing to his door with offers, including Harvard University Press, Harper & Row, McGraw-Hill, and Prentice-Hall. To each he sent a polite letter which in part read: "I have a long time and much work ahead in writing it [the history] before it will seem right to me to consider what to do with the manuscript."

The book, however, would remain an unfinished dream. By late 1966, Oppenheimer was telling friends that his cancer was spreading rapidly. On February 18, 1967, Julius Robert Oppenheimer died quietly at home. On February 25 there was a memorial service in Princeton University's Alexander Hall. Many old friends made special efforts to attend: Isidor Rabi, Cyril Smith, David Lilienthal, Leslie Groves, and many more. There were three brief eulogies—on Robert Oppenheimer the scientist, the statesman, and the institute director—given by Hans Bethe, Henry DeWolf Smyth, and George Kennan.

At the end, the Juilliard String Quartet played one of Oppenheimer's favorite musical pieces, the C-Sharp Minor Quartet, Opus No. 14, by Beethoven.

When the service was over, Kitty Oppenheimer took her husband's ashes to the Virgin Islands. From a small boat she scattered them into the quiet sea. For the man, at least, the journey was over.

Notes

Abbreviations

The following abbreviations are used in the notes:

DOE Department of Energy, Germantown, Maryland

JRO J. Robert Oppenheimer Papers, Manuscript Division, Library of Congress, Washington, D.C.

LASL Los Alamos Scientific Laboratory, Records Division, Los Alamos, New Mexico

MED Record Group 77, "Records of the Office of the Chief of Engineers: Records of the Manhattan Engineer District," Modern Military Branch, National Archives, Washington, D.C.

NA Records Group, "Office of Scientific Research and Development, S-1," Industrial and Social Branch National Archives, Washington, D.C.

PART ONE

1. A Matter of Risk

1. *The New York Times,* April 14, 1954, p. 1.

2. Emergence

1. Alice Kimball Smith and Charles Weiner, *Robert Oppenheimer: Letters and Recollections* (Cambridge, Mass.: Harvard University Press, 1980), p. 5.
2. Ibid. p. 39.
3. Ibid. p. 30.
4. Philip M. Stern and Harold P. Green, *The Oppenheimer Case on Trial* (New York: Harper & Row Publishers, 1969), p. 11.
5. Nuel Pharr Davis, *Lawrence & Oppenheimer* (New York: Simon and Schuster, 1968), p. 19.
6. Smith and Weiner, op. cit. p. 77.
7. Ibid. pp. 91–93.
8. Ibid. p. 93.
9. Davis, op. cit. p. 21.
10. *In the Matter of J. Robert Oppenheimer: Transcript of Hearing before Personnel Security Board* U.S. Atomic Energy Commission (Washington, D.C.: Government Printing Office, 1954), p. 7. Hereafter cited as *Hearings.*
11. Peter Michelmore, *The Swift Years: The Robert Oppenheimer Story* (New York: Dodd, Mead & Company, 1969), p. 31.
12. *Hearings,* pp. 7–8.
13. I. I. Rabi et al., *Oppenheimer* (New York: Charles Scribner's Sons, 1969), p. 18.
14. Hans Bethe, "Oppenheimer: Where He Was There Was Always Life and Excitement," *Science* (March 3, 1967).

15. Rabi et al., op. cit. p. 18.
16. Smith and Weiner, op. cit. p. 131.
17. Ibid. p. 135.
18. Haakron Chevalier, *Oppenheimer: The Story of a Friendship* (New York: George Braziller, 1965), p. 20.

3. Coordinator of Rapid Rupture

1. Alice Kimball Smith and Charles Weiner, *Robert Oppenheimer: Letters and Recollections* (Cambridge, Mass.: Harvard University Press, 1980), p. 207.
2. Richard Hewlett and Oscar E. Anderson, Jr., *A History of the United States Atomic Energy Commission: Volume I, The New World, 1939–1946* (University Park, Pa.: Pennsylvania State University Press, 1962), pp. 37–38.
3. Ibid. p. 34.
4. Ibid. p. 53.
5. Ibid. pp. 54–55.
6. Ibid. p. 103.
7. Letter from Robert Oppenheimer to Edward Teller, September 11, 1942. JRO.
8. *In the Matter of J. Robert Oppenheimer: Transcript of Hearing before Personnel Security Board* U.S. Atomic Energy Commission (Washington, D.C.: Government Printing Office, 1954), p. 12.
9. Ibid. p. 28.
10. Contract between the United States of America and the University of California, April 20, 1943. LASL.

4. The Secret Record

1. Philip M. Stern and Harold P. Green, *The Oppenheimer Case: Security on Trial* (New York: Harper & Row Publishers, 1969), p. 40.
2. *In the Matter of J. Robert Oppenheimer: Transcript of Hearing before Personnel Security Board* U.S. Atomic Energy Commission (Washington, D.C.: Government Printing Office, 1954), p. 822. Hereafter referred to as *Hearings.*
3. Ibid. p. 123.
4. Memorandum to General Leslie Groves from Colonel John Landsdale, July 6, 1943.
5. The interview appears in *Hearings,* pp. 845–863. All quotes are from this interview.
6. The interview appears in *Hearings,* pp. 871–886. All quotes are from this interview.
7. *Hearings,* pp. 152–153.
8. Ibid. pp. 167–168.
9. Ibid. pp. 273–274.

5. The Director

1. *In the Matter of J. Robert Oppenheimer: Transcript of Hearing before Personnel Security Board* U.S. Atomic Energy Commission (Washington, D.C.: Government Printing Office, 1954), p. 32. Hereafter referred to as *Hearings.*
2. Leslie R. Groves, *Now It Can Be Told* (New York: Harper & Row, 1962), pp. 254–256.
3. Minutes of the Governing Board, Los Alamos, May 31, 1943. LASL.
4. Minutes of the Governing Board, Los Alamos, August 5, 1943. LASL.
5. *Hearings,* p. 166.
6. Letter from Robert Oppenheimer to Robert Sproul, September 18, 1943. JRO.

7. Letter from Robert Oppenheimer to Richard Tolman, November 3, 1942. LASL.
8. Letter from Robert Oppenheimer to Hans Bethe, December 28, 1942. JRO.
9. Letter from Robert Oppenheimer to General Leslie Groves, November 20, 1942. LASL.
10. *Hearings*, p. 31.
11. Stanley A. Blumberg and Gwinn Owens, *Energy and Conflict: The Life and Times of Edward Teller* (New York: G.P. Putnam's Sons, 1976), p. 75.

6. The Task at Hand

1. Richard Hewlett and Oscar E. Anderson, Jr., *A History of the United States Atomic Energy Commission; Volume I, The New World, 1939–1945* (University Park, Pa.: Pennsylvania University Press, 1962), p. 251.
2. Minutes of the Governing Board, Los Alamos, June 17, 1944. LASL.
3. Hewlett and Anderson, op. cit. p. 252.
4. Stanley A. Blumberg and Gwinn Owens. *Energy and Conflict: The Life and Times of Edward Teller* (New York: G. P. Putnam's Sons, 1976), p. 135.
5. Hewlett and Anderson, op. cit. p. 252.
6. Letter from Edward Teller to Richard Tolman, October 6, 1944. LASL.
7. Letter from Luis Alvarez to Richard Tolman, October 4, 1944. LASL.
8. *In the Matter of J. Robert Oppenheimer: Transcript of Hearing before Personnel Security Board* U.S. Atomic Energy Commission (Washington, D.C.: Government Printing Office, 1954), pp. 954–955.
9. Alice Kimball Smith and Charles Weiner, *Robert Oppenheimer: Letters and Recolections* (Cambridge, Mass.: Harvard University Press, 1980), p. 288.
10. Letter from Robert Oppenheimer to General Leslie Groves, May 7, 1945. MED and LASL.

7. The New Age

1. Henry Stimson Diaries. Quoted in Martin J. Sherwin, *A World Destroyed: The Atomic Bomb and the Grand Alliance* (New York: Alfred A. Knopf, 1975), p. 5.
2. Ibid. p. 36.
3. Ibid. p. 198.
4. Memorandum from George Kistiakowsky to Robert Oppenheimer, October 13, 1944. LASL.
5. Kenneth Bainbridge, "A Foul and Awesome Display," *Bulletin of the Atomic Scientists* (May 1975), p. 43.
6. Vannevar Bush, *Pieces of the Action* (New York: William Morrow and Company, 1970), p. 148.
7. LASL, *Los Alamos: Beginning of an Era* (no date), p. 56.
8. Quoted in Sherwin, op. cit. p. 204.
9. Notes on the Interim Committee Meeting, May 31, 1945. NA.
10. *In the Matter of J. Robert Oppenheimer: Transcript of Hearing before Personnel Security Board* U.S. Atomic Energy Commission (Washington, D.C.: Government Printing Office, 1954), p. 34.
11. Letter from General Leslie Groves to General George Marshall, August 10, 1945. MED.
12. Transcript of telephone conversation between General Leslie Groves and Robert Oppenheimer, August 6, 1945. MED.
13. Letter from Robert Oppenheimer to General Leslie Groves, May 7, 1945. MED and LASL.

14. Transcript of telephone conversation between Robert Oppenheimer and aide to General Leslie Groves, September 15, 1945. MED.
15. David Hawkins. *Manhattan District History: Project Y, The Los Alamos Project,* Volume I, LAMS-2532 (Los Alamos: LASL, 1961), p. 294.

PART TWO

8. The Spokesman

1. National Opinion Research Center, Confidential Report. June 1946.
2. Cited in Peter Michelmore, *The Swift Years: The Robert Oppenheimer Story* (New York: Dodd, Mead & Company, 1969), pp. 119–120.
3. Quotes from speech by Robert Oppenheimer to the Association of Los Alamos Scientists, November 2, 1945. LASL.
4. Alice Kimball Smith and Charles Weiner, *Robert Oppenheimer: Letters and Recollections* (Cambridge, Mass.: Harvard University Press, 1980), p. 300.
5. Ibid. p. 308.
6. Ibid. p. 299.
7. Ibid. p. 309.
8. Excerpts from the Minutes of the Board of Trustees, Institute for Advanced Study, April 1, 1947. JRO.
9. Haakron Chevalier, *Oppenheimer: The Story of a Friendship* (New York: George Braziller, 1965), pp. 61–70.
10. Quoted in Philip M. Stern and Harold P. Green, *The Oppenheimer Case: Security on Trial* (New York: Harper & Row, 1969), p. 112.
11. Interim Committee Log, August 18, 1945. NA.
12. Interim Committee Log, September 28, 1945. NA.
13. Report prepared by Robert Oppenheimer for the Interim Committee, dates from 1945. JRO.
14. Richard Hewlett and Oscar E. Anderson, Jr., *A History of the United States Atomic Energy Commission: Volume I, The New World, 1939–1945* (University Park, Pa.: Pennsylvania University Press, 1962), p. 426.
15. Ibid. p. 437.
16. George L. Harrison, Memorandum for the files, October 11, 1945. NA.
17. House of Representatives, 79th Congress. "Atomic Energy: Hearings Before the Committee on Military Affairs," October 9 and 18, 1945, pp. 107–115. Hereafter called Atomic Energy Hearings.
18. George L. Harrison, Memorandum for the files, October 17, 1945. NA.
19. All quotes are from the Atomic Energy Hearings, pp. 107–115.
20. David E. Lilienthal, *The Journals of David E. Lilienthal: Volume II, The Atomic Energy Years, 1945–1950* (New York: Harper & Row, 1964), pp. 33–34.

9. A Matter for the World

1. Richard Hewlett and Oscar E. Anderson, Jr., *A History of the United States Atomic Energy Commission: Volume I, The New World, 1939–1945* (University Park, Pa.: Pennsylvania University Press, 1962), pp. 501–503.
2. David E. Lilienthal, *The Journals of David E. Lilienthal: Volume II, The Atomic Energy Years, 1945–1950* (New York: Harper & Row, 1964), p. 13.

3. *In the Matter of J. Robert Oppenheimer: Transcript of Hearing before Personnel Security Board* U.S. Atomic Energy Commission (Washington, D.C.: Government Printing Office, 1954), pp. 37–38.
4. J. Robert Oppenheimer, "International Control of Atomic Energy," *Bulletin of the Atomic Scientists* (June 1946).
5. Ibid.
6. Ibid.
7. Hewlett and Anderson, op. cit. p. 536.
8. Ibid. p. 539.
9. Lilienthal, op. cit. p. 28.
10. Bernard N. Baruch, *Baruch: The Public Years* (New York: Holt, Rinehart, and Winston, 1960), p. 365.
11. Margaret L. Coit, *Mr. Baruch* (Cambridge, Mass.: Houghton Mifflin Company, The Riverside Press, Cambridge, 1957), p. 573.
12. Nuel Pharr Davis, *Lawrence & Oppenheimer* (New York: Simon and Schuster, 1968), p. 259.
13. Lilienthal, op. cit. pp. 39, 41, 42–44.
14. Ibid. p. 54.
15. Hewlett and Anderson, op. cit. pp. 573–574.
16. Lilienthal, op. cit. pp. 59–60 and Hewlett and Anderson, op. cit. p. 577.
17. Hewlett and Anderson, op. cit. p. 582.
18. Baruch, op. cit. p. 365.
19. Lilienthal, op. cit. pp. 69–70.
20. Letter from Robert Oppenheimer to Harry Truman, May 3, 1946, JRO.

10. The Public Man

1. *In the Matter of J. Robert Oppenheimer: Transcript of Hearing before Personnel Security Board* U.S. Atomic Energy Commission (Washington, D.C.: Government Printing Office, 1954), p. 412. Hereafter referred to as *Hearings.*
2. Ibid. pp. 376–378.
3. Ibid. p. 179.
4. Ibid. pp. 380–381.
5. David E. Lilienthal, *The Journals of David E. Lilienthal: Volume II, The Atomic Energy Years, 1945–1950* (New York: Harper & Row, 1964), p. 137; and Richard Hewlett and Francis Duncan, *A History of the United States Atomic Energy Commission: Volume II, The Atomic Shield, 1947–1952* (Washington, D.C.: USAEC Technical Information Center, 1972), p. 30.
6. Norris Bradbury, Proposed Agenda for GAC Weapons Subcommittee Meeting in Los Alamos, March 22, 1947. LASL.
7. Hewlett and Duncan, op. cit. p. 61.
8. Minutes of the General Advisory Committee, April 3, 1947. LASL and DOE.
9. Lilienthal, op. cit. p. 186.
10. Ibid. p. 10.
11. Ibid. p. 239.
12. Cited in Lilienthal, op. cit. p. 217.
13. *Hearings,* p. 344.
14. J. Robert Oppenheimer, "The Failure of International Control," *Bulletin of the Atomic Scientists* (February 1948).
15. Hewlett and Duncan, op. cit. p. 270.
16. *Hearings,* p. 42.
17. Ibid. p. 17.
18. Ibid. p. 962.

19. All quotes from letter from Robert Oppenheimer to Harry Truman, December 31, 1947. JRO.

11. Threat from the East

1. Richard Hewlett and Francis Duncan, *A History of the United States Atomic Energy Commission: Volume II, Atomic Shield, 1947–1952* (Washington, D.C.: USAEC Technical Information Center, 1972), p. 141.
2. Minutes of the General Advisory Committee, October 27, 1948. LASL and DOE.
3. David E. Lilienthal, *The Journals of David E. Lilienthal: Volume II, The Atomic Energy Years, 1945–1950* (New York: Harper & Row, 1964), p. 288.
4. Ibid. pp. 454–456.
5. Cited in Philip M. Stern and Harold P. Green, *The Oppenheimer Case: Security on Trial* (New York: Harper & Row, 1969), pp. 121–122.
6. *In the Matter of J. Robert Oppenheimer: Transcript of Hearing before Personnel Security Board* U.S. Atomic Energy Commission (Washington, D.C.: Government Printing Office, 1954), pp. 210–215. Hereafter referred to as *Hearings.*
7. Haakron Chevalier, *Oppenheimer: The Story of a Friendship* (New York: George Braziller, 1965), pp. 80–81.
8. Hewlett and Duncan, op. cit. p. 331.
9. Letter from Robert Oppenheimer to Harry Truman, June 6, 1948. JRO.
10. Minutes of the General Advisory Committee, June 6, 1948. LASL and DOE.
11. Hewlett and Duncan, op. cit. p. 331.
12. Lilienthal, op. cit. pp. 367–368.
13. Hewlett and Duncan, op. cit. p. 355.
14. All quotes from Joint Committee on Atomic Energy, 81st Congress, "Investigation into the United States Atomic Energy Project," May 1949, Part I.
15. Hewlett and Duncan, op. cit. p. 366.
16. *Hearings,* p. 969.
17. Lilienthal, op. cit. p. 572.

12. Quantum Leap

1. Richard Hewlett and Francis Duncan, *A History of the United States Atomic Energy Commission: Volume II, Atomic Shield, 1947–1952* (Washington, D.C.: USAEC Technical Information Center, 1972), pp. 373–374.
2. Lewis Strauss, *Men and Decisions* (New York: Doubleday & Co., 1962), p. 217.
3. *In the Matter of J. Robert Oppenheimer: Transcript of Hearing before Personnel Security Board* U.S. Atomic Energy Commission (Washington, D.C.: Government Printing Office, 1954), pp. 775–778. Hereafter referred to as *Hearings.*
4. Ibid. p. 778.
5. Memorandum from Edward Teller to Los Alamos Laboratory Council, October 13, 1949; and memorandum from John Manley to Los Alamos Laboratory Council, October 13, 1949. LASL.
6. Telex from General John McCormack to Norris Bradbury, October 13, 1949. LASL.
7. *Hearings,* p. 407.
8. Interview with Norris Bradbury by author, 1977.
9. *Hearings,* pp. 242–243.
10. Ibid.
11. Ibid. p. 395.
12. Ibid.

13. David E. Lilienthal, *The Journals of David E. Lilienthal: Volume II, The Atomic Years, 1945–1950* (New York: Harper & Row, 1964), pp. 580–581.
14. *Hearings*, p. 785.
15. Lilienthal, op. cit. p. 582.
16. Minutes of the General Advisory Committee, October 30, 1949. DOE.
17. Ibid.
18. Ibid.
19. Ibid.
20. *Hearings*, p. 395.
21. Hewlett and Duncan, op. cit. pp. 642–643.
22. Letter from Robert Oppenheimer to Felix Frankfurter, December 9, 1949. JRO.
23. *Hearings*, pp. 717–718.
24. Ibid. p. 432.
25. Lilienthal, op. cit. p. 568.
26. Strauss, op. cit. pp. 219–222.
27. Denver *Post*, January 14, 1950.
28. Lilienthal, op. cit. pp. 623–624.
29. Stanley A. Blumberg and Gwinn Owens, *Energy and Conflict: The Life and Times of Edward Teller* (New York: G.P. Putnam's Sons, 1976), p. 213.
30. Cited in Nuel Pharr Davis, *Lawrence & Oppenheimer* (New York: Simon and Schuster, 1968), pp. 330–331.

PART THREE

13. Technically Sweet

1. *In the Matter of J. Robert Oppenheimer: Transcript of Hearing before Personnel Security Board* U.S. Atomic Energy Commission (Washington, D.C.: Government Printing Office, 1954), p. 220. Hereafter referred to as *Hearings*.
2. Letter from Robert Oppenheimer to Haakron Chevalier, February 24, 1950. JRO.
3. Minutes of the General Advisory Committee, February 1, 1950. LASL and DOE.
4. Memorandum from Edward Teller to Laboratory Technical Council, October 13, 1949. LASL.
5. Interview with Carson Mark by author, 1981.
6. Memorandum from Norris Bradbury to Edward Teller, March 15, 1950. LASL.
7. Interview with Norris Bradbury by author, 1977.
8. Richard Hewlett and Francis Duncan, *A History of the United States Atomic Energy Commission: Volume II, Atomic Shield, 1947–1952* (Washington, D.C.: USAEC Technical Information Center, 1972), p. 425.
9. Carson Mark, *A Short Account of Los Alamos Theoretical Work on Thermonuclear Weapons, 1946–1950* (Los Alamos: LASL, 1974), p. 2. Issued as LA-5647-MS.
10. Ibid. p. 10.
11. Hewlett and Duncan, op. cit. p. 439.
12. Ibid. p. 440.
13. Memorandum from Hans Bethe to Carson Mark, June 24, 1950. LASL.
14. Letter from Robert Oppenheimer to Harry Truman, February 23, 1950. JRO.
15. Letter from General Leslie Groves to Robert Oppenheimer, May 18, 1950. JRO.
16. Letter from Norris Bradbury to Robert Oppenheimer, May 20, 1950; letter from Robert Oppenheimer to Norris Bradbury, July 19, 1950; LASL. Hewlett and Duncan, op. cit. pp. 527–528.

17. Minutes of the General Advisory Committee, October 1–November 1, 1950. DOE.
18. *Hearings,* pp. 46–47.
19. Ibid. p. 46.
20. Ibid. pp. 685–686.
21. Ibid. pp. 787–802; and Hewlett and Duncan, op. cit. pp. 530–531.
22. Interview with Carson Mark by author, 1981.
23. S.M. Ulam, *Adventures of a Mathematician* (New York: Charles Scribner's Sons, 1976), pp. 219–220.
24. Statement released by the Department of Energy in 1980 in response to an article by Howard Morland, "The H-Bomb Secret," *The Progressive,* November 1979, pp. 14–23.
25. Memorandum from Edward Teller to Norris Bradbury, March 7, 1951. LASL.
26. Stanley A. Blumberg and Gwinn Owens, *Energy and Conflict: The Life and Times of Edward Teller* (New York: G.P. Putnam's Sons, 1976), p. 257.
27. Letter from Norris Bradbury to Robert Oppenheimer, June 11, 1951. LASL.
28. *Hearings,* p. 251.
29. Letter from Edward Teller to Gordon Dean, April 20, 1951. LASL.
30. *Hearings,* p. 85.
31. Letter from Harold Agnew to Commanding General, Wright Air Development Center, October 3, 1951. LASL.

14. Scorpions in a Bottle

1. Richard Hewlett and Francis Duncan, *A History of the United States Atomic Energy Commission: Volume II, Atomic Shield, 1947–1952* (Washington, D.C.: USAEC Technical Information Center, 1972), pp. 556–557.
2. Ibid. p. 570.
3. *In the Matter of J. Robert Oppenheimer: Transcript of Hearing before Personnel Security Board* U.S. Atomic Energy Commission (Washington, D.C.: Government Printing Office, 1954), pp. 747–749. Hereafter referred to as *Hearings.*
4. Ibid. p. 892.
5. Ibid. p. 497.
6. Ibid. pp. 748–754.
7. Ibid. pp. 757–758 and 763–764.
8. Hewlett and Duncan, op. cit. p. 519.
9. Letter from Robert Oppenheimer to Frank Oppenheimer, July 12, 1950. JRO.
10. Letter from Gordon Dean to Robert Oppenheimer, no date. JRO.
11. Hewlett and Duncan, op. cit. pp. 518–520.
12. All quotes from letter from Robert Oppenheimer to Harry Truman, June 19, 1952. JRO.
13. Letter from Harry Truman to Robert Oppenheimer, September 27, 1952. JRO.
14. *Hearings,* p. 97.
15. All quotes from Robert Oppenheimer, "Atomic Weapons and American Policy," *Foreign Affairs,* July 1953.
16. *Hearings,* p. 502.
17. Ibid. pp. 498–500.
18. Cited in Philip M. Stern and Harold P. Green, *The Oppenheimer Case: Security on Trial* (New York: Harper & Row, 1969), p. 206.
19. Copies of the Reith Lectures are in Boxes 276–279, JRO.
20. Ibid.

15. Our Science and Our Country

1. Oppenheimer to Strauss, December 22, 1953, JRO; and Philip M. Stern and Harold P. Green, *The Oppenheimer Case: Security on Trial* (New York: Harper & Row, 1969), pp. 229–232.
2. *In the Matter of J. Robert Oppenheimer: Transcript of Hearing before Personnel Security Board* U.S. Atomic Energy Commission (Washington, D.C.: Government Printing Office, 1954), pp. 836–838.
3. Jack M. Holl, "In the Matter of J. Robert Oppenheimer: Origins of the Government's Security Case," presentation before the American Historical Association Annual Meeting, December 28–30, 1975.
4. Herbert S. Parmet, *Eisenhower and the American Crusades* (New York: The Macmillan Company, 1972), p. 344.
5. Harold P. Green, "The Oppenheimer Case: A Study in the Abuse of Law," *Bulletin of the Atomic Scientists,* September 1977.
6. Ibid.
7. Stern and Green, op. cit. p. 224.
8. Letter from General Kenneth Nichols to Robert Oppenheimer, December 23, 1953. JRO.
9. Letter from General Kenneth Nichols to Robert Oppenheimer, December 12, 1953. JRO.
10. Telegram from General Kenneth Nichols to Norris Bradbury, December 23, 1953. LASL.
11. Holl, op. cit. p. 45.
12. Stern and Green, op. cit. pp. 245–246.
13. Letter from Lloyd Garrison to Lewis Strauss, February 3, 1954. JRO.
14. Stern and Green, op. cit. p. 246.
15. *Hearings,* p. 14.
16. Ibid. p. 19.
17. Notes of Legal Conference by Robert Oppenheimer, January 19, 1954. JRO.

16. The Hearing

1. *In the Matter of J. Robert Oppenheimer: Transcript of Hearing before Personnel Security Board* U.S. Atomic Energy Commission (Washington, D.C.: Government Printing Office, 1954), p. 3. Hereafter referred to as *Hearings.*
2. Ibid. p. 39.
3. Ibid. p. 53.
4. Ibid. p. 62.
5. Ibid. p. 71.
6. Ibid. p. 81.
7. Ibid. pp. 501–502.
8. Letters written on behalf of Robert Oppenheimer by Hans Bethe, Norris Bradbury, John Manley, John von Neumann, and Victor Weiskopf and Norman Ramsey, dates vary, Box 202, JRO.
9. Oppenheimer's testimony appears for the first time in *Hearings,* pp. 108–160.
10. *Hearings,* p. 153.
11. Ibid. pp. 167–168.
12. Ibid. p. 201.
13. Ibid. p. 229.
14. Ibid. p. 239.
15. Ibid.
16. Ibid. p. 241.
17. Ibid. p. 279.

18. Ibid. p. 306.
19. Ibid. p. 325.
20. Ibid. p. 372.
21. Ibid. p. 385.
22. Ibid. p. 421.
23. Ibid. p. 448.
24. Ibid. p. 513.
25. Ibid. p. 565.
26. Ibid. p. 649.
27. Ibid. pp. 659–661.
28. Ibid. pp. 698–708.
29. Stanley A. Blumberg and Gwinn Owens, *Energy and Conflict: The Life and Times of Edward Teller* (New York: G.P. Putnam's Sons, 1976), p. 359.
30. *Hearings*, pp. 709–710.
31. Notes by Robert Oppenheimer appear in Box 205, JRO.
32. *Hearings*, p. 736.
33. Ibid. p. 768.
34. Ibid. p. 888.
35. Ibid. p. 895.
36. Ibid. p. 936.
37. Ibid. p. 959.
38. Ibid. pp. 971–990.

17. A Failure to Enthuse

1. *In the Matter of J. Robert Oppenheimer: Text of Principal Documents and Letters* U.S. Atomic Energy Commission (Washington, D.C.: Government Printing Office, 1954), pp. 1–23. Hereafter referred to as *Text of Principal Documents*.
2. Cited in Philip M. Stern and Harold P. Green, *The Oppenheimer Case: Security on Trial* (New York: Harper & Row, 1969), p. 376.
3. *Text of Principal Documents*, p. 33.
4. Cited in *The New York Times*, June 2, 1954.
5. Cited in the *New Mexican*, June 7, 1954.
6. Letters to Robert Oppenheimer are collected in Box 202, JRO.
7. Letter from Lee DuBridge to Lewis Strauss, June 4, 1954. JRO.
8. Stern and Green, op. cit. pp. 397–398.
9. Letter from General Kenneth Nichols to Lewis Strauss, June 12, 1954. *Text of Principal Documents*, pp. 43–48.
10. Stern and Green, op. cit. pp. 399–401.
11. Letter from Norris Bradbury to Lewis Strauss, June 16, 1954. LASL.
12. Decisions and Opinions of the U.S. Atomic Energy Commission in the Matter of J. Robert Oppenheimer. *Text of Principal Documents*, pp. 51–67.
13. Statement for the press from the Atomic Energy Commission, June 29, 1954. JRO.
14. Cited in the Washington *Post*, July 1, 1954.

18. End of the Journey

1. Cited in *The New York Times*, July 4, 1954.
2. Cited in the Albuquerque *Journal*, July 13, 1954.
3. Letter from Robert Oppenheimer to Gordon Dean, September 25, 1954. JRO.
4. Joseph Alsop and Stewart Alsop, "We Accuse," *Harper's*, September 1954.
5. Cited in *The New York Times*, July 4, 1954.

6. J. Robert Oppenheimer, "Prospects in the Arts and Sciences," talk given at Columbia University, December 26, 1954. JRO.
7. Letter from Lloyd Garrison to Robert Oppenheimer, August 12, 1954. JRO.
8. Letter from Robert Oppenheimer to Haakron Chevalier, September 3, 1954. JRO.
9. J. Robert Oppenheimer, Presentation before Roosevelt University, May 15, 1955. JRO.
10. Letter from Lloyd Garrison to Robert Oppenheimer, July 1, 1959. JRO.
11. Cited in Peter Michelmore, *The Swift Years: The Robert Oppenheimer Story* (New York: Dodd, Mead & Company, 1969), pp. 241–242.
12. J. Robert Oppenheimer, Presentation before staff of Los Alamos Scientific Laboratory, June 16, 1964. LASL and JRO.

Sources

I. BOOKS AND ARTICLES

Alsop, Joseph and Stewart. "We Accuse!" *Harper's*, September, 1954.

Bainbridge, Kenneth. "A Foul and Awesome Display." *Bulletin of the Atomic Scientists*, May 1975.

Baruch, Bernard M. *Baruch: The Public Years.* New York: Holt, Rinehart and Winston, 1960.

Bethe, Hans. "Oppenheimer: Where He Was There Was Always Life and Excitement." *Science*, March 3, 1967.

Blumberg, Stanley A., and Gwinn Owens. *Energy and Conflict: The Life and Times of Edward Teller.* New York: G. P. Putnam's Sons, 1976.

Brown, Anthony Cace, and Charles B. MacDonald. *The Secret History of the Atomic Bomb.* New York: The Dial Press/James Wade, 1977.

Bush, Vannevar. *Modern Arms and Free Men.* New York: Simon and Schuster, 1949.

———. *Pieces of the Action.* New York: William Morrow and Company, 1970.

Byrnes, James F. *Speaking Frankly.* New York: Harper and Brothers, 1947.

Calder, Nigel. *Nuclear Nightmares.* New York: The Viking Press, 1979.

Chevalier, Haakron. *Oppenheimer: The Story of a Friendship.* New York: George Braziller, 1965.

Coit, Margaret L. *Mr. Baruch.* Cambridge, Mass.: Houghton Mifflin Company/ The Riverside Press Cambridge, 1957.

Compton, Arthur H. *Atomic Quest: A Personal Narrative.* Princeton, N.J.: Princeton University Press, 1956.

Davis, Nuel Pharr. *Lawrence and Oppenheimer.* New York: Simon and Schuster, 1968.

Dyson, Freeman. *Disturbing the Universe.* New York: Harper & Row, 1979.

Fermi, Laura. *Atoms in the Family.* Chicago: University of Chicago Press, 1954.

Gowing, Margaret. *Britain and Atomic Energy, 1939–1945.* New York: Macmillan Co., 1964.

Grodzins, Morton, and Eugene Rabinowitch, eds. *The Atomic Age: Scientists in National and World Affairs.* New York: Simon and Schuster, 1965.

Groueff, Stephane. *Manhattan District.* New York: Little, Brown & Co., 1967.

Groves, Leslie R. *Now It Can Be Told.* New York: Harper & Row, 1962.

Hawkins, David. *Manhattan District History: Project Y, The Los Alamos Project, Volume I.* Los Alamos, New Mexico: Los Alamos Scientific Laboratory, 1961. Appears as LAMS-2352.

Herken, Gregg. *The Winning Weapon: The Atomic Bomb in the Cold War, 1945–1950.* New York: Alfred A. Knopf, 1980.

Hewlett, Richard, and Francis Duncan. *A History of the United States Atomic Energy Commission: Volume II, Atomic Shield, 1947–1952.* Washington, D.C.: USAEC Technical Information Center, 1972.

Hewlett, Richard, and Oscar E. Anderson, Jr. *A History of the Atomic Energy Commission: Volume I, The New World, 1939–1946.* University Park, Pa.: Pennsylvania State University Press, 1962.

Jungk, Robert. *Brighter Than A Thousand Suns.* New York: Harcourt, Brace & World, 1958.

Kevles, Daniel J. *The Physicists.* New York: Alfred A. Knopf, 1978.

Kunetka, James W. *City of Fire: Los Alamos and the Birth of the Atomic Age, 1943–1945.* New York: Prentice-Hall, 1978. Paperback edition by the University of New Mexico Press, 1979.

Lamont, Lansing. *Day of Trinity.* New York: Atheneum, 1965.

Lapp, Ralph E. *Atoms and People.* New York: Harper and Brothers, 1956.

———. *The Weapons Culture.* New York: W. W. Norton & Company, 1968.

Lewis, Richard S., and Jane Wilson. *Alamogordo Plus Twenty-Five Years.* New York: The Viking Press, 1971.

Libby, Leona Marshall. *The Uranium People.* New York: Crane Russak and Charles Scribner's Sons, 1979.

Lilienthal, David E. *The Journal of David E. Lilienthal: Volume II, The Atomic Energy Years, 1945–1950.* New York: Harper & Row, 1964.

Lowe, George E. *The Age Deterrence.* Boston: Little, Brown & Company, 1964.

Lawrence, William L. *Dawn Over Zero.* New York: Alfred A. Knopf, 1951.

———. *The Hell Bomb.* New York: Alfred A. Knopf, 1951.

McPhee, John. *The Curve of Binding Energy.* New York: Farrar, Straus, and Giroux, 1974.

Michelmore, Peter. *The Swift Years: The Robert Oppenheimer Story.* New York: Dodd, Mead & Company, 1969.

Morland, Howard. "The H-Secret." *The Progressive,* November 1979.

Moss, Norman. *Men Who Play God.* New York: Harper & Row, 1969.

Oppenheimer, J. Robert. "Atomic Weapons and American Policy." *Foreign Affairs,* July 1953.

———. "The Failure of International Control." *Bulletin of the Atomic Scientists,* February 1948.

———. "International Control of Atomic Energy." *Bulletin of the Atomic Scientists,* June 1946.

———. *The Open Mind.* New York: Simon and Schuster, 1955.

———. *Science and the Common Understanding.* New York: Simon and Schuster, 1954.

Parmet, Herbert S. *Eisenhower and the American Crusades.* New York: The Macmillan Company, 1972.

Rabi, Isidor, et al. *Oppenheimer.* New York: Charles Scribner's Sons, 1969.

Royal, Denise. *The Story of J. Robert Oppenheimer.* New York: St. Martin's Press, 1969.

Sherwin, Martin J. *A World Destroyed: The Atomic Bomb and the Grand Alliance.* New York: Alfred A. Knopf, 1975.

Smith, Alice Kimball, and Charles Weiner. *Robert Oppenheimer: Letters and Recollections.* Cambridge, Mass.: Harvard University Press, 1980.

Smyth, Henry D. *Atomic Energy for Military Purposes.* Princeton, N.J.: Princeton University Press, 1947.

Stern, Philip M., and Harold P. Green. *The Oppenheimer Case: Security on Review.* New York: Harper & Row, 1969.

Stimson, Henry L., and McGeorge Bundy. *On Active Service in Peace and War.* New York: Harper & Brothers, 1948.

Strauss, Lewis. *Men and Decisions.* New York: Doubleday & Company, 1962.

Ulam, S. M. *Adventures of a Mathematician.* New York: Charles Scribner's Sons, 1976.

York, Herbert F. *The Advisors: Oppenheimer, Teller, and the Superbomb.* San Francisco: W.H. Freeman and Company, 1976.

II. ATOMIC ENERGY COMMISSION PUBLICATIONS

Atomic Energy Commission. *In the Matter of J. Robert Oppenheimer: Transcript of Hearing Before Personnel Security Board.* Washington, D.C.: Government Printing Office, 1954.

———. *In the Matter of J. Robert Oppenheimer: Text of Principal Documents and Letters of Personnel Security Board, General Manager and Commission.* Washington, D.C.: Government Printing Office, 1954.

———. *In the Matter of J. Robert Oppenheimer: Statement of the Atomic Energy Commission.* Washington, D.C.: Government Printing Office, 1954.

III. UNITED STATES CONGRESS

House of Representatives, Committee on Military Affairs. "Atomic Energy: Hearing Before the Committee on Military Affairs," 79th Congress, October 9–18, 1945.

House of Representatives, Committee on Un-American Activities. "Hearings Regarding Communist Infiltration of Radiation Laboratory and Atomic Bomb Project at the University of California, Berkeley, California," 81st Congress, April 22–September 27, 1949, two volumes.

House-Senate Joint Commitee on Atomic Energy. "Investigation into the United States Atomic Energy Project," 81st Congress, May 26–July 11, 1949, 24 parts.

IV. COLLECTIONS

The Library of Congress, Manuscript Division, maintains the papers of J. Robert Oppenheimer, which consist of 297 boxes of documents, including correspondence, reports, drafts of speeches and manuscripts, desk books, and material relating especially to Oppenheimer's security hearing in 1954. As part of its holdings, the National Archives maintains two collections of some interest. The first is the files of the Office of Scientific Research and Development, S-1, in the Industrial and Social Branch of the Archives. This collection contains the files and correspondence of Vannevar Bush and James B. Conant. The second collection is in the Modern Military Branch and is the Records of the Office of the Chief of Engineers: Records of the Manhattan Engineer District, Records Group 77. The Oral History Collection of the Massachusetts Institute of Technology contains oral history interviews with persons who worked with Robert Oppenheimer as well as with many individuals in leadership positions in science during Oppenheimer's professional lifetime. A surprising amount of historical material is maintained by the Department of Energy (formerly the U.S. Atomic Energy Commission), Division of Classification. Similarly, material of considerable relevance is maintained by the Los Alamos Scientific Laboratory, Los Alamos, New Mexico, by their Mail and Records Group. Unfortunately, neither collection is catalogued for use by the public and much of the material remains classified and unavailable. Papers relating to Robert Oppenheimer's direction of the Institute for Advanced Study in Princeton, New Jersey, have been retained by the Institute and are not available to the public.

Index